THE COGNITIVE DYNAMICS
OF COMPUTER SCIENCE

THE COGNITIVE DYNAMICS OF COMPUTER SCIENCE

Cost-Effective Large Scale Software Development

Szabolcs Michael de Gyurky

Computer Artwork by

Mark A. Tarbell

IEEE
COMPUTER
SOCIETY

WILEY-INTERSCIENCE

A JOHN WILEY & SONS, INC., PUBLICATION

Published by John Wiley & Sons, Inc., Hoboken, New Jersey
Published simultaneously in Canada

For general information on our other products and services or for technical support, please contact our Customer Care Department within the United States at (800) 762-2974, outside the United States at (317) 572-3993 or fax (317) 572-4002.

Wiley also publishes its books in a variety of electronic formats. Some content that appears in print may not be available in electronic format. For more information about Wiley products, visit our web site at www.wiley.com.

Library of Congress Cataloging-in-Publication Data is available.

The Cognitive Dynamics of Computer Science: Cost-Effective Large Scale Software Development
  de Gyurky, Szabolcs Michael

ISBN 13: 978-0-471-97047-7
ISBN 10: 0-471-97047-6

10 9 8 7 6 5 4 3 2 1

To Immanuel Kant

That wonderful teacher,
that exquisite mind and heart,
and beautiful soul.

CONTENTS

LIST OF FIGURES

ACKNOWLEDGMENTS

To my dear friend, editor, and critic, Mark Tarbell, whose artwork graces these pages: Thank you.

To my dear wife, Cheryl, for her criticism and encouragement: I could not have done it without your support.

In a systems development environment, ideally one learns as much from one's subordinates as from one's superiors. Subordinates and superiors are therefore equally teachers in their disciplines. So I'm fortunate to have had great teachers, from above and below, and it has been a privilege to have had the opportunity to work with truly gifted engineers and scientists here at the Jet Propulsion Laboratory. I thank our great team members, past and present, starting with my mentor and teacher at SHAPE in Belgium, Colonel, USAF, Joseph Bullers, my boss who taught me command and control concepts, and architectures on a global scale.

To Dr. Joseph P. Fearey at JPL, who as my partner, mentor, and teacher taught me the mathematical underpinnings of event-driven simulations expressed in computer software architectures and the art of computer modeling and event-driven simulation: Thank you!

A big thank you also to the championship engineering team members without whom I could never have done the jobs I have done successfully:

Henry Judd	John Guineau	Dan Zink	Sebastian Van Alphen
Rick Wissinger	Joe Galinsky	Mark Tarbell	Rod Iwashina
Willie Huo	Art Rinaldi	Louie Hirsch	Tom Collins
Larry Johnsen	Dan Wenrick	Edward Colbert	Diane Melin
Jerry Hill	Don Royer	Jim Brownfield	Paul Firnett
Sara Hyman	Mark Fujishin	Banny Winn	Charles Yamarone
Jay Braun	Mike DiLoreto	Larry Hawley	Joe Provenzano

Kent Thomson, for his unwavering loyalty to the JTCCS and support.

Carol J. Tarbell, for having contributed more to this book than she knows.

To all of you dear colleagues who prepared the requirements and the design, wrote the software, tested it, and maintained the budget and the administrative support flow, a sincere thank you! I especially thank you for never hesitating to tell me when I was wrong, and putting me back on the correct course. Open criticism and the stating of sincere opinions is the heart of Immanuel Kant's "Pure Ethics."

As you can see, we are not that big of a team. Out of all those people who came, stayed a while, and moved on, it was we who brought the cost of a quality system down in one case down to under $10 per line of code. I'm not saying that we didn't have lots of problems and big-time stresses, but it is winning that counts, and we won all of the games we played. "Played" perhaps is not the right word, because it was terribly hard at times.

However, a project should be a team to be effective, and a team is special. It is far more than a project, because on a team the members work unselfishly toward a common goal, and on a project people often work toward their own personal advancement, trying to outshine instead of support each other.

I will always believe that anyone can make software work, or build a system if enough time and money are thrown at it. The quality of the product, built on budget and on schedule, proves the worth of the manager and the team.

Finally, there are people in my two careers who taught me, mentored me, and led me by good example. Without these wonderful teachers I could not have written this book.

So I'm eternally grateful to:

Colonel Joseph W. Bullers USAF, for teaching me military command and control.

Colonel George Dornberger USAF, for teaching me the meaning and beauty of loyalty and integrity, and for being a true officer and gentleman wrapped in the person of a great fighter pilot.

Lieutenant General William Ginn USAF, for teaching me leadership in its finest form.

Lieutenant Colonel Edward R. Beaty U.S. Army, for setting the example and teaching me how to be a combat leader.

Dr. Thomas Thornton for being a good, steadfast boss, a great manager, and for his confidence in my engineering and management skills.

Mr. John R. Tupman for giving me an offer at JPL I couldn't refuse.

THE COGNITIVE DYNAMICS OF COMPUTER SCIENCE

1 Introduction

Computer software development has become very expensive in these United States, and there are a number of issues that high cost has brought with it. I suppose the most important of these is that the programming jobs are going overseas, along with most of our other manufacturing jobs. We can claim that we still do high-technology design, and the critical jobs of testing and integration. But these jobs, even if we did them well (which we don't always do), will also go overseas, along with the making of our beloved Levi jeans.

There is also a silent acceptance within the computer science community that the quality of American software is poor, to put it mildly. This is well known, even to our major publishing houses. They note that we write fewer and fewer "readable" books that our young and not so young practitioners can use. We forget that the academic preparation of young Americans is the foundation of their professional lives. It is hoped that a long and serious apprenticeship lies ahead of them, until they, too, become masters of their professional fields. A large portion of our publications and books is written just to publish, and not to teach the young professional. When I pick up foreign textbooks, I'm astonished at the pains their authors took to make them readable and truly useful to the reader. Foreign books are not written solely for one's academic peers; they are written to teach the reader.

We Americans are the great innovators and inventors, of course, but such jobs generally are restricted to a limited number of research houses, facilities, and universities. The earning of our daily bread as software professionals is becoming more and more difficult as the jobs are going away.

Yet, we *are* able to produce software of the highest quality, and at a lower cost, here in this country than anywhere else in the world. At present, based on my experience, the Federal Government pays between $350 and $800 per commented line of code for ground systems (the command and control software for aerospace and military applications). And for on-board flight systems—the software that is used in missiles, satellites, aircraft, spacecraft, instruments, and smart-guided weapons—the costs are much higher, ranging from $450 to $1,200 per line of commented code. Such systems are the very reasons for our global military superiority.

In contrast to these staggering costs, my colleagues and I here at the Jet Propulsion Laboratory have been able to reduce the cost of ground systems to about $10 per

The Cognitive Dynamics of Computer Science: Cost-Effective Large Scale Software Development,
by Szabolcs Michael de Gyurky
Copyright © 2006 by John Wiley & Sons, Inc.

commented line of code on our most recent systems. During the past 20 years, my teams and I have produced high-quality software at a cost ranging from $10 to $50 per line of commented code—depending on the mathematical complexity of the application, the availability of the technology in the marketplace, and the schedule to which we had to work.

1.1 THE RETENTION OF SOFTWARE JOBS

As a computer software professional, I am greatly concerned about the retention of software jobs within our borders. My colleagues are the very best in their fields, both in applications and systems software, and are pure technical innovators as well. They are highly paid and worth every penny they earn. I pay my programmers from $45 to $85 per hour, according to their years and levels of experience and skill qualifications (most of my computer scientists are contractors and consultants, as opposed to employees). Yet, we complete our tasks within the schedules and on the budgets we have committed ourselves to, producing a high-quality product at a cost far lower than anywhere else I know of in industry or in government.

Clearly, as a team, we are neither better educated nor more experienced than the rest of our colleagues throughout the country. So why is there such a difference in cost? Were it not for the fact that we are losing our livelihoods, this would be a moot point. But there are many "software guys" out there, including my colleagues, who are trying in vain to find jobs. They are worried and are asking me questions. We have professions for which we have invested large amounts of time and money, and we need incomes to pay our mortgages and raise our families.

So how does a project build software at $10 per line of code, while others build at $800 or more for the identical product? That is the essential question that this book is going to answer, together with:

What does it take to build quality software at a reasonable cost?

What are the major factors that influence the cost, quality, and development schedule in software design and implementation?

1.2 DEPTH OF EXPERIENCE

This book is a summary of my 32 years of experience in designing and building computer software: 7 years in the U.S. Army building software, and 25 years at the Jet Propulsion Laboratory. This period of accumulated experience also includes the information I gathered as a software management consultant to some of the finest and best U.S. corporations—indeed, the giants in our industry. The problems of quality, cost, and schedule have proven to be the same, end to end, wherever I was invited to help out. The phenomenon of schedule vs. cost vs. quality in computer science holds true for Germany, France, Holland, Denmark, and the rest of the European countries as well. I have no experience with Japan, China, or India directly, but there is no reason to believe that their computer scientists and software professionals are any different from ours.

I do not intend this to be "just another book on software," as some of my colleagues in industry have remarked dryly, but a worthwhile book to read. The intention is to pass on my accumulated experience in computer science, as well as the relevant experience gained in the combat arms of the U.S. Army, which in my case was the Airborne Infantry. Now, there will be those who will say, "What can you learn about computer science and software in the infantry?" Nothing about computer software, it is true, but everything about management, leadership, understanding people, discipline, planning, organization of work and people, as well as seemingly trivial subjects like how to staff through and coordinate action items efficiently. All of these are essential to our work in computer science and to the development of computer software. This is especially true for large systems—those above 250,000 lines of code with high factors of technical complexity combined with a short schedule. The absence of these skills will increase the cost of the product tenfold or more.

1.3   THE SCOPE OF THIS BOOK

The scope of Chapter 16, "The Autonomous Cognitive System," is much too large for the subject to be covered in one chapter and must be dealt with in great detail on its own. It is an essential part of the overall scope of this book, however, because it interprets the work of the great cognitive philosophers from the software architect's point of view. I began to approach the works of Kant, Hegel, and Schopenhauer as a way of looking at computer science many years ago; I never had the time to write my interpretation down until now. When designing and building large software-intensive systems year in and year out, back to back, one does not have the luxury to spend time writing, except for the design-associated books specific to a particular project.

The main theme of this book is *high-quality, low-cost software, built on schedule*; this theme will be re-emphasized throughout. It is a teaching point, and teaching points are just that: They are there to keep the mind focused, specifically on low-cost, high-quality products, on schedule. A minor theme is the inhibitors, those issues that prevent us from building elegantly, fast, and cheaply. These issues are also deeply rooted in the Kantian human thought system (the architecture) and the human thought process (the information flow), the understanding of which will enable a person to at least grasp the "why," even if one can't do anything about it. Understanding and learning from mistakes—one's own and the mistakes of others—is the great teacher and leads to ever better products.

It became very clear to me over the years that the successful building of computer software at a reasonable cost was dependent on several important factors:

- Leadership
- Management
- Communication

- Organization
- Understanding software development standards, architectures, and methodologies

A project lacking in any of these factors will see an increase in the cost of its software products. This book will discuss each of the factors affecting cost, from a practitioner's point of view.

1.4   THE NATURE OF COMPUTER SCIENCE

Additionally, two very important issues need to be discussed that also bear directly on computer science and the cost of computer software.

The first of these is raised by the following questions: Where do computer science and computer software belong in engineering? Should software be the dominant part in an engineering effort, such as an aircraft or spacecraft project, or should it serve a supportive role? This issue of computer science and its placement is causing a rub throughout the industry. It is an issue created by the mindset and outlook on the part of individuals. It is a divisive issue, and the resultant conflicts cost the customer money.

The second critical issue is raised by the questions: What is computer science really? Why did we rename it "information technology?" What is the complete definition of computer software? What is the role of philosophy in computer science?[1] Is it an important role? Why?

All one needs to do is look at the important recent publications in our field. We find that there seem to be no answers to our questions. Our profession used to be called automatic data processing. That evolved into computer science, then into information technology, and finally it has branched off into artificial intelligence and neural networks. What this really means is that while we are pushing the state of the art, we have no agreement as to a unifying science, like biology and chemistry have. Engineers deal with tangible facts and theorems, yet we deal in abstractions. Our profession is a combination of art, science, and engineering. So what is it? Why is it so important that we find a unifying principle?

1.5   THE FUTURE OF COMPUTER SCIENCE

We in computer science are headed full-bore toward total autonomy. This means we need to build a true robot, one that can be sent into space. This would be an autonomous system that, in an intelligent fashion and with an intelligence similar to our human intelligence, could explore our solar system and go to places where we humans cannot survive but from which we can benefit. As a starter, for the building

---

[1] Schopenhaur, Arthur. *Die Welt als Wille und Vorstellung* (The World as Will and Imagination) Gesamtausgabe (Complete Edition). Deutscher Taschenbuch Verlag GmbH & Co. KG, München 1998. Zweiter Band (Volume Two), page 149: "Every science has its special philosophy..."

of such a system, we need an architecture. We need a model that is rational, functional, and logical, and one that can be built. This poses a serious problem because it involves a paradigm shift in the way we think about our profession and how we work in it. Paradigm shifts are dangerous events, as we all know. Galileo was nearly burned for his ideas, and Bruno was. There is an inborn anger in some of us human beings when we are confronted with a phenomenon we don't understand. We either learn, or we are left behind.

I feel that here in the United States we have a few great issues at stake. One is retaining our lead in computer science, and in software programming jobs. Another is pushing the state of the art "through the looking glass." This *must* be accomplished, regardless of the opposition.

1.6   THE ESSENCE OF PHILOSOPHY

Why is the work of the great cognitive philosophers so important for the development of high-quality software at a reasonable cost? It is because they were the ones who researched how we humans perceive, think, decide, and act, and why we do what we do. *A thorough understanding of philosophy is therefore necessary to do what we do efficiently and thoroughly.*

The essence of philosophy comprises many factors:

- How we think
- How we organize our thoughts and our work
- How we contemplate
- How we pay attention and listen
- How we decide
- How we form value judgments
- How we communicate with others

Yet, above all, the essence of philosophy concerns itself with how we treat each other. To me, therefore, it is the greatest of all the sciences. Small wonder that many of the great philosophers were mathematicians and physicists. This discipline, philosophy, upon which all the sciences rest, is given scant attention in the curriculum of our universities and by those of us who earn our living in engineering and the other sciences.

The greatest teachers (and I have had the good fortune of having had quite a few) always used stories from their personal experiences to illuminate teaching points. As students, we were more attentive because the learning process was so much more interesting when it was related to historical events. The teaching of geometry and mathematics becomes exciting when related to Harpalus (a great Greek engineer and philosopher) and how he bridged the Hellespont for Xerxes and the Persian Army. Teaching and instruction become more memorable than watching and listening to someone writing equations on the blackboard. How did he build that 1.6-mile-long pontoon bridge between Abydus and

Sestus?[2] Why did he build it there? What was the outcome for Greece and Persia?[3] As a matter of interest, Harpalus can be justly referred to as someone we call today "a defense contractor," as were Archimedes and Histiaeus of Miletus[4] in their day. The Jet Propulsion Laboratory started as a U.S. Army Ordnance Laboratory, during the Second World War. Thus, before NASA was established, JPL, too, started out as a defense contractor.

There is one more very important aspect to using personal experiences in illuminating (or "adding substance" to) an object in a philosophical sense. As you will see in the architecture of the human thought system and the human thought process (Figure 1), the role of "experience" is one of the dominant roles in Kantian philosophy. How we apply our acquired knowledge, learned in the classroom, and solve problems depend largely on the level of our personal experiences (Figure 8). We acquire personal experiences by living life, and learning personally, or by having someone tell us of their personal experiences in life. Thus, the personal stories I recount in this book are to add substance to an "object" of a design, idea, or concept,[5] not simply to fill space.

Science and history taught together make learning complex subjects far easier. This is a method that is also used in the Army to reinforce a teaching point and to provide the student with a reference to the application of a skill, especially in subjects like engineering and tactics. It so happens that Combat Engineering was among the many skills I acquired through schooling in the U.S. Army. I specialized in bridge design and construction, pontoon bridges and timber trestles being my favorites.

I use stories from personal experience also to illuminate issues of management, leadership, and the architectural design process. I have a habit of doing this in my seminars and classes in order to reinforce the teaching point I am making. After all, the role of experience is one of the dominant themes of the *Three Critiques* of Immanuel Kant.

1.7   WHY AUTONOMY?

Why do we need a totally autonomous system, one that can act and decide on its own, without human intervention? The first thing that comes to my mind is the

---

[2] Herodotus. *The Peloponesian Wars*, Book VII, Chapter II. The Modern Library of the World's Best Books, Random House Inc. New York, 1942.

[3] J. F. C. Fuller. *A Military History of the Western World*, Volume I, Chapter I. Funk & Wagnalls Company, New York, 1954.

[4] Histiaetus and Thales actually built a 26-mile pontoon bridge over the Bosporus for Darius I "The Great." It collapsed with tragic consequences to those on it. For details, read *The Peloponesian Wars*.

[5] Since Chapter 16 of this book culminates in my first thesis for an autonomous system, the reader must understand the correct technical definition of the terms *idea* and *concept* as these dynamic processes relate to the human thought process. The definitions of how these are formed are found in *Die Welt als Wille Und Vorstellung*. Arthur Schopenhauer. Drittes Buch. Seite 316. Deutsche Taschenbuch Verlag GmbH & Co. KG. Muenchen, Germany, 1998. (*The World as Will and Imagination*. Arthur Schopenhauer. Book Three. Page 316. German Pocket Books, Publishers. Munich, Germany, 1998.)

Figure 1. An initial impression of the functional organization of the human thought system.

exploration of deep space. All of space is hostile to human life, in fact, to all of biological life. Mars, Venus, and Jupiter, for instance, are all hostile environments, yet we must explore them because of the categorical imperative: "I will, because I can." It would be infinitely easier to go to Mars if we had a crew of autonomous systems go ahead of the human crew. The autonomous systems would construct a fully life-supporting facility on Mars, test it, and provide the test data to the crew of the manned spacecraft prior to launch. There are also hazardous places on Earth, such as radioactive contamination sites like Chernobyl, the Hanford Reservation, and Oak Ridge that need cleaning up. Autonomous systems could perform the more dangerous jobs. Finally, there are the handling and disposition of biological and chemical agents, and the handling of unknown viruses and bacteria. All these tasks require autonomous systems that can learn, analyze, and decide on a logical course of action, with the human being still the suggesting superior, but not the controller.

One of the questions a colleague and friend asked me was, "What will we do if we build it, and it turns out that it doesn't like us?" Good question! I never thought that possibility through, and certainly I have made many mistakes in the past, not contemplating unforeseen possibilities. For example, as a young U.S. Army Special Forces demolitionist in 1962, I used to train with atomic demolitions ammunition. I had to disassemble and reassemble all of the uranium components with only a lead apron, lead gloves, and a pair of goggles to protect me. What all that did to me physically, I have no idea; I was only 24 at the time, and nobody told me about long-term effects.

So yes, we can build an autonomous system. How we control it is a question we have to resolve *a priori*.

1.8 AN ARCHITECTURE FOR AUTONOMY

The final chapter of this book is the chapter on autonomous systems. From the architect's point of view it describes the system architecture at a level that we refer to in computer science as a Level I architecture. Every system, by force of imperative, must have the architect's vision of how the system will look from an initially subjective point of view.

The greatest problem posed to today's professionals who are contemplating building a truly autonomous system is the architectural design. The reason is that current thinking in computer science is cast into the concrete of hierarchical-sequential logic. In the context that AI and neural networks are attempting to solve the problems posed by autonomy, this approach is unfortunately a "cul-de-sac," or dead end. Human beings who fall into the "normal" category have a completely dynamic, nonhierarchical, nonsequential, and nonlinear thought and reasoning process. Our "thought system" (our functional architecture), our "external sensory input," and our "thought process" (data handling) are so dynamic that they cannot be expressed by using simple traditional methods. The traditional approaches to illustrating the architectures of functional relationships are hierarchical and linear; these use the ubiquitous block diagrams and boxes.

It is in this arena of thought that the great classical German cognitive philosophers (e.g., Immanuel Kant, Arthur Schopenhauer, and Georg Wilhelm Friedrich Hegel) have laid the groundwork for us. When the collective "genius" of these three men is combined with the current state-of-the-art in the technology of computer science, we are looking at total autonomy as being within our grasp. Whether it is for the good of mankind or not is an entirely different question.

This still leaves the problem of how we are to express, illustrate, and articulate the architecture of an autonomous system. We must be careful at this point not to confuse software and hardware, and their equivalent in the human body and the human brain. The human brain is the equivalent of the computer hardware, but we are interested in the software that resides in the brain, the human cognitive system!

We would be using the human cognitive system as the model, but it must be done in such a manner that will be understood by those who will be building it. At this point the tools, processes, and methodology required to express the architecture become critically important, because if it is faulty or too complex, the engineering team will get lost in the details.

So, what is the alternative to the hierarchical and linear approach, to block diagrams and boxes? I personally have used spheres and circles in illustrating my designs during the past 30 years. I have expressed software architectures in this way because the systems I have designed and managed the development of were one-of-a-kind, unique, and mostly large systems built on constrained schedules with capped budgets. I have had a difficult time expressing these systems using the hierarchical approach and did not do so unless forced by my management. More often than not, they did not understand the context diagrams and architectural expressions anyway. The surprising thing was that my GDSS Design Team understood the concept, instantly, when I presented it to them in January 1986. As time went on, and my successes were followed by more successes, I was allowed to follow my methodology. I use Leibnitz "circles" and Euler "spheres"[6] to express the relationships between the functional attributes of the "human thought system" and the "human thought process." I also use them as a general approach toward the articulation and illustration of the functional relationship between computer software segments or subsystems.

1.9   OTHER NOTES

I would also like to bring the matter of the footnotes to your attention. Where I use references to foreign publications, it is only because that is the language I have read

---

[6] *Beitraege zur Berichtung bisheriger Missverstaendnisse der Philosophen.* Johann Michael Mauke, Jena, 1790. Theil von Abhandlung Nr. IV: *Ueber das Verhaeltniss der Theorie des Vorstellungvermoegens zur Kritik der reinen Vernunft,* S. 277–294. Gerhard Karls, Universitaet Tuebingen, Germany.

Contributions to the Commentary on the Misunderstandings of the Philosophers. Johann Michael Mauke, Jena Germany, 1790. Part of Essay No. IV, about the relationship of the IMAGINATION (with all of its attributes) to the *Critique of Pure Reason.*

them in. This is particularly true of the works of Kant, Schopenhauer, and Hegel. They are my main references and have had the greatest influence on my approach of how I manage and how I develop software. I translate the titles of the books for your benefit, but I cannot go back and reread the works in English for the benefit of this book; that would take years, and I'd never get finished.

My use of the German language in the original and in footnotes has its origins in my early college days. I started to use German books and publications for the clarification of technical and science problems that I didn't fully understand in my English textbooks, in particular, chemistry and engineering. This use of material in its original language became a habit and has remained with me throughout my professional career. I certainly would not have found the linkage between the classical philosophers and computer science had I not read their works in the original and developed an enthusiasm for them as a means of relaxation. While going about my business of designing software architectures and then managing their development, I suddenly realized that an autonomous system was doable and achievable in the near future.

As mentioned earlier, I use stories from personal experiences to illuminate issues of all the subjects covered in this book. I have acquired the habit of doing this from the teachers and instructors who were most effective in teaching me. I do this in my seminars and in my lectures to reinforce a teaching point I am making. There are many colleagues and acquaintants who cannot use personal experiences related to the constructs in computer science. These are friends who simply do not have the benefit of experience in the fields addressed here, or have only limited experience, having spent most of their career in the classroom teaching. They understand my style, however, and enjoy my references to practical and real situations.

Finally, the chapter on autonomy will be followed up with a volume purely dedicated to that subject, developed to a Level I architecture, enabling those who are interested and understand the systems concept to start the process of requirements and detailed design.

2 Prologue

This book concerns itself with the low-cost development of high-quality computer software and the factors that directly impact cost. I must admit that in pursuing my profession, nothing has given me quite the level of enjoyment as increasing the quality of a software product and driving hard to reduce its cost. In pursuit of this goal, and successfully achieving ever-lower cost and higher quality with each successive project, many phenomena appeared to manifest themselves. Over the last 30 years, these phenomena have become clearer and individually identifiable.

As I write this book, however, the question that consistently comes to mind is whether anyone cares about the cost of software projects anymore. I am of the impression that neither in industry, nor in DOD or NASA, is there any real interest in lowering the cost of computer software. If there is a true interest, I am not aware of it. Back in the 1970s, when I made the transition in my Army career to computer science and ADP (automatic data processing), people genuinely cared for a quality software product, on schedule and on budget. In fact, it was this professional attitude toward quality, budget, and schedule at the Jet Propulsion Laboratory that attracted me to JPL in the first place, and why I fit in so well.

2.1 HOW THIS BOOK ORIGINATED

This book started as a series of notes I was taking on Kant's *Critique of Pure Reason*. During this time I was designing and building two large ground systems. One was a design exercise for the prototype of a totally autonomous system. Initially, at the instigation of some colleagues, I referred to this system as the Immune Inspired Autonomous Cognitive Computational System (IIACCS); for a number of reasons, I renamed it Perseus.[1] Since a totally autonomous system could prevent illegal hacking into personal and classified networks and databases (among its many uses and functional attributes), I felt the name Perseus would be more appropriate and easier to remember than IIACCS.

---

[1] In classical Greek mythology, Medusa was a woman who was transformed by Pallas Athena into a Gorgon, a winged creature with serpents for hair. Looking upon Medusa turned one instantly to stone. Perseus cut off the head of Medusa.

The Cognitive Dynamics of Computer Science: Cost-Effective Large Scale Software Development, by Szabolcs Michael de Gyurky
Copyright © 2006 by John Wiley & Sons, Inc.

The other large ground system was for the Jason 1 satellite. Upon demonstration of the capabilities of the Jason 1 Satellite Telemetry, Command and Communications Subsystem (JTCCS), a number of my colleagues in industry and at the Jet Propulsion Laboratory asked, "How can you and your team build software so cheaply, while others are so expensive?" We build large complex systems for as low as $10 per line of code.[2]

The Jason TCCS is low-cost and truly elegant in its design and execution, containing 800,000 lines of new code, plus an additional 400,000 lines of adapted lines of code. The JTCCS is the latest and lowest-cost system of a long line of software projects developed by my teams over the past 25 years. So the questions I am going to answer are

- What does it take to build at low cost?
- Why would anyone build at low cost?
- What really is computer software, essentially?
- Where is computer science headed in the future?

2.2   THE IMPORTANCE OF MANAGEMENT

Surely, management is responsible for product quality, budget, and schedule, because responsibility and accountability are management functions. But there must be (and is) far more than that to these pressing issues. Efficiency is certainly an important factor, but efficiency in what areas? Clearly, efficiency is the key to reducing cost, but how, and in what way? We could first address management, but that is a very large and complex area of study, and many good books exist on management already.

Management is probably the most difficult of all skills if one is to do it well. A good manager is hard to find; a great manager is very rare indeed. Good managers make for great companies, lower product costs, and increased market share. Poor managers are those who don't have the necessary skills, dynamic energy, or experience in critical areas. They are simply not qualified to do the job they have been appointed to do. Such managers can bring an organization to its knees. They destroy organizations, companies, and enterprises.

I have applied my management approach to numerous tasks during the past 25 years, but I have used it almost exclusively for software development. I have discovered that the thing that has had the greatest impact on my approach was the influence of the great classical philosophers. I started reading philosophy, beginning with Plato and the Socratic dialogs, at the age of 15. Such examination of ideas

---

[2] The cost of a line of code, as used in this book, includes the source code, comments, all requirements, design, test articulation, user guide documentation, salaries, contractor award fees, facilities, and business-required travel, from the manager on down; in short, *all expenses* paid for by the sponsor and client.

taught me to examine closely every detail of a task that was before me. A second discovery, tightly coupled to the philosophers, was the analysis of how work is actually done. For these reasons, I came to understand that the interaction of people (regardless of academic discipline, training, and experience) and the mechanisms, protocols, and mediums they use to get the work done are of paramount importance in lowering the cost of a product.

After thinking over the question of why we build high-quality products so fast and at such low cost, it became evident to me that there was much more to the management function than met the eye.

Management is a position and a role, not an ability attribute of the human personality, as is leadership. Anyone can fill the role of manager, but to do it well requires certain functional attributes, as well as sufficient levels of experience in each of the attributes that make up management as an object. Key among such functional attributes is the ability to organize, including the ability to organize people, the work process, and the work environment. This includes the ability to visualize the product, to communicate extremely well verbally and in writing, and to understand communication not only as a transmitter but as a receiver also. There is the need for a very highly developed ability to visualize and synthesize from known constructs, to infer from these new and necessary constructs, and then to communicate this inference to others. All of this is a part of the *human thought system*—the term applied to it by Immanuel Kant—and how it senses, processes, and uses information. This has been the driving force for thought, study, and analysis by the great philosophers throughout the centuries.

2.3 THE TIE-IN WITH AUTONOMY

Closely allied with cognitive philosophy (cognitive dynamics + cognitive mechanics) is the concept of autonomy. To me, this means that if I know how I perceive, analyze, process, decide, and act, then it is this model that enables me to design and write computer software to help me perform these functions and tasks. It follows then, that computer software is an abstraction of the *human thought process*, not just of the human thought system alone. If this is true (and from my experience it is), then I can build a completely autonomous computer system, using *the human thought system as the model for the functional architecture* and *the human thought process for the functional data process*.

So now I have a model on which to build my autonomous computer or true robot, if one wishes to use that term. Note that a robot is not autonomous; it is an automaton, made up of programmed rules ("hardwired"), which it cannot of its own volition discard or modify significantly, nor may it truly act on its own accord. In contrast, an autonomous system is more like a human being: When it is given a set of basic instructions and then is taught to do the task, it will proceed on its own to learn, modify, and use its understanding as it sees fit, depending on its mental and physical abilities.

2.4 MAJOR THEMES OF THIS BOOK

Thus, from the question of why are we so cost-efficient in building high-quality software systems emerge two major themes and one minor. The first major theme is how we manage efficiently, and why. The second concerns what software really is, where we are headed in software development, and why. The minor theme is that if we know the answers to the first two questions, then we can build a totally autonomous system, and not at inordinate expense. The challenge, then, is to limit this book to under 300 pages so my friends and co-workers won't fall asleep reading it. Then, if there is sufficient interest in any one of the key chapters, e.g., Communication, Architectures, or Autonomous Systems, I'll write another dissertation on the requested subjects.

The most difficult product to produce at low cost while retaining high standards of quality is computer software. How this is accomplished is the focus of this book. For those who are interested in the subject of high-quality software at low cost, I have included many real-life experiences to illuminate and add insight into how people think, act, and perform their jobs. This was, and is, a scary thing in itself. Many of these experiences come from my 20 years of service in the U.S. Army, half of which was in the Army Special Forces (better known as Green Berets) and the U.S. Parachute Infantry in combat. The other half was in computer science and Psychological Operations. It was in the Army that I began to observe people under stress, while they were doing dangerous work. Some did it with great attention to detail and within the parameters established through training for their safety. Others, for reasons at the time incomprehensible to me, made huge mistakes by disregarding the rules and were killed or maimed. Why do people disregard rules, and often common sense? Worse, why do people disregard the guidance of someone more senior and experienced, only to make critical errors? These are all factors affecting the success or failure of any endeavor, but in particular computer software due to its cost to produce, maintain, and replace. In an age of spacecraft, fly-by-wire jet aircraft, satellites, and precision-guided munitions, software plays the leading role in effective and predictable performance and cost. And yet, low cost, if not demanded by the customer, is not an obligation. However, if a budget and schedule have been agreed upon with the customer, it is a sacred obligation.

2.5 THE CHALLENGE OF A NEW IDEA

Some years ago, I was presented with a formal challenge by a distinguished friend and colleague at JPL to come up with a new idea. He said that what we needed was a true "paradigm shift" at the Laboratory, one that would set us on a path to new discoveries and absorb all our mental and physical energies for a decade or two. At the same time, this new idea should allow us as an institution to pursue our great love, the exploration of deep space. There are two constraints to this challenge. First, it must fit in with our institutional mission objective, which is the exploration of deep space. Second, it must put us 20 years ahead of industry (and the other research centers) and give us, so to say, "a brand new technical bag," which would totally focus our talents as world-class engineers and scientists.

This was an interesting challenge. I am a builder of large software systems, not a researcher. People who design and build the software systems in support of our spacecraft generally do not have time to write and publish; we are too busy meeting schedules and committed to the launch windows looming on our collective and personal horizons.

My personal field of interest is computer science, specifically system architectures, their design and implementation. However, the challenge intrigued me and I decided to think about a new idea within the framework of the parameters of our institutional mission objectives. One of the major thrusts of research in our field of computer science (and its derivative, information technology) is robotics. As mentioned earlier, this means the designing and building of a true autonomous system, a real robot. This, of course, is true computer science. We have made little gains here and there in building semi-robots, like rovers and spacecraft, but these are only semi-autonomous systems, really nothing more than automatic systems. Such so-called autonomy is limited to the execution of tasks that have rule-based algorithms and therefore is limited by many constraints, such as computation speed, memory, and above all, knowledge on the designers' part. At the same time, I was aware that other friends and colleagues of mine were working on the mathematical representations of truly autonomous functions, such as self/nonself discrimination neural networks.

2.6 THE IMPORTANCE OF VISUALIZATION

As a software architect, I am used to laying out large, complex architectures and finding components that fit into the overall logical design. Furthermore, I also know from experience that having a subjective design is not enough; it must be accomplished by a grouping of the required disciplines and skill levels with the ability to communicate and work as a team. This process is paralleled by an understanding of what you want to do; it is a clear vision of the objective system you are trying to build. It also requires a thorough understanding of the object technology, as well as other associated technologies, and the academic disciplines underlying the systems architecture, methodologies, and management techniques that can bring it all to a successful conclusion.

There are three main contributing factors:

- Visualizing the product architecture
- Visualizing the organization
- Visualizing the methodologies and techniques

If any one of these is missing from the mind of the manager-architect,[3] the job can't be done at a reasonable cost or within a reasonable time.

[3] The concept of the "manager-architect" is discussed in Chapter 4.

(There is always the rare exception, of course. One such exception is when a superb, well-integrated, and experienced engineering team is available to the manager. The people on this team, with their high qualifications, will have worked together on similar projects over many years. They will, in an almost teleological sense, and with a thorough dialectic process, paint the *a priori* system object or architectural object and give it sufficient substance so it can be built.[4] In this rare case, the manager is and will remain a bean counter, an administrator, an electrical engineer, or a scientist, but not a manager-architect. In this exceptional case, the design team is not only the controlling element of the project, but also the principal systems engineer. This type of team has unto itself the vision of the architecture, which is the focal point of the team required to achieve the substantial object. However, there will always be delay factors, which means time and money overruns. As most of my old and experienced colleagues will agree, the systems engineer does not have the coercive authority to impose on the team; it is beyond a systems engineer's jurisdiction to decide on a course of action and punish those who do not carry out the instructions, either by firing them outright or by replacing them.)

How do you build a system you cannot envision in your mind? It can only rarely be done as a group. The vision is always formulated in one mind, the manager-architect's; it assumes substance within one mind, at the start.

2.7   THE MOVE TOWARD AUTONOMY

Furthermore, it is obvious to me and a few other computer science professionals that software is headed toward full autonomy. Where did I get the initial vision for a fully autonomous system? I needed at least a start, or *gerere*, to use that important Latin word meaning "to begin, to start."

One Saturday afternoon I was relaxing with the last of Immanuel Kant's three critiques, *Das Kritik der reiner Vernunft*,[5] and it hit me like a hammer on the head. I had found the answer on the three plane-levels necessary to build a totally autonomous system: the intellectual plane, the physical plane, and the technical plane. All three are equally important; it is not only important to know how to build a true robot (i.e., a true autonomous system), but it must be doable at a reasonable cost. What then is a reasonable cost in a time of tight budgets? How and why should we deliver a product at a good price? That is the other side of the equation.

So the credit of opening my mind to a new perspective and understanding of computer software and of computer science as a true science belongs to Immanuel Kant. I can see him in my mind's eye, sitting in his study late at night in Koenigsberg, Prussia, thinking and writing for us computer scientists who are often referred to affectionately as "code hogs." I'm sure he never thought, while writing away, that 200 years later his genius would have impacted a new science the way it has

---

[4] These philosophical concepts are discussed in Chapter 4.
[5] Kant, Immanuel. *The Critique of Pure Reason.*

with me. Now, as I think of my approach to designing and managing software systems at low cost, I realize that I owe it largely to the three critiques.[6]

What Kant is really talking about (as are Schopenhauer and Hegel) is the organization, functioning, and functional relationships among the subsystems and components of the human thought system, including how all that works, how it processes, how it decides and consequently forces the body to act. Computer science, software specifically, is no longer simply a tool; it is becoming an abstraction of the human thought process. The only models of the human thought system we have to start with are reflected in the works of the great cognitive philosophers.

The field of modern computer science, as it applies to my profession as a manager and architect, is therefore cognitive dynamics and cognitive mechanics. This also implies that it is in transition from its original electromechanical manifestation as a tool, toward becoming a biological identity with a chemical database storage system and neuro-electrical data transfer function, if not in its outward form, certainly in its architectural design.

It is a sad fact that university courses in philosophy and languages are not strictly required in the American curriculum of higher education for our engineers and scientists. It is almost a *sine qua non* that Kant and Schopenhauer should be read in German; I have tried reading them in English, but it is too difficult. Theodore von Kármán[7] recognized soon after his arrival in the United States that the American baccalaureate in Engineering lacked what he considered adequate depth to fully prepare a young individual to solve problems end to end in the manner he and other European engineers and scientists were prepared to by their education. Elton Mayo came to similar conclusions while at the Harvard Business School, although his discoveries are stated somewhat differently.[8]

2.8   WHY I WROTE THIS BOOK

This book is written because my friends and colleagues asked me to write it. So I write it for you, and for myself, as a summary of my experiences as a developer and practitioner in computer science over a period of 32 years.

Friends, colleagues, and co-workers are in fact who you are, because although I manage your efforts and have the responsibility and accountability for the systems we produce, every one of you has been or is an intricate part of the team. I have learned as much from you as you have learned from me, as each of you is a true expert in his field, with the commensurate depth of technical knowledge and extension into the intricate mechanics of computer science far exceeding mine in academic discipline and technical orientation. Indeed, I hire only professionals who

---

[6] Kant, Immanuel. *The Critique of Judgment, The Critique of Practical Reason*, and *The Critique of Pure Reason.*

[7] Theodore von Kármán, *The Wind and Beyond*. Little, Brown & Company 1967, Boston, Toronto, 156.

[8] Elton Mayo, *The Social Problems of an Industrial Civilization*, Harvard University, Graduate School of Business Administration, 1945. Printed at the Andover Press, Andover, Massachusetts.

are far more expert than I am, and who equal and exceed my own commitment to excellence and to the concept of winning. You are also the ones who have made me a success, much like the members of a championship football team make the coach a winner. With this, I'd like to thank my great team of professionals, you who have enabled us to win the equivalent of three software "Super Bowls" in a row, from 1986 to 2001. "Winning isn't everything, but wanting to win is."[9]

In software systems, this means three things:

1. A quality product
2. On schedule
3. On budget!

There is nothing wrong with this. Why not give the customer a quality product on time, for the money that you have agreed to provide it for?

And now, let me try to put together how we do it from the perspective of the coach (that's me). Here it goes, and if you disagree, your points are well taken. And yes, you did it all; I just told war stories to inspire you to greater deeds of software glory.

2.9   MERGING THEORY AND PRACTICE

The intention is to place computer science theory and practice into a closer relationship. I shall avoid the use of new terms like "information technology" and the like because I find "computer science" not only more inclusive, but also most appropriate to the subject.

Before going any further, let me say that there is a very interesting phenomenon in our profession. This phenomenon is that very few people who consistently work in software design and implementation have the time to write. On the other hand, those who do not work in software design and implementation as a profession do generally have the time to write; in fact, they put out a prodigious amount of great material. These people are generally educators, who must publish in order to survive. This means that their expertise is not completely based on practical reality or experience, but on study and research, which is idealistic. This creates necessarily a gap between theory and practice because truly correct decisions and value judgments can only be made *a posteriori*, that is, based mainly on the synthesis of the sum of one's experiences, and not on academically acquired knowledge alone.

There are many good textbooks out there, covering almost every topic in this book, e.g., architecture, management, organization, and so on. However, most of these textbooks are written by individuals who earn their daily bread by teaching

---

[9] Vincent Thomas "Vince" Lombardi (1913–1970). American football coach. Led the Green Bay Packers to six divisional titles, five NFL crowns, and two Super Bowl wins.

and doing research; thus, the textbooks they write are in the main theoretical-idealistic, or better said, *a priori*. This dissertation is intended as a source of information that is, to my knowledge, rarely covered in textbooks or professional journals. Every chapter in this book should (and will) have a volume written on it, as time permits. It is addressed to only a few interested software developers and practitioners, such as my co-workers and friends on my many successful projects. After 44 years of professional work, the lion's share of which has been spent in software development, I have learned many lessons. I have been asked by my friends and colleagues to pass these lessons on by writing them down for you and for others who might be interested.

2.10   THE PACE OF COMPUTER SCIENCE

As I write this, computer science, including software, is undergoing rapid changes and advances. The way I see it, every three years or so a major change occurs in the field of computer science, like it or not. I normally work on software-intensive projects that last on average 36 months. Regardless of how hard I have tried to build on the technology just completed, no matter how nice, trouble-free, and elegant, it is obsolete. So, my teammates and I must go to the next stage of sophistication if we want to stay current and employable. This means that we have to use new hardware, new application software, and new tools on the next project. Taking advantage of COTS packages (commercially available off-the-shelf layered software products) is another small factor in driving down cost, if you know how to select and use them.

Our software, here in the United States, is becoming more and more expensive. In fact, it is becoming prohibitively expensive. Why that should be is one of the questions I am going to try to answer. It is clear to every computer professional that more and more of our software jobs are going overseas. This is because it is assumed that those who are overseas, beyond our borders, can do it better and cheaper. This is simply not so; we can do it better in this country than anywhere in the world. My team here at JPL certainly has proven many times that no one builds quality systems and software cheaper than we do here. It is not hard to answer why that is. Some of the constants in software design that remain regardless of how fast new languages and hardware appear in the marketplace are architectural refinements, organization, process, implementation methodology, and communication. These remain because they are attributes of the human thought system and thought process; in other words, cognitive dynamics and mechanics.

Some time ago, in 1988, a friend and colleague of mine here at JPL was given a task to survey the cost of software across the country. It turned out that sophisticated ground control systems for satellites and spacecraft cost on the average $750 per line of code, while the satellite and spacecraft systems onboard cost about $1,200 per line of code.

First, let me digress a moment to explain what is meant by a "line of code." By my definition, the cost of code includes all development hardware, all software tools (e.g., design and test software), COTS packages, lines of executable code and comments, all documentation, all salaries, facilities, and contractor award fees. *In summation, the cost per line of code includes everything from the manager's salary on down.* The project we have just completed, the Jason Satellite Telemetry, Command and Communications Subsystem (JTCCS), cost under $10 a line of code for 803,000 lines of new code. This was all beautifully documented and fully tested and has been "flying" the satellite. Our successful team is made up of JPL and Titan Inc. employees and has a 16-year record of delivering equally elegant, sophisticated systems at very low cost. This includes the TOPEX/Poseidon Telemetry Command and Communications Subsystem (196,000 lines of code, at a cost of under $30 per line of code) and the Military Airlift Command's Global Decision Support System (971,000 lines of code, at a cost of under $40 per line of code).

Oh yes, it is important after the completion of each project to document the lessons learned and the metrics data accumulated on individual and team performance and productivity, the facility and robustness of various application software languages, rates of anomalies per line of code, the time to fix them and to document the fixes, and the associated costs.

There is no magic in our performance and how we build. Recently, I was told by an Air Force project manager that he was still paying about $750 per line of code. I was not completely surprised; still, it scared me somewhat. I do not want our software production jobs going overseas. More importantly, I don't want our national-security-relevant software to be developed in foreign countries.

There is no single parameter or function that alone dominates the cost factor of computer software. There are a number of them, all of which I believe have a great impact on how much a software-intensive system costs. I have divided these functional areas into distinct chapters. All of the chapters contain those elements of software design, implementation, testing, and installation that bear directly on cost. What percentage of the cost they account for is difficult to say. After I completed writing down the relevant chapters and their subjects, I was astonished to find how closely they resembled the Kantian *wells of experience*[10] that are required for making sound *a posteriori* decisions on the part of the manager-architect. (See Chapter 13 for more detail.)

Failure to pay close attention by not including each of the wells of experience in the formulation of a technical, organizational, or methodological value judgment in making decisions has caused me trouble in the past. The consequences were always to impact cost and schedule, but fortunately I have always been able to catch the problem before it went out of control.

Developing large software projects is in some respects like driving a car at high speed in a race. If you are the manager, you are the driver, and you can't let your eyes off the road for a second at 200 mph; your senses tell you how things are from the sound of the engine, the feel of the tires, and the motion of the chassis. When you feel and sense something is wrong you check your instruments. This of course

---

[10] Immanuel Kant, *Kritik der Urteilskraft* (*The Critique of Judgment/Decision*), Koenigsberg, 1790.

implies that the system needs to be delivered to the customer on time and on budget. If budget and schedule are not important, then it is not a race, nor is this book for you; put it down and forget it.

Software is exactly what it implies: it is "soft" and invisible, unless you ensure that it is visible on paper or some other substantive form. It is not like a mechanical engineering product or a chemical equation that you can look at, see the mistakes in, and correct. Yet it is similar because it is composition. It started out as a tool, a tool to aid us in calculations. Then it expanded to rule-based systems, which are more efficient tools to do difficult, complex work. Such tools help us do our work more efficiently, like flying a fighter aircraft, or guiding an unmanned vehicle to a target. Now we are headed into a great revolution in software, one that will be a true paradigm shift in the technology of computer science. We are on the verge of true autonomy, and autonomous cognition. It will be software based, which means that a machine will be able to learn, analyze, decide, and act. This new technology will require a new type of computation because of the enormous computational tasks inherent in autonomous systems. I have decided to call this new computational system "Monadics" in honor of Leibniz for the concept. It will be in nature *process cognitive*,[11] and will be based on the biology model.[12] It is an exciting new world for software, but we must be masters of our own house in cost and schedule.

2.11 THE IMPORTANCE OF COGNITIVE DYNAMICS

Let's start out with saying that we must understand the underpinnings of what we call computer science today, and where we are headed in the near future. We are already feeling our way toward autonomous systems. However, it has become equally clear that although we are making advances here and there in the mechanics, we are not able to converge on what we are trying to do in the dynamics. We are unable to bring it together into a systems concept, which has been available to us all along. The body of knowledge that has been absent from our engineering toolbox is philosophy, and the software term that I as an architect have come to use to describe my understanding of it is *cognitive dynamics*.

Cognitive dynamics—in computer science, engineering—is my frame of reference; it is the new designation and nomenclature of autonomous computer software. With cognitive philosophy as its foundation, it encompasses

- System architecture
- System design

---

[11] Mark Tarbell appropriately named the nature of the Monadics concept of computation "process cognitive." This means that the individual components of such a system know and decide autonomously what to compute, how fast, and when, much as biological systems do. See Chapter 16.
[12] Michail Zak, Dynamics of intelligent systems. *International Journal of Theoretical Physics*. Volume 39. No. 8, 2000.

- Theoretical and applied mathematics
- Neural networks
- Molecular biology
- Biochemistry and biophysics
- Robotics
- Application languages
- Computer hardware

Its other equally important plane of knowledge and discipline comprises

- Implementation
- Design methodologies and techniques
- Organization
- Communication
- Leadership
- Management of complex systems

We are heading very rapidly toward totally autonomous systems. It should be understood that computer science is a true science and does not take second place to any of the other sciences; in fact, it might well be the leading science of the future, along with molecular biology. Any country that puts computer science into a secondary or tertiary role will completely lose out technologically during the 21st century.

3 The Philosophical Foundations of Computer Software Design

Understanding the philosophical foundations of computer software design is important only if one wishes to do software well, and at a reasonable cost. If we are to
produce quality software products at a low cost, we must know the underpinnings of
the discipline we work in. I produce low-cost software because since my youth I
have had an abiding interest in cognitive philosophy, which models the human
thought system. I have also discovered that cognitive philosophy not only applies
to the craft of building software, but also to the applied work process around it that
makes it happen. The process could be labeled "management" and left at that.
However, there are functional elements of management that stand apart in their
importance. For instance, if a system is to work correctly, the subsystems must
be dealt with in equal consideration in order to fully understand their importance
to the whole. The subsystems that I consider crucial to the successful function of
management are represented in the chapters of this book.

Computer science is the science that strives to abstract the human cognitive process to the ultimate degree. The ultimate objective or target is the development of a
totally autonomous system that completely replicates our ability to sense, think,
analyze, decide, and act without outside interaction or the need for direction.

3.1 THE PHILOSOPHICAL ORIGINS OF COMPUTER SCIENCE

We must always keep in mind that the word *computer* means "counting machine";
human beings are counting machines, some very capable, some not. The first time I
thought about how important the fact is that we humans are biological counting
machines was when I came upon this statement by Kant:

> I hypothesize that one day, all visible and invisible phenomena in the universe will be
> explainable in mathematics.

The goal of Kant's search may have been for God, but in the process he and the
other great cognitive philosophers explored all of the subsystems of the human

The Cognitive Dynamics of Computer Science: Cost-Effective Large Scale Software Development,
by Szabolcs Michael de Gyurky
Copyright © 2006 by John Wiley & Sons, Inc.

mind, and the functional processes it uses to handle, store, and retrieve data. This they did over a great period of time without the aid of a modern computer, and with hotly debated antagonism amongst themselves, much like when we now dialectically debate design options.

It is a wonderful revelation that not only is the science of computation biology-based, but the way that individuals do work (how they work individually and in groups) is biology-based as well. Therefore, the thorough understanding of cognitive philosophy is essential to both the design of computer hardware and software products, as well as the design, organization, and direction of the people who are to do the work, down to the most junior programmer. A lack of this knowledge and expertise increases the cost of the products significantly. There are great manager-architects, like Kelly Johnson,[1] who understood the cognitive dynamics of design, organization, and leadership intuitively. Others, like Theodore von Kármán,[2] had the thorough academic grounding to achieve the same great deeds in engineering.

This is an introduction into the world of cognitive dynamics and how understanding it will reduce cost to acceptable and competitive levels. This is not an easy subject to keep confined to a couple hundred easy-to-absorb pages. Kant is not very easy reading. Arthur Schopenhauer is a little harder because he dissects Kant's propositions. But the fact is that computer science is computational science, and it is based on the human thought system and human thought process. Kant, Schopenhauer, and Hegel are required reading if we are going to build the systems of the future, such as use total autonomy, and if we hope to build quality products at affordable cost and remain world leaders in computer science, as well as remain competitive in the marketplace.

In the introduction of his wonderful work, *The World as Will and Imagination*,[3] Arthur Schopenhauer addresses his university colleagues by telling them

> When you read my book, and don't understand it, don't feel bad; put it down and forget it. If you have already bought it, and to your dismay don't understand it, I'm sorry. You can put it on your coffee table, to impress your friends, so your guests will think you are reading it. If you put it on your bookshelf, dust it off occasionally so your visitors will be given the impression that you are reading it. Don't even think of scanning it. I tried to make it simpler, and easier to understand, but gave up. I recommend that you read through the book twice. The first time slowly and carefully, the second time with deeper interest.

[1] Aeronautics engineer and manager Clarence L. "Kelly" Johnson (1910–1990). Led Lockheed's "Skunk Works" in development of the U-2 spyplane, SR-71 Blackbird, F-117 Stealth fighter, among many others.
[2] von Skolloskislaki Kármán Todor, a.k.a. Theodore von Kármán (1881–1963). Legendary aeronautics engineer and cofounder of NASA's Jet Propulsion Laboratory in Pasadena, CA.
[3] Arthur Schopenhauer, *die Welt als Wille und Vorstellung* (*The World as Will and Imagination*). Erster Band (Volume I), Deutscher Taschenbuch Verlag GMBH & Co. KG, Munich, April 1998.

3.2 INFLUENCE OF THE COGNITIVE PHILOSOPHERS

I read books on science, engineering, and mathematics very often in German. This language, to me at least, is the best tool for clarifying complex terms, theorems, and ideas relating to my profession. I neglected French long ago, except for poetry, music, and an occasional novel or magazine. I grew up with three languages, Hungarian, French, and German, and first learned English as an 11-year-old, when I arrived with my parents in this country. After that I added Latin, which has served me well, and Spanish because I wanted to read the literature of Spain. Hungarian is a fabulous, beautiful, and probably the most flexible language in the world. However, it is too hard to learn and command, and so very few people except the native speakers command it well. Even those born there and who emigrate soon lose the command of it unless they practice it constantly. So German and English are the main languages of the cognitive philosophers. Newton, Hume, Hamilton, and Locke are the English thinkers who influenced me the most.

This book should not be complicated. It is written from the perspective of a computer scientist and software development manager and architect for his fellow professionals. Thus, this is not a book on philosophy, but about cost-effective software development. For it to be most beneficial, however, you will need to read *The Three Critiques*, *The World as Will and Imagination*, and *The Science of Logic*. These are the essential works on cognitive philosophy, the science and system of human thought.

The science of human thought, cognitive philosophy, is to me as a software engineer *cognitive dynamics*; cognitive dynamics forms the baseline for computer science, cum software design. The other works, like those of Newton and Leibniz, are optional. Such reading will be a lot of work, but if you love computer science, it will be a wonderful experience; I guarantee it.

Human beings have developed tools over thousands of years to make life easier, functionally. Computer software, on the other hand, is not only a tool; with it we are striving to replicate the human thought system. The work going on today in robotics and artificial intelligence indicates that this is what is happening. There are many huge gaps, however; most are in the academic disciplines required for robotics and AI, as well as in the experience acquired during long apprenticeships developing software systems hands-on.

All of software, such as machine languages, operating systems, databases, communications, and application components, are abstractions of some component or subsystem of the human thought system. The study, analysis, and articulation of the architecture of the human thought system was the lifelong work of the giants of modern philosophy, Kant, Hegel, and Schopenhauer. They did not do it, of course, with computers in mind. They did it as a science, pursuing an understanding of how we think, how we decide, and how we formulate courses of action.

There are the other philosophers, too, the great minds of classical antiquity. I started casually with Aristotle, at 14, but it was too hard, so I picked up Plato's *Republic* and there received my first lesson in the dialogs. These lessons remain with me to this day. Actually, what motivated me as a 14-year-old to attempt

Aristotle was that I had read a biography of Alexander of Macedonia. In it, Alexander at a very young age mastered the great war horse Bucephala, after all the officers of his father had tried and failed. Upon being asked how he was able to accomplish this feat, he confided afterwards to his father, King Phillip, that he had observed that the horse did not buck when he was facing the sun. After the horse had thrown off all the riders, Alexander asked permission as a 12-year-old to try to ride him. First he faced the horse into the sun, and then mounted. He then rode the horse at full speed into the sun, until the horse was completely worn out, and obeyed only him from that point on. I really admired this insight, intuition, and keen ability to observe phenomena. It also became clear to me that I wanted to be as observant as Alexander. Well, his teacher was the great Aristotle, and I thought that I would make Aristotle my teacher, too, by reading his books, so I went to the Parkersburg Carnegie Library and checked out Volume one of his works.[4] I started to read it, but it was a very difficult read while caddying, mowing grass, and painting fences. I took a side trip and attacked and finished Plato's *Republic*,[5] which was far easier reading. Then I returned to Aristotle. I may add here my surprise, as a 15-year-old kid, reading in the shade of the caddy shack of the Worthington Golf Club, in Parkersburg, West Virginia, how much more there was to a simple word like "justice" once Socrates himself started to dissect it. This was the beginning for me, in my quest for analysis of the true meaning of words and objects. I never left off the questioning of others as to what they saw and what they really meant when they said something or described something. The dialectic is a wonderful tool in the toolkit of a systems architect or systems engineer. After finishing the *Republic*, I was perusing the shelves and found *Also sprach Zarathustra* by Frederick Nietzsche. I read first through the prologue to find out if it was worthwhile reading. In it I found a passage that made a big impression on my 15-year-old mind. The passage, paraphrased below, relates how human beings think, behave, and are motivated.

As Zarathustra comes off the mountain to return to live in the society of men, he watches a crowd assembled in a town square to watch a tightrope walker, who is earning his daily bread by putting his life into peril. He falls and is killed. No one bothers to take his body and bury it, because they all came to watch him fall and die. Zarathustra takes the body when night falls, and looks for a place to bury him. As he carries the body, he says to himself, "Verily, humanity is a filthy stream; one must be an ocean to take all this filth into oneself without becoming personally defiled." This quote took me back to the grizzly things I had seen and experienced as a 7-year-old boy, fleeing the onrushing Red Army into Hungary, and my

---

[4] Aristotle, *The Works of Aristotle Translated into English*, Volume I, CATEGORIAE and DE INTERPRETATIONE, ANALYTICA PRIORA, TOPICA and DE SOPHISTICIS ELENCHIS. Translated Into English Under the Editorship of W.D. ROSS, M.A., Hon. LL.D., Oxford University Press, London 1928.
[5] Plato, *The Works of Plato, Part I—The Republic*, Tudor Publishing Company, New York, 1933. p. 27, Book I, Argument.

later experiences in refugee camps, hospitals, and the German orphanage in Freiburg/Breisgau, Germany. Much later in life, as a U.S. Army Special Forces captain, I would sometimes be detailed to perform parachuting demonstrations for villagers and townspeople around the world. As I looked down on the crowd below at the drop zone, I would always have in the back of my mind that among the spectators was a number of people hoping to see a tragedy, and that my team and I were the tightrope walkers.

So you might say I became a Stoic philosopher at a very early age, not knowing what it was all about, but then having Socrates, Aristotle, and Nietzsche awaken in me the quest for understanding of how people think and behave.

3.3 ABSTRACTING THE HUMAN THOUGHT SYSTEM

I am not a philosopher, and this is not a book on philosophy. This is about the importance of understanding the basic philosophical constructs and how they apply to the art and science of software engineering. I pursue philosophy not as a student of philosophy, but out of curiosity and enjoyment, much like I read the Talmud, to see if there is anything I can learn from the authors. If I may use the term "fun," I'd like to, because Kant, Schopenhauer, and the rest are true delights to read. One must read them at least twice, but three times is best to get the most out of them. I read with the mindset of a systems architect, a manager, and a systems engineer who is trying to understand more deeply what he is doing, and how others around him think (or perhaps not think).

The more one understands how this works, the easier it is to build quality software at a low cost. In fact, I believe that knowing cognitive philosophy and understanding it enhance all architectural endeavors, be they building software, spacecraft, aircraft, or bridges. Again, for those of you who are not interested in low cost or short schedules, don't bother reading further. Whatever we do as humans can be done either professionally with clean elegance, or sloppily at great expense. Reading the giants and their masterpieces on the human thought system, I am amazed how lightly computer science is regarded by other academic disciplines. After all, Schopenhauer, Hegel, and Kant articulate mathematics and logic, not in the form of equations and formulas, but in words. Since at the time of their efforts there were no computers, expression of their concepts was restricted to verbal and limited graphical articulation. The works of the cognitive philosophers represent the product of 200 years of high-intensity effort.

Figure 1 in Chapter 1 is an initial impression on my part of the basic functional organization of the human thought system. Of course, it is articulated through the eyes of a computer scientist, specifically a computer software architect or software developer, as opposed to the eyes of a philosopher or software theoretician. Before I can build something, I must sketch it out as an architecture. Computer science is up there with physics, chemistry, and biology in importance; not in its primitive form, but in its mature present-day definition.

Computer software, therefore, is an attempt at the abstraction of the human thought system. It is at present still far from replicating it; for almost everybody pursuing robotics, this replication is a distant goal, but to a few initiates it is already within their grasp. The leap into replicating the human thought system is as great a leap into the technical future as the splitting of the atom was in its day. It will obsolete today's computation, it will make hacking into unauthorized systems an impossibility for many decades to come. It will permit landing on all the planets and their moons without exposing humans to those harsh environments, while accomplishing all the science and engineering objectives.

Welcome to the future, those of you young and old, who know what I'm talking about.

3.4 THE PHILOSOPHICAL FOUNDATIONS OF SOFTWARE DEVELOPMENT

The philosophical foundations of elegant, state-of-the-art, low-cost software development are

- *Intuition and reason*—Kant
- *Objectivity*—Schopenhauer
- *Dialectics and logic*—Hegel

These three are not the only philosophers who bear on human thought, but they are the ones who gave me the understanding of how we humans think, how we perceive, how we are motivated, and how we decide. Their ideas gave me an ability to model in my mind, *a priori*, anything I want or need to build. Therefore, it is important that every professional software manager-architect have a thorough understanding of cognitive philosophy and how to apply it to his work.

I would also like to establish right at the beginning of this dissertation that to me *the manager is also the architect* in this line of work; the two jobs are synonymous.

First among the several most important attributes of the manager is *leadership*. This means leadership as an intrinsic attribute, not just as a title. Without leadership, you have an administrator or an accountant, a bureaucrat or a bean counter. This type thinks and fully believes that by understanding where the money is being spent, he can understand the dynamics of an organization. Chapter 12, on leadership, encompasses the contents of 12 one-hour lessons, so it is difficult, if not impossible, to do any of the subjects in this book justice in a single chapter.

There are 16 chapters in this dissertation, and each is equally important if a large software project is to be a quality product produced at a reasonable cost to the customer, on schedule and on budget, with a healthy profit margin to the developers. How are all of these philosophically grounded functions handled by one manager-architect? I have been asked this many times. The shortest answer (which people hate) is: "It's Zen, man. It's Zen." The real answer, unfortunately, is still found in the concepts of Lao Tzu, namely Zen,[6] but much more complicated. It is covered in Chapter 13, on management. The manager is the master craftsman who makes it all happen; short of that, he is a failure and should take up some profession he is good at and is happy doing. Climbing to the top of something as esoteric and complex as software development is not fun, unless you love it. Those who can't produce as project managers should look for another job, like programming, testing, systems engineering, or even driving a big rig, which requires far less energy, and leaves more time for the wife and kids. But do that, for heaven's sake, and don't waste the customer's money.

3.5 THE PHENOMENON OF REALITY

Since my first encounter with Socrates, through Plato's *Republic*, I have been deeply interested in "reality" as a phenomenon. In everything I have done since my Army combat years in Vietnam, I have observed with fascination how people viewed, perceived, interpreted, and remembered events and impressions. The fact that any three people viewing one event would interpret it in three very different ways interested me even more. In order for me to get a better understanding of any situation, I began to question everyone who had viewed any particular event or phenomenon; then I would draw my own conclusions. In war this was very important in getting my mission accomplished and keeping my troops alive and in one piece. This habit of mine carried over into my Army engineering and computer science specialties as well.

My preoccupation with the concept of reality led me to read more deeply into the philosophers pursuing the cognitive process, from Aristotle through Locke and Hume. I finally arrived at my favorite philosophers, Kant, Hegel, and Schopenhauer, about the time I was going through my education in automatic data processing. As I started to design and program software, I noticed that some computer languages to me were easy and some were hard; in fact, some were almost unbearable to use. The ones that were easiest for my brain were IBM Assembler and GPSS, while the hardest was COBOL.

It occurred to me that the reason some languages were easier for me than others was that their syntax and structure were easier for me to understand and use. I arrived at the conclusion that the individual(s) who had invented the languages I liked must have had a mental process similar to my own, whereas the ones I disliked did not. So, the cognitive process has two elements: subjective recognition and objective recognition. This is also true of literature. I really like to read almost everything, but some books are very hard to read, in fact painful, whereas others are easy. The idea of cognition, and the understanding of how we humans sense, perceive, listen, observe, understand, communicate, decide, and act became of very great interest to me because it carried over into how I performed my job, alone as well as with others.

[6] Lao Tzu, *The Way of Life*. An American Version, by Witter Bynner, Capricorn Books, New York, 1962.

3.6   THE PHENOMENON OF SUBJECTIVITY

The more I read, the more I understood the phenomenon of subjectivity, and this carried over into my interaction with the people I commanded and managed.

To understand this, consider the careful directions I had given to one of my Army subordinates, on which his life depended. I reiterated my carefully worded instructions while looking into his eyes, and asked him to repeat to me what I had just said; he did so correctly. Within one minute he did exactly the opposite, and blew himself to bits. This is a great lesson in the cognitive process. Further and more significant is the fact that there were two other individuals there with him at the time who also had listened attentively, but ignored or totally disobeyed my orders. They were severely wounded for no reason whatsoever except the failure to pay attention and to follow instructions. The fact that this phenomenon was to repeat itself over and over again with the same sad consequences made me double- and triple-check every order and instruction and take measures to prevent these terrible things from happening. This usually meant that I had a few excellent noncommissioned officers who understood me and what I said; they would almost hover over the individuals doing their tasks. This understanding on my part of the importance of cognitive philosophy, however subjective at first, reduced my casualties to nearly zero.

As my career in the infantry ended and my career in computer science began in earnest, I carried this understanding of cognitive philosophy with me. As a basic hypothesis, I now assumed that what I said was listened to by only a very few. I also assumed that most of those who listened only understood a part of what I had said, and would retain only a fraction of that in an hour. My assumptions were correct. I now had to find ways and means to ensure that what I said was listened to and understood. One way was to write it all down, but sometimes what I wrote down was not read, and if read, not understood.

I knew that out of embarrassment or fear of being punished, demoted, or chewed out, those who did not listen, read, or understand would never come to me and say, "Sir, I wasn't paying attention during the design review. Would you please repeat it to me?" So I came up with a countermeasure. This countermeasure was at first derogatorily referred to as a BOGSAT—an acronym for a "Bunch of Guys Sitting Around a Table"—implying that nothing got done besides "slinging a bunch of BS." Nothing could have been further from the truth. It became much later a fine tool for me in how I approached architectural design. This methodology (and it is truly a methodology) became known as the "design hub," which I used consistently on all of my systems with great success.[7]

The cognitive process, as a tool in the manager-architect's toolbox, is of manifold importance. It enables the manager-architect to understand his own thought process, both subjective and objective, as well as that of others. It enables an individual in pursuit of excellence to mistrust his personal subjective conclusions, and

[7] See Chapter 10, The Development Process Methodology.

motivates him toward gaining an objective reality much more reliable than his own. This is also true of the cognitive process in others. It enables the manager-architect to build outstanding technical engineering teams, and then synthesize the effort of the team in such a manner as to reduce tension, improve the work environment, and produce a product of superior quality at a very reasonable cost to the customer.

Then there is the additional important factor in understanding the human cognitive process, and that is its importance in building an autonomous system. An autonomous system must have an architectural model before it can be designed in detail and built. It is also a truth that without an overall architecture, the components will never converge properly. And even if they eventually do converge somehow, it will be a cumbersome and very expensive system.

The human cognitive process is discussed in Chapter 16, "The Autonomous Cognitive System," from the viewpoint of a software architect and implementation manager. This idea that philosophy is an important element of computer science, in fact a dominant one, requires a new approach to our understanding of the cognitive process and reality. For this reason I use the term *cognitive dynamics* as the software equivalent of the human cognitive function.

3.7 LOW-COST SOFTWARE DEVELOPMENT

The overall purpose of this book is to enlighten those who are truly interested in developing computer software at low cost. There may be occasion for businesses, federal agencies, and corporations for which bringing in a system on budget and on schedule may be necessary. This could be when a company is in financial trouble, and there is a will to survive, or perhaps for some other critical reason, such as the sponsor or client threatening to cancel the contract.

I have seen software companies start with outstanding technical people and, from an initial impression, very capable managers. Yet it turned out that the managers had no intention of completing the project they were funded to do. For a while, I didn't understand this phenomenon completely; then I saw the salaries paid to the key managerial staff. It was then that I realized that they were getting rich, regardless of whether the product was delivered or not. It surprised me even more that there were other customers standing in line to pick up the pieces and continue funding the project. To these "entrepreneurs" it was monetary gain, not a reputation for doing a good job and making the customer happy, that was important. I'm not talking about large corporations who defraud investors, but small business undertakings that cost a customer only $100 to $200 million. These people are like small-time gangsters in computer science, the "Bonnies and Clydes" of software, as opposed to the Al Capone gangs that cost in the billions.

So, this book is not intended for everyone. I address this book only to those software professionals who are genuinely interested in lowering the cost of software development and who are interested in where we are headed in computer science. I address this book especially to those who would like to earn an honest living, have the capacity to absorb what I'm talking about, and would like to enjoy their chosen professions building great computer software products.

As mentioned briefly in the prologue, there are three key functions, *a priori*, in the activity involving the building of software systems:

1. The visualization of the product and its architecture
2. The visualization of the organization required to build it
3. The visualization of the methodologies and techniques required to achieve a quality product within a given time and budget

All three of these functions are the subjects of cognitive philosophy. The third function runs in parallel to the first two, and that is the ability of the manager-architect to visualize inferentially the required methodology for implementing the objective design from the subjective impression of the architecture and organization. All of the chapters in this book combine in the methodology; that is how these are used by the manager-architect and applied in the process of building the system.

The methodology and how it is used are based on experience gained in the U.S. Army, NATO/SHAPE, at the Jet Propulsion Laboratory, and as a consultant to some great American corporations (many of which have by now fallen by the wayside due to poor, inept, and incompetent management). My methodology is heavily influenced by some 20 years of experience as an officer in the U.S. Army Airborne Infantry and Special Forces units, of which nearly three years were spent in combat in Vietnam. The military influence comes from my observations of how people perceive things and events, how they react to events, and the conclusions they draw as evidenced by their reactions. As a young man, nothing interested me more than watching myself and others deal with, react to, and solve problems under pressure and stress.

Life in the Army was to me the real laboratory of human behavior. It is one of the reasons that I picked only the most challenging, dangerous, and stressful occupations and assignments I could find, and why I spent so much time in combat. I wanted to find out what made me and other people tick, how they got their jobs done, how they thought, and how they paid attention to the orders I gave.

Getting a job done well and expertly was to me always equal to the accomplishment of the mission without needless loss of life and resources. Failing to get the job done well and expertly because of negligence, lack of ability or competence, or someone else's negligence is something I can understand but not tolerate. To those managers who can't get their projects delivered by the standards I refer to in this book (to wit, a quality product, on schedule, and on budget): Do yourselves a favor and look for another profession. Don't be a manager. There is no dishonor in not being a manager; just go back to systems engineering, programming or testing, and be productive. There is no excuse in saying that this project or that is too complicated. A manager gets paid to manage and to deliver a product; the complexity is not an issue.

3.8 "ON BUDGET AND ON SCHEDULE"

As you know by now, the mantra of this book is the maxim: a quality product on budget and on schedule. To those who are not interested in this theme, don't read this book, as it won't do you any good; it will confuse you, and confusion leads to discomfort, and will only make you angry. But to those who think that being a software professional entails a love of one's work, pride in one's product, and having a happy customer who enjoys your product, this is for you. It is not intended to be a piecemeal, spoon-feeding approach to developing software with instant "solutions" to problems; there are many excellent textbooks dealing with such subjects. Rather, this is a summary in narrative form of experiences encountered over the course of a successful career building large systems from a hundred thousand to a million lines of code. This book should be a "beginning" for many of you to start you thinking about software in general, and about management, architectures, processes, and procedures in particular. It is not so much a roadmap as it is a checklist of important items that need to be considered when entrusted with a project. Granted, Kant's *Critique of Pure Reason* is not easy reading for most people,[8] but if you do read it, it will be of enormous help in getting the job done. It has been of great help to me.

The problem a software manager faces is more complex than that of a mechanical engineering project manager because there are no real blueprints in software design (at least, not yet). To get a project manager not familiar with computer software to understand that the articulation of the design in the detailed design document is our equivalent to a blueprint or mechanical drawing for a spacecraft bus is difficult. Yet without the software the aircraft or spacecraft will not work, much like without the nervous system the human body cannot function. These are simple analogies, but important ones. The Romans had a saying, "*qui bene distingui, qui bene docet,*" or "he who distinguishes well, teaches well." Use analogies in your daily work so others who are working on the project understand what you are trying to get at. The most misunderstood part of management and systems engineering is that a good software manager and systems engineer or architect is always a good teacher. Manager-architects "teach" their teams what they want done, how they want it done, and explain why. They listen attentively to feedback from the individuals who need to get their jobs done, like a football coach listening to a quarterback, running back, or tackle about his views on the execution of a play. Infinite patience, direction, and communication coupled to experience, intelligence, and expertise in the field are the hallmarks of a true manager-architect.

---

[8] In the copy of Kant's *Three Critiques* that I use (which is in high German for easy reading and annotated for better understanding), there is a statement by the interpreter-translator, Prof. Raymund Schmidt: "... wegen der sprachliche Unzugaenglichkeit der Kantische Schriften und wegen der historischer bedingt seiner Gedankenfuehrung dem Laien nicht ohne weiteres zutgemutet warden ...." This translates as: "... because of the linguistic inaccessibility of Kant's writings, and because of his historically determined and constrained thought process, its understanding will not be easy for the layman." Don't be discouraged. All this means is that the original text of his work is written in old German, and his readability is very cumbersome. Read the annotated version I use: Kant, *Die Drei Kritiken*, Eine Kommentierte Auswahl. Alfred Kroener Verlag, Stuttgart, Germany.

As with everything I have done in my career, I have always wanted to improve things in whatever I was working on. One of the things I strived for was the reduction of cost. Why cost? As a very young Special Forces operative I had to parachute with and carry everything I needed on my back. If I could reduce the number of explosives I needed to destroy a certain type of target, I had less to carry. This carried over into every part of my professional career, software engineering included. I constantly searched for ways to reduce the overall cost of my systems, and this translated into cost per line of code (as a practical measure of performance), code complexity, and faults per line of code.

3.9   THE TIME TO COMPLETION: SCHEDULE

The other aspect of cost was the time to completion, or schedule. This proved very interesting because it revealed areas that had great impact on cost, but that on the surface did not seem to be very important. Time to completion became one of the drivers of my goal in software development. Anything beyond three years is usually too long. Kelly Johnson, one of my all-time heroes, built the SR-71 in less than a year. Of course, it was an analog mechanical system. Today, it would take 10 years for our managers; Kelly would still get it done in a year.

Personally, four years is too long a time because I lose my interest and concentration. Almost all hard tasks generally should be completed in three years; the building of an autonomous system, however, will require from 8 to 10 years.[9] Normally, beyond three years, the engineering staff lose interest also and begin to look for more interesting things to do. The "technology turnover" in the computer science industry, with new products constantly coming onto the market, happens in three- to four-year cycles. Even an autonomous system project must be scheduled in three 3-year cycles, with deliveries scheduled in 9- to 12-month increments. This is important for the purposes of project design control, quality control, and staff motivation and retention.

There is also an additional reason for incremental deliveries. Whenever one starts a serious project, regardless of what it is, the people who "know better," "have nothing better to do," or simply want to be "important" will try to interfere with progress. Sometimes, simply out of bad intentions, they will do everything they can to stop the process of delivery. I have seen this often, so one must schedule a V1.0 release of a working quality product delivered no later than 12 months from the start; this must be something real and tangible so that you, the manager and the team, are left in peace to do your work.

Software professionals have to keep current with the marketplace and must learn new skills, languages, compilers, and tools. So, a three-year development cycle is really all you need; stretching it to four might work, but you risk personnel turnover with your key people leaving; then the delivery slips start for the obvious reason that you need to hire new people, who in turn need to learn the system.

[9] See Chapter 16, The Autonomous Cognitive System.

3.10 PHILOSOPHY AND SUCCESSFUL DESIGN

One of the most surprising discoveries I have made is the average attitude concerning the subject of philosophy. Even some of the most highly educated and academically highly qualified engineers and mathematicians I have met have an attitude that "philosophy, as a topic, is just sitting around, drinking beer, and talking about football and the opposite sex." I have heard more often than I care to remember statements at board meetings, design teams, and project conferences like, "What's your philosophy on this?" or, "His philosophy is to let everyone do his own thing." When an individual with a Ph.D., a Doctor of Philosophy, says something like this, I know that there will be at least a 50% cost overrun in the budget and schedule.

"Philosophy" is, in fact, the love of knowledge and wisdom. Initially, the idea that philosophy, or the lack of it, has a great impact on successful design completely surprised me. It should not have. I grew up with Socrates, Plato, and Aristotle. The idea that the human process of thinking—the sensing, perceiving, reasoning, deciding, and inferring—is a systemic process of the human thought system, just as is any other system (including a software system), was a revelation to me. Understanding this system, its functioning, its architecture, and its task assignments is of utmost importance to a software manager and systems architect.

4 The Philosophical Imperatives of Architectural Design

When considering the importance of efficiency and elegance in building something, most people never think of architecture seriously, or they think that it is an essential logical discipline totally grounded in philosophy with its two major components, mathematics and logic. When we think of building our lives and our careers, we rarely think of ourselves as the chief architects. It may be that most of us are unable to visualize a human life as an architectural undertaking. We are taught certain principles of construction by our parents in our early childhood, such as integrity, the need to study and make good grades, and to persevere no matter what life places in our path, thus learning the magic of discipline. Discipline is an awesome word, because above all it concerns the control we exercise over ourselves, which is an indispensable component of the process of building our lives and our careers. After the foundation on which we will have to build is laid, after the ground soil (granite, we hope) from our parents on which our edifice will rest is prepared, we finally go and pursue our education. Education, both academic and experiential, makes up the base of the life we build for ourselves. With some people, who build carefully, it is like a temple: The columns that support the roof are the experiences we gather in engineering, management, communication, organization, leadership, technical disciplines, and technology. This includes our understanding of our fellow human beings, how they think and pay attention, how they decide, and what motivates them. Finally, the roof of the edifice—our life and career—is formed from the projects we have built, the accomplishments we have achieved, and the good (or bad) we have done for those we have come into contact with.

None of the above may be considered relevant today, but this is the summation of philosophy and its components of mathematics, logic, and science. The fundamentals of elegant, cost-effective, and well-executed design of any edifice, be it a fighter plane, a ship, a spacecraft, or computer software (the most difficult of all), are deeply rooted in philosophical concepts.

4.1 THE MANAGER AS ARCHITECT

The first design fundamental is that the manager also *must* be the architect of the system.

The Cognitive Dynamics of Computer Science: Cost-Effective Large Scale Software Development, by Szabolcs Michael de Gyurky

Organizing people to the accomplishment of a job is also an aspect of architecture, in that organizations are also architectures, not of marble blocks or of computer software, but of people. The manager is not only the architect of the system, but of the organization that is going to build it. It follows that with experience and understanding we acquire the skill of compiling a number of methodologies and processes we use to get a job done with minimal confusion. This selection and modification of existing methodologies are the highest expression of philosophical operations in the mind; we call this "problem solving." Those manager-architects who are good at this are the ones who build best, fastest, and cheapest.

4.2 THE MANAGER AS TEACHER

The second design fundamental is that the manager-architect also *must* be a teacher.

Management is a teaching position. On the practical side, the manager presents his vision to the design team as the thesis. He expects the members of the design team to respond with the antithesis—their views and positions that represent their expertise; this is the reason they are there in the first place. They have the detailed knowledge in operating systems, databases, applications software, structural dynamics, and aerodynamics, all of which the manager-architect is not a detailed master of, nor can he be. What cannot be implemented in the thesis is presented in a semiformal context, resulting in an antithesis. After a lengthy discussion, a synthesis of the two different positions is formed; this synthesis becomes the new thesis, which is again taken and discussed. All the while, the manager-architect is present and teaches not only the methodology of the use of dialectics in software engineering, but also the methodology by which to arrive at an acceptable and balanced design, in a cost-effective manner.

On the theoretical/aesthetic side, the relationship between the manager-architect and project members is like a teacher and his pupils, or a football coach with his players, both collectively and individually. Such a coach was Vince Lombardi; working with his team, he taught them and directed them in what he wanted them to do, how, and why. He also listened attentively to the individuals who had certain problems to solve on the field, when executing the "architecture" of his plays. Being the member of a design team under a great manager-architect is like being a graduate student or research assistant to a great professor and teacher. The caring and attentiveness on his part are not only applied toward finishing an experiment, a project, or winning a game, but also toward the growth of his team, in knowledge, experience, as well as in spiritual qualities. The team then becomes greater than the sum of its parts. In football, it is like Paul Hornung carrying the ball for the extra yard and winning the Super Bowl. In engineering, it is like one fine young man picking up the pieces of a botched job and completing it, elegantly, with imagination, in time for testing, integration, and delivery. It is hoped that each project an engineer works on becomes like a postgraduate research experience, and he becomes enriched by the experience. The outcome is not only a salary and a product, but the deep-down feeling of gratitude to a good teacher from a pupil. The opposite scenario is as Lao Tzu said, "The worst thing is when they despise him," i.e., after leaving a project, successful or not, to hate the idea of ever working for the guy again. The greatest compliment therefore is when the project team members say, "We did this ourselves."[1]

With a good manager-architect there is never a "wrong" viewpoint, only an "interesting" one; all ideas are equally welcome and attentively discussed. In a hundred ideas there are at least five that will reduce the confusion and add a solution, which will bring the cost down.

Is this hard to do? No, but you have to be a manager *and* an architect *and* a good teacher *and* a leader. How do you get there? Through apprenticing, learning, and working hard.

4.3 THE MANAGER AS SOCIAL WORKER

On the totally philosophical plane, the great manager-architect is also a psychiatric social worker.[2] This means that if the individual is interested in a quality product at a reasonable cost, he is equally interested in the health and welfare of his subordinates and employees who do all the hands-on work. He is the first in the office and the last to leave, or should be whenever possible. It is in the early quiet hours when he "checks the pulse" of his organization. Some young people overwork themselves, or have problems at home, with no one to talk to. It is important for them to talk, and for the manager to listen. It is important for them to know that the boss knows what is going on, and appreciates all the hard work. When an individual looks sick, send him home; *make* him go home. Some people work 18-hour days without overtime just to get their jobs done. It is part of life, we've all had to do this, but the manager-architect is accountable and responsible for the product, so he must make a decision, regardless of the rules. When a project is inexpensive and good, no corporation will fire a manager for bending the rules. This is the "American way."

However, don't take this idea of being a "psychiatric social worker" too far, as some guys I know do. This extreme "touchy, feely" approach to management is disastrous. It's *not* the American way. Managers like these lose the respect of their subordinates, who simply collect their salaries; they would be fools not to. The talented ones leave for productive jobs led by good managers because it is imperative to their career progression, learning experience, and keeping up with technology to do so. No software professional learns from the experience unless a project is *completed*, except perhaps for picking up a new application software language, and maybe a new coding technique, but nothing serious for later in life.

---

[1] Lao Tzu, *The Way of Life*, New American Library, 1995.
[2] Kets De Vries, *Leaders, Fools and Impostors*, Josseys-Bass Publishers.

4.4 THE MANAGER AS AXMAN

Every member of the team is responsible and accountable for his own task. If he is found to be lacking, the manager tries to be of help. If there are no results, the individual simply must go; he is fired! That, too, is management responsibility. Remember that the manager is responsible and accountable overall for the product. It follows that it is unethical of an engineer not to do his job and thereby destroy the schedule and the quality of the product. An employee has no right to make the manager miserable, lose sleep, and get sick by conducting passive guerrilla warfare and sabotaging the project.

Suppose you fire such a person, and he takes you to court? It is a mighty judge indeed who will convict a manager who fired someone for not performing the job he was paid to do. Even if the individual is reinstated under the guise of "unfair" firing, one could ask the judge whether it wouldn't be more appropriate to put the individual on the state payroll, as opposed to paying him to produce nothing for the taxpayer or customer while demoralizing the workers who are doing his work and their own. Work is what made America great: hard work, like in that Merle Haggard song, "The Working Man's Blues." Work ennobles a person's character, regardless of how menial that work may be. It adds dignity to a person, to the human species.

Is it hard to fire someone? Yes, you bet! I have had to fire some of my best friends for not doing their jobs. In each case, I had to make a decision between accepting unethical behavior on the part of my friends, or honoring my obligation to the customer who entrusted me with the funds to build a product that he needed.

4.5 THE PHILOSOPHICAL IMPERATIVES OF ARCHITECTURAL DESIGN

If the system you are building is to be a quality product, on schedule, and on budget, you hope to produce it at a very low cost and make a decent profit. Consider the development approach of Phidias, when he built the Parthenon. After all, why shouldn't a systems architecture of software be as aesthetically appealing,[3] well-balanced, and clean as that of a temple? Achieve this by understanding not only the mechanics of design, but the great classical cognitive philosophy of Aristotle, Socrates, Kant, Hegel, and Schopenhauer.

The philosophical imperatives of architectural design are as follows:

- The vision or visualization of the architecture on the part of the manager-architect
- The presentation of the architecture as the initial proposition to the design team

---

[3] Kant, *The Laws of Perception*.

- The dialectical interaction of the design team with the architect, to arrive at a substantial architectural object
- The arrival at a point of acceptable reality when the work of development can begin

Throughout this process the manager-architect *must* be present. It is an intense period of activity.

This is probably the most important chapter of this book, because it addresses not only the foundations of system design, but also how the people who participate think and how they view the system that is about to materialize. If the design and implementation are to follow elegantly, efficiently, and cost-effectively, these are the rules of understanding.

4.6   AVAILABILITY OF THE MANAGER

The most important of all things in the development of an elegant, high-quality, and low-cost system is the constant presence of the manager. The manager must *always* be on the job. The manager is the "General" commanding his forces, which is the project. Another close analogy is the captain on the bridge of his ship, always available. If he is below decks during a difficult phase and not available because he is drunk, the ship runs aground. Availability must be kept to 99% of the time if the cost is to be kept within the approved budget. There are many historical examples of what happens when a manager is not available, and the tragic consequences for the manager who made that mistake.[4] The manager, being accountable and responsible for the project, *cannot delegate his responsibilities*; therefore, the manager's constant presence on the job is imperative.

4.7   PROJECT MANAGER: 10 KEY ATTRIBUTES AND RESPONSIBILITIES

The following list enumerates 10 key attributes and responsibilities of the project manager.

1. **The vision of the system belongs to the manager; he must also be the architect.** The manager must understand that his vision is a subjective impression and that it must be given substance through a dialectical process with the design team.

---

[4] During the Battle of Actium, 31 BC, while he was winning the battle against Caesar Augustus, Mark Antony took his flagship out of the line and sailed after Cleopatra's ship, which had left the battle. His departure from the battle caused the battle to be lost. For this reason, Mark Antony lost the Roman Empire. He should have kept his mind on the project at hand, instead of running after Cleopatra. He wasn't even getting "bonus miles" for that trip.

2. **The manager must have the experience in the critical areas of the project to a sufficient degree so as to make well-informed command decisions quickly.** Critical areas include the technical and administrative functions, knowledge of organizations, methodologies, processes, procedures, and effective communication.

3. **The manager must have sufficient dynamic energy to maintain control over the development process** at all times, and at all levels, if he would like to complete the job as planned. This is not too much to ask for,[5] because that is what is expected of a manager.

4. **The manager must provide an environment where even the most junior person can speak his mind freely, without fear of retribution.** The younger engineers and scientists are closer to the technical realities of the job and can contribute immensely to the better understanding of problems needing solutions. However, they are often intimidated by the fear of looking foolish, or are muzzled by their supervisors, either out of selfish interests or to cover up their own shortcomings. A good manager would rather hear a stupid question or solution than to hear nothing at all; worse yet is for others to tell him what they think he wants to hear.

5. **The manager must lead the design team, personally and daily, until the requirements and design are completed and implementation starts.** At the start of implementation he need not be present at all times, but must be available to make a decision as soon as a decision is required.

6. **The manager and key staff members need to understand that there will always be people who are not paying attention, even during critical design discussions.** Their minds drift in and out of lock, and much of the transmitted information is lost. One must probe constantly to ensure that the message gets through and to verify that others around the design table are also listening and understanding everything that is being said.

7. **To ensure clarity and retention, a technical writer *who is also an engineer* and who understands the software design standards used**

---

[5] Napoleon Bonaparte, Emperor of the French at the Battle of Austerlitz, knew where every unit and cannon of his army was, at all times. On the eve of battle, around 4 a.m., he rose to make a personal reconnaissance of the battlefield with his staff. Still in the darkness of early dawn, he stopped abruptly in an area and asked the Corps Commander the whereabouts of the battery of artillery that was to have been at that location. The Corps Commander was embarrassed, his Chief of Staff Berthier was embarrassed; no one even knew that a battery of artillery was to have been emplaced there. Napoleon, riding ahead, led the way in the dark, searching for it. They found the battery mired down in a muddy creek several kilometers away from its intended emplacement. Napoleon the Emperor dismounted and with his staff helped to push the artillery out of the mud. He then personally took the time to emplace them at the intended position. At Austerlitz, he defeated in quick succession the Russian Army, the Austrian Army, and the Prussian Army in a brilliant set piece battle, planned down to the detail of an artillery battery. This is management at its best. It reflects careful planning, design, execution, and detailed knowledge on the part of the manager, and it gives evidence of "dynamic energy" by the fact that one man could control the plan, the design, and the implementation.

should be putting all issues, action items, and design changes into a computer as they occur and are approved. A projector with a large screen displaying schematic and alphanumeric representations of the design or action item for everyone to see is a must. In this way, the manager and the design team understand the issue and are not excused from claiming that they never saw it, forgot it, didn't know it, or didn't understand it.

8. **No one is excused from a design team meeting, unless excused personally by the manager.** I have often been told, "I'm leaving; I have work to do, and this is wasting my time." There is a grave misunderstanding here! The manager is responsible and accountable for the achievement of the project objectives; the budget and schedule belong to the manager. The working engineer or subsystem manager works for the project manager. The manager needs all inputs and opinions, pro and con, from as many people as possible to add more substance to the design object or to the resolution of a problem. All personnel are at the convenience of the project manager; everyone will stay in the meeting, or leave the project.

9. **When starting a project, do so by always keeping a detailed record of activities.** Based on an initial understanding of the project, perform an *a priori* cost estimation, and write it down. Compare that later to the *a posteriori* cost estimation of the project. Estimate the costs in detail, and include productivity forecast estimates, like lines of code per day for all languages you are going to use, the software bugs for each language and how long it took to fix them, and document the fixes in the FRD, SRD, and SDD. Over a period of time, you—the manager and the team—will develop a great work-estimating ability.

10. **Prepare a detailed post-project "after-action" report.**[6] This is imperative, because for good or for bad this is the teaching tool for the entire project team. Take as baseline the elements in the original Project Implementation Plan:

- The cost estimate
- Organization
- Schedule
- Anticipated workflow
- Burn rate of project funds
- Original time allocated to programming
- Time allocated to unit testing
- Time allocated to going to meetings

---

[6] The Comparison of a Non-Standard Software Development Approach to DOD-STD-2167A, for the Global Decision Support System (GDSS) 30 March 1989, prepared at JPL for the USAF Military Airlift Command. JPL D-3216 by the GDSS Technical Writing Team.

- Time allocated to prepare and present reviews
- Time allocated for business travel

After the comparison of how the project started and how it was completed, it will be clear where mistakes were made and where good decisions were made. It is based on such unvarnished information, often unpleasant to accept, that the future project managers get real training. In the military, this is the "hot wash-up" after an operation. In sports, this is the "chalk talk" after a football game with the coach and the team, where the mistakes made are discussed and avoided in future games. It must be understood that the "after-action" report is the best teaching and mentoring tool for scientists and young and senior engineers alike. Schedule a one-week "project hot wash-up" in your schedule. It is time well spent for the company. This is how I train my staff, and how I trained my Rifle Company in Vietnam. This training, after every combat action, reduced my casualties to almost zero, while helping to achieve the tactical objectives.

4.8 PHILOSOPHICAL ASPECTS OF ENGINEERING

I discovered long ago the advantages of looking at philosophy as a software engineer, recognizing that software was an abstraction of the human thought system.[7] This allowed me to transliterate certain subsystems and functions into terms I could deal with more easily. Instead of cognitive philosophy, I called it cognitive dynamics, cognitive functions, and cognitive attributes. The cognitive attributes such as sensing, self/nonself discrimination, and so on are to me the domain of cognitive mechanics. The cognitive attributes that a human being has are being expressed in mathematical algorithms and algebraic equations today. Those of us in this field are on a journey of discovery, like Columbus & Co. sailing west, thinking they'd find a shorter route to India, but finding the Western Hemisphere instead.

A secondary aspect of philosophy as it applies to engineering is the exercise of the mind. Most of the cognitive philosophers were mathematicians or physicists, and their texts were in fact mathematics, mostly algebra. Kant hypothesized that someday all visible and invisible phenomena will be explainable in mathematics. Why? Because absolute objective reality can only be approached by means of mathematics or logic.

For the benefit of architects of complex software systems who are not aware of Hegel's concept of *reality as object*, I will explain. The object design, in degrees of reality, is substantiated dialectically to be sufficiently understood so that a design is acceptable and realistically doable;[8] the design process then continues on. The lack

---

[7] Kant, Immanuel, *Die Drei Kritiken*, Alfred Kroener Verlag, Stuttgart Germany 1975, page 90. The modeling of the human thought system (Empirische Gruende der Gedanken).

[8] Hegel, Georg Wilhelm Friedrich, *Wissenschaft der Logik*, Volume I (*The Science of Logic*), Felix Meiner Verlag GmbH, 1990 Hamburg, Germany.

of understanding of sufficient reality in the object results in literally volumes, indeed tons, of documentation being generated without a line of code being written. Often projects are cancelled because the manager does not know how to arrive at a sufficiently substantiated design for the design to work, although it may not be far from Hegel's *ultimate reality* or *absolute*. So, millions of dollars of the customer's or taxpayer's money are spent without anything to show for it. Nor is there at the cancellation of a project sufficient motivation or expertise for a rigorous technical review capable of estimating the status and the realistic time to completion. Most of the time, however, the design continues on and on, and due to pressure from the customer it is terminated without sufficient reality having been arrived at. Termination of the design phase and the start of the implementation phase must be a mutually agreed-upon point in the schedule, understood by the entire design team. If this point is not clearly defined, a disjointed implementation starts, which may never see completion. This phenomenon is so wonderfully alluded to by Baltasar Gracian,[9] who unfortunately predated Kant and Hegel by several hundred years; had he known them, he would have understood the root causes of the phenomenon.

4.9 THE IMPORTANCE OF FINISHING THE JOB

I have met many managers and engineers during the course of my career who have never actually completed a project. By that I mean they have never started something from the very beginning and finished it by writing the "after-action" report. If a project was started but not finished, then why was it started in the first place? There are many dangers should the engineers and managers not stay the course and never finish what they started. One only learns with relative certainty the positive and negative lessons after a project is delivered. So, in a very definitive sense, each project completion is a "final examination" to every member of the project team, and the project itself a "course" beyond the previous that one has completed. This is so because, at least in computer science, the technology makes a complete turnover in three- or four-year increments. During this period, new computer hardware and software systems enter the marketplace, and it is the next step toward advancing one's technical and managerial skills. The completion of a project is the proof of one's skill and level of abilities, qualitatively, in regard to cost and schedule as well. When interviewing applicants, I am very careful to look at the projects completed.[10]

4.10 VISUALIZING AN ARCHITECTURE

In order to make philosophy more useful as a tool in my profession, I have decided to rename the applied portion of it *cognitive dynamics*. Cognitive dynamics is the

---

[9] Baltasar Gracian, *The Wisdom of Baltasar Gracian*, Adapted and edited by J. Leonard Kaye, Pocket Books: Simon & Schuster Inc., New York, 1992.
[10] See Chapter 13, on management.

set of relationships of the major subdivisions of the human thought system with the major divisions of the human thought process. One of the subdivisions comprises *cognitive attributes*, which are very much like what we refer to in our software as "hardwired" or rule-based processes. Some of these cognitive attributes are self/ nonself discrimination, sensing, detection, and making *a priori* decisions.

The way I manage to build large complex systems so cheaply is by utilizing the philosophical constructs of architectural design and systems engineering. It became clear to me quickly that, at least from the philosophical perspective, a great, concise, and well-balanced design must be simultaneously intuitive, objective, and logical. These are philosophical terms and concepts, so I will explain further. The project manager of a software-intensive project can or should be able to, almost from the start, "visualize" the system he is going to be required to build. Only the project manager is expected to be able do this initially because the project manager is the one who sets the course that is about to be taken, *a priori*. The project manager is responsible and accountable for the product. That is, before anyone is hired, before anyone starts anything, it is the project manager who lays the architecture down, even if it is subjective at the start. Jack Northrop did not design the Flying Wing by asking people for ideas; he had the vision first, being the great aeronautical engineer that he was. Kelly Johnson knew what he wanted intuitively, and accomplished his mental vision at Lockheed with the interaction of many of the finest engineers in the world. To me, the SR-71 represents not only a magnificent machine, but an almost miraculous achievement of objective truth that is as close to reality in aeronautical engineering perfection as one can get.[11] Even so, the SR-71 was not able to achieve all of its design objectives, such as turning radius. In computer software, where blueprints are not available, the manager-architect must be infinitely more careful in the design, implementation control, and overview to avoid costly mistakes.

Software designers have an even greater problem: Software does not lend itself well to making blueprints or mechanical drawings. Today, software costs far more than computer hardware, spacecraft, or airplanes. Computer software people cost a lot of money. When you hire software people, you must be sure that you hire the right ones for the right jobs. You must be sure that they are put to good use early on, and that you get optimal performance for the salaries you pay them. This means that you understand the architecture of the object you want to build and the kinds of skills you will need to hire to design and implement each subsystem. By inference this means that you have completed your preliminary work and have the appropriate job descriptions already written, and a schedule to go with them. That is what cost-effective development is all about. After all, you have already been down this path many times, and have written numerous "lessons learned," and have been instructed in "lessons taught" by the people you have worked for over the years. Although your personally prepared Work Implementation Plan will not be perfect,

[11] Arthur Schopenhauer. *Die Welt als Wille und Vorstellung*, page 19.

it should sufficiently reflect an objective truth (as you understand it) to start hiring and to know who you need.

Visualizing an architecture is critical to design and implementation. Before you can build something, you must be able to visualize what you are going to build. This is one of the main reasons many technical specialists are assembled to contribute their input to the requirements of the system, especially in successful technically diverse systems. *You cannot build cost-effectively by using a process to arrive at a design.* The mental activity of visualizing a system happens in a *subjective* vein, within the mental process of the manager-architect. This happens to be called an *a priori* value judgment, or an impression with uncertainty, if you will. This is influenced by a scale of clarity available to the thought process of the person, which goes from the highest and brightest imagination to the darkest minimal imagination.[12] This is followed by the reference to the empirical knowledge sum of experiences of the individual, and the comparison of all possible cases encountered in the past. In other words, the sum of all possibilities and the probability of choosing correctly is then followed by the empirical, *a posteriori* proof called judgment or decision.

This process happens either autonomously, passively, as during an "idea" for an invention, or while listening to another person, such as a customer. In this visualization process, a mental picture is projected from the *understanding* part of the mental software onto the *reason*, very much like a motion picture projector projects an image onto a silver screen. During the continued input feed from the input source (which is usually verbal, but may also be from a whiteboard, etc.), this image, as an object of the mind, is provided with subjective substance from both the input and the knowledge parts of the brain, which in software terms is equivalent to a database. The database of the mind is what Kant refers to as the *wells of experience* and is a very complex subsystem of the mind. When the manager-architect has completed the process of autonomous analysis based on the sum total of his experience and postulates an *a posteriori* decision, he has arrived at the *recognition a priori* of the design.[13] Then begins the work of the design team, where the wise manager-architect, aware of the incompleteness of his experience and knowledge, begins the process of extracting the sum total of all the knowledge and experience of the project design team members.

For those members who are not familiar with the serious dialectic process necessary to the achievement of a synthetic judgment, this is a terrible experience. Many will quit the team, unable or unwilling to put up with the mental and physical stress inherent in the process. Not to worry! To quote Shakespeare:

The fire i' th' flint
Shows not till it be struck.[14]

[12] Kant, *Die Drei Kritiken*, page 10.
[13] Kant, ibid, page 110.
[14] William Shakespeare, *The Life of Timon of Athens* (Poet, act I, scene i).

When these individuals blow up in anger, that is when you know you have caught them napping, or you have gone beyond the reach of their mental faculties. The manager has achieved the first elegant objective of producing an organization, i.e., getting rid of the feeble-minded, the ones who lack the physical energy to bear through, the ones who are afraid to be wrong, or who are afraid to reveal to others how limited they are in experience, and those who lack commitment. I have had people quit at this phase who were eminently qualified from their academic training and whom I needed desperately for the project. One was a computer graphics program designer with a doctorate in computer science from one of our best universities. He suddenly started to curse at me and said that he would not put up with "this method of design." He got up and left, slamming the door behind him. I always try to impress on people that it is imperative that a design be as close to an acceptable reality as possible in order for the implementation to work efficiently. Furthermore, this process is the only methodology I know of that will achieve a close to identical understanding of the system in the mind of every member of the design team, enabling people to switch positions laterally and horizontally in the organization.[15]

4.11   THE ROLE OF INTUITION IN DESIGN

As a function, in its elementary definition, intuition is causative. In the human mind there is a subsystem we call knowledge, which is divided into two parts: innate and acquired. (It is not the intent here to give a lecture on the dynamics of acquired knowledge, and knowledge that is causative in origin, but to give a brief description of how this works in design.) As the input source provides information to the understanding, and the object in the reason acquires more substance, the reason takes a mental leap ahead and forms a hypothesis of what the object will look like. This is what is called the *thesis*. The first thesis of the design process is the manager-architect's. It is based on the earliest inputs received, and on experience. This thesis is an analytical judgment that is based on the axiom of causality. It is the foundation of design, and this mental leap is called *intuition*.

The manager-architect is the one who puts forward the thesis to the design team, which begins the dialectic process of the design. Sometimes in personal instances the intuition is irrefutable, like a perception or an understanding of what one must do. This is causative, and failing to follow one's intuition is more often than not wrought with serious consequences and painful results. The widening of perceptions is based on axiomatic rules. How this happens is probably based on the breadth and depth of an individual's experience database. The widening of the perception of comprehension or understanding is lightning fast and results in a

---

[15] On several occasions, I have had upper management make comments to me about seeing engineers shift positions overnight, from one subsystem to another. They were amazed that the people were able to do this without losing efficiency, and moreover were willing to do it. These managers were never able to understand the idea of cross-training and the design hub concept of educating the design team for overall efficiency.

synthetic judgment a priori, which is correct in this case, in the absence of external input. Kant reinforced this by stating, "The only irrefutable hypothesis is the human intuition."[16]

4.12 "SUFFICIENT REALITY" AND INFERENCE IN THE DESIGN PROCESS

Why inference? A manager-architect must understand how inference works in the human mind, and how it applies to the process of design. It has been proven to me repeatedly that my assumption that others thought like I did was not true. The essence of the masterwork of Schopenhauer is that everything in the world exists,

---

[16] Only once in 32 months of combat was I successfully ambushed. This happened in obeying an order, against my intuition, during the battle for Hue, Vietnam, in January of 1968. Never again would I jeopardize my life and especially the lives of my soldiers by overriding my better judgment in obeying a tactical order given by an officer drinking a cup of coffee in some far-away headquarters.

Much earlier, while in Special Forces, in late 1966, I set up an ambush along the Cambodian border where the Viet Cong were receiving their reinforcements. The ambush that I set up was on the bend of a large tributary stream flowing into a big river called the Gian Than. It was dark night, around 10:00 p.m., and I had just set up when we heard the ominous noises of a large number of sampans coming down the stream. This entire area of 50 square kilometers was not inhabited jungle and savannah, which the Viet Cong controlled; it was a free-fire zone, and they often attacked civilian boats, commercial traffic along the waterways, including attacking my camps. As we listened to the boats approaching, they suddenly ceased, and it became very quiet. Then we heard a lot of noise and cursing from around the bend of the stream masked by mangrove and bamboo. I began to think that they were local woodcutters because I knew that the Viet Cong were a well-disciplined, quiet, combat-experienced bunch of troops. It became evident that for some reason the Viet Cong patrol leader had decided not to paddle down the bend with his sampans because he got the queasy feeling that it was a death trap; in this he was correct. So, to avoid the bend, he and his men started to drag their sampans across the still somewhat monsoon-flooded field of weeds. When I realized what they were doing, but still thinking that they were "innocent woodcutters" there illegally, I told my Vietnamese sergeant to fire an illumination round over their heads. When he did that, the Viet Cong opened up on us at about 50 yards with all their weapons. I had with me about 10 Vietnamese and about 15 Cambodian (Khmer) mercenaries, who were terribly tough fighters. When we fired our mortars (which I had personally engineered onto some of my larger shallow draft sampans) and fought our way toward the Viet Cong sampans, the VC fled into the night. It turned out that there were five sampans, all loaded with money and mail. Counting quickly, by the red-filtered light of our flashlights, the sampans contained an a priori estimate of around 5,000,000 piaster, plus mail. Thinking that we had ambushed the advanced guard of the local Viet Cong Battalion, my Vietnamese allies fled into the night. We took the mail that had intelligence value, but the money, in crisp new bills, was very heavy, and there was no time for us to take it. So, we scattered all of it into the fast flowing river, thinking of the delight the poor fishermen and farmers downstream would have in the morning finding the bills. The average income of a Vietnamese farmer or fisherman in the area was about 150 piaster a month. Anyway, we didn't tarry long; we dumped the money and got back to our sampans and headed into the dark, flooded mangrove forests.

The intuition of the Viet Cong team leader had paid off; it saved his life, as my intuition would so many times save my own. How he fared with his commanding officer and political commissar I'll never know, but he had lost the entire payroll for the Viet Cong Battalions in my area of IV Corps Tactical Zone, plus all the mail for the troops, including a letter from the wife of the colonel who commanded the area. *This* is the *intuition* that Immanuel Kant talks about.

but only because I think it exists. Therefore, my view of the world is complete only to a very small degree of what reality is. In the process of developing an architecture and software design, if it is to be a good one and meet the minimum requirements, it must be as close as possible to an acceptable reality. This is what we seek, acceptable reality. *Absolute reality* is possible only in pure logic and mathematics, not in engineering or the sciences. If this fact is not understood by the manager-architect, the design will be incomplete and poorly done, or overdesigned and way over budget. There are individuals who overdesign, not merely because they are perfectionists, but also because they don't understand the philosophical concept of sufficient reality.

Sufficient reality is arrived at in a design process when everyone on the design team understands the object system sufficiently to start work.

But how does this work, and why is it needed? The completed design always rests on the completeness of the requirements. The stated requirements are never complete when they come from a customer, regardless of the expertise of a customer. The stated requirements identify a number of functional attributes that the customer needs in the system. From these stated attributes we infer first the *implicitly required attributes*, and once these are known, the *derived required attributes*. The implied requirements and derived requirements are often missing, incomplete, or never defined; when this happens, the cost overruns are huge. Most people are incapable of inferential reasoning. If the project manager-architect is unfamiliar with the engineering domain and is not able to reason inferentially, the project completion can easily be extended by a factor in cost and schedule, if not more.

4.13   DIALECTICS IN THE ACHIEVEMENT OF SUFFICIENT REALITY

What exactly is sufficient reality anyway? It is a point in the design process where every member of the design team has a *workable* understanding of the design. By "workable" I mean that each subsystem or element senior engineer, programmer, and manager has a thorough understanding of the overall architecture and all of the subsystems and how these relate to each other to form a system. The design team reaches this point of sufficient reality when the requirements and detailed design have been completed, which in computer science terms is the level of the SRD and the SSD-1. These two most important documents, having been developed in the group environment of the design team, are the articulation of all the ideas and expertise levels of each member of the team. To go beyond this point is usually not cost-effective at the present state of computer technology.

It is the dialectic process that permits the substantiation of a design. This fact is very interesting because although most people understand the meaning of the word "dialectics," very few relate it consciously to the design of a complex architecture. The manager-architect, who is and must be the first to understand the objective design; is also the one who presents the design team with the first thesis, i.e., *his* thesis. It then follows that he must elicit a response from the individual members of the team by whatever communication tools are at his disposal, such as persuading, coercing, cajoling, threatening, enticing, and tempting. The first thesis represents the best initial understanding of the architect, of how he envisions the system. The other members may have a completely different impression and view the thesis with skepticism. The response from another member of the team is called the *antithesis*. The dialog follows until the original thesis and the antithesis have evolved and merged into a synthesis, which then becomes the new thesis. Now it is the turn of the other subsystems to get involved; they present their antitheses and arrive at a new synthesis.

Why do this? As will be discussed in later chapters, unless this is done, the entire system will reflect the vision of one or two subsystems only. This is not because the subsystem/segment managers and systems engineers are the best of the bunch, or because their vision is technically better than the rest. Instead, it is generally because politically they have the most clout on the team or project. Clout, or power, is achieved by seniority or political power plays in an organization. Those who engage in such tactics often lack vision and current state-of-the-art technical knowledge, and are generally unwilling to listen to those who have this knowledge. They misunderstand their own limitations and are unable to accept recommendations from others less senior than they are. Because of this, they very rarely are willing to discuss design issues before the entire team. The tactic they most often employ to get around a technical confrontation is to say, "We'll discuss these issues offline."

This statement, "I'd like to discuss this issue offline with you," can have devastating consequences to the schedule and cost of a project. Requirements and design are activities that require the entire team be present if funding and schedule are important. The manager alone has the clout to force the team to cooperate. In software design, if this is not done, a system will look like "all database" or "all communications" or "all telemetry" for some time, until at a very slow pace the other subsystems infiltrate the single-subsystem-dominated architecture to get a part of the architecture that will help them work optimally. This process causes lots of delays, and that means lots of money.

4.14   THE RELATIONSHIP OF LOGIC TO SOFTWARE ARCHITECTURES

When is an objective systems design sufficiently defined and complete for work to start? This is an interesting question. Over the course of many years, I have watched great subjective forces at work destroy systems that had great technical potential. This is not only true of software systems but of computer hardware systems as well. There was a case, some years ago, where a very important project folded after an expenditure of $20 million or so. I personally was busy building GDSS, which I will use as a case study in a later chapter. However, although I was very busy, I still had enough time and interest to observe what was going on in the development process of this system. The system was managed by a fairly intelligent individual who would not, or simply could not, listen to his key and very expert engineering staff. He was not a computer scientist but a professional manager, who felt that by following a standard in its strictest possible interpretation (DOD-STD-2167A), he would ensure that a thorough and clean design would be the outcome. He had no personal vision of what the system would look like, but a vision that it would be forced to evolve through the requirements and design process as outlined in the DOD-STD-2167A and the Series 300 Air Force regulation. What happened was that the requirements were collected as stated, but because of a lack of design dialectics, neither the implied nor the derived requirements ever went into the FRD or the SRD. Furthermore, through the lack of understanding on the manager's part of a methodology, a development process, and a development technique (which can be gained only over many years of apprenticeship on projects), he forced his design team to have an FRD, SRD, and SDD down to the software component level, which is about the equal of a Level IV.

For clarification, such levels are organized as

- Level I: the system itself (as a whole)
- Level II: the subsystems or segments (satellite, ground, etc.)
- Level III: the subsystem elements (telemetry, communications, commanding, etc.)
- Level IV: the software components (decommutation, command translation, etc.)

This, of course, had many more drawbacks than met the eye. Not only did this create four levels of documentation, but four levels of managers, and all the complications and work required to coordinate such a hierarchy. The principal design engineers and senior programmers who knew the technical aspects and details of the system had almost no opportunity to formally share their information in discussions short of risking a reprimand by all of the many managers around. This left the technical conflicts to be resolved in writing by reviewing the documents. The writers used were documentation editors, not engineers. This means that they looked only at the format and the grammar, but not the contents. Engineers are notoriously poor writers. There are a few who are great masters of technical English, and most of these I met at JPL, certainly not in the Army or Air Force. I am privileged to have counted them among my friends.

In this case, the requirements and the design articulation were reviewed among the engineers and turned into an infinite loop, to use a software term. This "no methodology" process technique went on until more than four years later when the documents were completed. All of the funding had been spent, but not a line of code had been delivered. The customer was dismayed; the project was renamed, and a friend of mine took it over. After consulting with me, he managed to deliver an abbreviated version without the documentation after an additional three years of work.

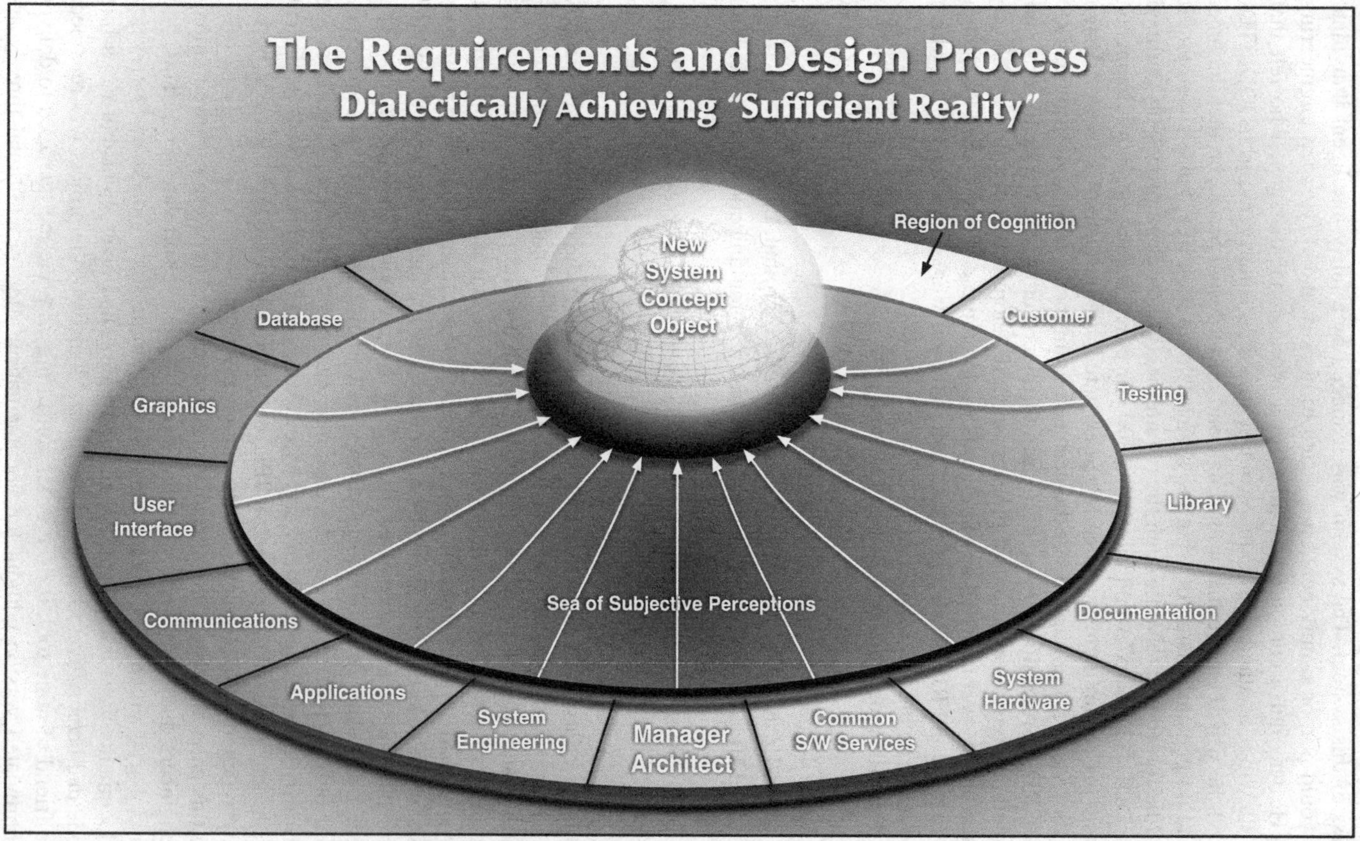
The Requirements and Design Process
Dialectically Achieving "Sufficient Reality"
Region of Cognition
New
System
Concept
Object
Database
Customer
Testing
Graphics
Library
User
Interface
Sea of Subjective Perceptions
Communications
Documentation
System
Hardware
Applications
System
Engineering
Manager
Architect
Common
S/W Services

Figure 2. Dialectically achieving a "sufficient reality."

I must add here that I was asked to consult with one of the all-time great American corporations that was having similar problems with a system of theirs being built for Norway, Denmark, and Germany. It folded after an overrun of $100 million, which the corporation had to pay out of pocket. Fixed-cost systems are hard on corporations when they put second-string managers in charge; cost-reimbursable projects are much more forgiving to companies because the customer is stuck with paying for the mistakes. It is all an issue of management.

4.15 THE LOGIC OF THE SYSTEMS DESIGN

So what about the logic of the systems design? In Hegelian dialectics, there is a point in the process of trying to find out what you want, where through dialectics you add substance to the design object of the objective system that you need to build. You, the project manager-architect and the design team, through this dialectic process, add substance to the object until it becomes *real*, or in other words, is understood by most of the participants equally. You thus arrive at a point called *sufficient reality* when all members of the design team understand at relatively the same level what they are looking at: the objective design. This is the point at which the manager-architect can ask those around the table what they see, and the answers all come back very close to the same, with something akin to a mathematical or logical reality. Furthermore, when anyone around the table asks a question of any other person representing another subsystem segment or component, the answer is still the same, reflecting a common understanding of the object. This is the logic of systems design, based on sufficient reality. Refer to Figure 2, "The Requirements and Design Process: Dialectically Achieving 'Sufficient Reality'."

This is the point when the work can commence. This is closure at the project level. After all, to go beyond the point of acceptable reality will result in overdesign and will make the system prohibitively expensive. Remember, the trifold theme of this dissertation is quality—cost—schedule. If any of these three is unimportant to a project, this book does not apply; put it down. I continue to repeat the fact that on most projects I have seen in the military and in my civilian career, cost has not been a factor. For a very long time I didn't understand why. It is therefore entirely conceivable that to many readers of this book also cost is of no consequence, so this book is not worth the time to read.

5 Project and Task Organization

The following rules apply to all organizations if the intention is to produce a quality product on budget and on schedule:

- Always develop the architecture of an organization to enable the manufacturing of the product you will be fabricating, in our case, computer software.
- Never use a preconceived organizational template, but look carefully at the workflow first and then organize the people around the workflow.
- When reorganizing a project, look carefully at the way the existing organization communicates, coordinates, and actually does its work, not the way the organizational diagram describes it.
- Reorganize by fine-tuning an organization to match the workflow, the coordination flow, and the way the staff actually communicate with each other.
- Every hierarchical and structured organization has its "secret communication network" that employees and staff who are bent on getting their work done use to bypass the obstacles and inhibitors that managers put in their paths. These are the "software patriots," our unsung equivalents to Sergeant York, who single-handedly or with a few friends pull the project out of a jam and deliver a product against all odds and despite the obstacles placed in their way by "management."
- Always ensure from the outset that the architecture of the organization is oriented toward open communication and good coordination. If you are the manager, don't just mouth "truth and openness," but be prepared to take the heat and listen to the opinions of others, no matter how junior they may be.
- Have as few "stem-winders" as possible, just enough to get your work done efficiently.
- The flatter an organizational architecture is, the more efficient and effective it is. It is a lot like a building, architecturally. Each story or floor removes an individual from those above and below by a factor in effective communication and coordination. This factor of removal is a delay factor, and if not directly an inhibitor it is a capacitor that adds time to the implementation schedule. The shorter the schedule and tighter the budget, the closer the staff must be located to the manager.

The Cognitive Dynamics of Computer Science: Cost-Effective Large Scale Software Development, by Szabolcs Michael de Gyurky
Copyright © 2006 by John Wiley & Sons, Inc.

This chapter deals with the organization of the design team and its members. Organization plays a very important part in the success or failure of a project, or any enterprise for that matter. Cost is the overriding factor in organization. Poorly organized projects cost a lot of money, mainly because of their built-in inhibitors to progress, such as infighting and territorial disputes over prerogatives, seniority, and authority in matters of design and implementation. The ability to organize is one of the great and fundamental attributes of outstanding managers and leaders. Effectively working organizations reflect the abilities of the manager and leader.

5.1 THE ROLE OF ORGANIZATION

The organization of any project, corporation, or political group reflects within a very short time the mental processes of those within it. To sum it up plainly, organization reflects the abilities of the manager and leader. Viewing an organization in this way is like looking into the brain and mental processes of a person. If an organization is lean, efficient, and highly productive without the undue exploitation of its members, you have an effective manager at its head.

In my experience, and as a student of history, the highest praises heaped on leadership, whether political or industrial, have always been statements to the effect of: "His ability to organize was remarkable," or "He was an outstanding organizer." Effective and elegant organizations cannot be accomplished as a team enterprise. First, the organization must reflect the vision of the manager like an architecture. Only after the vision of the organization is clearly defined should the design team interact with the manager-architect and provide their opinions and druthers.

Organization is most often one of the key elements of a military efficiency report and is instrumental to the advancement of a successful officer to higher rank. In industry, a corporation or government agency is lucky to have one of its really talented organizers get to the top, as opposed to a psychological charlatan, which I describe in the chapter on leadership.

A well-designed organization is one that is designed to produce a product efficiently and cost-effectively, because this is the American way and approach to doing things. There is a saying that was drilled into me long ago: "America's business is business." Even the word "business," if we stop and think philosophically about it, has serious all-encompassing connotations. For instance, a "business" is both an organization and a state of being, simultaneously a condition and an action. So by our very nature, our American philosophical position is "being busy." We are in the business of making money, keeping busy, and making a profit. The profit motive is one of the imperatives that made our country great. This idea is now lost on many, both native Americans and those who come to our shores. As a people, we take great pride in "working for our pay," and yet there are those corporate managers who claim that the American software professional is too expensive. So instead of exerting their little gray cells and finding ways to increase efficiency, these managers send the work out of the country because, allegedly, "foreign workers produce a better-quality product at a lower cost."

An organization, be it a company or a project, is just as much an issue of architectural efficiency as a building or a system is. It even carries with it aesthetic values to a practitioner or an interested and perceptive observer.

An elegant and efficient organization has many interesting physical attributes. It is first of all lean. By a "lean" organization I mean that it has only as many employees or members as is necessary to accomplish its mission or reason for existence. To this, one adds a 10% to 15% personnel overhead (no more than that) to ensure that the technical and managerial resource pool is available to cover gaps in the workforce, or to plug up holes that occur because of personnel turnovers and employee illnesses. When a level that is 15% over the required organizational strength is reached, an organization begins to become fat and bloated, like the human body, and is a burden to carry. This reduces profit, and makes for too much time spent going to meetings as opposed to being productive. Organizational efficiency is a manager's primary responsibility.

What this means in terms of computer software production is that it is far easier to have one senior expert designer working alone than it is to have him supervise a number of junior programmers, organize them to the task, supervise their work, and correct their mistakes. Each layer of programming staff adds managerial and supervisory overhead, which in turn means that the decision cycle extends by a factor. I have discovered over the years that having to hire an additional person to help someone out who was hired to be a senior design engineer often meant that I had made a mistake in hiring the guy in the first place. A senior design engineer who has through some mistake on my part gotten into a position for which he was not qualified will need technical and programming help. This certainly was often the case in my early projects. In a lean project organization, the manager-architect has direct access on an hourly basis with all senior design engineers if necessary. This is often the case when one is on a tight schedule. When someone needs help, it is always forthcoming, but it takes place in an open forum discussion within the design team, and not one-on-one with the manager. A lean, well-organized software team has members who help each other, and when as a group they feel that more resources are needed, they form that conclusion themselves. On the other hand, when a design team is "fat," the oversight and control of the organization weaken by a factor.

The military has spent much time over the last several hundred years on the study and analysis of organizations to make them more mission-effective and to reduce casualties in combat. In software development there are no combat casualties as such, but there are cost overruns, which are monetary casualties. If a launch vehicle or aircraft is lost due to faulty software, you have real casualties. An engineer should always keep in mind that it is his responsibility to the manager if the structure he designs collapses, be it an aircraft or a bridge. Overall, however, the manager of the project is responsible and accountable, even if he is not held accountable legally.

5.2   THE ABILITY TO ORGANIZE

The ability to organize is a rare skill, difficult to acquire. There are many aspects to project or corporate organization and reorganization. The organization and its architecture both enable the process flow. They set the manner in which people communicate with each other, how often, and how action items are resolved. It is critical to the schedule and to the quality of the software. Thus, the organization must be the vision of the manager, whose responsibility it is to organize and initiate reorganization.

An effective organization can never be designed through a group effort, because it is in the manager-architect's vision, as much as it is in the software product, that the architecture of the organization takes place first. Without the manager's vision, it is composed of the subjective views and impressions of the stakeholders. If, for example, a group is appointed to redesign or to reorganize a project or organization without the vision of the manager, it will always end up being the politically strongest stakeholder who will have his way, not the one most intelligent or visionary. When a situation occurs where they cannot come to a resolution, alliances are formed, and again those who are politically strongest will prevail. The others around the committee who are not well-connected will then simply give up, and eat donuts and drink coffee. Small wonder then, that the resulting organization is found to be inefficient. I have watched these power plays within my own projects and organizations so many times that I have become keenly aware of their impact on schedule and cost.

The mere fact that a manager delegates the reorganization of a project or organization to a selected number of employees or engineers and is not present at most of the work sessions is an indicator that he does not have what it takes to manage. Reorganizations are very complicated and difficult things to manage efficiently, which means they tend to be wasteful of resources.

Organization is an acquired skill; it takes much time and effort if you want to do it well. One should never reorganize just to get rid of incompetent managers merely because the reorganizing manager does not have the courage to tell a subordinate that he is not performing up to expectations. It demoralizes the organization as a whole, reduces efficiency for a long period of time, and shows that the reorganizing manager lacks the key leadership qualities called fortitude and strength of character. Weak character is a Machiavellian trait[1] that Americans as a rule find contemptible regardless of place and occupation. If you don't care what those beneath you think of you, it will cost a lot of slipped deliveries, and often personnel turnovers. The turnovers are never the people whom you'd like to see leave, but the people with the highest self-respect.

5.2.1   Traditional Hierarchical Project Organization

There are, however, several reasonable approaches to organization and reorganization if one is mindful of cost and efficiency and cares for the morale of the workforce.

---

[1] See Chapter 12, on leadership. Subheading: "The Machiavellian Prince."

First, consider the standard template (see Figure 3, "Project Organization: Traditional Hierarchical Approach: Isolated Control"). This reflects the functional mission of an organization and is derived from the work being done, which is the process of developing the Functional Requirements Document and the Project Implementation Plan.

This organization schema is the most popular, as it is easy to understand and use. It is preferable because it separates the organization into clearly defined, yet functionally oriented components, such as subsystems (the DOD equivalent is "software segment"), software packages ("computer software units"), and executables ("computer software components").

Each box represents both a work area, and the people who do the work. It is headed by a manager or task leader, and each horizontal line in the organizational chain has a time delay, and directive clarity component.[2] This means that given design, schedule, and budgetary directives, communication is subject to the same cognitive rules for each level, listening, understanding, analyzing, and retransmitting to those in the organization below. This is dependent on the managers and team chiefs in attendance, their attentiveness, ability to understand the language, ability to take notes, their understanding of the subject, and their willingness to meet with the next-lower level of management. And yet, the data loss is at least 25%, and the time delay can be as high as two or three days. The lost data and time cannot be recovered on a schedule already in motion. An additional aspect of this organizational architecture is that the managers and team chiefs have their own subjective impression of the work, and control their subordinates tightly. I have seen it happen more often than not that individual software engineers and programmers don't readily bypass their chiefs for fear of losing their jobs. Further complexity is added by the competition between managers, team chiefs, and program leads for advancements and visibility for career progression. At times, this makes lateral communication, sharing knowledge, and helping colleagues akin to career suicide. All this happens at the expense of the schedule and the funding, and often the quality of the product suffers.

Meanwhile, the inexperienced project manager, who does not have an adequate set of acceptably full "experience personal data files" or *wells of experience*,[3] believes that everyone in the organization is in possession of the exact data set he instructed his subordinates to pass on down the organization and implement. Nothing could be further from the truth! In the military, it is called the "fog of war" when the troops in the line or on patrol are working on incomplete information and false assumptions. At least in the military, combat operations are carefully and painstakingly planned, reviewed, approved, and signed, based on a commander's concept.

[2] "*Klarheitsgrad*."
[3] See Figure 8, "The Kantian Thought Process: Decision Making Schema."

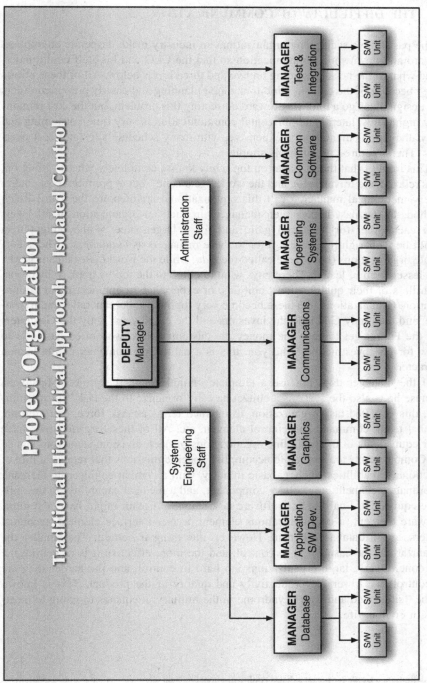

Figure 3. Traditional hierarchical organization—front view.

5.3   THE DIFFICULTY OF COMMUNICATION

In the past I have seen many organizations in industry make desperate attempts at upward and downward communication so that the CEO and his staff could understand what in the heck was going on two and three levels below. All of these efforts failed because of the built-in inhibitors. Good planning and clearly presented orders and design plans go a long way toward correcting this problem, but the cost remains very high. Thus, lateral and horizontal communication is very time-consuming and risky; their implementation is expensive, with many schedule slips and cost overruns. The structured hierarchy is simple.

This implies that the manager on top rarely knows completely what is going on; he is relaxed and travels a lot, and the work "gets done" but at premium cost, and in a very methodical manner. I call this organizational architecture the Third Reich method. In the past I have seen managers in such an organization at all levels fight each other for territorial gain, and for a larger slice of the budget than would be their rightful share. I refer to these managers as *Gauleiters*.[4] The subordinate organizations (boxes) are called the *Gau*, while the word *Leiter* means guide, or a lesser form of leader. These guys want to climb to the top by hook or by crook, regardless of their qualifications, abilities, or experience in engineering or administration. Organizations like these become very top-heavy, bureaucratic, and expensive, and then may God help the investors and the employees. Only the Gauleiters and the Führer get to keep the money the customer pays, who often has little to show for his investments. Mind you, this is a natural phenomenon of the human character.

If the manager does not use a template or understand the project objectives, because he is also the systems architect he can "organize to the task." In the military, this is called task organization, using such terms as task force, battle group, combat team, command and control element, etc. All of these organizations have their equivalents in the basic line organizations of fleet, division, squadron, and so on. Combat teams are formed to accomplish specific missions that require a mix of functional capabilities, such as basic infantry, with a combat engineering element, an ordnance element, an artillery component, and a medical capability. In the software equivalent, I call them "software task teams." A team might have a systems software element, a communications element, a user interface element, technical writers, and a database element. However, one thing is certain: The smaller the organization, the easier it is to control, and the more effective it is in getting the job done. Overly large organizations are hard to control, and the harder they are to control, the lower the productivity and quality of the product. This is known as the "sit around and wait" syndrome in the military; it equates to going to meetings in civilian life.

---

[4] By definition, a *Gauleiter* meant a district political official in Nazi Germany; by extension, a Gauleiter is a local official who is dictatorial. From German *gau* "administrative district" + *leiter* "leader."

5.4   THE TITLE OF "MANAGER"

One of the most costly aspects of software development environments is the bestowing of titles such as "manager" too lightly, and the designation of some size of work as a "project," when in reality it is nothing more than a simple task. Something very interesting happens in the minds of most individuals when they are appointed "managers." I have watched this over many years. There is in the dimension of the human mind a database containing concepts, both correct and incorrect, that have been acquired at some time in the past. It could very easily be that they either misunderstood the original scope and meaning of the terms entailed, or never really underwent the apprenticeship of having worked for some great managers, and were never selected for greater responsibility.

To most people I have met during my career, the title of "manager" brings immediately to mind a vision of a large office, an administrative assistant, and fancy executive office furniture. It seems to conjure up from abstract portions of the concepts database the entitlement to travel and to collect huge amounts of bonus miles flying all over the world. It brings up images of the executive lounges at airports like JFK and Heathrow, and of giving lectures (which few understand and no one criticizes, because it is impolite to do so). It is almost audible from a thin cranium when the *understanding subsystem* cries out in delight, "Executive dining room, here I come!"

The two sayings, "Oh God, I've made it! Wow!" and "Oh, now I have to perform; this will be tough," I have seldom heard together. The idea that a person is completely responsible and fully accountable I have almost never heard.

5.5   THE FLAT, NONHIERARCHICAL ORGANIZATION

So how do you organize to the task? What does task organization look like? Task organization is dependent on the creative mind and the experience and ability of the manager. It reflects his understanding of the work at hand and is organized for optimal control and free-flowing communication, laterally and horizontally. For this reason the organization is flat, as opposed to hierarchical. It is not completely flat on the diagram (Figure 4), but it is when you look at it from above (Figure 5). Figures 4 and 5 are two views of the same flat (nonhierarchical) optimal organization.

The segments are rarely managed by managers, but almost always by team leaders. The subordinate software units are made up of one to three programmers, with a senior programmer in charge. The segment managers have an administrative assistant and senior engineer, but the senior engineer is usually the team leader. The architecture in Figure 5 is akin to the spokes of a cartwheel leading out from the hub, which represent the manager and his support staff. What happens in this environment is that each segment and software unit has its design problems to solve within the context of the overall architecture of the system. By human nature, the segments pull in the only direction they can go, away from the middle and

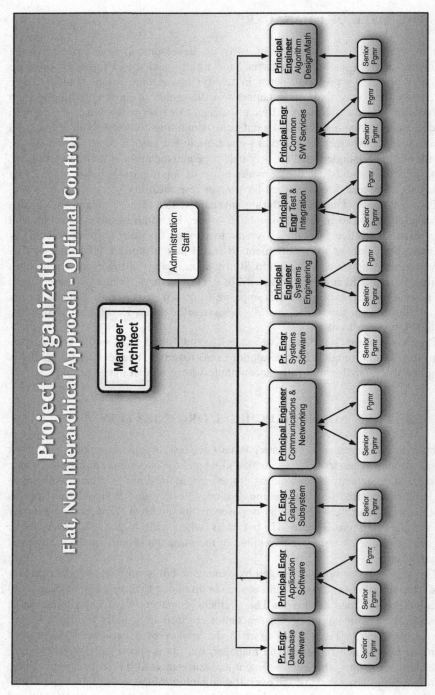

Figure 4. Flat, nonhierarchical organization—front view.

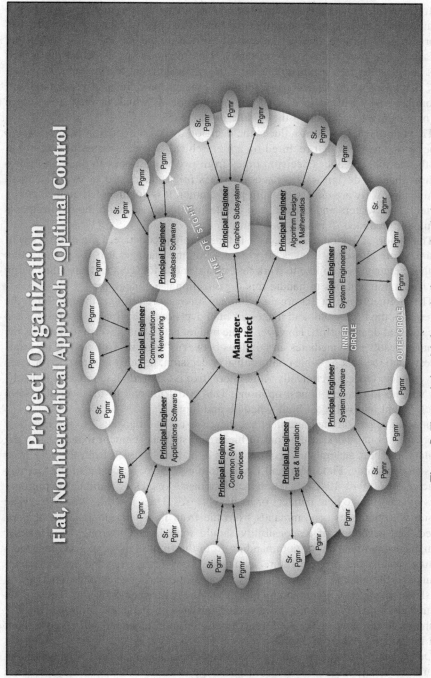

Figure 5. Flat, nonheirarcichal organization—overhead view.

central control. This is natural and is to be encouraged by the manager, who needs to know all of the design issues, all of the time. The only way the manager gets this information is through varying the control exerted on the subordinates, and letting the arguments flow freely and constantly. This methodology is called the *design hub*, and it is the best arrangement for a flat organizational architecture. Individually, managers, team leaders, and senior engineers have their own personalities, accompanied by a need to control, the application of which is very stressful on the manager, who is stuck in the middle of the team.

This approach, however, reduces the decision cycle on an action item or design issue to one-tenth of that required by a hierarchical organization architecture. Put in other terms, it reduces decision times from two work weeks to one day. It also ensures that the design issue or action item is fully understood by every segment team leader, software unit, and senior programmer. It is documented on the spot by the technical writers and entered into the design document, with the requirements document amended to reflect the change.

The flat organizational architecture is thus highly productive; I prefer this type of organization. However, it takes effort to control and manage; it is the organization for those managers who like to work fast, clean, and at low cost and have the energy and leadership abilities to handle this organizational architecture.

The architecture of a flat organization has some shortcomings, though. First, the manager is the focal point and makes all final decisions. This makes it stressful and takes a great deal of effort. However, if the budget is tight, it is worth it. Second, the manager resolves or mediates all conflicts between "warring factions" if he wants honesty and the best possible compromise or decision; he must not muzzle for mere convenience. Once a technically valid alternative is ignored or suppressed unjustly, you will no longer get honest opinions. This is detrimental to the overall system development and will cost both schedule and money.

In a flat organizational architecture, there are no "bottlenecks" to the free flow of organizational work in the control hierarchy, such as segment managers. In the military, the best generals and commanders in history have led from the very front lines (for example, Field Marshall Erwin Rommel, the commander of the German Africa Corps, 1940–1942). Is it a demanding task? Yes. Does it dilute the prerogatives of subordinate commanders or managers? Yes. Does it work? Yes. Why? The person who manages or commands from the front is usually courageous, experienced, and accepting of responsibility should something go wrong. This manner of manager involvement or commanding from the front is the way good managers nurture, teach, and prepare future managers. They learn over and over the finer points and the mistakes made. There is always time during a break or quiet period to ask the manager or commanding officer why he made such decisions. These good commanders do give candid, unvarnished answers to valid questions during hot wash-ups in the field or the conference room. A good manager will always admit to a mistaken decision or a wrong move.

During such discussions with poor or mediocre managers, I have often heard that a particular project was very difficult and large, and that it was not the manager's fault that it was over budget, and that the schedule for delivery was very uncertain.

This is not even an issue. It is not the difficulty of the job, but the ability of the manager that. is in question. A manager gets paid to do a certain job; if he can't, he shouldn't be managing. I don't want to hear how hard it is; everybody knows it is hard. It is your responsibility to get the job done. This is why the element of experience in a manager is so important. This is why you get a set of executive furniture and a large paycheck.

A flat organization is extremely demanding on the manager because the management function is at the hub, or center, of the project team. The idea that all submanagers and project members have their own subjective views, agendas, and druthers does not change. It only means that their direction of movement and thought, and their interpretation of the directives and orders are not necessarily identical to those of the manager. This makes them drift with great force outward and away from the hub.[5] In order to maintain control and optimal efficiency, the manager exerts gravity on the would-be runaway satellites. This keeps them close enough for good control and production integrity without the manager becoming a constraining factor, but not far enough to be out of range and not fit into the project design efficiently. The stress on the manager can be very great and requires what we call dynamic energy. Without it, it doesn't work cost-effectively.

Defining what is meant by all the terms and positions is very important for cost-effective operations. Giving away titles of "manager" is very dangerous, because although it may be done with good intentions, the individual appointed to such a lofty position may have subjective ideas of what it means to be a manager. It will mean many different things to many different minds. The first definition that large organizations should be made aware of is titles. "Project" is a very important title, also. A project is a very large task. To an organization in industry that survives by the products it manufactures, the project managers are the generals. They make or break an organization, much in the same way as poor generals lose battles, lose lives, and often lose the wars they fight. But there are many "projects" and many "project managers" that are not really anything more than task managers at most, or task leaders. Somehow, through ambition, subterfuge, and "working the scenes," they have managed to reach the top.

5.6   PROJECTS, TASKS, AND WORK UNITS

How does one put order into an organization where jobs, tasks, and positions are vague? An organization should formally establish absolute criteria for qualification to the next higher position. Look at the Kantian *Quellen der Erfahrung* ("Wells of Experience") required for a particular level of management, and compare them to those of individuals in an organization who are qualified for filling a job. Then a board of officers should meet and review the performance records of all available individuals and appoint the most qualified individual. It should be a cut-and-dried

---

[5] More on this in Chapter 10, subheading, "The 'Design Hub' as Implementation Tool."

selection process; the individual selected might not even want the job. Nevertheless, he is duty-bound to accept, because the company depends on him to get the job done; otherwise, it has no use for him. This process is by no means perfect, but it comes closest to locking out the ambitious "Prince."[6]

- The title of PROJECT I should be reserved for systems funded at $500 million and above.
- The title of PROJECT II should be reserved for systems funded at $300 million and above.
- The title of PROJECT III should be reserved for systems funded at $100 million and above.
- Only managers of true projects should have the title of PROJECT MANAGER.
- The title of TASK should be used for funding levels of $50 million to $100 million.
- Only managers of tasks should have the title of TASK MANAGER.
- The title for any work under $50 million is simply a TECHNICAL WORK UNIT. Individuals managing work at or under $50 million should have the title of TECHNICAL WORK MANAGER.

The reason for the above is that the high-level managers must really be the most experienced individuals, and should have the prestige of those positions to work for, with the commensurate authority. People who have reached each tier of management by definition would have built many smaller tasks at low cost and on schedule. It is simply a matter of apprenticeship, the learning from more experienced professionals, over extended periods of time. Regardless of how many doctorates you have in computer science, physics, or engineering, if you have not built and delivered over many years consecutively better and better products, you are not qualified to lead projects. True, there are instances where dynamic young persons can be promoted up, skipping the level directly in the next step of their advance. These should be rare cases, and should have as reasons the individual's accomplishments of several consecutive assignments and the completion of quality software products on schedule and on budget. If these don't exist, don't promote! Safeguard the organization from the fast talkers and the profilers, and above all, from the "nice, pleasant people" who "really fit in."

5.7 LARGE ORGANIZATIONS AND STAFFING

One of the things I get a big enjoyment out of is managers who derive their sense of status and importance from the organization chart. There are people who have what we in the industry call "chartsmanship." This means two things. One is that the

---

[6] See Chapter 12, on leadership, subheading: "The Machiavellian Prince."

individual is very good at preparing briefing charts, and the other is that the larger the organization chart of his organization (i.e., the more boxes there are), the more important he is. In itself, the large organization chart is not necessarily a detriment. If the organization requires a lot of people, then it must reflect that. However, there are many who use large organizations for their own sake, and this means form, not substance. The idea that the larger a manager's organization is the more important he is in comparison to his peers was a surprising discovery to me; I started to notice it about 15 years ago.

The biggest problem with large organizations is that most managers quickly lose control. There are some truly great managers and commanders who can run large organizations efficiently, but it has been my experience that most people do not have the talent for large organizations if one is to insist on optimum efficiency. The optimal level of control for one person is to interface directly with around 7 people; the maximum is around 14. This is reflected in the tactical organization of the U.S. Army Rifle Squad, which in the old, time-proven TO&E (Trained, Organized & Equipped) team had 12 members. The Special Forces A-Team has 12 members, for optimal control. Large organization charts are okay if, like Napoleon, an individual can control a huge organization effectively. However, smaller is far better: The control is better, the oversight is easier, and the cost is lower because the burn rate is lower.

Several factors in the issue of organization affect cost. The first is the problem of controlling the organization and getting it to follow cost-effective methodologies and sound engineering practices in the performance of the work that is required to be accomplished. The second is controlling the burn rate. Both are equally important, and both will destroy the budget and schedule if they are not totally under the supervision of the manager.

Both of these factors are questions of productivity. If the burn rate is high, and the productivity of the team is high, then the development process is in harmony or balance.

When the burn rate is steady, but the productivity is low, due to improper scheduling or inappropriate control over the organization, the budget is in trouble.

The primary reason a disharmony between productivity and burn rate occurs is staffing up using a standard template for the organization without considering what the product of each of the positions is, and when they must become available for the next staffing increase. For the organization to be in harmony with the burn rate, the productivity is of primary importance.

How to develop the organization of the design team without losing control over its activities is an important issue in keeping the cost low and the work of its members efficient. There is pressure to staff up quickly in order to accommodate the burn rate once a project has been funded. This usually results in the selection of an organization template, which is then hastily filled with personnel before the job descriptions and role statements have been completed. This creates a time when confusion reigns; funding is consumed going to meetings that have no specific agendas, but are for gathering of information only.

Business travel is another large burner of budgets, in particular if the manager-architect and other key decision makers are on the road as well. Delayed decisions sound like well thought-out *a posteriori* decisions, but bring productivity to a stop, or at best a crawl. No progress is being made, except for endless meetings, and travel to do studies, meet with people, and play golf in exotic places and have dinner at exotic restaurants. Sadly, many managers I know measure the level of their productivity and importance in an organization by the amount of traveling they do. This is a real "bummer" to the budget, and to the customer. My ideas, of course, are unwelcome because traveling is fun, it gets you out of the house, and that is another important aspect of travel. Even those managers who have spouses they love and care for consider getting away on travel as the only way to relax and get a vacation or a little private time. To the ethical manager that considers the product he is to deliver for an agreed-to cost, having staff that travels for all possible reasons is unacceptable.

So how does one synchronize the staffing process to organizational control measures and cost-effective productivity? This is easy, if you really care for a cost-effective product. The basic software organization of a software-intensive project is composed to reflect the basic computer software functional areas, while retaining control over the organization. There are many reasons for this, primarily the initial selection of staff, the need for the manager-architect to understand them thoroughly, and for the staff on an individual basis to understand the manager.

The manager-architect in current terminology means that the individual is both the manager of the project and the technical principal of the project as well. In essence, this means that the technical staff as a group becomes an extension of the architect's technical mind. The administrative staff become the administrative extension of the manager's mind. Both halves, the technical and the administrative, are equally important. Neither is permitted to act as the primary, if the budget is sacred and the schedule and product quality are to be kept as a primary focus.

The members of the technical staff (engineering and science) must understand not only their individual roles and responsibilities but the roles and responsibilities of each other as well. In software this is important for interfacing each other's products, such as segments and software elements. In the case of my teams, the individual members understand each other's functional areas so well that they can exchange roles when it occasionally becomes a necessity. Under the direction of the manager-architect, the individual members of the technical staff synchronize their minds to each other. The same happens with the administrative staff of the project. The administrative staff are as important to the project as the technical staff, for it is in this part of the team that the schedule and budget reside. It is this part of the staff that administers the implementation methodology and the processes and procedures required to keep track of cost and productivity. Both the technical staff and the administrative staff are an integral part of the design team. This integration is not very popular, but it has saved my budget over and over again. During the design team meeting sessions, which initially go from 0800 to 1300 hours daily, the administrative staff are also present, because the discussions almost always have cost aspects.

5.8 STAFFING UP: THE INITIAL TEAM

The initial team becomes the nucleus of the project. Anyone who does not "fit" into the nucleus must be replaced for the organization to evolve smoothly, and in harmony with the manager and with each of the other members. The organization and its team harmony (or lack of it) can make or break a budget. The initial team is easy to control because the span of control is small. It allows for the role of the manager-architect to be the teacher of the team in the implementation methodology and process, while at the same time laying out the vision of the architecture of the project and the organization.

5.8.1 The Initial Team

The required members of this team:

- Project Manager/System Architect (Manager-Technical Principal)
- Assistant Architect/Systems Engineer for the functional domain
- Administrative Assistant
- Business Manager
- Chief Technical Writer

The required products of this team:

- The Level I Systems Architecture
- Project Implementation Plan (first draft, plus organization charts)
- Functional Requirements Document (first draft)

In this initial phase, the manager has many pressures to contend with. As is frequently the case, if the sponsor is managed by a "bean counter" with little technical or managerial experience, he will consider the financial burn rate as the primary objective and is irritated by under-running. What this means is that he measures, at least initially, all progress by how fast money is being spent. It usually means that he will force, or try to force, the project manager to staff up fast to meet the monthly burn rate forecast. If the project manager acquiesces, he is in trouble, because there is no way that he can possibly know what he needs to do or what the architecture will really look like once the dialectic process is completed and presents the sufficient and acceptable reality for the next step. Nor is the conceptual organizational structure or architecture completed. If the staffing is done too fast, with little thought for skill fit, level of experience, and manageability of those being hired, there is real trouble ahead. Misunderstandings, infighting, and undermining of authority will start.

The task of the initial team is to work out the *a priori* Level I architecture of the system. This requires the help of the Chief Technical Writer, who is also the Systems Engineer for Standards and Specifications, in selecting the appropriate standard to be followed in expressing the architecture and organization for implementation. The team then prepares an implementation plan, which will contain the work breakdown structure as well as the first cut at the staffing requirements.

The staffing requirements are of utmost importance, for they contain the job descriptions for each identified position to be filled. At a minimum, these include the statement of work to be accomplished by that position, the academic qualifications needed for that job, or the equivalent in years of technical experience in that type of work. There is the need to show examples of work done on past projects. In the software industry, this means looking at programs written by an individual (and the comments on the code), as well as documentation he has prepared in the past. Finally, references *must* be carefully checked out.

It is very important to match a person's maturity and experience level to the position to which he is assigned. The academic qualification is a small but important part of the required skills, except in the case of hands-on programming in specialized areas. At this level, the Ph.D. is the "knowledge worker." This is the level where all of the critical technical work is done, whether developing new propellants, engines, or aerodynamic forms for aircraft. These positions require high technical expertise gained in the classroom, such as required in the design and programming of instruments to be flown on a spacecraft. One key indicator of the experience level of an individual is the number of projects completed, the size of each task, and its complexity. An average task and project is approximately three years in duration. If the individual has left a project prior to that without having completed his task, he does not get credit.

What this thorough preparation does is to lay clear the path for meritorious, qualification-based, unbiased selection of staff members.

Poorly written and vague job descriptions guarantee great troubles. The interview for a vague job description is based on personal likes and dislikes, and subjective value judgments on part of the interviewer. The interviewer may or may not be a good judge of human character, and may or may not know the greater details of the technical aspects of the job. Indeed, it is nearly impossible for managers to keep pace with all of the latest hardware and technical advances taking place. The effort put into the job descriptions will also keep one from hiring one's friends and those people one likes who may not be the best qualified for the job, or even qualified at all.

As an aside, it is interesting to see how this lack of insight affects everything: success or failure, cost and budget. For example, a board may pick a project manager or program manager based on academic credentials and achievements though the individual has never delivered a system of any size or managed a credible organization in a large effort to completion. One would think that project managers, or managers of large administrative organizations, would be selected on experience or substance as opposed to form.

5.8.2   Phase One Team Expansion

The additional proposed members of this team:

- Systems Engineer for the Project Functional Domains (e.g., ground system)
- Systems Engineer for Design Standards and Specifications

- Systems Software Senior Design Engineer/Senior Programmer
- Common Software Services Senior Design Engineer/Senior Programmer
- Communications Software Senior Design Engineer/Senior Programmer
- Hardware Senior Design Engineer
- Applications Software Senior Design Engineer/Senior Programmer
- Software Test Engineer
- Software Librarian

The required products of this phase:

- The Functional Requirements Document (final draft)
- The Project Implementation Plan (final draft)
- The Software Requirements Document (final draft)
- The Software Design Document (final draft)
- The Software Interface Specifications Document (final draft)
- Common Software Services Subsystem (initial operating capability)
- Communications Subsystem (initial operating capability)

The Phase One team expansion now acquires the next level of engineering staff, whose special qualifications in software-intensive systems are key to the mission and project success. With the Level I architecture completed, and with the job descriptions completed, the key positions are filled for the development of the Level II architecture.

In my case, I select first and with great care the systems design engineer/senior programmer, who happens to be the expert on the operating system and computer platform we will select. Then we select with great care the common software services senior design engineer/senior programmer who will design and program the "abstraction layer" on top of the operating system. This is a very important position, because this position is first among equals on the team. This individual enforces the coding conventions to be followed by the subsystem senior design engineers and programmers. On the design team chaired by the manager-architect, and participated by all members of the technical team, the conventions are enforced. Only after thorough examination of the circumstances and a rigorous evaluation of alternatives are exceptions made to this rule. The common software service layer provides the layered and modular aspect of the architecture, which will allow the seamless replacement or repair of components and subsystems without forcing a costly redirection of work.

This is followed by the selection of the software senior design engineer/senior programmer for communications, who will immediately become the technical lead on the network design, the selection and use of communications, and file transfer protocols for the project. This position is especially important when there are many nodes to a system.

Before any subsystem designs start, the common software layer and the communications layer should be up and running. Then the other subsystems will have from the start a working functional base to interface and code to.

With a small design team, control is excellent and productivity is very high. All the while, the feared "burn rate" imposed by the sponsor, who may be a number cruncher or administrative type with little hands-on management experience, will be under-running the budget. Don't worry, however; the technical and leadership or organizational problems that are inherent in any project will cause enough budget problems that you will be happy that you under-ran up front, early on. To my mind, unless there is a very critical reason, like a launch window imposed by planetary configurations, being over schedule but still on budget is a forgivable flaw in implementation.

5.8.3 Phase Two Team Expansion

The additional proposed members of the team:

- Database Senior Design Engineer/Senior Programmer
- User Interface Senior Design Engineer/Senior Programmer
- Computer Graphics Senior Design Engineer/Senior Programmer

The products required of this phase:

- Software Test Plan (master, final draft)
- Software Test Plans (for releases 1.0, 2.0, and 3.0)
- Software Operators User Guides (for releases 1.0, 2.0, and 3.0)
- Software Maintenance Manual
- Applications software, all subsystems (releases 1.0, 2.0, and 3.0)

The Phase Two team expansion fills out the team for the completion of the Level III and Level IV architectures. Understand that these are not set rules. The database senior design engineer/senior programmer on my projects in the past has been there at the start. This was necessary because at the time, relational databases were in their infancy and we had much work to accomplish on them to make them work for us. As I will discuss in a later chapter, the user interface senior design engineer/senior programmer was also among the first on the Phase One team. There was also a variation in the organization, imposed by a very short schedule and a very limited budget. I had to do an architecture that I called "inferential", used where there are no formal requirements, and no time to document such a huge system. I combined the position of subsystem senior design engineer/senior programmer with the user interface senior design engineer/senior programmer. That system, GDSS, is still very much in use by Military Airlift Command, and I shall discuss the implementation of it in Chapter 14 in detail.

The main thing that a manager must always keep in mind is that a large design team is difficult to control and orient, and to oversee. The organization, no matter what the expertise of the members, must learn to work together on a small scale first, and expand carefully, as the scope of the project unfolds. Those who are not team players must be gotten rid of quickly. This doesn't mean that they are not good people, but that they just do not fit into that particular organization. This has happened to me often in the past. In fact, there is a term called "personality conflict" that is very real and must be taken seriously. It can destroy a budget. It is not the fault or the culpability of any one person, but it can create chaos, conflict, and lack of cooperation; it lowers team morale, and makes good people quit, resign, or just stop producing. It is one of the most costly problems in an organization. The tough-minded manager is aware of it and deals with it instantly.

In government organizations, where firing people from a project is next to impossible, it can be easier and cheaper to sideline a troublesome individual where he cannot cause problems, rather than keep him on the team. Pay the salary, even if there is no work in return, rather than have an entire subsystem lag behind and produce poor-quality work.

5.9   BALANCING HARDWARE AND SOFTWARE

The basic software development organization of a nonsoftware-intensive project is composed to reflect the engineering functions of the project that require software support and development. A nonsoftware-intensive project can be for things like a spacecraft, a combat vehicle, an aircraft, a warship, or a submarine. In each case, although the software enables the object to operate (unless it is purely mechanical and analog), the software design team is a support organization to the primary project object (the vehicle). Unless this is clearly established by the project manager-architect, confusion and infighting over prerogatives will result. Here is the problem of *Anschauung* or "vision" again. Some IT managers or self-styled "gurus" actually view the system backwards. Instead of viewing their role as the people who enable a piece of hardware to work, they view the computer software as enabling a system to exist. This is a very flawed vision. I had to fire a very good friend of mine who had such a faulty vision. Not to say that it cannot work, but to view things totally upside down and to force one's flawed vision on a group of very talented engineers is to cause the good ones to leave and find other work.

I view computer software like the nervous system of a biological entity. While we are using the software as a tool, an extension of the human using it, it is like a communications network, an extension of the nervous system of the human using it. Once it becomes autonomous, it is like the nervous system with the brain being the operating system, or as I call it, the central control semaphore as the director of the system.

Aeronautical and aerospace engineers can have a hard time accepting something they don't understand; they build tangibles like aircraft. So a high level of mistrust comes about, causing conflicts and cost overruns. The project manager must have a good understanding of the software and the hardware, and have two assistant project managers, one for computer science and one for hardware. The hardware guy must be the one who carries the biggest word for the machine, not the software. Balancing the two individuals, along with keeping the design team in harmony and marching along toward the same goal, is what managers get paid to do. The development of the requirements and the design should have the business manager present so that fluctuations in cost are not overlooked. In the past I have always asked my business manager, "Can we afford this? Maybe we should build our own?" This, in fact, keeps the budget manageable and always on everybody's mind. Again, it is more stressful than letting everyone work on his own and just submitting the cost overruns to the customer. The answer, of course, is to follow the dialectic process developing the architecture of the organization in a small group. Much of the organization is the vision of the project manager, and he is the first to map out the organization. Architecture of the system follows, a Level I or perhaps Level II architecture, so that there is a clearer understanding of how the organization is going to have to look to implement it.

The balance and harmony between the segment engineer (such as an instrument, spacecraft, propulsion, or attitude control engineer) and the supporting applications software engineer can only be enabled by the project manager. The software applications engineer is the junior partner. The mechanical design dominates and must have the prerogative. It is a surprising fact that the software part of a system, unless it is purely a computer software system, is always regarded as one of secondary importance, yet almost always it is the software costs that ruin a budget. The software is as important in the overall system as the hardware, the former without the latter is of no use and the latter without the former will not work.

As always, prepare the implementation plan immediately after the architecture has been hammered out. This takes some time, but the implementation plan has the important role of defining (in accordance with the software management standard) what the documentation tree will look like, what the organizational interfaces are going to be, and which protocols will be used. It will also have the initial job descriptions that will prevent careless hiring of unqualified people to fill positions.

To me, a task-oriented team means that the product is not software alone, but perhaps a missile guidance system, a tracking system, or an aircraft. Computer science people typically are not experts in guidance systems, tracking systems, or scientific instruments. It is the computer software that makes the system function as a system, as opposed to the way analog systems used to work in the past. (I call to mind the Kugelfischer mechanical fuel injection system, as opposed to the computer-controlled fuel injection systems of today.) Computer science people are software engineers for the most part, and not mechanical or aeronautical engineers. Thus, they must be teamed to the lead engineers, from the project manager on down to the engineer responsible for the smallest mechanical component in need of integration with the software of the system. Hence the project manager/systems architect's type of right-hand man must be the project software manager. As it starts with the design and the selection of the standards, all of it must have computer science input into the design architecture, completely, at all levels.

At first glance it looks expensive to have a software counterpart, but it saves time and money in many ways. Far fewer mistakes are made, the requirements are parallel and traceable to the hardware components at all levels, and in particular, the software interface specifications are well prepared and easy to understand. Without interface specifications, the system is a "hack job" and will ultimately cost terrible amounts of money to keep going.

It should never happen that a computer scientist take the lead on a hardware project. As their primary assistant, the subsystem managers have a computer scientist design the software aspects of the subsystem. The computer scientists have many important roles on a project. They help to evaluate COTS packages, select subcontractors for the project, and ensure that the contractors can do the jobs they are hired to do. They prepare the FRD, SRD, SDD, and the SIS and the software RFPs and RFBs. They also ensure that only qualified computer scientists are hired onto the project. In other words, they are an important part of the project team, but are a service part and not the lead. Internal conflicts between the flight or ground hardware engineers and the software engineers must be carefully arbitrated. This is a part of the project manager's responsibility and must not be delegated, because it can cause serious money to be squandered.

5.10 INCREMENTAL DELIVERIES

There are many ways to get around the problem of hiring too many computer science people and software engineers. One way is to have incremental deliveries of the software, and perhaps even the hardware, but the software for sure. I began to issue incremental deliveries in 1986 for several reasons. The first was that the challenge of the size of the Global Decision Support System was coupled to severe schedule and budgetary constraints, and I was forced to improvise. The second reason was that the Defense Systems Management College, at Ft. Belvoir, Virginia, had issued a memorandum[7] recommending what I was in the process of beginning to do. The memorandum suggested an approach of "build a little, test a little, and field a little." This confirmed to me that my hypothesis was on the right track, and that others were thinking along the same lines I was.

The methodology to do what I was intending to do remained to be developed, and it worked out in an excellent fashion, saving the American taxpayer a bundle of money.

An excellent way to do this incremental delivery, i.e., "build a little, test a little, field a little," is to build a computer simulation of the system with an equally outstanding test bed, before starting, and to test all software components as they are being delivered into the "System Simulator Test Bed" (SSTB).

Once one set of software components is programmed, compiled, linked, unit tested, and integrated in the SSTB, the programmers can take on the next systems component or subsystem incrementally and sequentially. This is better than doing the work in parallel, which to control always requires great physical and mental energy of the manager. This energy is called dynamic energy, the

---

[7] *"Joint Logistics Commanders Guidance: For the Use of an Evolutionary Acquisition (EA) Strategy in Acquiring Command and Control (C2) Systems."* Defense Systems Management College, Ft. Belvoir, VA. March 1987.

energy to understand, comprehend, make decisions, and see things through to their completion.

5.11   FUNCTIONAL ORGANIZATION

As I mentioned above, most of the technical and administrative positions on a project require a software counterpart in the role of a junior partner to the subsystem manager, design engineer, or team leader/senior engineer. Depending on the scope of the job, additional persons can be added, but only after careful consideration. Remember: To be effective, a staff should be as small as possible. When a team works together as a team and all participate in the design, each of the members becomes very familiar with all of the subsystems and can help out anywhere there is a need. A good senior programmer is a good senior programmer, and it really doesn't matter whether the software is written for an instrument, a fire control system of a tank, a spacecraft on-board computer, or a ground system. The only criterion is that there be a spacecraft team chief or senior design engineer who thoroughly understands the functional performance and characteristics of the hardware and sensors, and can clearly and succinctly communicate this to the software engineer who supports him. On the surface it may be somewhat intimidating to think that each key principal position is doubled with a software engineer and a technical writer. However, this is the way a project is going to be cheap. Cost is not only salaries and people; it is also time. The less time is wasted, the sooner a project will be completed, and the less it will cost.

The functional organization of the design team depends entirely on the mission objectives of the systems to be developed. Let's take as an example GDSS, the very large U.S. Air Force command and control system built from 1986 to 1989. The Global Decision Support System is Military Airlift Command's tool for controlling, on a worldwide basis, all of its airlift missions: aircraft, cargo, personnel, air crews, ground crews, mission tracking, and aircraft maintenance. The project was to support an average of 800 cargo and personnel airlift sorties daily, capable of expanding to 1,600 sorties during time of war, when the national airlines were supporting the war effort. It turned out that during the Persian Gulf campaign, it supported up to 6,400 sorties of all types (the expansion was due to the aircraft provided by our allies, England, Egypt, Germany, etc.). This was accomplished without a single breakdown in software. The initial system was built in 21 months at a cost of $16.5 million and comprised 550,000 lines of code. An additional $7.5 million was provided for a 12-month extension period to add additional subsystems and expanded capabilities. The implementation and design used the "Inferred Architecture Methodology" of which I'll talk later in Chapter 10.

The GDSS system is divided into the following functional subsystems:

- Command Post Subsystem (DOC)
- Crisis Action Team Subsystem (CAT)

- Current Operations Subsystem (DOO)
- Diplomatic Clearance Subsystem (DIPS)
- Logistics Subsystem (LRC)
- Special Assignment Airlift Mission Subsystem (SAAM)
- Airfield Database Subsystem (AFD)
- Transportation Subsystem (TR)
- Graphics Display System (GFX)
- Airfield Database (AFD) Appendix Subsystem
- AUTODIN (ATD) Appendix Subsystem
- Computer Aided Scheduler (CAS) Appendix Subsystem

Each of the above subsystems had a team chief, who was also the principal programmer, and a technical writer for support. With the system being software-intensive, the organization was reflected in the basic software organization above.

5.12   INTERFACE PROTOCOLS OF THE ORGANIZATION

If a project is to move ahead at high speed with a view toward conserving resources, verbal and written communication should be as open as possible. This is not to say that the team chiefs, systems engineers, and project manager are bypassed, but that technically important data and coordination flow smoothly. The project manager and the subsystem managers are kept informed through the daily coordination meetings, and through the technical writers as well. Many project managers and team leaders do not feel comfortable with the approach of people sharing information among themselves. However, this is a big saver of funds. The important decision-requiring issues are discussed by the implementing engineers themselves; the decision makers, who have enough to keep them busy, are confronted early by a coordinated action item that has support across group and subsystem boundaries. This also requires that the management team be ever present to approve action items and resolve conflicting views on an hourly basis. The best way to track action items and the status of their coordination is the "Staff Action Memorandum." This is the most sacred document in a decision action needing coordination and approval. It is a summary of the technical, schedule, and cost impact of the recommended course of action.

5.13   COMPLETION OF THE TASK

The meaning of "completing a task" is as follows:

- Full participation in the preparations of the requirements for the appropriate level of the project or task, including the FRD, FDD, and SRD

- Full participation in the design, coding, and unit testing of the software
- The appropriate commenting of the code written by the individual
- Testing and integration of the entire product

These are the *sine qua non* for a professional. It is only at the end of a project or task that an individual understands the errors made per lines of code, the error rate between languages used, etc. The lessons learned can only be understood after the completion of the system.

Individuals who leave a project before it is completed have the following characteristics, which may not be universally applicable, but are a reliable indicator most of the time:

- They have difficulty committing to serious work and seeing it through to the end.
- They have not matured to the next level of professional competence, with all that entails.
- They are not team players, and may not be able to get along with a team.

5.14   DETECTING THE "FRAUD"

A person is a fraud who talks a good game, has a great memory, understands the rules and syntax of the various computer languages, but cannot design and write a functioning module of software, much less an entire program, to specification. I have known this type; one such person managed to get through a screen of five expert software professionals by simply overwhelming them with his academic expertise in a language. This costs a lot of time and money, especially when a manager hires such people into key positions. Often the individual is not even intentionally a fraud; he simply cannot write a concise, well-balanced design. It is analogous to someone with an expert understanding of English grammar and syntax who is unable to write a sonnet or a poem in free verse, much less in iambic pentameter.

The chapter on leadership elaborates on this because it is of utmost importance to understand the dynamics of this type of person. The fraud can and will ruin a schedule and a budget. At the peer level, these individuals will often succeed in their attempts to dominate the rest of the design team. In the absence of the manager-architect sitting in on design issues, the peer group has a problem recognizing that something is wrong. These individuals have all the answers, are self-assured, but somehow things are not going right. Depending on the workload and how urgent their tasks are, others are reluctant to challenge them. When an action item is not resolved for several weeks, it is an indicator of a fraud, or at best, simply an immature or inexperienced person. In any case, the manager can only inquire into the problem with little, if any, hope of success.

What this means is that the individual in question has been hired into a position for which he was entirely unqualified, but naïvely thought could do the job, and convinced the interviewer of such. It could also mean, though, that the individual willfully misled the interviewer as to his qualifications, was hired without a background check, and "slipped through the cracks" and got the job. If this is what happened, the individual is (or certainly feels) in control.[8] He feels that the engineer who hired him is far too embarrassed to inform the boss of his mistake. Or as it often happens, the engineer may be overly busy; he would like some answers as to why the job is not getting done, but puts it off. Unpleasant things are often put off, and it takes an especially seasoned and experienced veteran manager to understand the consequences of no action down the line, and to take action as soon as the problem is known.

It may, of course, be completely easy to explain. The individual may be new and have a hard time communicating the need for direction, input, receivables, etc., and thereby is unable to get the job done. In this case, the manager with experience will get things done quickly; he will reorient both the team leader and the engineer, and progress will be made. However if the individual is indeed a fraudulent person, he will immediately threaten to file a lawsuit. In this instance, most managers will back off, leaving the individual to intimidate them; the managers will work around the problem. On a team or project this has a demoralizing effect, because people who work hard have to pick up more work, while they see that certain individuals hardly work at all. Sooner or later the nonproductive individual will have found a "new opportunity" to improve his career, and will inform his boss that he would like to move. The poor, overworked boss is only too happy to pass the fraud on to the next boss, without saying a word. Nor is the individual's new employer likely to call the old one for a reference, for fear that he might miss the opportunity to hire such a "great find." The fraud then makes a career of moving from job to job, never staying longer than 9 to 12 months at any one of them, changing jobs just before a delivery.

[8] Kets De Vries, *Leaders, Fools and Impostors*. Josseys-Bass Publishers.

6 The Philosophy of Communication

For some reason I have almost always worked in environments and on projects where time was short and funding was very low, and I was forced to depend very much on clear, timely, and complete communication. Well-structured, concise instructions, whether organizational, technical, or administrative, are cost-savers, because there is no need for additional clarification.

Without good communication there is no cost-effective product. Communication means clear, concise, unambiguous verbal and written exchange using correct technical English. However, even with these parameters, communication is not complete unless one has *visual* access to the communicator and to those receiving the communication. I consider written communication such as e-mail very incomplete because I cannot see the facial expression, the body language, or the eye movements of the individual I am "talking" to. By using only written communication, one does not have access to the tone and emphasis of the message as one does with visual and verbal modes of communication.

Communication is the sensory connection to the outside of the human thought system and human thought process. Much of it is transmitted in code and masked by the anticipation and the likes and dislikes and aesthetic preferences of the communicators. What has impressed me the most is that as trusting and familiar to the open communication environment as my colleagues and engineers are, they still hide information from me and from each other. Even though I have over many years emphasized the importance of totally open and frank exchanges of ideas, opinions, technical facts, and technical issues, they still hold back. Sometimes even the most outspoken and intelligent individuals I know are reluctant to "tell it like it is" for fear of offending their colleagues or looking stupid themselves.

The inability to communicate on part of the communicator occurs for a variety of reasons, one of which is a perceived or real lack of training in verbal or written communication; in other words, a poor command of the English language. I have seen this often: A highly placed individual is reluctant to communicate in writing because he feels vulnerable and embarrassed about his lack of writing skills. Writing skills are greatly lacking in engineers born and raised in this country.

These phenomena, the natural inhibitors on part of individuals to communicate freely, drive cost up because decisions are made on incomplete data, much like incomplete intelligence in the military results in wrong decisions.

6.1 "SANITY IS AN ACHIEVEMENT!"

In the immortal words of the late Dr. Pierre Janet:[1] "Sanity is an achievement!" One of the heroes in my career is Elton Mayo.[2] He performed studies in teamwork and team and individual productivity in the American workforce between 1934 and 1947 as a member of the Harvard Business School. Were he alive today, he would have a "field day" with us, because, if anything, we have gotten worse at what we do. Our individual performance on the job, our productivity, and the cost of our products to the American taxpayer and customers in industry, private or public, are worse now.

It is almost certain that everyone in the software industry has encountered the shy young engineer with super academic credentials, who talks little, asks no questions, demands nothing, and sits quietly in his cubicle, immersed in his computer. He programs at a great pace, even before the requirements are completed and the software design is thought of. Everyone is happy to have the young engineer on board, and all praise the individual for insight and initiative. One glance into the cubicle of this individual reveals a couple dozen crumpled cans of Coca-Cola and a wastepaper basket full of Snickers or Mounds wrappers. He usually comes in to work at 9:30 or 10:00 A.M. and works late. He may or may not be plugged in to some kind of music. He is almost always late for reviews and design team meetings, but participates little anyway. One must drag the information out of him about when his product will be either debugged or delivered. "One or two weeks," comes the typical response, quietly and on the defensive. Of course, since there is no design the systems engineer can review, there is an awkward feeling of guilt on part of those who need the product.

Another type of individual one encounters in the workplace is the one who, at the mere mention of a one-on-one meeting with the project manager or task manager, breaks down in tears, and begins to sob. This, of course, puts you—the modern manager—on the defensive, thinking, "Maybe I'm asking too much. Maybe I'm being too hard. Maybe I'm not an 'in' person. Here I am being unreasonable, cruel, and threatening." Then, after a useless discussion on why the software module or program is not ready, the individual leaves your office with an agreed-to two-week extension on his schedule. As you lumber off to the cafeteria for a bite to eat, you realize that you really are not being unreasonable in demanding a product for wages paid.

Who are we talking about? We refer to these individuals affectionately as "nerds" and "geeks." Elton Mayo refers to the 1947 equivalent of a nerd as a "psychoneurotic." "A psychoneurosis is the consequence of insufficient social discipline and practice in the capacity of receiving communication from others and responding to the attitude of others in such a fashion as to promote congenial participation in a common task." It is a lack of sufficiently developed social skills in an individual with highly

---

[1] Elton Mayo, *The Social Problems of an Industrial Civilization*, Harvard University, Graduate School of Business Administration, The Andover Press, 1945, Andover, Massachusetts.

[2] George Elton Mayo (1880–1949). Australian-born business theorist and professor emeritus at Harvard.

developed technical skills. Such psychoneurotics are usually a product of our universities, where the technical curriculum is all-consuming at the neglect of the humanities such as philosophy, art, literature, and political science.

One would like to think that nerds and geeks are great assets, and often they are. However, for them to be useful, they must work directly under the supervision of a very senior and experienced engineer, who mentors them and brings them slowly out of their shell. It is usually not the fault of the nerd alone if the job doesn't get done. It is the manager-architect and senior design engineer who fail to communicate the task adequately and clearly, so that it is understood, not only by the design team, but by all of the other psychoneurotics on the project as well.

This communication issue is not as easy as it sounds, and the cost of the project will depend very much on clear, concise, well-articulated verbal and written communication. In times of war, a commander's incomplete communications can cost lives; for a project, it costs money, stress, and more money.

6.2   GAUGING UNDERSTANDING

There are several tools available to the manager-architect that will permit him to gauge the degree to which his message is understood. This is rooted deeply in philosophy, specifically, cognitive philosophy. Am I getting through to the team how I want things done? Nodding heads and approving smiles mean nothing; in the mind a lot of things are going on, and the manager or systems engineer has not the foggiest idea of whether the listeners in the audience are "in lock" or "out of lock," to use a communications term. They may be present and completely attentive, but they may also be mentally "out to lunch" on a golf course, at a concert, hunting antelope, or at the beach. There is no way of telling, except through facial expression, body language, eye movement, and verbal response. In fact, if managers knew how little people paid attention when they were talking, they would ensure that everything they said was written down and published. After the design team meeting it will be a rare individual indeed who, having missed a critical transmission, will call the manager saying, "I'm sorry, but I missed the bit about coding conventions on the telemetry subsystem; I was thinking about my girlfriend. Would you repeat your presentation for me?"

This may sound overblown to some people, but missing 30% to 80% of a design presentation and not recovering it for a guaranteed 4 to 8 weeks really throws production into trouble. During the presentation, the manager must scan his audience closely and fire off questions at the first indication of individuals going out of lock. This of course irritates the individuals on the receiving end, so it must be done elegantly, with finesse, so that the message gets through and you don't lose a good engineer.

6.3   INTERNAL TEAM COMMUNICATION PROTOCOLS

Protocols are rules governing the manner in which we interface with each other, and the manner in which we communicate, both within the organization and with those outside a project. The protocol for communicating with each other is established at the outset of a project by the project manager, covering formal and informal communication, verbal and written, the "need to know," the trivial, and the technical and peripheral data that we exchange. These rules should be included in the Project Implementation Plan, where all aspects of the project's implementation are found, such as job descriptions, design and coordination meetings, etc.

Some team leaders and managers wish to be made aware of and control all communication flow within their organizations. Control of communication is one of the great tools of power, not only on projects and organizations but politically as well. It is one of the tools of the Machiavellian Prince.[3] Controlling communication within a project can be done, but it is expensive. What I am talking about here is the time delay factor involved in the coordination, review, and approval process of problem reports, action items, and change requests. There is also the aspect of gathering information on the part of individuals who need it to get their jobs done. The delay factor of having to go and get approval from a team chief who in turn has to speak to another team chief and get his approval so one of his can talk to one of theirs used to be common in the past. In the military, it can have terrible consequences on one's career. Whenever you ask for assistance or information, there is a philosophically implied condition that you ask because you don't know. To a rational person, not knowing everything is a given. But trying to save yourself lots of time and pain by doing research on your own, when all you have to do is ask someone who sits in an office a short distance from yours who knows the answer, is just wasteful.

An irrational person, one who is unable to communicate effectively and is very ill at ease with himself, finds the asking of questions to be traumatic for fear of revealing that he does not know what he should know. It is an unacceptable agony. Trouble mounts when such an individual, because of his ability to climb politically, reaches the upper management levels. He is still insecure psychologically with his position and with his level of expertise, and for his own subordinates to communicate with other organizations is an absolute *no!* I experienced this several times in the Army, most dramatically while I was in combat in the 5th Special Forces Group. Interestingly enough, I have also experienced it here at JPL. Both persons to whom I was subordinate were what we today would call "control freaks." Stepping outside the chain of command, even to report time-urgent events with possibly terrible consequences, was against the rules. Green Berets did not go directly to the source of help without going through five layers of chain of command. This I had done, but it turned out that the messages were not considered important and not passed up the chain of command. Three weeks later I was in Saigon in transit to go on R&R. I was sitting at the bar of the compound MACV J-2 and asked a senior officer sitting next to me from that command chain why no one was responding to my recon reports, for I had sent three in three weeks. He was visibly shaken at the breakdown in communication; only by the grace of God did I get away with it. There are occasions when the communication of inaccurate,

[3] See Chapter 12, on leadership, subheading: "The Machiavellian Prince."

incomplete, or faulty data can have unpleasant consequences. However, when I figured out which was worse, no data or all the data I could get, the latter won out. I learned early to correlate and triple-check everything to prevent incomplete information from causing me to make a faulty decision. Open and unconstrained communication in engineering and science is very important.

Similarly, suppose you have a solution to an urgent problem in robotics, but you don't belong to the organization that is responsible for robotics, nor do you have the credentials to be considered as someone who might be allowed to be on the periphery of the priesthood of robotics. You simply will not get to talk to anyone in the robotics organization. The best you can hope for is that an individual will steal the idea and use it to solve the problem, while you have only the satisfaction of having provided the idea.

As a manager-architect, if you understand human dynamics and human nature, you can circumvent the bastions defending individual and collective rice bowls. Aye, "fiefdoms" are the greatest curse to schedule and budget! Picture the project as a stream or river; it should flow at an easy pace without blockages. When it runs into a landslide or dam and the water can't flow and overflows the banks, it takes out bridges and buildings downstream, and it is all very costly. For team leaders and senior design engineers it is imperative the team does work as a team. The collective effort of a well-designed, well-led team produces four times as much quality product as a "team" made up of individuals reporting to one person.

6.4   EXTERNAL TEAM COMMUNICATION PROTOCOLS

One of the most interesting phenomena I have encountered in my professional life is the manager who, with a truly military attitude, has no tolerance for individuals going outside the "chain of command." In his organization, discussing official issues such as design, implementation subjects, proposals, and items of this nature with those outside and above his position in the organizational structure is forbidden and not tolerated. Anyone doing it is on the Q-List, and these types do get even at raise time, promotion time, and performance evaluation time. Most of these manager types are the ones who use the "management by intimidation" technique. In software engineering, engineering in general, and in science, the open exchange of ideas and the discussion of technical issues are of paramount importance.

It is true that in the military, breaking the "chain of command" can be and often is very disruptive, so there is little tolerance for it. Anyone who does it is marked, in more ways than one. But the mission of the military and its organization is by its very nature structured, and only in specialized units with high-risk and relatively independent missions are things like that sanctioned. Some examples are the Cavalry Regiments and Separate Parachute Regiments of the Army, and Special Forces units in combat.

In engineering and science, however, *not* breaking the chain of command when necessary is detrimental to the accomplishment of the task in a timely manner. It is understood that the managers at all levels must be informed of the event, action, and the status. This is necessary, and courtesy requires it. In science and engineering it is of the utmost importance that communication flow smoothly and without impediment, horizontally and laterally, without fear of reprisal on the manager's part. The maturity and self-confidence of the manager are indicators of the rate of flow of communication. It may take a proposal or an action item 30 days to get through the appropriate channels for approval, when a simple telephone call or a face-to-face meeting between the responsible individuals can make it happen in less than a day.

6.5   TECHNICAL ENGLISH AS THE MEDIUM

English is the *de facto* language of science and engineering in today's world. In software, more so than in mechanical and electrical engineering, the pure, unambiguous, explicit, and clear use of the English language is a must. Most students graduating from our universities are not taught to prepare written communications without ambiguity; in fact they are very poor at it. I am an immigrant, born in Hungary, and had to attend a language laboratory in college. The examinations at the time, regardless of discipline, allowed for only one grammatical error and only one spelling error in the text. Anything beyond that was an automatic F. I had to learn English, how to pronounce the words, and how to write compositions. I grew up with three languages simultaneously, German, Hungarian, and French, which were not much help in being fluent in English. Let me say that there is nothing more distracting and frustrating to an audience such as a design team than when the presenter of a concept either mispronounces almost all of his words or does not know how to structure sentences, be they simple, compound, or complex. Compounding all of the problems of paying attention and keeping focused on the object being designed, poor English ability on behalf of the speaker forces those in the audience to attempt to interpret what is being said, serving only to hasten one and all to go "out of lock."

Losing lock is an awful waste of time. I shudder to think what portion of the average budget is consumed because of faulty communication. I had to attend the language laboratory at my university because the English Department felt that my pronunciation and enunciation were poor. I had been in this country for only 6 years, and academically had been at the top of my high school class. However, complicated subjects such as chemistry, biology, and mathematics have to be understood by the student, not only from what is written down on the blackboard but also from the verbal articulation of the professor presenting the subject. Then, of course, there is the aspect of how well the individual who is doing the teaching presents the subject, and how good his command of the English language is. In the Armed Services, since one of the primary missions of a Special Forces soldier is to be an expert teacher, we had a saying: "The student fails to learn because the teacher failed to teach." Today, in our multi-ethnic, multilingual society, we Americans must accept that in order for us to succeed in a cost-effective fashion, we must do it in English, and we must do it well.

It is not incorrect to tell someone, "I don't understand what you are saying. Would you please rephrase it for the sake of clarity?" One of the most important classes we need to send all levels of management personnel to is the class in the English language (I am not kidding). Furthermore, the "how to make friends and influence people" classes, as well as "Toastmasters," are just as important as classes in the latest technical developments. In my observations over the past 45 years, there is nothing that turns the "listening switch" to OFF more quickly than someone who is not transmitting correctly.

Each listener has two ears (antennae) he can array for audio reception, and two eyes (telescopes) he can array for visual observation. The combination of the two separate sensory subsystems provides for an ideal reception of data, when kept in lock on the presenter and subject. Even when the *external sensing* function picks up the transmission, if the *inner sensing* function cannot compile the data and send it to the *abstraction* function in a state sufficiently complete to be interpreted, the *reason* function shuts the external sensing down. There is a scheduler or controlling function that has auto-prioritization of activities to be performed in the reason. The receive mode is shut off if there are more urgent data to be processed, such as with resolving a personal issue, or thinking about one's domestic problems. I always scan the receiving faces of my transmissions, but many still slip by me where I fail to spot that they are not paying attention, but are far away. By them not "being there," my budget is jeopardized.

It is an understatement for me to say that excellent English grammar, diction, and pronunciation are critical to getting a technically complex job done quickly. In many languages the dialects vary so much from one village and county to the next that it is nearly impossible to understand what is being said. I used to speak fluently in a Bavarian highland dialect. After an absence of 10 years in war and back in the States, I returned to the Garrison of the 10th Special Forces Group on a visit. I worked out and went to our steam bath where three natives sat talking. They didn't know I spoke German fluently, but assumed that I did, so they switched to the dialect of Finsterwald and Miesbach. I was locked out! It was a terrible experience. I tried to concentrate on key words at first. That didn't work, then on to sentence structure and speed. That didn't work either. It took me one hour sitting there in the heat to start getting meanings from sentences and then inferring the missing data before they left. Yet, they were speaking German.

This is exactly the experience people have in a design team or a technical review who do not understand the spoken communications. They are afraid to ask or speak up, thinking that they may look stupid. If only they knew that two-thirds of the audience feel the same way! Instead, almost all go away cheated and frustrated. It is an insult to the audience not to present in fluent English if time and money matter. If not, then it is okay.

Then there are the endless viewgraphs and presentation slides that say nothing meaningful. They are full of boxes and arrows, relational diagrams, and schedules that add little technical value to accompany the presenter's already miserably poor presentation. This is a disaster to the project schedule and funding profile.

6.6   ENGINEERS AS TECHNICAL WRITERS

One way of dealing with an engineering and science team unable to articulate a design concept or implementation plan is to have a large number of engineers on the team who write well and have a great command of the English language. There are people like that, serious engineers and scientists, who understand the technical domain. Spacecraft propulsion systems, molecular biology, computer science, electrical engineering all are disciplines that have professionals who are not employed in the fields they were trained and educated for, but write extremely well.

Once the technical writers create a first draft of the design using input from the design team meeting notes and the design articulation process, each senior design engineer and senior programmer is interviewed by a technical writer, who then completes the applicable section of the detailed design. Once this is completed, it is thoroughly reviewed by the responsible senior design engineer, who corrects it and returns it to the technical writer for finalization. It is then presented to the design team for approval. This takes far less time than the process of having engineers read each other's comments and redlines, and circulating the document around and around until everyone is satisfied. This reduces the design time by two-thirds.

6.7   DOCUMENTATION: ARTICULATION OF THE REQUIREMENTS AND DESIGN

The problems usually start with the preparation of the *proposal*. This is a very important document, as it is the cornerstone of how the project will proceed, and holds the secret of how much it is going to cost. It tells me at once how the project manager's mind is organized. I'm not looking for Kantian perfection, just logical organization. The proposal tells me how the individual whose signature is on the document thinks. Is it well organized? Is it clearly architected so that the requirements, design, and testing documentation will flow easily out of the proposed product? Can I, the reader, sponsor, or customer, visualize the end result? In other words, if I am the customer, I have a general idea of what I want in the product. When I receive the proposal, it should tell me that those who are responding to my request understand what I need, or have a close enough understanding of what my needs are for me to trust their initiative. The proposal is the keystone that connects the customer with the client in a clear, unambiguous, logical, well-organized fashion. Then, once this understanding is established, it connects the proposal authority or project manager to the initial design team, which prepares the requirements.

The proposal should state at a minimum the task the system is to perform, the way it is to perform its task, the development approach to be taken (e.g., MIL-STD-498), the development methodology to be used (e.g., rapid development, prototyping, traditional hierarchical), and the estimated cost[4] in hardware and software (lines of code per function, task, and instrument). The standard mandated in the proposal, after it is tailored to the task, will enable the estimation of the documentation count, which as a rule of thumb is usually pages of documents per line of code. This will vary from project to project, depending on the technical complexity of the task. Mathematically highly complex systems such as new types of radar or laser communications would require much more documentation than simpler systems, such as a ground system.

Documentation is the "blueprint" of computer software. If it is not done in a disciplined fashion, both online and hardcopy, and kept under tight configuration control, you are asking for trouble. Errors in the software then become ambiguous, and trying to fix these is expensive because the systems software engineer and the manager have no insight into the code without having to take excessive time to go at it. Well-documented software is easy to fix, and the schedule and budget are not impacted. All these items are of utmost importance to the development of computer software systems.

Let me restate the importance of clearly prepared and unambiguous systems *articulation*, usually referred to by inexperienced and self-impressed engineers as *documentation*. One of the first things I do as I begin the task of defining a system is to impress upon my team the importance of properly defining terms and roles. In my terminology and by my definition, when I refer to "documentation" I mean things like birth certificates, driver's license, health and dental care records, performance evaluations, diplomas and such. These are documents! To computer science professionals, when referring to software systems requirements and design records, these are the equivalent of blueprints for hardware engineers, and are sacrosanct to quality work. Therefore, these documents are the articulations of the requirements and design.

6.8 THE SRD: SOFTWARE REQUIREMENTS DOCUMENT

Unless the system parameters are carefully and meticulously articulated, you have a very costly task ahead of you. Let's take the importance of the Software Requirements Document, the SRD. Why have one? There are many projects that don't bother with such things. The SRD is your contract with the customer. Who is your customer? Generally for a segment, it is the system implementation manager. If you are the systems manager, it is the end user like the Army, Air Force, or NASA, depending who entrusted you with the funds to build the system. If it is incomplete, how do you know as a customer what you have coming to you? As a producer of software, how do you know what you have to deliver for the money you have been paid if you have an incomplete set of requirements?

---

[4] Cost estimates are usually very sloppy these days. They need to be broken down into hardware and software components, at a minimum. Regardless of whether the "host" is a flight system or ground system, all of it works because computer software makes it work. We are past the mechanical age and cannot exclude software from our estimates if we are sane, care about cost, and take professional pride in the work we do.

This is double jeopardy; I don't like it. One of the techniques that some customers use to get the last drop of blood out of the implementer is to say something to
the effect of, "Gee, this application doesn't work right." This puts you on the spot
and gives you feelings of guilt or makes you feel stupid for having forgotten it,
when in fact the function might not have ever been a requirement. An SRD is an
SRD only if, at a minimum, it has been signed by both parties. It helps if two
management tiers above have reviewed it and concurred to make certain that
some critical application was not left out accidentally.

The project Software Requirements Document is the contract between the customer and the client. It follows that it must be treated with due respect. Not having
one would be equivalent to an individual saying to a contractor, "I want you to
build me a house. There is the lot, and here is the money. Let me know when
you are finished." No honest person would accept a job like that; I certainly
wouldn't.

The Software Requirements Document is very complex. It contains all stated,
implied, and derived requirements needed by the project and system. I would estimate the contents of the SRD are about 60% stated requirements, 25% implied
requirements, and 15% derived requirements. Only the stated requirements origi-
nate from the customer. The rest is originated through dialectical examination of
the proposed objective design. This is not an easy thing to do. On GDSS, the entire
system depended on implied and derived requirements, which represented a good
two-thirds of the total cost.

Moreover, the project test plan is based on the SRD; all test cases and test procedures are based on the SRD, so a project cannot test a system that does not have a
completed, signed off Software Requirements Document (or System Requirements
Document for system hardware, like spacecraft, aircraft, or missiles). Without an
SRD, the customers don't know what they are to get, and you don't know what
they want. Worse than just looking like a fool, you will take a lot of abuse—not
name calling in today's politically correct environment, but the kind of abuse
that makes you feel like a fool, a novice, a greenhorn. The stress is awful: Your
cholesterol climbs, you eat big burgers with everything on them to control your stomach acid, and you gain weight. Your best people leave and you have to hire new
people who may or may not be good at their chosen professions. They need "break-
in time" to familiarize themselves with the project, systems, and personnel; nevertheless, your blood pressure goes through the roof, and it affects everything. Even
this could be acceptable if the individuals who push you around were technically
competent and serious individuals who understood the conditions. But they are not;
they are anything but experienced and knowledgeable computer scientists. They
may have a B.S., M.S., or even a Ph.D. in computer science, but have never delivered a significant system from start to finish. They are "professional managers"
whose interest is in career before product. So, the SRD is very important to all concerned, and above all to the project and implementation managers.

If a fully agreed-to SRD does not exist, the project is not being managed correctly. In fact, there is no way realistically to cost a system, hardware or software,
unless the requirements are completed and signed. An expert manager can estimate

very closely what it will cost, but it is not the real thing. As far as "creeping requirements" are concerned, the meaning of this term is "we don't know what we are doing; we are novices." A customer always knows what functionality a system must provide. It is the project manager and his team whose job it is to figure out the detailed requirements, and based on those, the detailed design.

When going out on a competitive bid for implementation, if funds matter, the project design team writes the FRD and the SRD. Based on these two documents, the project manager prepares the Project Implementation Plan (PIP). The Request For Proposal, RFP, contains only the FRD and SRD, and is the package that needs to be sent out. When the proposals come back, the costs proposed can be compared to the PIP, and then you can see relatively clearly who is and who is not rational about cost and schedule, if the funding profile is important, of course. I am saying this because in my experience the funding was rarely important to most projects in the military. The rare exceptions were instances like GDSS and JTLS, because the acquisition of a new technology had priority and urgency.

The FRD is the project manager's contract with the customer, while the SRD is the project manager's contract with the implementing organization. No one would invest in building a house without a contract, yet projects do the equivalent of this all the time. All government agencies do it; it's no small surprise, then, that our national budget is so overrun. We taxpayers are paying almost 100% percent more than we need to for our products. Only the private sector is anxious to get value for the money.

7 Software Management Standards

The software management standard is one of the most important tools at the disposal of a manager-architect and systems engineer. In my point of view, it is the "Talmud" of computer software development. I don't like to even think about developing a system without it. In my career in computer science, I have only once built a system without using an software management standard. It is certainly a great help in keeping cost down, the development on schedule, and the quality of the product at a professional level. When a decision is made to waive a standard, it must be made with great caution. Only those managers, architects, and systems engineers who understand software standards thoroughly should be permitted to forgo the use of one. In such cases, the manager and systems engineer already know it by heart and will substitute improvised methodologies that reflect the fundamental approach of a specific standard, or a combination of several.

It is sad indeed that software management standards are not included as a required subject for a degree in computer science in the curriculum of our universities. Not that a standard is a substitute for courses in management or systems design, but it forms a clearly articulated framework around the process of systems development, like the structure of the five-paragraph field order does to Army operations, planning, and implementation. If one uses a standard properly and consistently, it becomes second nature to one's mental process, and ever easier to apply and use. In a definite sense it becomes a teacher to the users as well, as discussed in Chapter 10, "The Development Process Methodology."

7.1 THREE GOOD STANDARDS

There are numerous software management standards around; all are good. The most important ones are DOD-STD-2167A, MIL-STD-498, and JPL-STD-D-4000. These are the standards that my team and I prefer to use, primarily for their flexibility and elasticity. They are not so detailed as to impose unreasonably long hours for anyone to study and understand. They leave much of the policies and processes open to the interpretation and requirements of the users, manager-architect, and systems engineer.

The Cognitive Dynamics of Computer Science: Cost-Effective Large Scale Software Development,
by Szabolcs Michael de Gyurky
Copyright © 2006 by John Wiley & Sons, Inc.

7.1.1 JPL-STD-D-4000

JPL-STD-D-4000 is structured as an open standard because it is a synthesis of the many engineering development standards we have used at the Laboratory over the years. We are a unique engineering research and development laboratory, doing unique, one-of-a-kind projects, so our standards must be flexible and elastic to accommodate a wide variety of special and unique systems.

The Department of Defense software management standards are more detailed and exacting. They encompass a very wide variety of applications, ranging in the categories of dependability, accuracy, availability, and maintainability from low, medium, to very high. They cover software applications ranging from low-risk systems such as financial packages, through high-risk systems like missile warhead guidance software, and everything in between. A DOD manager who does not thoroughly understand the standards and the Army and Air Force regulations that govern their use and the degrees of compliance for each application should not be managing. The cost of the product will reflect that ignorance.

7.1.2 MIL-STD-498

The most important companion of the military manager interested in the acquisition of DOD systems at a reasonable cost to the American taxpayer is MIL-STD-498. This is not only a necessity to conserve public funds, but there is also a purely professional perspective to this. Any officer entrusted with the responsibility of managing the acquisition of a large and important system for Uncle Sam has the unique opportunity to acquire great management skills. The "mil spec" is a great outline for the functional skills a person needs to acquire and develop an expertise in. When an Army or Air Force officer follows the standard and takes courses that functionally represent the areas outlined in the standard, he will develop an expertise highly sought after in industry. The SPO, the manager with the military background, already has the leadership skills so often lacking in his civilian counterpart. Add to that leadership, engineering skills, and such functional processes represented in the standard as requirements analysis, functional design, software design, and testing. After retirement from active duty, such a manager will have no difficulty in finding exciting employment opportunities.

Even experienced and expert managers should use a software management standard. Those managers with fewer than 15 years of experience in software development, and with less than a million lines of code delivered in several large systems, shouldn't even think of building without one.

7.1.3 DOD-STD-2167A

The very best of the software management standards was the old DOD-STD-2167A. It was done at great effort and expense to ensure that DOD software acquisitions were of uniformly high quality, delivered at a reasonable cost, and easy to maintain. "Assuring" that the foremost criteria of quality, cost, and timely delivery were present in all software acquisitions was a complicated task.

It must first of all be taken into consideration that the Department of Defense has many categories of software, each with varying degrees of "assured" dependability, reliability, and availability. These are specified in the requirements. For example, the dependability, accuracy, reliability, and availability criteria for nonreal-time logistics cargo tracking software is far removed from the criteria required for ballistic missile targeting software.

Years ago there was a snafu with the toilet cover in an Air Force C-5A Cargo aircraft. This got the press excited, because the toilet covers cost $5,000 apiece. I suspect that the reason for this was a lack of familiarity with the standards and specifications used at the time. This kind of unfamiliarity with standards and specifications is dangerous. It results in the overdesign of an item or a product. The vendor/ manufacturer may know better, but may not say anything for fear of alienating the SPO, of risking not getting the contract, or both, for too many reasons to mention. But when the requirements are written in clear, unambiguous engineering terms, leaving no room for misinterpretation, the cost will be equal to the fair interpretation of the functional requirement.

I had several experiences while in the service with software acquisition SPOs at the level of colonels. These SPOs were not about to study, understand, and properly tailor DOD-STD-2167A, and received in the end no product whatsoever, but at great cost to the U.S. taxpayer. If creating many jobs in industry (as a high-ranking friend of mine told me once) is the intent of the project to begin with, then it is "understandable" (jobs that serve as placeholders for certain skills critical to the defense industry are important, however).

I once illustrated the reason for high cost, using a nonsoftware example, to my colleagues by writing a set of requirements and the design, test, and integration criteria using DOD-2167A and applying the strictest interpretation, using AFR (Air Force Regulation) 300-10 series as guidance for a toilet paper dispenser. It easily topped $35,000 had someone been foolish enough to have wanted one. Just to set the upper and lower limits of the revolutions per minute for the spool under the diverse climatic conditions of Arctic and Amazonian humidity and temperature will make the cost prohibitive. Let's add to that a favorite of some managers: the fudge factor. Then, contract out the spool assembly, the spool housing assembly, and the attachment multipurpose mount assembly, for both flat and concave bulkheads, and you have a nightmare of a test and integration plan.

7.2 ASPECTS ADDRESSED BY A STANDARD

To a manager-architect, a software management standards package addresses the most important aspects of development, much like a pilot's preflight checklist:

- The management aspect itself
- The philosophy that provides the guidelines for interpretation in order to avoid the pitfalls discussed above

- The system and subsystem design phase
- The software design phase
- The software implementation and test phase
- The subsystem and system integration test and delivery phase
- Software management and planning
- Software configuration management and control
- Work implementation and planning

All these are of great importance to the developer and practitioner. As time goes on, experience is gained, and a team of experts is formed. Some of these practices are modified and adjusted to meet the cost and time constraints placed on the system; experts can do this, but novices should not do it lightly. Each package of the selected standard should be read by the design team, and then discussed in sessions led by the chief technical writer, who is the systems engineer for design articulation. All systems and subsystems must be thoroughly and accurately documented, otherwise it is only maintainable at great cost.

7.3 PREPARING TO SELECT THE STANDARD

Selecting the appropriate standard and specification is one of the imperatives of cost-effective software design. The chosen standard and its supporting regulations define to the developer the standards of performance that are expected by the customer of the product. It is the standard, tailored to the project needs, that permits an accurate tracking of the progress of development of the product, and provides for controls and insights into what is expected of the developer and to what detail. Few managers use this approach, and I don't understand why. The actual contract to a software developer is, at a minimum, the Functional Requirements Document (FRD), but in most cases it is not enough. The Software Requirements Document (SRD) is really the backbone of the system, and it is the real definer of what is required in the scope of work. The SRD then forms the basis for two other documents, the Software Design Document (SDD) and the Software Test Plan (STP).

The Software Design Document represents the architecture at Level III. The developer uses the SDD-1 to build the system, while the manager and his test team prepare the Software Test Plan as a separate document under management or sponsor control to ensure that the system meets the customer's requirements. You rarely should task the vendor or developer to write the Final Test & Integration Plan (FTIP) or Acceptance Test Plan (ATP); that is like having the fox guard the chicken coop. The customer may be a corporation itself, levying the work on its own systems division. That is no way to ensure quality, by which I mean that the software meets or exceeds the requirements of the customer, is free of known defects, is easy to use, and is easy to maintain, modify, and enhance in the future. After all, a system is a big investment for a customer. Big money is invested, hard-earned money, by a corporation or by the federal government to get a product that is hoped will make their operation less cumbersome and more cost-effective. In industry, profit margins count. On the government side, one has the American taxpayer as the sponsor, so why not give the taxpayer the maximum bang for his hard-earned buck?

The first thing I do after I receive a task or project is get my preliminary team together and decide which standard we are going to use in getting the job accomplished. This must happen first. Then the systems engineer for standards and specifications along with the systems engineer for the technical domain spend a week or so with me, reading the standard so we understand it thoroughly. When the Project Implementation Plan (PIP) is completed in final draft, but before it is signed, the Phase One Team Expansion is assembled. The new members of the design team are then briefed in detail on the project standard, and everyone gets his own copy of the standard to be thoroughly understood, along with the PIP. One week of presentations and discussions follows, dealing with issues such as coding conventions and the detail and clarity required in articulating the requirements and design. As the project manager-architect, I give the first thesis or proposition on how I envision the system to look and what I expect; I invite arguments of every kind. These arguments will range from objections and outright rejections of my vision architecturally, to acceptance *en toto*. There will be objections to the standards and specifications that were selected, and to the content and detail of the scope, which each specification demands to be complied with. All arguments and objections are valid; they represent the subjective realities (*Schelling*) of the participants' antitheses and are reduced dialectically to a synthesis and a new thesis of what are valid and invalid expectations.

It must be remembered that the DOD-2167A spec encompasses a software scope ranging from the complexity of, say, a nuclear warhead-armed ICBM to the simplicity of an accounting system for the Army Finance Corps. If you design an accounting system to the rigor of an ICBM guidance system, the accounting system will cost as much as the ICBM software. The converse is true also; you would have an ICBM system with only the reliability and availability of an accounting system. So there needs to be a long and patient discourse on how the design team understands the objective system, and the minimum detail it requires in the application of the standard.

The standard is just that: it is a standard way of approaching something you are going to do. It tells you sequentially what you must do, and how to write down what you are going to do so that others understand what you are doing. In a large software system, the written and graphic articulation of the work being done allows the manager-architect and systems engineer to have a look and scrutinize the product being developed. It permits the reviewer quick access into the work over a large organization, at a glance, with an *a priori* expectation of what to expect. The reviewer can go to the status of a given module in the Detailed Design Document from the Software Design Document, and compare the two. If required, he can then look at the code and read the comments. I guarantee this: If the individuals are not following the agreed-to and directed conventions, you will not have a quality product at a reasonable cost.

7.4 STANDARDS FOR IMPLEMENTATION

At first, the main issue is the resolve and commitment as a team to use and apply one standard. This standardizes the approach of the team and project if it is a large system. We at JPL are very successful at building great one-of-a-kind systems, like the Voyager spacecraft (exploring the outer solar system) or the Viking spacecraft (landing on Mars). This is because we use and apply engineering standards very strictly, and depending on the classification of the subsystems, apply them as cost-effectively as possible. In the past, we had a set of standards for each directorate: Planetary Flight, Deep Space Network, Instruments, to name a few. As the missions became more complex and sophisticated, and the demands of our software more extensive, the Laboratory consolidated all of the software standards from the directorates into one: the JPL-STD-D-4000. We had an outstanding team of professionals do the work, and it was greatly influenced by DOD-STD-2167A, for many reasons. JPL started originally as a U.S. Army ordnance laboratory before being converted to NASA for the launching of our first U.S. satellite, Explorer, and then hitting the moon with the Ranger project. Many of our senior engineers and managers were veterans of World War II, and had returned from combat in the Pacific and Europe as captains, majors, and commanders, and took up their professions once more as engineers. JPL is now an engineering outfit; it is unique, the only one of its kind in the world. Engineers work to strict, no-nonsense specifications, even with the one- or two-of-a-kind prototype products like our great spacecraft.

As I have mentioned, the tailoring of the selected standard is important because it has serious implications. A standard like DOD-STD-2167A is a broad set of rules, so it must be tailored through careful discussion of issues such as required precision, criticality (single points of failure that can cost a spacecraft), availability (percentage uptime), dependability, accuracy, and maintainability. Will the system be needed in ten years, and in that case should it be portable to new platforms and operating systems? What about the usability of the system? Who will use it, and at what levels of expertise? Who will maintain the system? What is the expected turnover rate of the maintenance team? All of these issues will bear directly on the tailoring of the standards and specifications.

The tailoring process further contributes greatly to the synchronization of the minds of the design team, and permits the project manager-architect to evaluate the thinking process, or absence of it, in the members of the design team. During this period of indoctrination and familiarization, the team begins to understand the objective design, not from the architectural perspective, but from the logic of the activity flow of the participants.[1] It also establishes the discipline and commitment required of the team, and the parameters expected in their interaction together.

---

[1] Hegel, Georg Wilhelm Friedrich, *Wissenschaft der Logik*, Volume I (*The Science of Logic*), Felix Meiner Verlag GmbH, 1990, Hamburg, Germany.

7.4.1 Waiving the Standard

Standards may be waived for various reasons. The first and foremost reason is if a true and valid time constraint exists, such as when the software simply must get done, say, for reasons of national security, or to meet a launch date. This is a very difficult approach, and the manager-architect must not only have a complete understanding of the system, but must transfer this understanding in real time to the key designers of all the subsystems, on a daily, even hourly, basis. Other reasons would be if the customer waives the formal standard requirement (for cost or time concerns), or if it is a small rapid-prototyping project.

When proceeding without a standard, all of the details are kept in one place, the manager-architect's head, and in one document, such as a design logbook, and maintained on an hourly basis by the technical writers. There are no requirements documents, and only one design, which is interpreted by the subsystem senior design engineers in real time. Systems engineering in this case is a four-person task:

- The Systems Engineer for the Technical Domain
- The Systems Engineer for Design Articulation and Standards
- The Systems Engineer for Action Items and Coordination
- The Systems Engineer for Workflow

This was the case in the building of GDSS. The risk was extremely high, because in the event the manager-architect should get sick or fall out, no one would have a design. The architecture was completely of the inferred type, which meant that in lieu of a top-down or bottom-up design, it was inferred in real time from a number of known user points, perspectives, and needs. The probability of success was only about 5%, but it worked out marvelously. This is the most stressful environment a manager-architect can imagine. I do not recommend it. It requires you to keep almost all architectural, development, and organizational data and status in your head. You have to deal with the stress by exercising daily and taking a disciplined approach to relaxation, preferably meditation. This might sound odd coming from a modern architect, but it helped me to get through 32 months of combat with little sleep. Projects that are high-intensity, short-duration, and under tight schedule and budget are to me like infantry combat, minus the bullets and grenades. I fully believe that the stress on the nervous system, digestion, and mental operations are identical, and if overdone, will destroy one's health quickly.

8 The Estimation of Software Cost

Probably the greatest pain for a manager, if he is an honorable, duty-conscious person, is to go to upper management and ask for more money. There are feelings of guilt about not having managed the funds correctly, and there are feelings of embarrassment, because it reflects on one's competence in managing. Money in American business, as in private life, separates individuals into classes of people. Our national vocabulary is filled with terms like, "he is worth every dollar," and "his word is his bond," very clearly establishing the dollar as a measure of an individual's worth, honesty, ability, value, and social standing. This is perhaps because of our work ethic, and the fact that as a people, we shy away from other handles of social standing, such as titles of nobility. With respect to the work ethic, it is drilled into most American children that we start working early in life, making money by delivering newspapers, mowing lawns, painting fences, caddying at the local golf course, and saving what we earn to start a savings account as early as possible. The savings account and its uses give most of us an understanding and respect for money and budgets, resulting in a conscious effort to treat the money of other people with the same respect we treat our own.

The chapter on leadership covers the great Kantian attribute of ethical behavior. Nevertheless, it is expected of us as individuals to respect a budget we have been given as a trust, at least as much as our personal savings account, if not more.

A budget therefore is a trust. It is an honor to be entrusted with funds belonging to an individual customer, a company of investors, or the American people, and be expected to provide in return a product specified by those individuals.

In a very serious sense, it is a scary thing to contemplate that if we as a people ever lose sight of our obligation to respect the money of others, we become a bunch of charlatans, liars, cheats, and thieves. We become dishonored not only in the eyes of our colleagues, but in our own eyes, too. To be branded a cheat in America is a terrible thing. To be branded as incompetent in the serious world of management is deprecating. There are those among us who will shrug it off, saying, "Others cheat, so I'm doing it also." This attitude doesn't change the meaning of the American term for a cheat. There are others in business who redefine cheating by calling it "padding the budget." This doesn't change a thing. Why does a manager need to "pad" a budget by two or three times the true cost? This is a dishonest measure to

The Cognitive Dynamics of Computer Science: Cost-Effective Large Scale Software Development, by Szabolcs Michael de Gyurky
Copyright © 2006 by John Wiley & Sons, Inc.

deceive one's superiors and means that the individuals who do this are liars and unworthy of trust.

Sound business practices do include an operating reserve in the budget. Depending on the complexity of the technical work, one can legitimately ask for a 20% or even 30% reserve. Based on an honest cost estimate of a project or task, it is fair to ask in writing for a 20% reserve in one's budget. If you are not provided with sufficient reserves and an unforeseen event occurs, then the problem shifts to the individuals who did not authorize the budget reserve.

8.1 SPONSOR COSTING ISSUES

However, there is to me nothing more embarrassing than having to ask for more money, and thank God, I have never had to. Worrying over budgets is a terrible thing, even when you have done a thorough job of estimating and know almost to the work week how much funding is required for a job. Yet, the sponsor disagrees and estimates it at 1/3 of the cost, and at 1/3 of the meticulously estimated schedule. Keep in mind also, that budgets are used by some sponsors as weapons and tools over the implementation manager. You worry and can't sleep; you sweat up the pillow, stay up all night, night after night, because you'd love to build this system. It is a wonderful, doable, technical job! You also need the work, and the sponsor knows it.

The sponsor, as it happens, may not be an honest or ethical individual. This type of person loves to manipulate, knows the real cost fairly well, and also knows that if you accept the conditions, you are his slave. He can be abusive and condescending, and savors the fact that he judged you correctly—that you're as spineless as he happens to be. Meanwhile you are doing great physical damage to yourself. The stress a manager is under in such circumstances results in overeating to control stomach acid; heart attacks occur in the coming years, followed by cancer or strokes. The employees working on such a project, being honest, needing the job, and wanting to succeed out of professional pride, are also caught in the jaws of this vise. They work longer and longer hours, without pay, just to get the job done. This is the great attribute of the American working professional, to get the job done, regardless how difficult, because of commitment and pride in one's work. They believe in themselves, but the consequences are severe. Families suffer, resulting in divorces, and their health declines; "burn out" is the term. And, to the business at large, the loss of a great engineer or scientist is incalculable, because he takes his great experience and knowledge base with him, when he could otherwise be teaching the younger people coming on the job.

Meticulous cost-estimating ability on part of business and project managers is among their most important tools; it protects them from the insane or corrupt habits of exploitive character types. There are two incidents I will mention before going on with the methodologies of cost estimation.

In one instance, a program manager out of DOD assumed control of a project while I was in the process of doing the Functional Design Document, in accordance with DOD-STD-2167A, a process the individual did not understand.

The requirements had been approved by the previous program manager, so the functional design was not difficult in itself. Technically, as far as computer software is concerned, it was just within the realm of being doable. My team and I completed the FDD and SRD, and I wrote a Project Implementation Plan. Having accomplished all this, my team and I worked out an implementation schedule for this very large software-intensive system. The result was an estimated $62 million over approximately 7 years. When we briefed the program manager, he flatly told me that we would build it for $16.5 million, and we would build it in 36 months. He had a large staff of his own, a personal staff of about 30 officers and senior NCOs. We had a terrible cost review. The individual was overbearing and abusive. I was unable to sleep. There was no way that we would be able to do it for that amount of money and on that schedule, even though I was used to building efficiently and at low cost.

He and his staff, confident that he would be able to force us to comply, went back to their site, and I had another sleepless night. We had completed the first phase of our project, the analysis phase. All we had to do was accept the funds and start development. I had a review scheduled with my division manager the following day. We needed the funds badly; I was well aware of that. After the preliminary design review was over, my division manager congratulated us and said that we could proceed. I told him that I disagreed, and that we should terminate our relationship with this program. He was surprised and upset, and asked me if I really wanted to be the project manager. I explained that, yes, I wanted to be the project manager, but not at the expense of our collective reputations, and all the embarrassment to me, to him, and to the Laboratory. I reiterated the delta between our cost and that of the DOD program manager. I recommended that we return the unused balance of the funds, and terminate the relationship. This was done. Years later, we read in the trade papers that the program had been attempted elsewhere, yet terminated due to large cost overruns.

In another instance, I had agreed to design and build a system, also a very large one. The program manager and I agreed on the cost, and we proceeded to work. Once again, a "timely" reorganization occurred, and a new program manager came in. He promptly cut my funding in half. I actually knew the individual well, and went to see him and brief him on the cost. He didn't budge. I asked him to tell me why he had cut my budget in half.

He simply informed me, "You know I never give you more than half the funds you need, Mike."

"But I can't do a proper requirements and design phase with half the funds, and you know that," I protested.

"I know," he replied.

"So then tell me, why did you cut my project budget in half?"

He leaned back in his chair and laughed. "Oh, you know—I like to see you thrash!"

I believed him. I knew this type of manager, this type of commander, from the Army and from other corporations I had worked with. I went off, and took another project that was already in the queue and waiting.

This kind of game is played up and down all over, from sea to shining sea. These character types (described in Chapter 12, on leadership) occur in all walks of life, on both large and small scales, even down to the family unit. So, making correct cost estimates are not only important to the project implementation, but for the protection of all.

8.2 TYPES OF COST ESTIMATES

There are three types of cost estimates: an *a priori* estimate, an *a posteriori* estimate, and a *detailed cost analysis*. Among serious professionals, an *a priori* ("up-front") costing is rarely necessary. It is used primarily by the project manager and systems engineer as a personal reference for better understanding the parameters of a work unit. But, there are sponsors on rare occasions who will still ask for a "ballpark figure," or a "rough estimate," without having time to go into the details, or for reviewing or discussing the budgets and schedules of another project, not one's own. In this case, an *a priori* cost estimate is proper.

There are a few people who, for the lack of a better word, are "naturals" in the fields they have chosen in life, be it music, engineering, or management. There are also a few people who can estimate cost at a glance, which is an *a priori* estimate but frequently comes very close to the actual cost at completion. This ability has its explanation in philosophical terms: It is *intuitive*. Functionally, the intuition is the interaction between analysis and reason and is based on a sum total of the individual's experience in building systems over many years and participating in costing exercises. So in many ways, it is very much a decision process with cost as the decision object. If it is an *a priori* estimate, it is based on a template of experiences, rather than a detailed analysis of one's own personal experiences.

8.3 "LINES OF CODE" METRICS

The costing is done in U.S. dollars, and the template has two units of measure. There are a number of good ways of sizing a project; one way I prefer is in terms of source lines of code, minus comments (SLOC); another is in terms of source lines of code, plus comments (LOC). Whether estimating software cost *a priori*, *a posteriori*, or in detail, I use dollars per lines of code, or dollars per module. I realize there are many opponents to both of these approaches, but in my 30 years of software development I have not found a better, more accurate or pragmatic way to estimate cost. I suspect that there are several reasons for the inaccurate cost estimates today. The errors are due to the methodology applied in the estimations, the parameters used in the estimates, and the inexperience of the estimators.

The use of lines of code in cost estimation is most accurate when you are replacing an existing system, or building a new system but with an application you have built in the past. The "workdays of effort" estimation method is more accurate when building a system from scratch, one that is not completely familiar to the architect or to the design team. The workdays of effort approach is more familiar to senior programmers and principal design engineers who can relate to the work required to produce a module of software.[1]

The cost in terms of dollars per line of code (budget and schedule) includes *all* associated costs from the project manager on down, including all salaries, benefits, travel, holidays, sick leave, facilities, computer hardware, COTS packages, compilers, tools, business travel, programming, unit testing, meetings, testing and integration, and systems design. In summary, the cost in terms of dollars per line of code includes everything that the sponsor's money pays for.

When doing an *a priori* cost estimate on the redesign of a system, the following works very well for me. I anticipate mentally that I will need to reduce the size of a system by about 30% in the source lines of code count, throwing out software that is no longer functionally usable. The reprogramming, depending on the languages used, along with new requirements added for such things as more automation, will increase the system by 50% in size.

All of the code will be new code, of course. I have never really been able to reuse old code in a tightly integrated way, even from the systems my teams and I have built together. The new platforms, operating systems, and application languages available every three to four years, plus changing vendor support, generally makes code reuse expensive and impractical. Furthermore, the programmers, the really professional ones who work for me, cannot afford to be left behind technically while advancements in the state of the art are being made. Programmers are not all alike. A good programmer will have an inclination toward elegance, practicality, and simplicity. With a poor programmer, however, overelaboration of the code is difficult to control because of his prevailing mental attitude, preferences, and work habits.

The required comments per line of source code must then be added to this, which increases the size further. I then mentally arrive at a total lines of code estimation. Depending on the level of complexity of the programs, I select an average cost per line using past projects, such as those described in Chapter 14, and come up with a cost, plus 20% for reserves. When the reserves are not used (and they rarely are), they are returned to the sponsor.

For the estimation of the completion of the project, the anticipated productivity rates are added. I use generally two types of productivity categories. The first one is technical productivity (programmer lines of code per day), and the second one is implementation productivity (which includes me, and everyone else on my staff). I prefer to use the implementation productivity rate, *a priori*, to estimate time to completion in the cost of a project. I do this because the technical productivity metric is misleading. It does not include the technical writers, testers, software librarian, systems engineers, configuration control engineers, and so on. I habitually break the productivity down into two major areas: systems software (networking, common software services, database, and graphics) and applications software (telemetry, commanding, user interface, automation, etc.). Over a period of 30 years

---

[1] A module of software, in general, will vary from as few as 50 to as many as 250 lines of code.

collecting data on my projects, tasks and work units, I have come up with an overall average productivity rate, and a range for both the technical and the implementation productivity. From adding the salaries to the cost per line of code and the productivity rate, based on complexity issues, I have a very good idea of how much a project is going to cost and how long the required schedule to implement will be. I'm rarely off my *a priori* estimates by more than 10%, and these estimates are usually on the "under run" side.

The programmers of the applications programs perform at an average of around 45 lines of code per person per day, and a range from 30 to 85 lines of code per person per day. Systems programmers working on the common software service layer and the operating system directly are the slowest, at around 20 lines of code per person per day, due to the greater complexity, with a range from 15 to 25 lines of code per person per day.

Workdays of effort are easier to estimate on completely new systems because it is easier for the individual senior programmer to visualize a chunk of work to be programmed. It is the manager-architect's task to dialectically round out the workdays through sometimes exhaustive questioning on what seem like side issues, but which bear directly on getting the job of estimating done. For example, if a programmer states that one module of a certain type of telemetry processing takes approximately three days to program, he may be anticipating that the module will be about 75 lines of code. He rarely at first considers that after he coordinates his work with the communications and user interface senior design engineers it will have grown by an additional 150 lines of source code plus comments, making the work of programming actually 225 lines of code, at a rate of 45 lines per day, plus a sick day, for a total of one week of work. However, this one week doesn't include the time required to unit test and document the work, nor does it take into account the time required to go to meetings, which count as workdays of effort, not lines of code. I must add that I have been fortunate to have had the very best software professionals in the world working for me over many years. They are not only great programmers, but also have the creative genius to solve difficult design problems quickly.

8.4   THE MAJOR WORK AREAS, FUNCTIONS, AND TASKS THAT MUST BE INCLUDED IN THE ESTIMATION OF COST

Over the years I have developed a software work estimate worksheet (see Figure 6). It fundamentally is based on the Software Requirements Document; however, the SRD represents only a part of the time spent on development. The work that is not in the SRD can only be estimated in workdays of effort.

Although this is not strictly an accurate way of estimating scope of work, it is nevertheless very important, because a lot depends on it. Once an estimate has been completed by the manager-architect, it may become evident that the task scope of work is far too large (for the subjective impression held by the sponsor or customer) and the proposed schedule and funding entirely inadequate. If that is evident, you

Estimation of Software Cost
Software Work-Estimation Worksheet

PROJECT / TASK / DELIVERY: DATE:

REQMTS	DESCR	A. Meetings, Egr Training, Reviews, Coordination	B. Analysis, S/W Design	C. Programming, Unit Testing	D. Documentation	E. Integration Testing	F. Anomaly Correction, Contingency	G. S/W Configure / Installation	H. Demos, User Training	TOTAL: Work Weeks	PROGRAM AFFECTED	Cognizant Engineer / Programmer	ANALYST	TECHNICAL WRITER
TOTAL: Work Weeks														

REMARKS:

Prepared by: Date:

Approved by: Date:

Figure 6. Software work-estimation worksheet.

should turn it down, at once. I have done this before. But, there are instances where it is so imperative to get the job done, that it simply must be done, and there is no way out of the time to delivery and the level of funding. In this case, one must utilize the genius of the manager-architect and the skill, expertise, and loyalty of the team to find ways to shorten the schedule and deliver. This should be done only once in a professional career, because it is very stressful, and stress is a killer. You must have assurance that the good will of the management above you is on your side and will do everything necessary to support your effort. If they just want to use you to get one step higher and take credit for your work, turn it down. I have turned down many offers in the past. And don't think for a minute that you will be listened to, even with every tool available to you to prove that the risk is too great. In fact, on one project, an outstanding, outside, uninvolved engineering team did a survey and estimated the cost with a probability of success at 32% at the given level of funding. The sponsor embraced it, and decided that a probability of 32% was acceptable. It failed, at a cost of $52 million, yet money is still being spent happily on it, now in the vicinity of $100 million, with no end in sight.

Turn it down! Don't try to be a hero. All it does is ruin your health. It is important for software professionals to be able to look back on every project completed and draw from the lessons learned for their own base of expertise and for the benefit of the next project. If you are not permitted to complete a project, you will have no metrics data to refer to for the next job. You will have only some negative lessons learned.

This is a mental process that can only be described accurately by first understanding the system of human understanding, perceiving, processing, inferring from known points of reference, and coming up with an estimate on the scope of work. Personally, I have the first impression of the proposed task (i.e., the hypothetical system) to rely on. However, to be able to do this, you have to have many projects behind you as a database for your reasoning process.

8.5 THE DETAILED COST ESTIMATE

The detailed cost estimate cannot be accomplished without a completed and signed-off Software Requirements Document. The SRD is the contract between the implementing organization and the sponsor. It is the most serious of all documents. Sometimes I go to the extreme of including data couples and controls on the dataflow diagrams to ensure that what I want is understood clearly by all. The other reason is that the Detailed Design Document, the DDD, may not be required because the SRD may be adequate to meet the need. I did this on the TOPEX TCCS SRD, because with a 21-months-to-launch timeframe there was no time for doing a DDD. Until TOPEX, I had never done a spacecraft ground system, so I had to be careful, though I was in a hurry. Launch pad reservations at the Kourou Launch Facility in French Guyana are very expensive. Had my software subsystem not been on-time and launch-ready, it would have cost an additional

$5.6 million. This was the cost of a reservation for an Arianne IV-42b launch vehicle, and, in fact, was equal to the total budget of my subsystem. Add to this $1.0 million per day for each day you are not launch-ready, up to five days, after which you go to the back of the line and wait your turn. So, it behooves one to be launch-ready.

Now, the SRD and Software Design Document (SDD) are the most important documents, with requirements stated, implied, and derived all annotated and numbered, traceable vertically and horizontally. Each item in the SRD has a number and a technical specification describing what it does. Additionally each requirement has a number of valid time-consuming attributes:

- Meetings, reviews, coordination, and training
- Programming and unit testing of commented code
- Documentation
- Integration and system-level testing
- Anomaly correction, debugging of contingencies
- Software configuration and installation
- Demonstrations and user training
- Total work week calculations
- Affected programs assessments
- Senior engineer and programmer involvement

8.6 THE SRD AS A CONTRACT

When I say that the SRD is a contract, I mean it very seriously. The SRD directly indicates the requirements for the Systems Interface Specification Documents, the SISDs. Every major system or subsystem that the object system interfaces to must have a SISD that specifies the interface to the bit level and describes the data connectivity and timing. If you don't have a signed-off SRD, then you cannot have completed SISDs, and thus you have no system; it is like forgetting to reconnect the nerves, muscles, and tendons after an operation.

One of the failings we have as humans is forgetfulness, perhaps with a dose of downright orneriness. We forget what we should have written down. Once, during a pre-delivery review, I was accused by the project systems engineer of failing to provide a certain critical function. I was caught off-guard and felt like a fool, and all eyes from the project manager on down were on me. It was a very critical function of the command segment. How could I have made such a mistake so close to launch? I was fortunate to have my roughly 780-page SRD with me, complete with foldouts. I opened it up to the segment he had referred to. Lo and behold, the answer was there. It had been crossed out three months before at a design meeting chaired by the manager, and approved by the board. The reason? Cost. It had been decided that it was not required.

My accurately maintained and up-to-date SRD had deflected an attack, which was hostile in tone, and perhaps unintentionally but nevertheless painful to me. But with time to launch set at 9 months, for me to add the function now would require a stop to all ongoing work to get it in. This would mean significant redesign, documentation, testing coordination, and reshuffling of resources and money. More than money would be needed to get the item into the architecture, to get the requirements on the schedule completed, and to get caught up with the milestones. Time was the constraining factor. We alone had to do the job; new personnel couldn't be hired to help out because the time to familiarization would take too long. All of this increased the implementation of that function from a former estimate of $100,000 to $400,000.

9 The Exercise of Project Control

For a project manager, control of the development of activities that bring about the completion of the project is of the utmost importance. The manager is being paid to deliver a product and therefore is responsible and accountable. The subjective assumption that everything is being taken care of and getting done, just because people tell you so, can and does have disastrous consequences. Do not believe that the briefing you are given is the truth. Consider human failings, sloppy work, inattention to detail, and even downright lying.

Once, on a major project, I dropped in to visit a colleague who was managing a subsystem in the same program office my system was in; he was preparing for a review the following day. I had great respect for him, for he had helped me out technically years earlier while I was working on the Voyager project. He was a serious guy, with a Ph.D. in physics, and was articulate and smart. I owed him for helping me out when I was new at JPL. As we were talking, I picked up the presentation package of the viewgraphs lying on his desk, and started to leaf through it.

I was very familiar with the technology that he was using, and the status of his progress, which was very far behind schedule. As I read through the briefing, I realized that almost nothing in it was true—most of it was totally made up! I was completely devastated.

"But this is completely wrong. You know this is totally misleading."

He sat in his chair, totally calm and disinterested, and replied without emotion, "Yeah, I know. But that's what they want to hear, so that's what they're going to hear. I'm tired of talking and trying to persuade a bunch of guys who will not accept the truth and don't understand my problems."

He then laughed, and told me that he was looking for a job, and had several offers "back East." I understood only too well the program manager he was talking about, so we had a good laugh. The big review was 8 a.m. the next day, with all of the top-level management and review board in attendance, as well as the sponsor.

The briefing went very well, and everybody was happy. I sat in the back of the conference room and took it all in. This to me was a major workshop, call it Project Management 702 for Postdoctoral Work in Cognitive Dynamics. I must confess that I was very much interested and taking notes.

The review drew to a close, and everybody filed out of the conference room. The program manager, who was the last to leave, stopped by my chair and told

The Cognitive Dynamics of Computer Science: Cost-Effective Large Scale Software Development, by Szabolcs Michael de Gyurky

me cynically, "See how great this project is going? Now why can't you manage like he does? Why can't you give a briefing like this one?"

I answered, "I guess I'm good, but not that good." Now, my system was delivered on time and on budget, which is what I cared for. The system that was presented at the review went on for a few years more, and was eventually delivered after going through three more managers.

The moral of this story is if you care for a quality system on time and on budget, don't take anyone's word for the state of the system. Be there personally to manage and supervise. You can't manage when you are collecting frequent flyer mileage and savoring gourmet food.

9.1   THE FUNCTIONS OF PROJECT CONTROL AND OVERSIGHT

The functions of project control and oversight, the understanding of their functions, the roles they play, and their importance throughout software development, especially during critical phases, are of incalculable importance to the manager, as well as to the design team as a whole.

So how do you control what mechanisms, processes, and procedures are available to you? Why are there phases, and what are the control parameters and methodologies?

Each phase of a project, regardless of technical complexity, scope of work, and sheer size of the staff, has its points of vulnerability and weakness. The project manager can establish a number of checkpoints along the way that will indicate during each phase what is going right and what is going wrong. Digging for facts is an important part of the project manager's job; keen observation of the workflow is another. If the cost is to remain low, the manager must always be there. It is of course his decision: the responsibility is there at the manager's desk and person. Corporate profits, if nothing else, should be a motivator. At NASA and in the governmental agencies the motivator would be the respect of the taxpayers' money. If as a manager you travel, and if it is not unavoidable, then you have an alternative, undermining agenda. If you can do it and still keep the cost per line of code at or under $50 per line of code, okay! My team of colleagues and I here at JPL don't expect anybody out there to produce code and deliver large systems at the cost we do. However, by now, with the wonderful "outsourcing" of software and engineering positions, we should all be worried about our jobs.

There are very few people who have the ability to retain all important data in memory. To compensate for this limitation, and to assure control over events, the manager, systems engineers, and team leaders must have a plan for checking for progress and ensuring quality. This is not a difficult thing to do; you become better at it with practice.

In the Army, I used a technique that had become obsolete by 1968. I named this technique "pre-combat inspection." A company commander doesn't have time to check everything before getting into an aircraft for an assault in a place where the enemy is entrenched. So I made myself a list. I assembled my troops and knew what they had to have, because I had given them specific instructions as to the amount of ammunition, water, food, first aid items, clothing, and so on. As soon as the troops were assembled, I'd walk down the line and look at them. When I spotted one who had a button unbuttoned, I almost always was correct that the rest of his gear was not up to par. I then would check the magazine for his weapon and find the ammunition dirty, the safety pin on the hand grenades lose (a very dangerous thing in an aircraft!), a canteen that was half-full when he had to have four quarts. All of these things were of critical importance in order to stay alive. When I found discrepancies, they would be corrected on the spot. Squad leaders, platoon leaders, and the first sergeant would ensure that these were accomplished. The shortfalls are a problem of the mind, inhibited by not paying attention to instructions, and not paying attention to detail. Whatever the reasons, combat fear, feelings of helplessness, etc., they are to me detailed in the thought process of Kantian philosophy. The problems are much like software failures that are caused by inattention to instructions and inattention to detail. To fix or "debug" my troops took time, and the aircraft were waiting. So, you get up earlier and muster for inspection, which is a lot like a "code walkthrough," and it must be done. There can be no jammed weapons on the battlefield, or sloppy software at launch time.

There are many who would think that a military analogy to something as "civilized" as engineering and computer science is grotesque or out of place. Many of the advances in industrial efficiency derive from the ways the U.S. military functions in and out of combat. The ways in which the military does its job are carried over and refined in the private sector in areas such as the logistics and infrastructure required for the distribution of food to supermarkets, for example.

No other country today is as efficient as we are, and this is largely from our military lessons learned, refined in the civilian sector, and then reintroduced into the military. The Jet Propulsion Laboratory, you may recall, started as a U.S. Army ordnance laboratory, and our leadership during the heyday of pioneering space comprised Army and Navy aviators, most of whom were combat veterans of WWII and Korea. To these guys, the skills of discipline, organization, communication, inspection, and decision were as natural as their skills as engineers and scientists. These skills are no longer with us, because although we do have great engineers and scientists, they have very little experience in leadership, organization, and communication. Above all, many of the young and not so young engineers in America these days cannot make a decision. One look at Figure 8, the diagram from the *Critique of Decision,* and you will see why: the lack of proper experience. This planning for eventualities and probabilities is just as important to the successful accomplishment of a project as the technology and engineering is, provided you care about cost, schedule, and quality.

9.2   THE REQUIREMENTS PHASE

It is during the requirements phase that the operating procedures for the project are set. The meticulous preparation of the functional and software requirements is key to the success of the project. The team must be small (see Chapter 5, Project and Task Organization), staffed only by the most essential technical and administrative members of the project. The manager-architect must not only chair but lead the process, although the systems engineer does most of the leading in the discussions. I use a projector with a computer to project the requirements onto a screen. The computer is operated by the senior technical writer, who is the systems engineer for standards and specifications (JPL-STD-D-4000). He knows exactly what information is needed and the degree to which it is articulated as required in the standard. Unless the manager is present, the team members tend to ignore the technical writer's request for clarification; even the systems engineer is often not given full-hearted support.

Once the document outline and formatting have been accomplished, the stated requirements are included easily enough. It is the implied requirements, such as the required bandwidth for communications, that require much discussion and elaboration to ensure that nothing is left out. In this day of mass communications, it might be hard to believe that bandwidth is still an important issue in design, but it is one that has not been solved, not because there are no easy solutions, but because of the inhibitors to the thought process.

Finally, the derived requirements must be identified. This is often overlooked. This part is tedious, frustrating, and time-consuming because it requires inferential reasoning over long periods of time. Derived requirements are identified from two or three already identified requirements. I regret to say that only a small percentage of the population is capable of reasoning inferentially. So it is the manager-architect who prods and pushes the process. Often individual members of the team feel picked on and can become angry. It is always a genuine surprise to me how much resentment there is on the part of certain individuals when I probe their minds for answers to problems. As intelligent and well-educated as they are, they resent me looking into the murky darkness of their minds. I have a certain sympathy for them, but I do have to get my job done. That is what I get paid to do. Some members will want to leave such discussions with the claim that they have work to do. One thing must be clearly established during this phase: The manager is in charge, and no one leaves to do anything on the project until the manager is satisfied that the phase is done.

9.3   CONTENTS OF THE SOFTWARE REQUIREMENTS DOCUMENT

Now that the functional requirements are completed, signed by the manager, and concurred by the sponsor or customer, we have a contract to start work. Now the work can be controlled, requirements item by requirements item. After the completion of the Software Requirements Document (SRD), it is reviewed, approved, and signed by the project and the customer.

Let's look once more at this most important of documents, the SRD. It is the lynchpin to getting all of our work done. It contains at a minimum nine chapters, five appendices, and a glossary:

Chapter One contains the segment level description data and other introductory materials.

Chapter Two contains the functional overview, to reiterate the functional aspects, and an overview of the segment.

Chapter Three describes the external interface requirements and constraints, as well as the man/machine or user interface requirements. This is a serious chapter, but is often not taken seriously. In a large communications network, with hybrid systems requiring interfaces to the segment, the external interface requirements or software interface specifications can amount to 30 or 40 large volumes of engineering design, each anywhere from 50 to as many as 250 pages.

Chapter Four contains the program set functional requirements in terms of input, output, and processes.

Chapter Five describes the general performance requirements, and details the performance requirements by Computer Software Units and Computer Software Components.

Chapter Six lists the reliability, maintainability, and availability (RMA) criteria and requirements for the segment.

Chapter Seven contains the delivery, installation, and environmental requirements, and points to the relevant documents that describe how the segment fits into the software system to which it belongs.

Chapter Eight describes the design and implementation constraints, assumptions, dependencies, and the criteria for each Computer Software Unit within the segment.

Chapter Nine establishes the general criteria by which requirements detailed in other chapters of the SRD can be verified.

Appendix A contains the requirements traceability matrices.

Appendix B contains the list of TBDs ("To Be Defined").

Appendix C contains the Dataflow Diagram and the Data Dictionary Balancing.

Appendix D contains the Data Dictionary.

Appendix E contains the List of Acronyms.

The SRD is the control document, a.k.a. the "mother of all documents." It is the software manager's contract with the project, and with each senior design engineer and senior programmer on the segment. Would you build a house without a contract or a blueprint? It's fortunate that people don't have to live in a software segment.

Whenever there is an impartial third party that is responsible for external oversight to ensure that the product is qualitatively correct, he is required to concur on the document. This is wise because it protects the project from inadvertent mistakes and oversight. We now have a contract between the customer and implementation team. The SRD is also much easier to quantify, in terms of scope of work and cost. At the level of detail I require when implementing a traditional architecture, the dataflow diagram allows for a very reliable way of identifying the number of modules; then you can estimate cost based on the size in lines of code per module. Control during this phase of the implementation is easy; you have all of the staff participate in the preparation of the SRD.

9.4   THE DESIGN PHASE

During the design phase, the design team is expanded by the addition of the senior programmers, the testers, and the librarian. The manager-architect chairs this rigorous effort as well, and indeed must. There are two computers and two projectors required for this eye-watering process, with a technical writer behind each computer. One writer follows the format of the Software Requirements Document (SRD); the other writes down the text of the Software Specifications Document (SSD-1). The SRD contains the dataflow, and the SSD-1 expands it into the data structure. The technical writers articulate the dataflow and data structure diagrams and add the information required by the traceability matrix. In following the production of the software, the matrix is very important if mistakes are to be avoided. It reduces the time spent on backtracking and repairing careless code.

It is at this point that the manager-architect presents his conceptual design based on the SRD to the team, whether it is a traditionally derived architecture or an implied architecture. Every member of the design team is required to interact freely. Criticisms and objections are given and taken until an acceptable design object evolves and comes into being. This in turn becomes the second thesis, and so on, until the system at Level III is clearly understood by all, and accepted. The most important goal of this process is to have control over the design. The second goal is for the design to be objective; that is to say, it is balanced as closely as practical from the perspective of all Computer Software Units, rather than the design representing the vision or "willpower" of just one or two CSUs or senior design engineers.

In a balanced design, by adding substance to the objective design (representing what we are going build) we achieve a sufficient reality, representing the understanding by all, from all perspectives. Work can begin on the implementation since every subsystem, software component, and module is now directly traceable to a specific requirement. The critical and necessary documentation tree with all of the volumes has been designed so that the members of the design team can estimate the work required to complete these. Among the most important documents are the Software Interface Specifications Documents (SISD) and the Coding Conventions/ Programming Rules and Conventions.

9.5   THE IMPLEMENTATION PHASE

The implementation phase begins with the design team in session. The first team to start coding is the common software services team, building the common software layer onto the operating system; this is followed by communications. Without the common software and communications layers in place and running, programming of the other elements shouldn't begin if control over the design and implementation is to be maintained. While the work of building the common software and communications layers is in progress, the design and writing of the SISDs and the preparation of the cost estimates must be accomplished. At this time, the user interface screens are designed with direct input from the users and operators. The estimation of the detailed cost is now possible and should be done. It should not show a cost that deviates by more than ±10% of the one that was completed for the SRD.

As implementation begins to move forward, every morning the individual team chiefs, subsystem managers, senior design engineers, and senior programmers report on the progress of their subsystems to the manager and the design team. Each discrepancy, software anomaly, and change request is resolved in real time, and adjustments to the design are documented. For those whose most productive time period is early in the morning, the design team can accommodate the review and design in the afternoon. It is easy to check the progress based on the modules being programmed, and also by timing the effort of programming and unit testing.

At the time that actual implementation starts, the test team assumes the primary control point in the project. The first people to brief the project manager in the morning at the design team meeting are the testers (the entire test team). Here the manager gets a good idea of the quality of the software being produced. The individual programmers may be called in to discuss their bugs and their software problems. Many things converge at these meetings with the testers and programmers. The testers, being among the best programmers on the team, can and do point out solutions to the senior programmers.

It is worthwhile to discuss this issue in detail. The software testers are not simply that; they are computer science professionals in their own right, and are as good in programming as they are in testing. The only difference between tester and programmer is in the role that is assigned. A good analogy is the difference between a writer and an editor. The editor, too, knows how to write. Likewise, the testers, looking at the code, can see issues that the programmer might have overlooked. The discussion that follows is a great teaching forum for both junior and senior computer software professionals; this is mentoring in the finest sense of the word. There are times when the programmers are "swamped" with work for a critical delivery. In a team environment, the tester may well tell the programmer, in the presence of the manager-architect and the systems engineer, "I can fix this problem, if it's okay with you." If the programmer says, "Okay, I don't have time, so that'd be great. I really appreciate it," then the issue is closed. The tester fixes the software bug, and the technical writer (who is present with the systems engineer and the manager-architect) approves and concurs without wasting time and money with another meeting. This happens often, and makes for the development of young software engineers into experienced software professionals who can design, program, manage, and write in good technical English.

Deliveries are made to the software library on a weekly basis. These are in the form of logically linked modules, routines, packages, and even computer software components. It is the software librarian who compiles and links the delivered products. At the start of the design team meeting in the morning, it is the software librarian who has the first say. To facilitate this "ongoing design team meeting," the conference room is chosen to be the manager-architect's office. It usually starts at 0800 hours and continues uninterrupted until 1300 hours. As things progress into full-time production, the only ones who are needed to be in attendance are the test team, the systems engineers for standards and specifications, and the librarian. The others, like the systems engineer and the senior design engineers, are busy and need to attend to their duties. If there is a pressing need for a decision or opinion, they can be called in selectively and on an individual basis, or the manager-architect can look them up.

After the design is complete, the manager can track the progress from his workstation and the SSD-1. He reads the status reports, reviews what works and what does not, and why. He finds out who does and does not follow coding conventions, comments his code, keeps programmer's notes, or updates the design book (or in case of traditional architectures, the SRD and the SSD-1). Every control measure is designed to reduce the number of software bugs and the time it takes to correct software discrepancies. When you have good control, stress is kept to a minimum, the development is kept on schedule, and the cost of the software is kept down.

To monitor the system to an even higher degree, especially when my time is already tight, I have installed a third systems engineer on the team. The job of this systems engineer is the monitoring of the progress of the development, and keeping track of action items. A systems engineer for action items is needed only on very large software projects, and when the implementation is nontraditional, such as with an emergency rapid development environment.

Accurate and meticulously kept and maintained requirements and design are very important. If the project loses an important person on the team, it need not be a devastating and costly situation if the replacement has up-to-date documentation to understand where to pick up the work.

It is not acceptable to rewrite the code, which happens more often than not on sloppily managed projects. Often, on a well-architected organization that runs smoothly as a team, a programmer can be replaced by a software tester (or a senior programmer from one of the other computer software units) who understands the software package of the individual who quit. This, too, is easily done, because the requirements and design development environment have made each senior design engineer and senior programmer intimately familiar with everyone else's software domain. When I have done this in the past, other project managers were always surprised. The inexperienced managers have the impression that functions such as telemetry or commanding require specialized skills, and both cannot be present in one good software engineer.

If the manager has done his job, everything is well in place and tested at this point. The librarian knows how much code there is, what problems there are with the build, and whether the code is properly documented. Beginning a new module, when for some reason the original approved design does not work, is appropriate, but it must be authorized by the manager, or the design team if he is not available. Time is money.

9.6   THE TEST AND INTEGRATION PHASE

During the test and integration phase, the software librarian is moved to the office adjacent to that of the manager. The software librarian is the person who can say what works and what does not work. The testers and engineers are busy testing and debugging the system, and the programmers are busy fixing anomalies, so they need not be tied down attending meetings. The technical writers and systems engineers for software standards are also key in this phase, because they will check the software, too. How often have the technical writers been the ones to inform me that "Joe hasn't followed the design," or "The software produced by that engineer does not match with his design." The technical writers, being not only good software engineers but excellent architects as well, have saved me a lot of money and much potential embarrassment in my schedule by bringing inconsistencies to my attention.

"Why bother if it works?" asks the novice manager. Well, for starters, I am not running a sweatshop that produces junky, sloppy software. I have to know each individual who works for me. In the long run, my career is dependent on developing better and better software engineers who understand their professions thoroughly, and who can be depended on to deliver a consistently superior quality product at a progressively more competitive scale. This means reduced cost, tight schedules, higher profits, and less stress on all individuals, including me, where all the stress comes together. This makes for a higher profit for a company; if government funded, for a more reliable system at a lower cost to the taxpayer. In order for me to properly mentor and educate my apprentices, I must know how they think, how they reflect, and how consistent they are in their work, not only with the overall design, but with their own personal attention to detail in the design of a module that they have designed themselves.

9.7 PERSONNEL ISSUES

If a person remains inconsistent with his own design, and does not follow instructions and rules, he will need to find another job. I'll be glad to rehire him at some time in the future if he has matured. Interestingly enough, there are software virtuosi whom I have met who have no discipline in their work habits. I keep track of these "special" people. When they work on my projects, they work directly under my supervision, and not under a senior design engineer who doesn't know how to direct and focus the creative energies pent up in this type of individual. Generally they will not become members of my personal group of colleagues, co-workers, and friends. I suppose the terms "colleagues" and "cronies" are reserved for those special people whose abilities, honesty, dependability, and energy I admire so much, and who like my skills and traits as well. We keep in touch wherever we happen to be, and we come together on projects whenever an opportunity arises.

I am quite willing to spend extraordinary amounts of time teaching and instructing people who are intelligent, who are willing to learn, and are ethical in their outlook on life. But I will not waste my time on individuals who do not "dig in" and learn, improve, and progress through self-discipline and diligence. After all, one of my traits is that I like to work myself out of a job. Every project I have ever accepted and started during my career I have completed and delivered to my customer;

as a result, my colleagues and I were out of a job, and needed to find new work. There have been only two exceptions to this. One exception was for a large enterprise, where the management simply didn't want a completed product. This was because of the psychological need on their part to maintain a large workforce and organization chart. Had the system been permitted to be delivered, the workforce and organization chart would have gone away.

The other exception was a large, complex system where the program manager was a novice. As a colonel, he should have been a capable manager, but he was technically and tactically not qualified, and I returned the remaining funds to his department after completing the requirements and the design. The issue was a total lack of understanding on his part of the scope and cost of the project. This action was necessary for many reasons. The first is that it would have been unethical for me to accept a job that I knew I could not do or deliver. The second reason is that when I take a job that is totally out of scope, and I have a good, hardworking, conscientious design team, they always try to get the job done in spite of the inhibitors. They spend endless amounts of overtime, without pay, working out of pride in their profession, trying to prove the impossible. The ensuing stress is a killer, a destroyer of families and happiness. This is something I don't permit, and especially not for a person who has built unrealistic images of himself and of the world around him. There are many people in industry like this, and you find them in surprising numbers in the military.

When I spot-check around, I usually plop myself down in a programmer's cubicle to see if he has anything interesting to say, or if he has problems. Of course, I do select a person before I go for a visit, with specific questions in my mind. Performance measurements, like rates of coding (e.g., lines of code per person per day) interest me in about the same way that Elton Mayo was interested in rivets per hour, per riveter.[1] On large projects with 70 programmers and numerous languages in use for various reasons, I find it interesting to note which languages have the highest productivity rate, average and mean, sustained over the extent of the project. This includes software bugs, or software failure reports, per language per thousand lines of code. So, I take the time out around mid-morning, and look at my SSD-1 that is on my desk. Since I have a general idea what each person is working on, I select the name of a programmer, look at the SSD-1, and find the module I expect the individual will be working on. I enter his office or cubicle and say hello, and ask if there is anything I can do to be of assistance. If not, I'll just watch him work a bit. If the implementation is not what the design book or SDD-1 describes it should be, then there is a problem. It can affect the entire architecture and must be corrected. Either the design is incorrect, or the programming is incorrect. I can also look at the individual and see if he is commenting his work.

You may ask, with all this tight control over the development, how can such controls help in building quickly and cheaply? After all, I'm just interfering with a senior design engineer or senior programmer, and taking up his precious time,

[1] Elton Mayo, *Teamwork and Labor Turnover in the Aircraft Industry of Southern California*, Harvard University Press, 1944.

right? I have heard this often in the distant past, but lately I haven't had complaints by many. Even my more junior programmers appreciate the honest interest I take in their work, and they learn how much cheaper it is to plan and organize their work efficiently.

Following a military standard and doing meticulous planning and production control is not the cause of the high cost of software development. Rather, it is the sloppy code, often written by talented but undisciplined programmers who work for sloppy, undisciplined novice managers who do not know their profession. That is the cause of the high cost of software development.

Undisciplined programmers produce undocumented code, done on the fly, out of a muddled head; this is code that cannot be tested or integrated, and it must be reviewed, rewritten, retested, and the documentation updated to reflect reality. That is where the cost is. That is why a "code slave" somewhere overseas is getting your job! Slinging code without an SRD and SSD-1 is called "hacking." Hacking is not acceptable, except under special conditions. Such conditions are extremely stressful on the manager-architect, as well as the design team. Professional implementation means disciplined work, using well-proven standards and mature methodologies.

9.8   THE HACKER AND OTHER PERSONALITIES

What can you do about hackers, or those engineers who have a misconception about their responsibilities and a subjective view of their own personal worth? I have frequently run into very intelligent and well educated people with powerful self-images who had their own ideas about what they needed to do, and how. Asking these people nicely to remain at a meeting and participate and contribute to the sub-stantiation of the design object is useless. Strangely enough, their answer is usually, "I have work to do. I'm already behind. I don't have time for this."

With these responses, at first, even an experienced manager-architect is caught off guard, thinking, "Maybe he is right. Maybe I am wasting everybody's time. Wasting time is wasting money, and I don't have the right to waste the customer's money." The individual gets up and leaves. Well, now what? The rest of the team realize that they can leave also, since maybe the absence of a key member of the design team leaves an incomplete definition, or an imbalanced definition of the design object. Okay, as the manager-architect, you relent and dismiss the remaining part of the team, letting them go back to do their work; there are many things and action items you must attend to anyway.

But after attending to some administrative and engineering action items, you start to think about the issues.

"How can this guy go and program if he doesn't have an overall design?"

"How can anyone program if there is not even a completed set of approved requirements?"

"Do I really need to take this kind of attitude from an engineer, his magnificent academic credentials notwithstanding?"

"Is the input from this guy indispensable to developing the design to the point of acceptable reality?"

"If I am the manager and architect, I am supposed to be in charge of the project, and I am held accountable and responsible for its delivery by my management. True or false?"

I had confronted this situation before, and it irritated me once I thought about it. After I arrived home, I went running for four or five miles, thinking about it. I got angrier and angrier. After finishing my run, I was still so upset I had to go to the gym and pump iron for an hour. Finally, I came home, had a Stolichnaya vodka martini with two olives, and answered my own questions.

"No, no one can program meaningfully without a design!"

"No, I don't need to take this kind of attitude from anyone working for me, no matter how great his academic credentials!"

"Yes, one can arrive at an acceptable reality with less than a complete team. All it means is that the technical discipline of the individual not attending is not represented fully. He may complain about being unhappy with the design, but he'll have to live with it."

"Who is really in charge of this project? I, the project manager, am in charge, and the individual who does not comply with the project manager's direction is gone, off the project."

In this instance, the guy with absolutely eye-watering academic credentials in mathematics and computer science left my project. He tried teaching at one of our best universities, and finally wound up becoming a mail carrier for the U.S. Postal Service. He had great talent, but no personal discipline. I still like the guy; he is simply not cut out for serious work.

In such instances as these my response is, "I'm paying your salary, and you will do as you are told. If you don't want to do it my way, there is the door." There are people who seem to think that the high salaries paid to them as software professionals are their birthrights as American geniuses who, having had the good fortune to graduate from a top academic institution with an equally great academic record, are entitled to be the recipients of homage from the toiling masses of the uneducated. *Wrong!*

9.9 THE BUCK STOPS AT THE TOP

The manager is the only one who can say,

> This is what the Work Implementation Plan says, and this is what you do. Your time belongs to me, because if you fail, I fail, and you don't have the right to make me look bad, incompetent, or stress me out just because you don't want to do as you've been told. Only I have a right to stress myself out, to fail, and to look bad. Sorry about that, "American programmer," we need to be competitive, and we can be. We, the country, need software cheap, or at a reasonable and competitive price, and we don't have to go to the 'Cyber Pass' to get it.

If a customer can get it from the Jet Propulsion Laboratory, here in Pasadena, California, home of the Rose Bowl and the Rose Parade, then a customer should be able to get a similar product at a similar cost from any other computer science company here in the U.S.A.

The manager is accountable and responsible to the customer for a product, for which he and the team are being paid their salaries. In this line of argument, the manager's vision and architecture with the accompanying authority give him the right to demand compliance with the rules set forth in the Work Implementation Plan. The buck does and should stop here, at the manager-architect's desk. There is no wiggle room.

Many managers say that the project objective is too complicated or too hard; that's understandable. However, the job being "too hard" is not the issue. The issue is simply that that is what you are being paid to do, so you do it. If you can't do the job, just say so, and I'm sure there is a Kelly Johnson or Jack Northrop out there who will be only too glad to get it done and collect your salary. There is always the issue about a manager in some company who needs to be placed somewhere, simply because he is out of a job. So, he is given a software-intensive project, even though has never written a line of code or been a team chief supervising a team of programmers. He came up through marketing or line management, but he is well liked by the boss, so he gets the job regardless. Now we have real trouble on our hands.

I don't mean that there are no mechanical engineers or geologists who can manage software development; there are a few, and that is what they have done for many years as a choice. There are equally few Spruances[2] who can go from commanding cruisers to aircraft carriers and win a decisive battle, like the Battle of Midway. Intelligence, leadership, professionalism, dedication, and loyalty will go a long way, but you need to understand the domain of your profession. This understanding can come through academic or on-the-job training. Apprenticeship to the facile mind is as good a teacher as the classroom.

To transition from one discipline to another without skipping a beat is difficult. Understanding how it happens, and why only about 2% of the population can make the transition, is revealed in the work of the cognitive philosophers.

Again, if money and schedule are of little importance, as it appears to be in our corporations, judging by the almost nightmare-like cost overruns and fraudulent practices, well then by all means give the position of CEO, COO, or project manager to the individuals you like. But maybe in some rare instances corporate profits do count; in those cases, give such positions to the persons with the best track records for effective management, and who know how to manage to a budget.

Computer software is "complicated" only to those who are not practitioners. Computer science is an art and a science; as such, it is not easily taught. Programming

[2] Admiral Raymond Ames Spruance, USN (1886–1969). Led Task Force 16, with two aircraft carriers, during the Battle of Midway. His decisions during that action were important to its outcome, which changed the course of the war with Japan.

is an important part of it, but a small part. Other equally important parts are architectural design, systems engineering, object orientation, communications, user interface design, computer hardware architecture, machine and assembly languages, technical writing, the proper uses and applications of software management standards, software testing, configuration management, systems analysis and code walkthroughs, statistics in software development, and the list goes on and on. Computer science is not an academic discipline easily taught, because it requires extensive apprenticeship in the field, as well as in leadership and management, above and beyond academic instruction.

I use the term "the dog in the manger" often. It is a very important term for software managers to understand, as it concerns the way we think, act, and decide. The phenomenon is of someone who needs help but cannot do the job. There is another individual who is not only willing to help but also can do the job, and easily at that. The person with the job who can't do it blocks any attempt to be given help. This way the development process comes to a screeching halt. This is the "dog in the manger." The dog makes itself at home on the straw in the manger. The cow comes into the barn to eat, and tries, but the dog barks, and drives it off. Of course, the dog does not eat straw, but remains on the hay to keep the cow from eating, so both starve to death. In terms of a software project, this is the phenomenon I have encountered most often. It is one of the major occupations of a project manager to drive the dogs from the manger, and keep the workflow going.

9.10 HOW PEOPLE THINK, PAY ATTENTION, AND REMEMBER

One of the reasons that understanding the thought system of the human being is so important in keeping a project on schedule is that you can get an impression, or at least an idea, of how much of the instruction and project-related communication the communicator is actually getting through to the team and the individual. This understanding helps dramatically in getting the message through. Even the best managers and engineers in lead tasks often wonder why they were misunderstood when they felt they gave a very clearly detailed set of instructions to the staff, short of writing a book. Well, the individuals you talked to do not misunderstand you. In most instances, they were not even "there." Who knows where they are mentally, at any moment? Surfing at Waikiki? Skiing at Aspen? They fade in and out of lock while you are transmitting. You are certainly not getting through. This may sound trivial to most readers, but for a manager to understand this phenomenon, its importance cannot be overemphasized.

Can an attentive manager, engineer, or communicator spot this? How important is your budget and schedule? If they are not important, then don't worry about it. Otherwise, take steps to make certain that whatever you are saying is really getting through, to the tune of: "I can look into your eyes and see the color of your socks!" (And I realize, to my horror, that there is nothing there.) The assumption that all in the conference room are fully involved with what an individual is saying can be very costly to a project.

I have always read philosophy, so when I entered the Army I was surprised by what I saw. I began to infer that people were not only not paying attention, but they didn't even read what was in front of their faces, with costly consequences. Some events may be funny now; they were tragic then.

One of the earliest examples was an incident at Ft. Knox, Kentucky, while I was going through advanced armored training. I entered the Army as an enlisted soldier based on two romantic notions: One, that I should learn from the bottom up, by learning everything before getting a commission. And two, that I should take Napoleon's saying, "In every soldier's knapsack is a field-marshal's baton" to heart.

After basic infantry, I wanted to learn all about tanks, how to drive them, maintain them, and how to shoot the weapons on them. Now, on the bulkhead of the M-48A2 Medium Tank (official designation: "90mm Gun, Tank M-48A2"), right in front of the driver's eyes and directly under the driver's periscope, there was a stenciled message. The message was painted in bold white capital letters about 2 inches tall and said:

DRIVER! DO NOT LEAVE YOUR SEAT WHILE ENGINE IS RUNNING!

We had received instructions on this over and over again.

The reason for relating this story is to give an example of how people think, remember, act, and make *a priori* or *a posteriori* decisions. This lesson to me personally was but the beginning of many incidents I observed in the Army that often had tragic results. Sadly, this type of decision happens as often in engineering, science, and all walks of life as it happened on that day in 1959.

We were getting ready for an inspection of our M-48A2 medium tanks after we had spent two weeks in the field on the firing range at Ft. Knox, Kentucky. We had been qualifying on the 90mm main gun. We were now back at the regimental motor pool, taking turns at the wash rack. I had finished most of my work and was hosing down my tank, washing off the mud with a hose about the size of a normal fire hose. Also on the wash rack were several other tanks being cleaned as mine was. The one next to mine had the engine idling, and the driver was somewhere inside. I didn't take notice, until suddenly he stuck his head out of the tank commander's hatch and pulled himself out. He climbed down the turret and jumped off the fender skirt to get something from his toolbox. The big Continental V-16, with 750 HP, was idling, and I was about to holler over the noise that he should turn the engine off, when the transmission slipped into first gear! When this happened, it started to move forward. Since he had it backed into the washing slot, there was no tank directly in its path to stop it as it moved forward. The path was clear to the drainage ditch, then on to a four lane highway; beyond that there was a 12-foot chain-link fence. Behind this chain-link fence was the parking lot of the 1st Training Regiment Armor, the U.S. Army Training Center Armor (USATCA), filled with the cars and pickup trucks of the cadre officers and non commissioned officers of the regiment.

Well, the 50 ton M-48A2 tank in first gear has so much torque that it travels on 1st gear at about 15 mph without any pressure on the accelerator. There is no way anyone would risk life and limb trying to get on board when it is moving. So it simply moved, or lumbered, across the road. Fortunately, the traffic was light because it was about 0930 hours (back then, reveille was at 0530, so everybody was at work). The traffic halted, and the tank moved across the highway. It moved over the chain-link fence like it was nothing, and then started across a row of cars and pickups. All of the troops and the standers-by were amazed, and we ran behind it. It was headed for a company mess hall. In those days we had company mess halls and the food was absolutely fantastic because all the company mess sergeants competed for best mess hall in the regiment; we ate like kings at Ft. Knox.

Thank God there was one of those large tractor-trailer trucks delivering milk to the "chow hall"; it was a Foremost milk truck. The guys on Kitchen Police (KP) got all excited seeing this big piece of steel coming their way; they spread the alarm and cleared the mess hall. The tank must have very casually demolished about 15 to 20 cars before it hit the trailer of the truck. The power of this V-16 Continental was so great that it simply pushed the trailer over on its side. It arched up, almost making it over the top, when it finally stopped. There was not enough engine rpm at idle in first gear to climb over the trailer, so the engine simply died.

Obviously, the reason for never leaving the driver's seat before turning off the engine was that it was unsafe. It had a three-speed hydramatic transmission, and the "Neutral Park" position was located directly up at 12 o'clock, with 1st gear at 1 o'clock, 2nd gear at 2 o'clock, and Reverse gear at 6 o'clock. A bad design, to be sure, because the vibration from the engine had a tendency to shake the shifter lever loose and slip it into 1st gear.

For this reason, we were given hours and hours of safety lectures on every aspect of the tank, but above all, we were instructed never to leave the driver's seat while the engine was running! This was literally "hammered into our brains." So with all this training, with all these lectures, with all the inspections and tests and pop quizzes, why did this driver fail to remember? The answer, as Arthur Schopenhauer so well explains, is that as we human beings process information and decide, we often make *a priori* decisions. These decisions are almost always wrong. I was a 20-year-old kid with two years of college and lots of philosophy reading under my belt. These phenomena simultaneously fascinated as well as dismayed me. I became a witness to terribly tragic incidents, during both peace and war. (Even I, who always tried to be very circumspect and aware of what could happen, would make a decision, which but for the grace of God, would have cost me life and limb.)

For this reason, I am very careful during systems requirements, design and implementation to be absolutely focused on the members of the design team. To ensure that as we discuss each segment, subsegment, software data set, module, and routine they are clearly understood by everyone sitting around the table, and that they all are carefully documented. Then, during implementation, I can check with reasonable assurance that every programmer is doing what we agreed to do as a team. I can also reasonably predict when each task will be completed. With all this caution, I'm still sometimes caught off guard, but at least I can correct the problem.

Looping back to the story with the tank, allow me to draw an analogy to spacecraft control systems. Think of it as a software compare, an "equal to" instruction, in the mind of the tank driver as having caused the destruction of about 20 cars. An average car at the time cost $1,500 (we drove mostly Chevrolets and Fords), but those dollars were silver dollars, which today cost $10 a piece, and add inflation on top of that. So at $20,000 per car, you are talking about $400,000 for this software error. At $200,000 per engineering work year (burdened) you are talking about a big loss in time and money. To recover in software from that much loss, and still retain the schedule, you have to triple that sum in money and time. If you have blown $400,000, and you have to catch up while the rest of the team is working (this includes the design upgrades in the documentation set and test plan), it will take the $400,000 + $400,000 to come up to where you were supposed to have been on the schedule, plus an additional $400,000 to come abreast of where the rest of the project is on the schedule. Now this seemingly small and isolated mistake costs $1.2 million. That should answer the question: Why does NASA and DOD software cost so much?

10 The Development Process Methodology

If funding is tight and a conservative development approach is required, methodology will play an important role. Development methodology involves the selection of a number of techniques and procedures to be used in the implementation of a system. In my world of low-cost implementation, the process of selecting the correct methodology is an exciting, creative, intuitive process in itself. In terms of Kantian concepts, a methodology is the selection of the appropriate organization, communication, development, and control functions from one's wells of experience, and the application of them to the project to be developed. There are standard approaches for development when the schedule and budget are adequate for the job. Then there are the additional factors of experience. A manager-architect with a high level of experience in the technologies involved (and in communication) may not have an adequate level of experience in organizations; he will not be able to select an appropriate organization necessary to keep the development cost down.

There is good news here, and bad news. Like everything else, process and methodology can be learned from books, but that's the toughest way. I did it initially from IBM and Army instructors, and not very long after that from some outstanding experts who had written indispensable books that I devoured over the years. While I was still working as the assistant architect for the Allied Command Europe, Command Control and Information System, at Supreme Headquarters Allied Powers Europe (SHAPE) in Belgium, I ran across a wonderful book titled *Standardized Development of Computer Software*.[1] Volume I became one of my basic manuals in software development. I asked the author to update the books, but he never did. Everyone interested in software development must read his two volumes. They cover many aspects, including production.

My guide and mentor during my three years at SHAPE was a fabulous systems engineer and technical thinker, Colonel Joe Bullers. He was a chemical engineer by education and a USAF B-47 pilot by profession. He had been Gen. Curtis LeMay's systems architect for the command and control system of the Strategic Air Command

---

[1] Robert C. Tausworthe, *Standardized Development of Computer Software, Part 1: Methods, Part 2: Standards*, Prentice Hall, 1977

The Cognitive Dynamics of Computer Science: Cost-Effective Large Scale Software Development, by Szabolcs Michael de Gyurky
Copyright © 2006 by John Wiley & Sons, Inc.

Bomber Fleet. He was handpicked for SHAPE, and he handpicked me. He was an innovative and creative thinker, and we formed a great team, the two of us. Besides being the only one who could read his handwriting, I was able to elaborate in writing and graphics the ideas and concepts he would mumble in fragmented bursts. He was a good teacher. When our tours were over, and we retired from the Service (he with 30 years, me with 20), we were replaced by a high-powered academic team of 32 members.

Little did I anticipate that one day soon I would have some of these great thinkers working for me. Why would some of these outstanding people, whose books I had read, come to work for me? Since I had methodology, I would become friends to many of my colleagues here at this wonderful place called Jet Propulsion Laboratory. My methodology is actually an amalgamation of military engineering methods, IBM systems engineering instruction, much reading and practicing, and, of course, philosophy.

10.1   THE "DESIGN HUB" AS IMPLEMENTATION TOOL

The idea of the *design hub* came about because of a rather bad situation. The TOPEX[2] project had only 21 months remaining on the calendar to launch, and only $5.6 million left in the budget. This left little time for coordination and fooling around. The lowest bid was for $14 million and 48 months. My division manager called me in and told me that I was going to take on this job, like it or not. I certainly didn't want to do it, because I was happy with what I was doing at the time. However, because it was also an honor that he had that much confidence in me, I was committed.

But how could I get all this work done in such a short time? I had to create an environment where all design issues could be resolved almost immediately. This meant not only collocating the team, but collocating them in such a way as to have them working in their own spaces for privacy and concentration, but, at an instant, being able to hold a meeting, just by turning around in their chairs. I selected a large room, and put the individual cubicles along the walls. In the open area in the center was a large conference table, which could be reached by merely turning around in one's chair, and scooting six feet. There was also a long whiteboard, a pull-down projection screen on the long axis of the room, and a workstation to drive a projector. See Figure 14.

The design hub allows the manager to resolve action items and monitor work constantly while getting all the work done without delay.

There were many objections along the lines of, "I can't work this way!" but the only other option was to leave the project. Besides, the key members of my staff had delivered GDSS with me only 9 months earlier, so they trusted me. After a while, they came to like the methodology. In the design process, there can be no secrecy. The dialectic approach is now ready to assume its work. This environment,

---

[2] See Chapter 14, subheading: Case Study Three: The TOPEX TCCS System.

where everyone is forced to interface, cooperate, and communicate, is no place for the psychoneurotic of Elton Mayo.

The design hub approach to software development is actually a true methodology and has a physical, organizational, and process architecture. The physical components are the layout of the workspace (i.e., the integration of the individual workspaces of the personnel) and the conference room rolled into one unit. The organizational component is reflected in the presence of all key members of the design team in the physical unit. Only a really well-integrated and mature team can work together at close quarters over an extended period of time. The systems engineer, systems programmer, communications programmer, database programmer, applications programmers, technical writers, testers, and hardware are all collocated in the presence and under the chairmanship of the manager-architect. The objective of the design hub is to reduce the number of design and programming mistakes made. This occurs due to the reduction of time spent in coordinating the design, and the reduction of programming and test turnaround time. The loss of some privacy on part of the individual members of the team is a small price to pay. Individuals in this environment work at a slower pace, but this slightly reduced pace is more than offset by the time that would otherwise be wasted going to and from meetings. Also, being able to resolve software issues on the spot and to correct bugs with the help of colleagues in real time are great timesavers.

The process component is the manner in which the entire system is built. The design team assembles around the large conference table under the chairmanship of the manager-architect. This assembly is called the "design team meeting in session." There is nothing further that is necessary for the individual members to do than to swivel their chairs around from their workspace cubicles and scoot over to the conference table. Two projectors are set up, and hooked to the computer with an outline of the project documentation tree to be discussed and agreed to. The one projector is dedicated to the text and the other projector to the graphic representation of the requirements, design, or any other related subject. Each of the computer terminals serving the projectors has a technical writer/engineer inputting the information provided by the design team. The technical writers, who are engineers and who are a part of the systems engineering component, ask questions to clarify statements concerning the scope and content of the requirements or design issues at hand. Clarity and exactness as represented in unambiguous technical English text and correlated graphically are big eliminators of misunderstandings and software problems. In philosophical terms, this is called "adding substance to the object," which in our case is an architectural design as visualized by the manager-architect.

10.2   THE ARCHITECTURE DEFINITION PROCESS

The process by which a group defines an architecture in real time is similar to the way a football coach describes a play to his team. The coach presents the play on the blackboard, and the members of the team respond by adding their own situations and needs to the overall strategy required to execute the play correctly. Note that the coach in this case is the manager-architect, not the systems engineer. The systems engineer is the project equivalent of the quarterback of a football team. The SE understands the practical environment and the functional technology but does not always see the big picture. Above all, the SE doesn't have the authority to bring discipline to the meeting; he is first among equals. Many times I have seen the lack of cooperation from some of the more egocentric and senior members of the design team. The manager-architect, on the other hand, is the individual who has hired and organized the individuals for the job; the time is his, the schedule is his, and so is the budget. How he chooses to develop a system is his personal responsibility and prerogative. The methodology he chooses is also his, because it is he who is accountable and responsible overall for the delivery of the product on time and on budget.

I have had disagreements on this hypothesis. Certain members of the team feel that they are wasting their time and need to be programming, to my chagrin, with or without a set of detailed requirements or design. It has taken me a long time to impress on some of these highly talented but inexperienced professionals that they will not program until the design has reached a state of sufficient reality to do so. By "sufficient reality" I mean that we have defined the design object to the degree that all key members of the team have contributed equally to it. In this way the design is well balanced, and all senior design engineers and engineers on the team have a clear understanding about what needs to be done and how we are going to get there. Furthermore, the design has been written down by the technical writers into an SSD-1 that is compliant to a standard.

All members of the team must know what is expected from every other member of the team, and not only from one or two individuals.

The team is a well-organized and well-led grouping of experienced people. It has an interesting component that never ceases to surprise me, what I refer to as the *work multiplier*. This phenomenon becomes apparent when the team as a whole "gels" and becomes much greater than just a collection of individuals. This is when the total production of the team exceeds the highest productivity rate I originally predicted based on the individuals in the team. The schedule milestones are beaten one after the other through a natural increase in productivity, as opposed to being forced to do so by schedule manipulations, as high organizational management often does. The natural increase happens when a manager-architect and systems engineer provide the kind of leadership and environment that reduces friction within the team to almost zero. It happens through leadership, management, and organizational methodology that the work environment becomes so pleasant that the staff have a hard time going home from work. Again, good leadership is the key.

At work, as in war or competitive sports, winning becomes an obsession to the American professional. The meaning of winning has many important facets, such as having a product one is proud of, and one can say without flinching is the best. It also means that we built it ourselves, and it was on schedule and on budget. As Coach Lombardi used to say, being second is being a loser; only God and family come before winning. Since anyone can be successful in software if enough money is thrown at the project, cost becomes an important factor in being the best.

In this manner, by using the team environment in a design hub, the time-consuming process of documenting the stated, implied, and derived requirements is accomplished. By strictly following the tailored outline of the software development standard selected for the project, such as MIL-STD-498 or DOD-STD-2167A, every requirement will be fully defined and assigned a reference number, which is correlated to other requirements. The assigned reference numbers in the software requirements document (SRD) are then mapped into the software design document (SDD-1). If the SDD-1 is clearly defined and complete, an SDD-2 is not needed because the software code itself is sufficient (i.e., if the programmers follow the mandated coding conventions and comment their code faithfully).

Certainly, when the programmers see a break to exploit an idea or resolve a problem, and program a module or two before they lose the idea, they can swivel around and program, without the rest of the design team breaking up from the concentrated work. The documentation is going ahead, sometimes in parallel with the programming effort. The proximity of the programmers, systems engineers, and testers to the manager-architect also permits him to pay attention to the progress and quality of work and the adherence to the coding conventions. Even so, individual team members, no matter how expert, dependable, and mature, tend to transgress the rule of the conventions without informing the other team members. On certain occasions where I caught some team members a week late in their implementation, the recovery took three weeks. One week of coding on part of some of my top programmers, say at a rate of 50 LOC per day, represents about 5 modules of code. (A module may vary according to application and the programming language used from 50 LOC to 250 LOC.) This requires an average of one additional week to debug, and another week to catch up on the schedule, which includes updating the SRD and SDD-1. It often impacts the work of the other applications programmers, depending upon the modularity of the system.

10.3   THE USE OF LARGE-SCALE REPRESENTATIONS

I have noticed over the years that written communication and design representations are perceived and understood differently by each individual. I have paid attention to how people write, read, and comprehend; in fact, some do not comprehend at all.

Again, for getting the message across, I find it easiest to use a projector and a screen for displaying text with symbols; the manager can interact line by line with every member of the team and make modifications to the design. This is communicating, truly, and getting through to people who are otherwise unable or unwilling to participate. Many don't know much beyond how to program an already designed routine or module; this forces them to come out of their shells and be team players or to leave the project. This forcing of people to communicate and to cooperate in the development process is one reason why many design hubs are empty. They will not enter the great Amphitheater, the "Coliseum of Gladiatorial Communication."

They don't have the proper weapons; they were never trained by their educational system in the dialog and the dialectic. They know only to use political coercion, not syllogism and rhetoric, to get their way in the design process.

Another positive aspect of this methodology is that once the process starts, the participants quickly realize that if they don't cooperate, they risk losing their share of the subsystem to territorial losses. Functions that naturally belong to the data communications subsystem may be picked up or occupied by the database subsystem, etc., making the accomplishment of a clean, well-designed system that much harder.

To better understand any situation at a glance, it is far easier to look at the big picture than at small individual representations of it. There are very few individuals with the Napoleonic ability to retain and keep track of innumerable individual events. Most of us can understand better when looking at a large display. For this reason, Military Airlift Command insisted on a 12 foot by 36 foot situation map in their operations center at Scott AFB, Illinois. This permitted the commanding general and his staff to understand at a glance the disposition of all MAC assets, and query for detail by clicking on an individual item for status of the flight, cargo, and maintenance issues. So it is with the design team and the architecture of a system under development or review. By looking at the overall architecture people individually and collectively get a better understanding and can zero in on a problem by clicking on a particular module to see what it looks like. This is also of tremendous help in doing code walkthroughs.

10.4 DESIGN TEAM MEETINGS

In a fast-moving situation when development is severely impacted by schedule, the daily meeting of the design team is a necessity. Every member must completely understand the design. In Hegelian terms, this means to understand the acceptable reality of how the thing will work, and what level of detail and understanding of the object is necessary to start work. Every key member must know this, at a given level of expertise. It has to be thought about and dreamed about; it must be ingrained. Thus, the design "team" is more than just a team. It is a classroom of senior engineers. It is a conclave of the manager, first among equals, who reports to the customer.

The team in session begins the meeting with a review of the activities of the previous day. Then, the status reports by each team chief or subsystem manager are reviewed. This is followed by a resolution of action items, and then by the settling of disputes. The action items and disputes are settled with the individuals who are responsible for the pieces of work that need attention. Never trust the subjective interpretation of someone else, regardless if he is senior or is the supervisor of the "action item" engineer. One distortion can cause days of delay. When you have a burn rate of $25,000 per day, unintentional misinterpretations of an action item can easily cost $100,000 to $200,000; that is equal to the annual earnings of three or four American families—the ones who pay our salaries. And yet you say you don't care? Because you are the manager, "big medicine" is required indeed.

So the design team meets from 0800 till 1300 hours, 5 days a week during the requirements and design phase. If for some reason a senior design engineer cannot attend, he must send a representative; all of the work doesn't get done this way, but there is no backtracking if it only slows progress a little, which is okay.

10.5 RAPID DEVELOPMENT VERSUS PROTOTYPING

The terms "rapid development" and "prototyping" are often used by upper-level management who want to give the impression of being practitioners, yet have never built software of any type, nor programmed as much as a module. A very high-level JPL manager once decided that doing GDSS at the pace at which my team and I did it was a "good" thing. He wrote up a concept briefing titled "Quicker, Better, and Cheaper" and had it circulated and briefed to NASA, to industry, and worse, to the Air Force. He never once asked me how I was able to bring the cost down from $750 to $37 per line of code. He never inquired as to the methodology and process involved, or whether I recommended it or not. He made a big splash with it anyway, and other managers equally lacking in experience bought into it. I don't blame the generals and managers who took it in good faith. After all, it followed a new DOD guidance, was signed by the logistics chiefs of all three services, and was put together by a Brigadier General I knew and often talked with at the Defense Systems Management College, Fort Belvoir, Virginia.

Rapid development and prototyping are two different things entirely! Unfortunately, at the higher levels of management, the two terms appear to be close enough to be used interchangeably. Because of this, when you build a prototype with the intention that the prototype is to be just that, *a prototype*—not to be used as a part of the production model, but to be discarded after it is finished—it is not documented nor rigorously tested. It is an exploratory effort to see if an idea really would work, *and that is all*. Unfortunately, because it looks good and credit is to be had for a "fabulous" piece of work, it is integrated into the production model, even though it does not have the stability, reliability, or availability of the rest of the system. This is very costly in terms of what it will take to debug, integrate, and maintain a system containing the prototype.

Rapid development, on the other hand, is a very disciplined approach at implementing, by necessity, a system on a short schedule and low budget. The stress on the manager-architect and on the team or project is terrible. I can assure you that the mental and physical stresses are equal to my serving nearly three years in Vietnam as a Special Forces officer (Green Beret) and commanding a parachute infantry company in combat. Trust me! Don't try it unless you understand that. My cholesterol went from 162 to 287 mg/dl in a year and a half, not so much because the technology we needed to build was that far out ahead (it was), but because the managers imposed above me had no idea what it took to do the job technically, procedurally, or methodologically, not to mention in leadership or management.

First and most important, before one can do rapid development, one must have had vast experience in developing by the book, and I mean *by the book*. The strict adherence to and intimate knowledge of a standard like DOD-STD-2167A is required for the manager and his team to know which steps can be skipped and which can be modified and made simpler to save time and money. In its essence, it's Zen. Since the time I was very young, Lao Tzu's book *The Way of Life* has never been far from my side.

You have to have the ability to lead and challenge and participate to get the work done. If the manager goes on travel and is not there, the individual members will slack off (more about this in Chapter 12, on leadership).

10.6   THE TRADITIONAL DEVELOPMENT METHODOLOGY

Traditional development methodology is a safe and proven approach to getting the job done. The manager in this approach is really nothing more than an administrator. He selects a proven standard like DOD-STD-2167A, tailors it, and follows a routine of monthly reviews of hiring and purchasing, looking over the budget, but not getting involved in technical decisions. In traditional development methodology (see Figure 7), the technical decisions belong to the systems engineers and the senior subsystem engineers. The methodology may be top-down or bottom-up. The workflow will be the waterfall method; this is good and safe, and relatively acceptable in cost. The progression is predictable, and there is reasonable assurance that the system will be ready at a certain cost because the only variables, really, are the technology and the complexity.

Were it not for COTS packages and other readily available tools, I could never have developed the systems at the cost and schedule my team and I were able to. There are great commercial off-the-shelf products out there, built by smart, talented, software engineers. There is also a lot of junk, and one must be careful in what one buys. As the requirements and software design documents are being completed, the senior design engineers, systems engineers, and senior programmers will already be visualizing their work and the problems they will need to solve. During this period they will nominate products, languages, and compilers that they have read about, heard about, and would like to try out.

During "design pauses" one can take as much time as one needs to discuss these COTS packages and notify the vendors of the interest in a demonstration and briefing. I use the design pause as tool to refresh the team from the hard work done on the design. There are stories and analogies that relate in abstraction to the problems at hand. I also use the development of ideas as a technique to relax the mind, while concentrating on a related problem.

The design pause can be used to discuss tools, listen to briefings by vendors, and watch demonstrations. The COTS products nominated are then put on hold and later tested by the team, based on the requirements of the project. It is very important to understand exactly who uses the product, what they think of it, and to see the vendor's test plans and test procedures. A vendor proud of its product will furnish these; one who has something to hide will not. Do not buy a product that is not mature; it will kill your project!

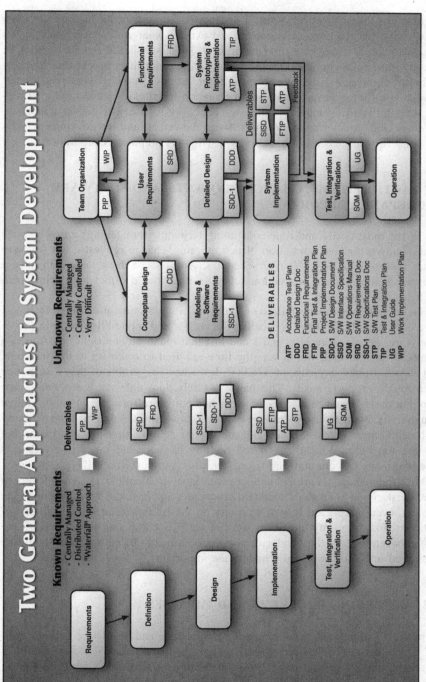

Figure 7. System development approaches with known and unknown requirements.

There are times, however, when a product is far from being mature, not even tested really, but the concept is correct and exactly what you need. Even if it has a long way to go, it will save time and money. Then you should consider getting it, but only if the following conditions are met: The vendor must accept the engineering help you are going to give them, and the product must be developed jointly between you (or the government) and the vendor. It will still be the vendor's property, though the government will have the benefit of its use. This means a hand-in-glove working together environment between the vendor and the government. This was done very successfully on GDSS with Digital Equipment Corporation.

10.7   ACTION ITEMS, CHANGE REQUESTS, AND SOFTWARE DISCREPANCY REPORTS

One of the most costly and time-consuming (schedule-threatening) items of work is the approval for and correction of action items, change requests, and software failure reports. This is a killer of schedules. Any one of these items can have a devastating impact on a production schedule if it should affect the critical path and leave others waiting.

I had a system hardware failure once during programming and critical testing. I had a burn rate of $25,000/day. I called the vendor and wanted it fixed *now, immediately*; my people were idle, and I had lost that much money right off. Add two additional days to that, which was the time required to catch up to the schedule. That meant a three-day slip, or $75,000, for a one-day problem; this was money that I couldn't recover easily. This happens rarely now, unless it is a network problem, but in this instance it was a network and hardware/software anomaly, simple enough to fix internally from drawing on one's own resources, but then the warranty on the equipment is lost. So you call the vendor and maintenance contractor, but they are too busy. What then? If the funding is short and the delivery date is close and many of your staff are sitting by idly, you fix it yourself.

When the manager is present and an exceptional problem like this occurs, he can make the decision to forgo the standard procedures and have the system team fix the problem, even if it means loss of warranty on the computers or other such consequences. Most often my engineers were at least as competent technically as the engineers sent out by the vendor or support contractor. Of course, this should be considered only if money and schedule are important.

10.8   RESOLVING PROBLEMS AND IMPASSES

All projects and organizations are made up of people, and people are political entities. There are egos based on subjective views of one's personal worth, qualifications, and status within a project. There are territorial disputes between equals, managers, and systems engineers, all of whom establish technical and political territories, and then often succeed in acquiring the territory of a neighboring subsystem. This happens all the time, and it is part of life, but it also sends costs through the roof. It demoralizes intelligent young people who don't understand the fundamental stupidity and selfishness on part of the "techno-warlords," "feather merchants," and charlatans who have nothing to offer but political infighting and trouble.

This is an area that is fraught with problems. Often, to see what is inhibiting progress, the manager must makes his rounds, listening and watching as he goes about the offices of his team. He should not get anyone to complain and point fingers, because the subordinate managers are warlords and will hold a grudge. Besides, many warlords are outstanding technically and you need them to get the job done; everybody has flaws, after all. Such unresolved issues only serve to alienate a young person with little experience from the team leader and the team. What the manager does is establish and re-establish policy; he must pay careful attention that this is being complied with. If that doesn't work, you must resort to removing the obstacles to getting the job done.

11 The Development of System Architectures

One of the most interesting discoveries I have made during my career working in computer science is the role played by philosophy in architecture. Specifically, there are philosophical aspects to the ways in which people think, perceive, listen, decide, and work together toward a common goal. Architecture is more than a mere physical representation of the structure of a system; it is a projection of the architect's vision of the subject, the hypothesis of what he perceives the architecture to be. It is a subjective impression on the architect's mind, and far from what the objective design will be in the end.

The architecture of a building or a classical temple is simple compared to that of software. The form, proportion, and size of a structure are limited by the materials available to carry the load. Since a model can easily be constructed, the vision of the architect can quickly be implemented to scale and shared with others. The customer can make comments and ask for refinements in a process that "adds substance to the object," which also helps the architect gain a deeper understanding of what he is trying to accomplish. Sometimes the vision is incomplete. It is only the initial incarnation of an idea, after all. When a physical model is actually built, it may surprise the architect, for it may look far different from what he had imagined.

I can only ask myself how others think and envision what they build. I have in reality not the foggiest idea of how to do so unless I can visualize the product of their minds. Architecture is a thing of harmony and beauty, and it is a product of the mind, like a picture or a painting. A photograph represents an event in time, as seen through a lens. It may have the photographer's imprint in a combination of his abilities in composition, light, contrast, and subject. However, it still is an event captured. One can imagine Ansel Adams waiting for a month or two to capture the exact sunset that was on his mind for years. A painting is different; philosophically it represents the artist's interpretation of what he sees and feels, if he possesses the talent to combine them into a picture.

As a young boy, I often wondered why Pablo Picasso made that terrible painting of Guernica. I hated cubism. Then, as time went on, and I read and reread the great classic philosophers, I began to understand a few things about this school of art that

The Cognitive Dynamics of Computer Science: Cost-Effective Large Scale Software Development,
by Szabolcs Michael de Gyurky
Copyright © 2006 by John Wiley & Sons, Inc.

Pablo had founded. After my maturing in Vietnam, and adding to that my childhood experiences during World War II, I began to understand what he was saying with that painting. He was unable in the classical style available to him to capture all of the event of Guernica: the scene, the terror, the individual pain, and above all, the scream of agony of a town under attack. He painted not from the visual rubble, ruin, and dead bodies, but from a part of his mind called *inner sensing* in Kantian philosophy. This is where the impact of the external sensing function is converted into mathematical format for processing and sent to a function I think of as *abstraction*. Here, in the abstraction, the mathematics is reconstructed by combining the algebra, geometry, sound, smell, motion, mass, and so on for further processing, analysis, and storage. I am not saying that I am completely correct, but it is because of my understanding that I place high value on architectural design and how it works, and understand why it often doesn't work. Obviously, when it doesn't work, it has a great impact on cost.

This phenomenon influences not only our understanding of how we visualize, but how we perceive and interpret an object. Not being able to understand something does not mean that it is not correct; all it means is that our ability to understand another's vision is limited. You could say that it is a limitation imposed by IQ, but that is unfair. IQ is a flaky subject; the results of IQ tests can be influenced by culture, language, and age. An idiot savant may be able to do sheer magic with theoretical mathematics, but have no other talents whatsoever. I have known several individuals like that. Dismissing what a subordinate engineer or scientist is saying because you do not understand him puts the entire architecture in jeopardy, schedule-wise and budget-wise.

11.1 PUSHING THE ARCHITECTURE

The process of putting forth one's vision of a system involves forcing the design team to sit around a table and a computer and have each member give his personal impressions of it. This is of immense value in arriving at a completed design, what I refer to as the *point of acceptable reality*. This is when we have discussed the architect's hypothesis, come up with the antithesis, synthesized a new thesis, and so on until the architect feels that everyone key to the project has an understanding of the design that is close to his own.

The benefits of this are many. Not only has the design team, through a laborious process, arrived at an understanding of the design, but the design has been evolved and refined to the level necessary to begin work. This is a Level IV architecture, the level of the computer software component (CSC) and the primary executables. This is the level of design required for optimal control and oversight of implementation. Next, the traceability is added to the requirements (in the FRD and SRD). Now, with traceable requirements and a crisp design, the systems engineer or manager-architect can simply sit down with a senior programmer and be fairly certain of what he is doing at any particular time. (This issue is discussed in greater detail in Chapter 13, on production control.)

Another benefit in pushing the architecture that has a positive impact on cost is the contribution made by the more junior engineers, whose opinions are rarely heard. For example, during the design process we often run into very worthwhile discussions on possible solutions to design and implementation problems. These range from the "What you're asking for is technically impossible" to "Maybe . . . I think I've heard of someone in industry who is trying to do this, too. Let me check it out."

This dialectic process is very important to software architectural development. Our industry changes steadily, year to year. There are complete changeovers every three to four years or so, and no matter how hard a manager-architect or systems engineer tries to keep on top of the state of the art, he cannot. The younger engineers, on the other hand, have more time to focus at the executable level, where the application software languages and tools are used.

These ongoing sessions are important not only as a way to reduce cost, but also as a teaching tool by the manager-architect. His interaction with the team enables him to learn about the latest tools, compilers, and platforms available in the marketplace from individuals who are far more "in the know." In turn, the younger members of the team learn the all-important lessons in technical management, design methodologies, techniques, and the design process. This includes how to chair meetings, how to listen carefully and beneficially to every member of the team, and above all, how to impose the required discipline to get the project accomplished on an agreed-to schedule and budget.

In cases where such discipline is not present or exercised by the manager, the lessons are not learned, apprenticeship doesn't happen, and the cost of software goes through the roof.

The manager-architect's vision of the architecture in software should be as clear to him as the design of the Parthenon was to Phidias before he presented the first model of it to Pericles. Software, too, must be modeled, but it requires more than the visualization of an artist. The skills of many similar but varied disciplines are required to achieve harmony; thus, a great group effort is required. By the way, it was often thought that columns and arches were Greek inventions. They were, in fact, first used by the Sumerians about 5,000 years ago (3000 B.C.).[1] We concern ourselves with columns and arches in software design because software design is architecture, albeit not of physical structures. If it is to be elegant and cost-effective, it is still architecture, and the thought process for its definition is still the same as it was in 3000 B.C. These concepts are very important, as building computer software systems relies on the same connection and synthesis required between the art and engineering disciplines as building physical structures.

11.2   THE POINT OF "ACCEPTABLE REALITY"

The organization of the personnel on a design team and how they are expected to perform their work is in itself an architecture. As I have watched others work,

---

[1] Sir Leonard Wooley, *Excavations at Ur*. Thomas Y. Crowell Company, New York, Apollo Editions, 1965.

I have noticed that the most important issue has always been "reality as a concept." Reality affects how I as an architect view the system I am about to build, and how I as a manager organize the people who are going to build the system. Reality affects how I understand my team; it affects the clarity of my communicating what I want and what I need from them. I find I must pursue the issue of closing the gap between theory and reality if I am to have any hope of building an absolutely fine system, regardless of size, but always at a very low cost to the customer. The *theory* is how I subjectively imagine the system will look when it is completed; the *reality* is what my engineering staff and computer scientists agree to, within the constraints of the state of the art. This is not much different operationally than pursuing reality and theory in physics,[2] except for the fact that we in computer science architecture deal in approximations and fuzzy sets as opposed to the clarity and elegance of physics and mathematics, where one is in control. Contrast this with building a large complex system, where one can only lead the dialectic process in the hopes of evolving an architecture that can be built. This is the point where the "buildability" is reached; I have designated this the *point of acceptable or sufficient reality* of the system.

I have watched other systems architects and managers thrash and strive, at great cost in time and budget, trying to reach the point of buildability without knowing where that point was, or why they were doing it. The result of these efforts was usually an endless set of requirements, brought about through an unending cycle of collecting and documenting requirements, and getting large customer organizations to approve and "sign off" the requirements. The customer organizations were often reluctant to sign off because they didn't know what they really wanted either. In the first place, they came to an organization that was expert and experienced in the field of software design, and depended on contractor computer scientists to tell them how to get the process, requirements, design, and implementation in place for a set of stated requirements, and to test and install the system. The fact that the stated requirements left huge gaps in the equation (variables I refer to as "implied" or "inferred" requirements) only left the task they faced nearly impossible to complete, and even if completed, it was done so at a huge cost to the customer. For a government-funded agency, such costs are usually not very important, but to a commercial customer it is a financial tragedy.

I have observed this phenomenon to very often repeat itself: A large contingent of people spend several years traveling; they gather, document, and review requirements and incomplete designs. Finally, after the expenditure of vast resources, the project is cancelled. Why? Simply because no one understood the objective or the concept of acceptable reality, and because everyone was always blaming the customer for "creeping requirements." To the professional computer scientist or manager-architect, creeping requirements should never amount to more than 2% of the total and should definitely not become a show-stopper or come as a surprise. If they do, then the individual understands neither his job nor the knowledge domain he is working in.

---

[2] *Albert Einstein: Philosopher-Scientist.* Edited by Paul Arthur Schilpp, Volume VII in the Library of Living Philosophers. MJF Books, New York. 1970, pg. 250.

There are many people reading this who have experienced this phenomenon, where the system is overdocumented and overdesigned, and never implemented due to cost. Take one such example, not in our line of work but in the field of photography. When I was young, while stationed in Germany with the U.S. Army, I bought two 35 mm cameras, the Zeiss-Ikon CONTAX IIf and a CONTAX IIIf. I also owned a Franke & Heidecke Twin Lens Rolleiflex that was much larger and bulkier. I soon found that the Rolleiflex was much handier to use, because it was simpler. They both had the wonderful Zeiss Planar lenses, but the CONTAX was overdesigned, and although a great camera from an engineering point of view, it was not as elegant to use as the Rolleiflex, and required many accessories that I did not need with the Rolleiflex.

There is an issue of sufficient reality in all architectural design, and it is the manager-architect who must know intuitively where that point is; after all, it is a responsibility inherently and part and parcel of the job description of the manager-architect.

If one divides the responsibility of manager from architect, my experience tells me that the cost of the system will be increased by one factor. To those would-be managers, or managers who feel that there is no need for a manager to know the technical details of a system, look at your budget and schedule, and you will know that you are wrong.

This book is being written with the sole purpose of keeping computer science technology at home here in America. There are two sides to the issues raised in this book. One side is that we, American computer scientists, *can* build software at a much lower cost than anyone else. The other side is that we *refuse* to build it at a lower cost, because our managers are preventing us from doing it, virtually by saying, "Over my dead body you will!"

How often have I heard the statement, "I don't understand it, so you won't do it!" I have heard this on several critical occasions, which stopped greatly needed leaps in technology from being developed in DOD, NASA, and the country.

11.3 THE IMPORTANCE AND IMPERATIVE OF VISUALIZING PHENOMENA

I have repeatedly encountered how hard it is for even experienced people to begin a project technically. Some years ago, I was starting up a large software project for the Navy. I was also committed to another very important project, and therefore I gave one of my smartest and most experienced engineers the task of doing the conceptual design and layout of the architecture. Weeks went by, and I kept asking what progress was being made. "Well, none," came the reply. Then the chief technical writer on the team, who had also worked with me over many years, told me that the problem was that they really didn't know how or where to begin. I honestly didn't believe what I was hearing. First of all, these individuals if anything were much more technical and expert in their fields than I was; they had been with me to see the customer, and they were in contact with the customer. They had worked for me over many years, so what was wrong?

Vorstellung (imagining/picturing/conceptualizing/visualizing) is a philosophical term, and a concept unto itself. If the manager doesn't have this mental attribute, the project is in trouble already, because it will be an object designed haphazardly, done by people mentally wandering about. I was very surprised when my senior engineer told me to write down what I thought the system was going to look like.

"Just write down the concept, Mike. You know, the systems architecture." This made me realize that I just couldn't push the architectural vision over onto them; I had to bite the bullet and take two weeks away from pressing work to write the architecture, the concept of operations, and the structure of the implementing organization, along with the implementation plan outline. Two weeks later, I had completed the outline, and gave it to them. They rolled off for a couple of weeks, and the system was defined; they were happy, and it looked great. But why didn't they know how to start? That is perception, inference, and the ability to visualize *a priori* a design. This is the domain of the manager-architect. If you don't have such a person at the head of a project, it will cost a lot of money. It certainly is much like the definition of leadership and the leader, as in the Latin word *agere* (to set in motion, to lead) and in the Greek word *archein* (to begin, to lead). These definitions may in themselves be unimportant, but taken as lessons they mean big savings in software implementation.

11.4 TRADITIONAL ARCHITECTURES

A traditional architecture evolves top-down and bottom-up and is a structured yet simple edifice. It is usually a hierarchical design, similar to structured hierarchical organizations, where the interfaces are formal and converge at the top. Almost all of us are limited to think that way consciously, and we also act that way. But our primitive logic is not sequential; it is the opposite. It is, however subconsciously, inferential and selectively prioritized. This selective prioritization is based on our survival instinct and is a different architecture. So, as we develop architectures, we find they reflect the same "stove pipe" and hierarchical schemata as those of the organizations we live in.

In a hierarchical architecture, the software requirements are followed by the software design of the software system, the software segments, then computer software units, computer software components, and finally the computer software component units. It is a systematic, hierarchical approach that works very well and is a guarantee to a cost-effective system; it is the approach I like to follow. It is well documented in DOD-STD-2167A and MIL-STD-498, as well as in JPL-STD-D-4000. All of the process reflects the development of a documentation tree and the organization containing the minimum number of personnel with the correct mix of skills that will produce each volume of the documents (more on documentation in Chapter 5, on organization). The discipline and the methodology used still apply throughout the development cycle. However, since a proven standard is followed, and provided it is tailored correctly to reflect the system requirements, schedule, and budget, its implementation is not particularly difficult or stressful. You can determine from the category of the system, being a single point of failure or not, just how exacting and meticulous the execution of the design is to be followed. Then, based on the complexity of the computer software units and the skill of the programmers (as reflected in their productivity rates), you can determine when each delivery can be expected. This is the easy part. This is also the best approach for developing the design of the architecture.

11.5   THE INFERRED ARCHITECTURE

The methodology used to develop a systems architecture under the pressures of an unreasonably short schedule and perhaps an unreasonably low budget is entirely different from the traditional one. There are times when for some reason, be it an emergency or the incompetence or inability on the part of higher management to plan properly, one is stuck with a high stress job. To begin with, as a well-meant warning to those manager-architects, systems engineers, senior design engineers, and senior programmers who are caught up in doing such a job: Be careful, and never do it twice in your career. The stress of doing what was mistakenly labeled "quicker, better, cheaper" is so high that a healthy person with lots of personal discipline can get away with it once without doing permanent physical damage to himself. Understand also that human nature being what it is, most of those above whose careers and reputations are at stake don't really care about the health and welfare of the people doing the work. This is not a condemnation on my part, but an observation based on my experiences of several years in combat and in the workforce, and on my readings in philosophy and history.

It is considered heretical to most who portray themselves as caring managers and caring political leaders to voice these sentiments. There are only a few who care. I have had the good fortune of having had a few great bosses, leaders, and mentors who became my role models, but there were only a few.

Inferred architectures are not based on written requirements, much less on written and well thought out software designs. Software-intensive projects like these usually start by someone high in an organization saying something to the effect of, "We need this system, and we need it now!" The term *inferred* means that the requirements will be based on certain well-known points. These known reference points are the user functional requirements.

This is a very interesting methodology and approach to systems development. The first task is the manager-architect's visualization of the systems architecture and its articulation in sufficient detail for the other members of the design team to understand what is meant. This is followed by the articulation of the end-to-end network architecture and its software segments. In this way the design team has an inner core with the manager-architect and the systems engineer at the center and is in session from the beginning of the workday. See Figure 5.

The outer circle of the design team is composed of the software segment (application software only) senior design engineers (SDEs) who develop the user requirements in conjunction with the end users of the system. These user requirements are usually in the form of the data required by a user in the performance of his work, on an hourly, daily, and weekly basis. The required data are displayed in written text, spreadsheets, reports, and graphics for each subsystem and user interface to the system.

The user tells the SDE what information he needs at his workstation, the needed data sets, the window layouts, the preferred user interfaces, mouse interactions, and so on. A picture emerges for those subsystems that have a number of specialized users established, and the data refresh frequency determined for each user. Initially, the SDE reports to the design team meeting after a thorough session with the end user, and presents the user requirements to the design team; each SDE does so in turn. The requirements are discussed and integrated into the architecture. In the case of a system such as this, it is entered into a computer with a large screen projector, so that the design object is clearly visible to all. Years ago, instead of using a projector, the requirements were taken from either copy boards or personal computers and were formatted to the architecture on large, corked wall-sized surfaces. As the user requirements became more clearly defined, the requirements on the system segments became clearer. The system software segments comprise the communications segment, the common software services segment, the database segment, and the graphics segment of the user interfaces.

The following data, inferred from the users, are formalized:

- The size and design requirements of the database
- The bandwidth required for communications and networking
- The need for and extent of graphics
- The interface requirements to other systems from which data are needed
- The size of the programs needed to implement the system application software
- The size (power, capacity) and type of hardware to implement the system

There are several implied requirements here for the computer hardware system. As soon as development starts and the software segments have been identified, a local area network representing the exact design of the actual system must be installed in a laboratory. The deliverables for which the application segment SDEs are responsible act as the user interface to the system for the end user of that segment, who is generally an operator. They are responsible for delivering a user guide with each software release. There are no other releases. The first software releases are delivered to the software test engineers. Once they have tested the software, and all problems have been eliminated, the delivered software is turned in to the project librarian, who compiles the software release and links it. If there are problems (and usually there are many), the senior engineers and programmers work with the testers for as long as it takes to clear the software and make it trouble-free.

The project software librarian works directly for the manager-architect and sits in on the design team. All software deliveries must be approved by the librarian before being integrated into a build. The design team is in session from 8:00 A.M. until 1:00 P.M. All disputes and design issues are discussed and arbitrated by the SDEs, with the oversight and in the presence of the manager-architect. During this time of design, programming, and testing, the technical writing team prepares the user guide, and through interviews with the SDEs and the users, they begin to prepare a maintenance manual for each subsystem. Since the architecture is totally modular, the user interface is not uniform, nor does it need to be. Getting all users to agree on one standard user interface takes a lot of debate, discussion, and wrangling. It is one of the paramount attributes of a successful system to get the system into the user's hands, in the manner the user is most comfortable with. The user interface can be reconfigured at any time to suit the needs of the individual operators.

This methodology for developing a systems architecture is a tough way to go; don't do it unless there is a bona fide need and they pay you well for it. It is a very difficult thing; in fact, it's the most difficult of all. There are no requirements or design documents, and you, the systems manager-architect, have to keep all the details in your head. You cannot travel, you have no time for much else but to watch the development day and night. You cannot bypass the Software Interface Specifications; these must be formally written. Only after the completion of the system is the articulation of the design completed. Each release of software has a User Guide/Software Operators Manual to go with the delivery. These are a must; without these you cannot test the system.

11.6   THE REDESIGN OR UPGRADING OF EXISTING SYSTEMS

The redesign methodology and development approach is the easiest system for me to calculate, *a priori*, and it is the cheapest to deliver. The reason for an accurate *a priori* costing is that sometimes there is a sudden requirement for rebuilding an existing system, and thus the need for a ballpark cost figure (maybe not the final figure, but a figure reliable enough for planning purposes). None of the program managers understands software anymore than the DOD managers do. Over a period of time, and based on experience, they may trust the software manager-architect if his record is good. The additional motivation is to get a chance to build a great system and have a salary coming in.

Most great American corporate managers and CEOs no longer care about keeping the jobs at home, and no longer trust American engineering. I know where most of these guys drifted in from. They made their mark in administering budgets with no restrictions on the limits of spending. Now the hard times are coming, and the poor guys are ill-equipped to manage tight budgets while having little to no experience in software engineering.

I have used successfully the following cost estimation rule of thumb, developed over the course of the past 30 years:

1. Given the total lines of code in a system, a redesign will *reduce* the total by 25%, due to modern tools, faster platforms, and new application software languages.

2. The redesign and reprogramming will add an additional software segment or two, plus a new user interface, which will *increase* the system by 50%.

3. Then, based on the design team and their level of experience and rate of production, the cost will be

   - *High*, up to $80 per line of code
   - *Medium*, from $30 to $60 per line of code
   - *Low*, from $10 to $30 per line of code

This is the *overall* cost and includes *all* salaries, hardware, facilities, testing, travel, and documentation.

Often there are undocumented mathematically intensive subsystems. It must be first inferred from the code if they are mathematically intensive. If they are, then the equations must be reconstructed, documented, proved, and then programmed. In such cases, the line of code count will certainly be up an additional 40%. Depending on the complexity of the code, the cost is established as an overall average and can be close to $80 per line of code, including the profit margin. This includes all the parameters mentioned earlier.

11.7 THE APPROACH TO NEW SYSTEMS

New systems must be approached as the standard requires. Over the years, I have asked my managers whether they were sure that they wanted me to deliver the system. They were always surprised, and asked what I meant. I would explain that if they really needed me to do the job professionally, on cost and on schedule, they had to be sure. Once I started, I wouldn't stop until I completed it, and I would not tolerate interference, screwing around with petty politics, usurping credit, and haggling over what someone understood or not. I will not spend a half a day, much less entire days or weeks, trying to explain technical and philosophical issues to illiterates. It is a waste of time. To use the old American adage: "You can't teach a pig to sing; it wastes your time, and annoys the pig!" So follow the standard and the organization I spoke about in the previous chapter.

Really—what would a geologist or biologist know about software and Kantian cognitive dynamics? Worse yet, what would a scientist know about management? Of course, if money and schedule are not an issue, please give the job to such people; they'll be only too happy with a large office, nice furniture, an administrative assistant, and plenty of frequent-flyer bonuses. I'm not interested in that; blame it on my training as a Special Forces officer.

12 The Impact of Leadership on Software Development

Leadership is the art of influencing and directing people in such a way as to obtain their willing respect, confidence, obedience, and loyal cooperation to get the job done.

The ultimate objective of leadership in any organization is the accomplishment of that organization's mission. The accomplishment of the mission is reflected in a quality product, on schedule and on budget. This is, of course, the recurring theme of this book, but I cannot overemphasize the importance of excellence in engineering and science. All of these objectives are achieved through an effective, highly proficient, and well-disciplined organization, possessing high morale.

The organization that produces high-quality computer software at or under $50 per line of code can lay claim to good leadership; the others cannot.

These are perhaps hard words to hear, but they are true. This criterion, by the way, is not only valid for software development, but is just as applicable to an outfit doing interior decorating, a lumber mill, or an aircraft firm. Young individuals possessing positive leadership traits in an organization should be identified, nurtured, and carefully observed by upper managers to ensure that the leadership indicators are correct and sincere, as opposed to "put on" or faked.

Personally, I view an overriding honesty as the dominant trait, followed by duty and obligation as elaborated by Immanuel Kant. The worst trait of all is the lie.[1] There seems to be nothing worse in the world than to be a liar and to be caught in the act of telling a lie. After you lose your honesty, you become a person without honor. This terrible trait is followed closely by cowardice. This is the inability to stand up for what is right, proper, and true. These two negative traits—dishonesty and cowardice—destroy budgets, schedules, quality of product, and quality of life. They are the destroyers of great companies, organizations, and families; they destroy countries and peoples.

12.1 RECOGNIZING GOOD LEADERSHIP

Almost any organization, corporation, or company can be recognized as having good leadership at the top, the minute you walk in through the front doors. Good

---

[1] Immanuel Kant. *Von der Luege* (*Essay on the Lie*).

The Cognitive Dynamics of Computer Science: Cost-Effective Large Scale Software Development, by Szabolcs Michael de Gyurky
Copyright © 2006 by John Wiley & Sons, Inc.

leadership is manifested by the high morale and enthusiasm of the workforce. Looking more carefully, you will see that the work gets done even without constant supervision or micromanagement, and that the software is well documented, on schedule, and of high quality (i.e., fewer than 2 software discrepancy reports per 1,000 lines of code). This is a sure indicator of superior performance among all employees. The American worker, blue collar or white, expects much from his leader. He knows that if he does his work well, the leader will ensure that there is more work for him after what he is doing is completed. This trust is based on honesty and integrity, and it is a two-way street between the leader and those being led. Of course, a person can be a manager without having leadership traits worth mentioning, but the cost of the product goes up proportionately.

Leadership and leaders are a fact of life, and a part of life. Leadership is a group phenomenon, an interaction between the leader and the led, and so leadership never happens on its own or in isolation. When the management is devoid of leaders, which is the case more often than not, good workers seek them out by using the "secret communications network" to find them. Many of these are people who are known for their experience, learning, and their "love of wisdom." There it is again, that word philosophy! All it means is love of knowledge, tempered by understanding, curiosity, unselfishness, and an interest in and commitment to truth.

These "leaders of thought and information" are the people who are sought out by others. They carry projects to successful conclusions but never get the credit, nor seek credit. It is rare indeed that positive, unselfish leaders rise to the top of an organization. When they do, those of us who have had the privilege and luck to work for them will always cherish their memory. They lead by example. The negative types lead by intrigue and intimidation. A good leader never intimidates; yes, he gives a corrective counseling (a "chewing out") when appropriate, but he does not intimidate. It must be said here that there are many negative leaders who intimidate, but who nevertheless manage very well. Even these leaders are to be preferred over those managers who have no positive or negative leadership traits worth talking about. One can have a Machiavellian Prince[2] for a boss and still achieve good results. But too many princes destroy organizations and companies through their constant infighting, using up precious time and resources undermining each other instead of getting their jobs done.

The American type of leader has one great task that never goes away: He must keep these Machiavellian Princes under control. First of all, these princes have a lot of energy, and their energy must be channeled toward the accomplishment of the organizational mission and not dissipated in personal struggles for supremacy. Second, these princes are selfish power-seekers and are often after the leader's own job. Don't throw the baby out with the bathwater. Don't get rid of the princes; instead, control them, and use their often more than abundant talents and intelligence for the benefit of the company and the country. If the leader lets these princes get out of control, however, he must get rid of them. In the American sense of leadership, as expressed by Ralph Waldo Emerson, they are on the whole a contemptible

---

[2] See subheading in this chapter, "The Machiavellian Prince."

lot. Never fall prey to them, and that requires a tremendous understanding of people and social dynamics, as well as extensive physical and mental energy.

Take Napoleon, for example. Essentially he destroyed himself by becoming a "prince" type, whereas he had started as a "hero" type. He couldn't get rid of Talleyrand, for reasons hard to understand. Talleyrand betrayed him, and in the end was his destruction. Here was a man totally bereft of honor and integrity, and yet even with all the power at his disposal Napoleon was unable to get rid of him. The thing to remember is that to a prince, power is virtue. He attains this power through communication. This type will never take a risk or commit himself to a cause while striving for high management positions. This is done not for the good of the firm, but only for personal advancement. Avoidance of exposure to failure and risk is the trademark of the prince. If you go into the office of a highly intelligent and admired manager who always listens intently and praises your ideas, yet nothing ever comes of it, you are dealing with a prince. If your engineering design is good, and your ideas are sound, then for the good of the project and the firm a good leader will take it forward. This type of leader is the American hero type, who is a mover, a shaker, and an innovator. The hero type is the one who makes things happen, who pushes the envelope in his field. He will never give up his vision. The strong prince prevents unified action; the hero enables and encourages team play and unity of effort.

12.2   THE CONCEPTS OF MANAGEMENT AND LEADERSHIP

Management is an organizational function and position. Leadership is an attribute of the human character. Sadly, most individuals lack the attribute of leadership. Worse than sad is the fact that most of our "leaders" don't even know the meaning of the word, much less the philosophically positive definitions of leadership as a talent and trait. We admire good leadership qualities in a person, in particular the positive traits, which are the great virtues of humanity. The negative traits, however, are the embodiment of the Machiavellian Prince. This is the type we find in the American workplace today. It is simply a human trait. Even if one cannot change things, if an intelligent individual is at least aware of it and understands it, the charlatans who have the negative traits are easier to stomach. To the American computer scientist, who is a very intelligent and creative individual, it can even be entertaining to watch the political intrigues and struggles, the Lorenzo dei Medicis and Vespasiano Colonnas[3] fighting each other for supremacy.

Then, suddenly, the weakened company sees a hostile takeover, much in the fashion of the German Captain Frundsberg[4] during the Renaissance, and 12,000 *Landsknechts* (mercenaries) marching over the Corporate Alps and subjugating the little warring factions, who have through their selfishness destroyed the company, but made off with a lot of plunder. However, regardless of whether our leaders

---

[3] Julia Cartwright (Mrs. Ady) Isabella D'Este, Marchioness of Mantua (1474–1539) *A Study of the Renaissance Volumes 1 & 2*. John Murray, Albemarle Street, London. 1923.
[4] Ibid.

are idealistically motivated (as we Americans like to see our heroes) or are in love with power, in the final analysis the leader is the reason for success and failure. This includes the cost-effectiveness of a product and the schedule. A power seeker will always try for the top. In the military, as well as in civilian business, we attempt to put in safeguards against them. This often fails, to our detriment. This results in the loss of market share, the loss of projects, or even in the loss of products that are very costly, be they computer systems, weapons, or automobiles.

Good leadership is good leadership, be it acquired through long apprenticeship (by observing and interacting with others much more experienced) or as a natural part of our personality. It is probably the most dominant factor in the successful accomplishment of any project, particularly a computer software-intensive project. By successful accomplishment I mean, of course, on schedule and on budget. The fact that a project may be very complicated and intricate is irrelevant. A leader is selected and/or appointed to lead a project and is paid to do the job. If the person appointed to do the job seems to be incapable of handling the responsibilities of that position, you need to look for someone who can. The inadequacy of a leader to the appointed task is the cause of low morale on the workforce, and the low morale can be counted in terms of dollars over budget.

Throughout my career there was never anything that scared me more or made me feel more uncomfortable than when somebody would tell me, "Everything's great," or "It's all okay," or "It's well in hand." The minute I would hear those words I would start looking and digging, usually to find that things were as bad as I suspected. The second thing that has caused me to recoil is praise about my abilities. I hate praise. I know exactly what my mental status and my mental and physical abilities are, and almost always the compliments, even when well intentioned, fall far short of the realities, making me instantly alert to the intention of the compliment.

There are some people who love compliments; I don't. They always remind me of the story of the Crow and the Fox, written by La Fontaine for young Francoise I: "*Maître Corbeau, sur un arbre perché, Tenait en son bec un fromage. Maître Renard, par l'odeur alléché, . . .*"[5] The upshot is that a crow is sitting on the branch of a tree with a nice piece of cheese in its beak, out of the reach of a fox. The crow forgets momentarily about the cheese and makes an *a priori* decision to thank the fox for complimenting him on his looks. He opens his beak, as if to say, "Thank you, Mr. Fox," and drops the cheese. The fox eats it, saying, "A flatterer lives at the expense of those who listen to him." Ever since I was a little kid, because of the stories of La Fontaine, I distrusted compliments and preferred criticisms, which I knew were always warranted.

12.3 REWARDING FAILURE

As the first indicators become visible about a problem in leadership, upper management (or the appointing authority) realizes that the appointed individual is incapable

---

[5] La Fontaine, *Fables*. Edition critique de Jean-Pierre Collinet. folio classique. Printed by Gallimard.

of performing effectively. It is now the responsibility of the appointing authority to correct the error, and admit to having made a mistake in judgment by reassigning the appointee to a job more suitable to his ability. There is nothing wrong in making a mistake or admitting to having made a mistake; people make mistakes all the time. What is terrible is in realizing that a mistake has been made and nothing is done to correct it. Appointing someone to a job in management and later realizing that the individual is incapable or unsuited for the position is not unusual. The individual who has been wrongly placed should not feel bad either; everyone has made mistaken appointments. If you do not correct these mistakes, you are jeopardizing a project or a company by condoning the waste of resources that results from not taking corrective action. This is either unethical or stupid or both. What I value above all is candor and honesty.

I informed a manager once that he rewarded failure. He promoted a person who had bungled a very large and important project by giving him another important project. His reply was that the individual was a "learner." This is an interesting philosophical issue of a lack of ethics and fortitude on the part of the manager involved. No matter how much we may like certain people, they should not be learning management and leadership on half-billion dollar projects.

A high-level manager at the corporate level who cannot admit a mistake and continues to hope that by adding more money to the budget of the appointee he will eventually succeed, lacks positive leadership abilities himself. This is double trouble for a corporation or business trying to make a profit. When those in the chain of command in the organizational leadership hierarchy are lacking in positive leadership qualities necessary to correct mistakes, the organization loses market share and profits, and goes out of business.

The inability or unwillingness to correct a mistaken appointment is an indicator of the lack of leadership in an organization. This condition, if left unchecked, eventually will ruin any organization, even a country. The lack of good leadership brings chaos to any enterprise, and it will certainly ruin a project. Leadership, in its finest expression, is the most important asset of an organization; it makes things happen smoothly. By the American definition of the word, a leader is a person who is admired by colleagues, superiors, and subordinates alike.

Some years ago, I was invited to conduct a one-week software development workshop at the computer sciences division of one of our largest corporations. It so happened the corporate CEO was making the keynote address. He was one of the best I have ever seen. He informed the leadership of that division that unless they complied with his directions, he would fire the lot of them. He said it was cheaper for the corporation to outsource the software work he and his directors needed than for them to take up office space and use up funds inefficiently. For some unimaginable reason, the division manager and his staff ignored the threat, and they were outsourced. The lower-level managers and engineers were calling me, asking me to help them get through to their chief, but to no avail.

A similar incident happened to me with another famous American corporation, which is now defunct. I had made a bet with the president of the company that

I could deliver GDSS[6] on the schedule and budget I had committed to. He had a software system similar in scope and function, which he was building in Europe. He, moreover, was overrunning his budget by $60 million, just as I was starting up. Twenty-one months later, I had completed my task, and my system was running like a top. He invited me over for my reward—case of Budweiser—and told me that he had to come up with an additional $45 million out of corporate funds to finish the job. It was a fixed-cost project. I held a symposium for his managers, but it was sort of like the saying "the spirit is willing but the flesh is weak." I realized that all these top-level managers had not only lost the technical edge, but individually no longer possessed the "dynamic energy" required for their positions of leadership. The losses to this corporation, a famous, large, and distinguished corporation, were so great that although my friend fired the computer software division, it was too late to save the corporation.

Leadership is a full-time job and requires energy, *dynamic energy*, and a deep understanding of philosophy and how people listen, how they think, how much they retain, and what motivates them to higher achievement. Did these older, run-down people who spent their time collecting frequent-flier bonuses and sampling the fine dining and golf courses around the world have the right to destroy one of our major American corporations through their incompetence? No, they did not! A workforce, small, large, or very large, has a sustained "burn rate," and that burn rate must have a commensurate product that accounts for the expenditure.

I should note here that having been a "philosopher" from the time I picked up Plato's *Republic* at the age of 15 in Parkersburg, I was not so much interested in going to the top in management or the military, professionally, as I was interested just learning as much as I could about life. I had an attitude much like Lao Tzu taught in the Tao Teh Ching: "The way to do is to be." I risked my life in combat over a long period to find out what I was made of, and what others were made of. The energy and effort required for becoming a high-ranking general was channeled into computer science psychological operations and engineering. I think that I wanted to be more like the sage by doing less and loafing more, like Walt Whitman, but I had too much curiosity and too much energy. Besides, you can't loaf in combat with the parachute infantry.

12.4   THE LEADER'S SUBORDINATE

In good leadership, it is the subordinate who is the most important to the leader, not one's superior. It is the subordinate who does the work that makes the leader successful and propels him forward to positions of greater responsibility and authority. It is also equally true that it is the subordinate, who for a number of reasons, and in countless ways, can and will bring the leader down and destroy his career. Thus, leadership, in its good and positive form, is very important to the leader, the follower, and the organization.

[6] See Chapter 14, Case Study Two.

In leadership, there are by definition leaders and followers. There is nothing demeaning in the word "follower" in our vocabulary. There are many very talented people in the world who prefer to do hands-on work to that of being responsible for the work of others. In fact, there are probably many more recipients of the Nobel Prize who are not leaders than those who are. Leadership is a very demanding task, and there are those who simply don't want to pay the price in time, stress, and effort.

The set of relationships, interactions, and behaviors between leader and follower is called psychodynamics.[7] Psychodynamics can at times have disastrous effects on a venture, be it in war or business. Thus, the quality of leadership is either effective or ineffective, constructive or destructive. However, the bottom line is always the leader's ability, and not the follower's. As I stated earlier, leadership is not only the most important element in success or failure, or cost and quality, but it is also the determining factor of organizational efficiency and employee morale.

There are, of course, leaders who use their charm, psychological insight, and intuition to climb the organizational ladder, through the flattery of their superiors, and through manipulation. The exploitation of human weaknesses in a superior through flattery to gain access and promotion is the negative side of leadership. Even great leaders like Julius Caesar and Napoleon used this technique. Caesar exploited the weakness of the dictator Sulla to gain the office of Consul, and he went on to greatness from there. Napoleon married Josephine, the mistress of Barras, one of the most important members of the government of Revolutionary France. However, both of these individuals knew how to exercise power effectively, which is what leadership is all about.

12.5 INDICATIONS OF POOR LEADERSHIP

The lack of effective leadership in the workplace has several key indicators, such as the loss of market share and declining profits. These indicators are generally followed by a decline in the quality of the product, which is usually a reflection on workforce morale. Low employee morale is also reflected in slipped milestones and cost overruns.

Individuals in leadership positions who lack positive leadership qualities are the greatest threat to an organization.[8]

However, in the American industrial world of high technology, tight schedules, and budgetary fluctuations, the American type of leadership is still the successful one. To be sure, it is an idealized type of leader that unfortunately is becoming rare to find.

The first thing I learned about leadership is that nothing escapes the perception of those being led. The opinion of one's leaders by those being led is very direct and to the point, both in the armed forces and in industry. If some of the leaders I know

---

[7] Kets De Vries, *Leaders, Fools and Impostors*, Josseys-Bass Publishers.
[8] Ibid.

were aware of the contempt and low opinion they had from their subordinates, they would be very upset. Yet to many a leader, the opinion of the subordinate doesn't count. However, a person in a leadership role who cannot lead affects morale, and low morale is reflected in schedule slips and increases in the cost of a product.

Having said all this, what is leadership? Well, first of all, it is a far broader area of knowledge, study, and interest than we might think. This chapter cannot possibly cover the knowledge base of the subject. Elsewhere I have written a seminar of 12 one-hour sessions on this subject, and yet only scratched the surface.

The U.S. Army has a saying, "Leaders are made, not born," and in the Army this argument goes on and on. Some scholars of leadership are convinced that leadership is an inborn character trait or attribute of those who have it. Whatever the truth is, we humans cannot function without leaders; when we don't have one, we look and find one. When someone is appointed over us who we feel is not up to the job, we hate it. We Americans are hard on our leaders, and expect much from them.

12.6   LEADERSHIP AND ETHICS

It is largely a psychological phenomenon and activity between the leader and his followers that we should expect from our leaders an idealized subjective behavioral pattern, much like what we have developed of ourselves in our minds, but personally do not follow. When we see in them those traits we dislike in ourselves, even if we don't admit to them, we feel that we have been betrayed and let down.

So then let's say that leadership traits are personal qualities of which there are positives and negatives. The positive leadership traits we would like to see in ourselves, but are willing to suppress for personal gain; the negative traits we more often than not dislike in ourselves. However, most of us are willing to use our negative traits, setting aside our scruples, for personal gain. These scruples are called personal ethics, or simply *ethics*. What we are really talking about when we discuss the subject of leadership is behavioral ethics. Ethics by itself is a category of philosophy.

When we see unethical behavior, we instinctively know it, even if we don't fully understand it, and even if we choose to disregard or ignore it. The ideals we would like to see in ourselves form the thesis; the antithesis is the contrary behavior on our part or that of the leader. This creates a great emotional conflict and impacts our behavior and how we perform on the job, at home, and in our communities. On the battlefield it costs lives.

Great high-quality leadership, therefore, is of utmost importance to getting our work done with efficiency, at low cost, and on an acceptable schedule.

12.7   THE ATTRIBUTES OF LEADERSHIP

What then are the traits we Americans hold in such high esteem in ourselves and in our leaders?

12.7.1   Unselfishness

I suppose I would put on the top of the list UNSELFISHNESS. A good leader will put the work at hand as the most important item on the priority list.

12.7.2   The Welfare of Others

The second on the list is the WELFARE of the subordinates, colleagues, and co-workers, who do the actual work of designing, programming, testing, maintaining, and operating the systems we build.

12.7.3   Ambition

Next comes the leader's personal AMBITION, and his likes and dislikes. Leaders also would like to rise above their peers, as is natural, but not at the expense of the job being done, and the people who do the work. Keep in mind that this may not be a reality today, but it is the American ideal.

12.7.4   Integrity

The next trait on the list of the positive leadership traits is absolutely beautiful, because it says it all: It is called INTEGRITY. The Latin word "integritas" was the parole by which a Roman citizen soldier of any rank would address his superiors. It means his unimpaired condition, soundness of health, moral purity, uprightness, the unimpaired condition of his weapons and equipment, the absolute correctness of his obedience to the laws of the Roman Republic, and his willingness to give his life in its defense. Not many leaders today can touch their hearts when facing the public and say, "Integrity is the code by which I live and work."

I must admit that only in my third reading of Immanuel Kant's critiques did I begin to understand the full meaning of integrity and the relative worth of the inner dignity of a person living by these rules. This is the hypothesis that in the reasoning being, man in his highest moral form, acts out of a sense of duty. That duty is the *categorical imperative* of the rules of ethical behavior to act unimpaired by personal gain, by likes or dislikes, by fear of higher authority, or being rejected by peers. It's worth quoting here from the great master:

> Duty! You noble, illustrious, you great name, you who carries in your nature the integrity to love nothing that carries flattery as a companion. This integrity within you that demands submission of your senses and desires, but never threatens the moral laws or the disposition of your spirit and your soul.[9]

What this means in the workplace is that the good leader will act always for the greater good. This is the synthesis of the accomplishment of the project as a quality

---

[9] Kant. *Die drei Kritiken*. Page 243. Compiled by Raymund Schmidt. Alfred Kroner Verlag, Stuttgart, Germany, 1975.

end product, out of respect for the customer and for oneself, having been entrusted with the task and the resources. It is also out of respect for those who do the work, by listening carefully to their opinions, regardless how tedious that is at times. Finally, it is out of respect for those who will use the product and try to maintain it. Duty as the categorical imperative of pure ethics carries with it the attribute of *truth*. This means that a person who has a correct answer to a problem, but decides for whatever reason not to speak up and provide the information, is as unethical an individual as one who has willfully mislead a person by providing wrong information.

The fact that pure ethics is only possible to a person possessing a free will means, interestingly enough, in a syllogism, that anyone who is unethical does not have a free will. We are constrained from telling the truth sometimes, because we are afraid for our jobs, because we know that the boss does not want the truth, because it will upset him, it will ruin his weekend with worry. Also, we keep the truth hidden because we want people to fail, so we will look good and get their jobs, or just to be able to say, "I told you so." Or, we say the things others want to hear so we will be liked, get promoted, and get pay raises. All of these acts mean that the individual does not have a truly free will because of the constraints on the will by agendas, appetites, likes, dislikes, and so on.

The real leader will never hold the opinion of anyone, high or low, in disregard. He will never punish when someone discovers a personal mistake; even a serious or potentially catastrophic oversight is forgivable if the individual comes out and tells the truth upon discovery. In this way, integrity creates an ethical work environment, and this impacts the work being done in such a positive way that the work speeds up, almost effortlessly.

12.7.5 Loyalty

Very closely on the list follows LOYALTY. This is an interesting trait since it hangs with integrity, in that it means first of all loyalty to one's ethical behavior. It follows then that one is loyal to those by whom one has been entrusted to do the work, and with the resources to get the work done. This is a great trust and honor, to be entrusted with funds, and it carries with it that special word again—*duty*—to one's superiors and subordinates. More than that, it carries with it the obligation to the company one has chosen to work for and that is paying one's salary. On part of the leader it carries the responsibility to ensure that the engineers, scientists, and administrators have no fear of the next job after the one they are working on is finished, because the leader is planning for their next job already. Loyalty among staff is a work unit multiplier. Loyalty, again in the idealized sense, builds strong teams and in some ways extended families based on respect and trust.

12.7.6 Knowledge

A leader must have KNOWLEDGE, not only of the technical work on hand, but of all of the ancillary areas associated with it.

A computer software-intensive system comprises not only programming languages, but systems architectures, engineering, functional design, communications, databases, applications, and systems programming. It includes the technical functions that the applications software is to support. Then the individual must also understand and like people, and help solve both the technical and administrative problems encountered along the way. The leader must have knowledge of his job, and continue to learn and improve. Knowledge includes the continued interest in how the system is evolving, by asking at all levels for information to gain an insight. There must be a thorough understanding on the leader's part about what the individual staff members need to be more effective, and to provide the needed support.

12.7.7 Tact

TACT is important, and I must admit that I have been told very often in the Army and in the workplace that I lack tact, so I know something about it. One blunder people make is that they mistake the truth for a lack of tact. Here I have to say that one of the reasons I loved JPL so much when I first arrived was the absolute uninhibited telling of the perceived truth. The mission of the Voyager spacecraft was so critical and its success so imperative that the exchanges between scientist and engineers during meetings were uninhibited. I loved it. The science provided by each instrument was of such importance to each principal investigator that a centimeter's worth of data on the tape recorders during occultation at Jupiter was worth fighting about, verbally of course, no holds barred. I was the General Science Data Team Chief, and I can assure the reader that every error on the science data records was duly noted in no uncertain language. People of the present generation call it verbal abuse; I call it "telling it the way you see it." Being uninhibited in language with me and with each other prevented us from making more mistakes, and on any project mistakes are made. In any case, when being chewed out on the phone by one distinguished scientist after another, I just held the phone a foot away from my ear. As far as foul language is concerned, I was used to it from the parachute infantry, where we used the same vocabulary. Today it is different. One way I deal with personally using expletives is telling my team to use them right back, and many of them do. Stress on projects can be mind boggling, and cussing releases stress. There is an old German saying that translates to "cursing is the laxative that purges the soul." Just be sure that when you curse, even accidentally, you have only friends around you. This is one important reason why it is good to have only the finest, smartest people, and those you respect above all others, working for you.

Never curse or use expletives in front of people you don't care for, those you don't respect or trust, and above all, never in front of the stupid or illiterate. They will take you to court thinking they can make a few dollars off your mistake. Better lose a project or slip a schedule at a cost of millions than curse. This is a sign of the times. The primary culprit is that we have done away with our personal interface protocols. Today, we address almost all people at all times as "guys." The terms "gals," "sir," and "ma'am" are gone. Even terms like "ladies and gentlemen" and "dear colleagues" are seldom heard. The use of the "he" and "she" definite articles have brought terror to the workplace, for fear of offending someone who doesn't understand the more intimate rules of the English language. I envy the Hungarian language for having an animate third-person singular and plural pronoun devoid of gender specifics. But then the Hungarian language has triple the vocabulary and term listing of English or German. However, one should not envy the Hungarian language for its scope and flexibility. For simple foulness, it is equaled only by Yiddish and Russian.

When my father taught me to tell the truth always, he never told me that as a young man he had read it in one of the essays of Kant. I had to find that out myself. The second thing he never told me was that I would take more punishment in life for saying the truth than for any other act. It seems that truth is not something that people like to hear or want to be made aware of. People often claim that when you say the truth they are offended, and that you lack tact.

12.7.8   Judgment

JUDGMENT, as a component of value judgment and opinion, is a complex cognitive dynamic process if one is to model it in software architectural terms (such as I do in the chapter on autonomy, using the model built from the Critique of Judgment[10]). In this case, it means that the leader is technically and tactically able to make a correct *a priori* judgment, which is the synthesis of his experiences in connection with the selection of a process to solve a problem on the spot, or in real time. "Technical and tactical" competence means that the manager-architect knows, understands, and visualizes not only the architectural concept, but also the organization required to build it, with the correct mix of skills, the appropriate communication protocols required, and the methodology needed to complete the project in a certain time. All of these functions are separate and distinct skill requirements, and the manager synthesizes all of these into an *a priori* decision. This is a Napoleonic *a priori* decision, like the one he made at the Battle of Austerlitz, but here it is a technical-organizational-methodological decision, not a military one.

Judgment also includes the ability to integrate the knowledge and the experiences of other team members with the leader's own to make a correct *a posteriori* judgment. Formulating the correct value judgment of a situation and making the correct judgment saves lots of time—and time is money. This ability is totally dependent on the level of one's experience and knowledge as it applies to the work being done.

12.7.9   Initiative

INITIATIVE means that in the absence of direction, orders, or approved plans, one assesses the situation correctly, or reasonably correctly, and moves on one's own volition. A dominant trait of true leaders[11] is the ability to see the task in three

[10] Immanuel Kant, *Kritik der Urteilskraft* (*ein Kritik des Erkennens*), 1790.
[11] *The Wisdom of Baltasar Gracian*, Pocket Books, 1992.

dimensions, by visualizing the object technically, and simultaneously visualizing not only the required actions that are needed to be taken, but also the type of people needed to do the task, and the methodology and process to be followed. These are in the mind in the form of two databases: One contains concepts/templates, more or less complete, and the other contains the wells of experiences empirically governed and used to enhance a hypothesis. The speed and success of a value judgment and the ensuing decision resulting in the initiative are dependent on the successful retrieval and understanding of the problem to be resolved. Hesitation means a lack of knowledge and courage that is based on experience.

12.7.10   Bearing

BEARING is a positive leadership trait because bearing is an outward manifestation of inner qualities. Our bearing is one of the modes of communication among humans and animals. Bearing communicates our attitude, our confidence in ourselves, and in particular, our worth and self-esteem, or the lack of it. This trait encompasses the way we walk, the way we talk, the way we carry ourselves, and the way we dress. Our physical appearance and the way we present ourselves almost always reflect the way we feel about ourselves. There is a passage in the Talmud, Tractate Sabbath, where one of the great rabbis comments on putting on your best clothes out of respect for the people you are going to visit, those whom you might run into during your day's work, and out of respect to your own person. There are very few people I have met in my life who surprised me by their bearing and dress. One was Admiral Kidd,[12] for whom I worked as a staff officer while he was at CINCLANTFLEET. When he walked into any room, no matter how attired, you knew this was a *man*, and that he was in charge. You may not know who the person is who just walked into the room; he doesn't have any outward indication of being special, but you mentally snap to attention and salute. That was Admiral Kidd. He also had great war stories and knew how to use the English language effectively, but never harshly. He was probably the best leader I have ever met.

12.7.11   Courage

COURAGE is an awesome trait. It is, in fact, a virtue. Great moral courage, coupled to integrity and thoughtful contemplation, is like magic. Through integrity and obligation to say and do what is right and honorable, and not to count the costs, is the kind of courage that created the great American Republic. It is the trait of the leadership type we call the *hero*.[13] Most men slink around, worrying about what to say, to whom to say it, and if to say it at all for fear of being wrong, falling out of favor, being fired, or not getting a promotion. The individual with the moral and

---

[12] Admiral Isaac C. Kidd, Jr. (1919–1999). More than 40 years of naval service, retired October 2, 1978. He served in command of destroyers (divisions and squadrons), Cruiser-Destroyer Flotilla 12, and the 1st and 6th U.S. Fleets in the Pacific, Mediterranean, and Atlantic.

[13] Eugene E. Jennings, *An Anatomy of Leadership*, McGraw-Hill Book Co. 1960.

physical courage, on the other hand, understands the risks, but has no choice left to him by his sense of duty and personal ethic, and says and does what he knows needs to be said and done. Not having the courage to communicate problems upward in engineering and science loses projects. In combat, it loses lives and battles. Courage is a trait and a quality that never recoils from truth. In fact it probably takes more courage to listen to the truth than to tell the truth. Those leaders and managers who are afraid to listen and make corrections to a bad situation lack courage and a free will and are unethical.

12.7.12 Decisiveness

DECISIVENESS is based on the ability to form sound, rational, timely, and well-thought-out value judgments. Decision making and the probability of whether a decision is correct or not depends on the experience of the individual making the decision, not only in the technical arena of, say, the expertise in matters relating to computer science, but in the ancillary fields as well. The decision of selecting one database system out of three candidates is a technical decision, based on technical constructs. However, there are other criteria for the decision, such as the time to evaluate and benchmark the performance of each, and to evaluate the cooperation of the vendor to get the job done on time. There are issues of proprietary information sharing, visibility into the product, of safeguarding the schedule and cost, and seeing through the hidden agendas of the advocates for and against a decision. These are managerial and political in nature and are issues of experience in communication.

Decisiveness is of paramount importance in a project manager, as is his ability, which is based on the sum total of his experience of seeing through the minute issues impacting an issue. It is the *reason* that constructs the concept or hypothesis of whether a solution is correct or not, and to the degree[14] that it is based on this, whether a decision can be made *a priori* or *a posteriori*. Lacking sufficient broad-based experience for sound decision or acute intuition will make a decision either faulty or completely wrong. This is what costs money and schedule. Hesitating to make decisions ("indecisiveness") is the result of a lack of confidence in one's own ability, and is the result of a lack of experience in an individual. Good leaders are decisive (for the right, informed reasons), poor leaders are not; when a poor leader makes a decision, it is usually based on the analyses of committees or other ad hoc groups, which is usually a time-consuming and costly approach.

12.7.13 Dependability

DEPENDABILITY is a special character trait that a successful leader must possess. It enables an organization to entrust a person having this trait with directing a job to a successful conclusion. In an individual engineer or scientist, it is the trust to get the task accomplished in a pristine fashion. Having dependable managers and

---

[14] Arthur Schopenhauer, *Die Welt als Wille und Vorstellung*.

employees reduces the amount of time spent on supervision and reviews. It reduces cost and therefore increases the profit margin to the company. The best endorsement one can make of a professional person is that the individual can be depended on to get the job done correctly!

12.7.14 Dynamic Energy

DYNAMIC ENERGY, or endurance, in the leader is essential for the success of a project. The lack of it makes the forward momentum of building software slow, tedious, and costly. All well-executed tasks and projects in modern computer science require great attention to detail, and constant awareness of the activity flow and perturbation in the process of getting the job done. Attention to detail is a leadership responsibility; it includes all aspects of the development of the product, the monitoring of the workforce, individual as well as group performance, along with the budget and schedule.

There is a temptation here to say, "We do not like to be driven like slaves, and we are not slaves to our work." I believe that the workplace, on local and national levels, is a competitive environment. My experience has been that Americans love being competitive; they thrive on competition. Most Americans, regardless of occupation, love to think of themselves as being the best at what they do. It is not hard work that demoralizes them, it is poor leadership and a poor example at the top. Americans expect to be led from the front. The boss must be there; he must be seen involved in the work being done, and involved with the people who do the work. If he is interested, attentive, connected, and accessible to resolving problems, even in the middle of the night during critical testing, a magic-like thing occurs: The team is "energized," they "follow their leader," and they are happy to be working.

Kelly Johnson of the Lockheed "Skunk Works" was this type of leader. Bob Parks, Bill Pickering, and Jack James here at JPL were like that. They would show up in the Spacecraft Assembly Facility at 2300 hours, and sometimes remain until 0600 hours because the work was interesting, and they got involved with technical or procedural problems. These great managers were true leaders by the very definition of leadership.

So the work being performed by the top person, the *leader*, has a multiplying effect on the entire organization. The leader's presence resolves the squabbles that will always exist in any workplace, in an efficient, timely manner. Let us suppose that you stay in the production facility until 0600 hours. Then you go home, take a nap, get up, shave, and shower, and you are in for an 0800 meeting. You can do this enthusiastically and with commitment if the work is well-organized, interesting, and everyone is doing his best and loving it. This endurance is called dynamic energy; great leaders have it in abundance.

In computer science and software development, the demands for dynamic energy are even greater than in spacecraft and launch vehicle development or instrument design and construction. In computer science, the design of a system is based on the minutiae of requirements represented in often mind-boggling detail. There are no engineering blueprints such as we have in electrical or mechanical engineering, yet a mistake in the requirements, the design documents, or the test plan can have catastrophic consequences. The leader must expend the energy required by the attention to detail to ensure that every thing and every item is correct. He must be open to all suggestions and be perceptive to signs that something is wrong or could go wrong. In time, and with experience, the good leader develops a Kantian database of experiences and templates that enable him to take shortcuts and save time, but never at the expense of the product.

Clearly, as we get older, we cannot maintain a thorough pace of 60- or 80-hour work weeks, and this is not necessary. It is the manager/leader's job to plan well and pace the work, his own as well as the work of the engineering and programming staff. In many ways, having to work more than 8 hours per day just to get things done is an indicator of poor planning, poor work habits, and poor organization. Overtime is something that is required on occasion, but it should be done only when an unforeseen emergency occurs. Overtime because of poorly organized workflow and incomplete steps in the software lifecycle process is an indication of poor planning.

In badly organized projects, the amount of required overtime is a sure indicator of stress in the workplace. A stressed-out employee who is forced to thrash wears himself out, cannot concentrate, and makes more mistakes. This type of activity then becomes a vicious cycle, in that the longer the hours, the poorer the quality, and the more hours are needed. On occasion I have found myself working for people who really had no leadership abilities. And, although I succeeded in producing a very successful system, my cholesterol shot up from 162 to 287 mg/dl in just a year and a half. To deal with the idiots above me, I took to eating large hamburgers with fries in order to counter the rising levels of acid in my stomach. I managed to keep these turkeys away from my engineers long enough to get the deliveries accomplished. So, good leaders lead from the front, are always on the job, and take care of their employees.

Where can you optimize your time, where can you get the time to spend on the job where it counts most? *You can cut down on travel*; that is where you start. Get a good deputy whom you can trust; the deputy can travel and take care of coordination issues. Good leaders, after all, are mentored and taught by older and more experienced leaders. If someone proves untrustworthy to represent you, get someone else. Good leaders make quick decisions; they don't do too much agonizing. The deputy is the one who should do most of the traveling. The leader's place, except on rare occasions, is in the workplace if budgets and schedules are important. If not, then by all means travel, but you should know that if you have slips in the schedule or cost overruns, they are entirely *your* fault, and not the fault of "migrating requirements" or "technical complexity."

12.7.15   Enthusiasm

ENTHUSIASM is also a magical trait. Some jobs, projects, and campaigns are terribly hard on a manager, leader, or commander. The world is full of people who only see the negative side of an issue and who tear down the morale of an organization. This is particularly true of detractors on the sidelines. The leader who is unselfish and believes in himself and the task at hand will generate his own enthusiasm, is always positive, and inspires the organization with enthusiasm. Enthusiasm is infectious even when there are extremely hard times. People love to believe in positive things and not negatives. People love to believe in success, against all odds; this is the trait of the quintessential American or Democratic Hero, the people's leader, the great teacher, the great coach who embraces hardship and almost insurmountable challenges and leads the team to victory. He raises the confidence of the individual members of the team and doubles and even triples their personal worth in their own eyes and in the eyes of their teammates. This is the trait of a Vince Lombardi. It comes out of years of experience, contemplation, and the conscious drive to do the correct thing.

Although I have studied leadership, and read about it extensively, I'm not a scholar of leadership; I'm an observer and experimenter. It became clear to me during my enlisted service in the U.S. Army and as an American "citizen soldier" (private individual in a working environment) that a leader is someone whom you will never fool with a "put on" attitude for very long. Other nationalities have different expressions in the leaders they pick, for good or for bad. The American character is different. Americans in general are almost anarchists at heart. They don't like to be told what to do, and do not want constraining laws and regulations forcing them to obey anyone. This makes us all independent people at heart with a drive to do things our way, and not the way someone else wants us to do it. Nor do we as a group want to lead, and are only too glad to let someone else do the job, provided it is done reasonably well. Since we are very reluctant to yield our independence, we require very high standards of those who lead us. "Show me what you can do, and show me why I should trust you!" That sums up the American attitude in the services and in the workforce. If well-led, the American worker, blue collar or white, will shoulder almost any task, no matter how difficult, simply because he'd like to believe in the good and the worthwhile, not even for personal recognition or gain, but just to have done it!

The employee values the best; be therefore the best if you want to lead. I personally have found that in 45 years, only twice were my positive efforts on behalf of subordinates rewarded with ingratitude. One occasion was in the Army, in Vietnam, and the other was while developing a very complicated software system here in Pasadena. That is a very low failure rate, and we all would be happy if the systems we built were as trouble-free and reliable as the reciprocal action of the American working professional.

There is, however, a reality that impacts productivity through leadership in a negative way: If you don't have positive leadership attributes by the time you have reached your mid-20s, you probably never will. Leadership is an attribute of the human character that is developed over time, through practice, apprenticeship, training, and study. Napoleon studied it as a young boy, by incessantly reading Plutarch,[15] studying and observing while attending the Military School of Paris and

[15] Plutarch, *The Lives of the Noble Grecians and Romans*. Bennett A. Cerf and Donald S. Klopfer, The Modern Library, New York. Random House, Inc.

at the Military College of Brienne. He devoted most of his free time reading political science, a natural outcome of his interest in leadership and people as well as mathematics and science.

It is well worth noting the value of military experience as a school for developing leadership and the practice of discipline. The fact that later Napoleon caused the demise of the cream of the youth of France, some 3 million of them, and that his wars set France into the rank of a second-rate power from which she has never recovered, is the negative side of leadership.

Thus good, positive, American-style leadership is not by appointment, or bestowed; it is earned through the respect of one's peers and fellow citizens.

12.7.16   Empowerment

You can be appointed to a position of leadership, it is true, but most likely you will fail if you don't have the ability to lead. Years ago I had a senior engineer working for me who frequently asked of me, "Give me power and authority, and I'll show you what I can do." I tried over many years to make him understand that leadership, at least in my book, was not by appointment. Had his co-workers, colleagues, and peers sought him out for help and praised him to me for his diligence and abilities, then I would have "empowered him," but they did not.

EMPOWERMENT is a term we use so freely these days. This is good only if used in the context of seeking information, advice, and initiative in one's work within the framework of discipline and adherence to sound engineering practices. Empowerment with close supervision and performance monitoring is very positive. It enables solutions to problems that easily can escape 95% of the population.

Empowerment is the free communication of ideas without fear of retribution from superiors and peers. Positive leadership, not the management function, sets the environment for empowerment. Closely following empowerment is recognizing the contribution of the most junior person on the team for a great idea, or the solution to a problem. Positive leadership is exemplified in this quote by Vince Lombardi:[16]

> The leader must be willing to use it. His leadership is then passed on truth and character. There must be truth in the purpose, and willpower in the character. Leadership rests not only upon ability, but upon commitment and upon loyalty and upon pride and upon followers.

This quote blends in well with what was drilled into us in the parachute infantry: "Winners never lose, and losers never win." Americans are that way; they hate losers and they hate losing.

The attitude of young American professionals has not changed much from the soldiers I served with. For the most part, they start off very idealistically, although

---

[16] *Vince Lombardi on Winning, Success, and The Pursuit of Excellence*, Edited by Gary R. George. HarperCollins Publishers.

there are exceptions. Seeing, however, that their would-be leaders had nothing to offer in terms of leadership, they quickly become cynics and join the crowd on the way up, forming a group of people who "strive" for upward mobility with few, or incomplete, qualifications. These are the guys who "politick" their way up the management ladder, but who either lack the understanding of what it really takes to do a good job, or are not willing to put in the time to qualify.

This incomplete understanding of self caused the decline of many a great company I was invited to consult with. It is an interesting intellectual experience to find out what some people really think of as leadership and management. It should also frighten the board of directors. I know a great number of managers who assess their level of importance in an organization and the work they accomplish by how much they fly. Yes, business trips are to some the primary measure of importance. Then there are those to whom the size of the office and the type of office furniture are the indicators of position. Finally, I had a colleague who measured everyone's position in an organization by the size of his annual budget. He was a friend of mine, who passed away some years ago. I didn't hold it against him that he thought little of my striving to build at low cost, which made my budget one quarter of comparable budgets. It is just the way he saw the world. I would not have been able to understand or appreciate him had I not read Arthur Schopenhauer's *The World as Will and Imagination*.

12.8   THE RAMIFICATIONS OF FAILURE

To managers, failure of a project (failure to deliver a quality product, on budget and on schedule) these days is not considered that significant. However, to the rank and file engineering and administrative staff, the failure of a project is still very significant because of the frustration of losing after working endless hours with great stress and personal sacrifice, while the leader is playing golf in New Zealand or being served gourmet meals in Rome. The fact that the leader or manager is not present and is unable to make on-the-spot decisions and resolve conflicts impacts cost and schedule in a measurable way. The distain of the workforce is manifested in a different manner: The quality of work goes down, deliveries slip, documentation is substandard or nonexistent, and the product cannot be tested adequately. I have observed this phenomenon on several occasions. After all, if the manager doesn't care, why should the workers? Absenteeism becomes frequent; excessive sick leave, long lunches, late arrival at work, and early departures for home become the norm.

In fact, Americans expect their leaders to be the first into work and the last to leave, to be there and to solve their problems. They honestly don't begrudge them their perks and salaries (as they do in many other countries) if they live up to their responsibilities. They also see through the ones who pretend to care, but don't. If a leader cares and leads, he is always on the job and keeps the workforce moving ahead at a comfortable pace; this produces enthusiastic involvement on all who participate. A good leader in the American workplace finds he must often drive his workforce out of the office and force them to go home. He should check by the office on Saturdays and Sundays to make sure that people don't sneak in and work. That is leadership. However, if the leader is not in his office, but flying off to distant places, amassing large quantities of frequent flyer bonuses, that individual cannot solve problems, nor does he give the impression of being overly concerned about the work being done. So the worker doesn't do more than "get by." In any enterprise, no matter how hard one tries, one cannot get around leadership as a powerful influence for success, and its absence for failure. Leadership types are found in all walks of life, in engineering and science as well.

12.9   THE ABSENCE OF LEADERSHIP

Having considered the positive attributes of leadership, now we consider the signs of poor or absent leadership in an organization. The first indicator of organizational problems is a loss of market share and the declining quality of the product. It stands to reason, as discussed earlier, that a lack of positive leadership has a very negative impact on the workforce. The good programmers leave, because they understand that they have their expertise and consequently their livelihoods at stake. A truly good computer scientist or programmer must keep current with the marketplace, using the latest and best computer hardware, software tools, and operating systems. Equally important are the best and most cost-effective approaches to software development, the standards and specifications to be followed, and the often overlooked development methodologies and procedures. Only by using the latest and most robust techniques does a computer scientist keep current with technology and therefore remain in demand by other potential employers.

This is almost as demanding as in the medical field. A physician must constantly keep current on the latest developments in pharmaceuticals and surgical and operative techniques. It is an all-consuming task just to remain current. If, therefore, the latest technology is not used, good programmers leave and look for other jobs where they can maintain currency. The consequence of the aforementioned is a rapid decline in the quality of the product being produced. In computer software this is manifested in bugs (lots of them), poor documentation, and difficulty in maintaining the systems. On the vendor side, it means the inability to support the product over its expected lifecycle. Easy, low-cost maintenance is a very valuable system feature to the user. This enables a system like the TOPEX Poseidon TCCS, which was built in-house, to operate the spacecraft at low cost over 10 years in parallel with other systems, maximizing the benefits to science for a relatively low investment. A low-quality system, poorly documented, and requiring high-cost maintenance would have meant shutting down the system after its extended mission phase.

Organizational problems originating in a lack of leadership are also manifested in milestone slips and frequent schedule changes and delays, which invariably result in cost overruns. Let's be completely blunt about this: When an organization has good leadership, there are rarely cost overruns. Cost overruns are almost always the result of a lack of leadership and management oversight.

12.9.1   Absenteeism

Let's take ABSENTEEISM as a factor of poor leadership. Absenteeism cannot be laid at the feet of the knowledge worker alone, who may be demoralized and unmotivated. When a manager is absent in body, he is absent from his job. It is immaterial whether he is traveling to a seminar or symposium, or presenting a paper to a corporate meeting at a resort hotel or a conference. The absence of the manager over a period of time, like a week, puts almost all decision making on hold. In this, too, the manager with his lack of leadership qualities is a malingerer. By "decision making" I mean solid, well-conceived, and thoroughly reviewed *a posteriori* decisions.

On the management level, there is another reason for absenteeism. This is caused by the inability to cope with problems at the workplace. A leader feels "at home" in his environment, regardless of whether it is in a corporate executive suite or a simple cubicle with 10 programmers. The executive who does not have the leadership attributes to deal with strong subordinates effectively tries to avoid confrontation and finds every excuse not to be in the office. In cases where an executive or manager has a solid background in science and research, for example, he will escape to the familiar surroundings of the research laboratory, where work has no confrontation associated with it. Or, he might go back to his university campus, if it is close by, and work there, where the satisfaction denied to him by his subordinates and assistants at the corporate office is found in the reward of new discoveries and peer recognition in academia. However, such behavior also costs time and money to the organization the "leader" was entrusted with.

In the government agencies, including the Department of Defense, the taxpayer's money is essentially "funny money," and the fact that they are wasteful and thereby unworthy of public trust doesn't even enter their minds. It is their "due," a position they have earned through study and academic achievement (or in the military, as graduates of one of the service academies). They consider themselves as the chosen high priesthood of national privilege. There is essentially nothing criminal in this, because it is rarely premeditated and willful; rather, it has been drilled into their minds by teaching and apprenticeship. Nevertheless, the company suffers because the "Chief" can't get himself to tell his powerful deputies, "You are not performing to my expectations. I am reassigning you to a job I know you can do. You are going back to engineering, or science," or maybe, "You are not doing your job! From now on I will personally approve all your travel. Is that clear?" Of course, anybody can get the job done eventually, if enough taxpayer dollars are thrown his way. I'm talking about the essential American manager/leader who respects his fellow citizens as customers to whom he owes a quality product, on an agreed-to schedule at an agreed-to budget.

12.9.2   Hidden Agendas

HIDDEN AGENDAS on the part of individuals in management positions are also indicators of a lack of leadership. A leader's responsibility is the delivery of a quality product, and the well-being and profitability of his organization; any deviation from that is a loss to the organization. Typical hidden agendas include the "princely" behavior of power-seekers, and the political intriguing to get to the next higher position on the ladder of corporate power. Hardly has an individual occupied his new position when he is found to be planning his next move. By planning one's own moves excessively, realistic and serious planning for the organization suffers. Planning for the gainful employment of the workforce is much more important in leadership than is planning for one's own personal advancement.

12.9.3   Communication Gap

Almost always, people in management positions who lack positive leadership traits have a COMMUNICATION GAP, or are the communication gap themselves. The most important tool a leader must have is a thorough understanding of the qualifications, the mood, and the motivation of the workforce. It is a lot like a physician making his rounds in a hospital, looking at his patients, taking their temperatures, and asking questions. The intermediates in organizational leadership most often don't pass up the line the really important information, like employee morale; instead, the good leader goes about seeking information and truth, which either has been accidentally glossed over and ignored, or willfully withheld. Good leaders make sound decisions based on the best and most accurate information they can obtain. Most often, information isn't willfully withheld from the boss by the middle-level managers. What happens is that the middle level is often overwhelmed by work, and information slips through the cracks. As a good leader, you must explain to mid-level managers and leaders that you are not invading their territory out of distrust, but just making certain that nothing falls through the cracks. They need to understand this, otherwise they will feel insecure. It is part of the mentoring process of good leaders. There is nothing wrong in getting information; no one can know and remember everything, especially when overcommitted to the work at hand.

12.9.4   Poorly Defined Goals

Another sign of a lack of leadership is POORLY DEFINED GOALS. Good leadership includes well-thought-out and well-written project implementation plans. The Project Implementation Plan really should be written by the manager; this is a leadership responsibility because the PIP sets the tone of the work to be done, the organization required to do the job, and the methodologies to be applied in reaching the project objectives. When organizations and projects drift away from a well-defined objective, it is like a military combat operation that is not following the operations plan and order. Keeping the organization going in the desired direction is a leadership responsibility, and it is a full-time job.

Such are the attributes and psychological characteristics of leadership that cause great corporations to go under, and on a smaller scale cause projects to either succeed at great cost to the customer, or to fail outright.

12.10   THE BASIS IN LEADERSHIP FOR FAILURE

12.10.1   Personal Struggles

The PERSONAL STRUGGLES of individuals in the workplace for power and position in the organization are very costly to the project and the customer. It is the manager's responsibility to keep the struggle for power among the subordinate leaders and engineers under control. Poor managers who have no confidence in themselves are unable to bring order to the project organization. This incessant strife is as natural to human beings as is eating and sleeping, and if used appropriately it is beneficial. The energy is channeled toward the goal. People are not punished for stepping out of line unless they are dishonest or otherwise unsavory ethically. In the second instance, it is the flawed character and lack of ability of the leader who does not have the ability or the qualities of a good leader, and therefore pits one individual against another to exercise control, as opposed to imposing discipline and taking responsible action.

The political struggles consume energy and dilute the concentration and the momentum so important for keeping software projects on budget and schedule. It may be surprising that I should bring this up as having impact on the cost of the product, but it is as important as organization and architecture. The focus on the task at hand is of greatest importance. Struggles for the upper hand, for the ear of the boss, and for the supremacy of one idea, however ill-conceived and foolhardy, all take away from the major objective: the accomplishment of the job. It is the manager-architect and leader who must impose his will on the organization without stifling productivity, and force would-be "technical warlords" along the path of cooperation and team play. Often these junior warlords are willing to go to any length to have their way, and often do, through cajoling, fast talking, getting on the inside track in the project, and otherwise undermining their colleagues to dominate. To dominate in some way or another is in the human nature (Nietzsche).[17] The trick is to control these would-be dominant personalities, and channel their energies through persuasion, teaching, and supervision without losing their technical abilities (i.e., causing them to leave your project). The good leader develops in the mini would-be technical warlords their own personal gifts and abilities for leadership, their understanding of ethics, and technical expertise. This act of mentoring, teaching, and guidance, exercised during software product development, is a great challenge to any senior leader and manager. There is in short nothing wrong with power struggles, provided the top managers maintain control and direction of the organization.

---

[17] Friedrich Nietzsche, *Der Wille zur Macht (The Will to Power)*, Alfred Kroener Verlag, Stuttgart, Germany, 1996. It is translated widely into English. Don't be afraid of reading Fred Nietzsche; he had a lot to say, was very, very bright, and was just a bit outspoken.

12.10.2   The "Machiavellian Prince"

Power politics are a part of human nature and are just as applicable in the workplace as in national politics. Niccolo Machiavelli observed that the Italian city-states struggled so greatly among each other that none acquired sufficient power to stop France from coming in and conquering them. He was puzzled that there was not enough common sense and unity of purpose to make them stop contending against each other and unify to stop France. He concluded that the power to change things rested only in the hands of one superior talent.[18] On this conclusion he wrote his great work, which became the foundation of the field of political science. The diversity of opinion and the struggle within an organization for position and power can be very positive if the leader has the physical and mental energy to channel this struggle toward the accomplishment of the job. This is a very time-consuming, energy-consuming task and requires the commitment and constant presence of the leader. It is not unlike driving the four horses in a chariot race at the Circus Maximus. This is what makes a good manager-architect much like a great Roman charioteer. You need to know the strengths and weaknesses of every member of your staff, and harness them to the project "chariot" so they compliment each other as a team, according to their abilities; then you win the race. If you hitch the horses into the wrong positions, regardless how great, powerful, and enduring they are as individuals, they kick and bite each other and the race is lost. (There are a few people, by the way, who resent my analogy of the project to a chariot race, and of my best software engineers to racehorses. I have no problem with how they feel.)

Know your people, teach them, lead them, use them correctly, and you will come up with winners. Always keep in mind that no one can change human nature. To try is a waste of time and energy. What a good leader can and must do is channel the energy and talent of the employee or subordinate in such a way as to accomplish the project or mission of an organization effectively. Each project, task, and job is like one game of professional football that one must win. After the game you plan for the next game. It is the project and game that count; winning is the objective, not losing.

12.11   THE IMPACT OF POOR OR NONEXISTENT LEADERSHIP

The effect of poor or nonexistent leadership is more often than not catastrophic. One can argue and make excuses for costly budget overruns and slips in production schedules, but there are no real excuses. By definition, a leader is responsible to deliver a product on time and on budget. In the military, it is the loss of life and materiel that indicates poor or missing leadership. In corporations, and industry in general, this is disastrous to investors.

So how do these poor, unqualified people get into top management jobs, even to the level of CEO? This is easily done. There are two basic types of individual

---

[18] *The Prince*, Niccolo Machiavelli.

approaches to getting to the top. The first type of individual is the one who enters his profession with the desire to excel at what he does. A person from this category begins to work and learn the technical details of the job. He enjoys the work, and soaks up the details of the job and everything related to it like a sponge. He takes pride in his work, makes improvements to the process he employs, and his skills increase dramatically over time. Then, as he becomes more expert, he goes one increment higher, maybe managing one to four others whose jobs he understands, so he can mentor these and teach them the way he was taught by his superiors. Such people always hope to have a great senior engineer as teacher.

The fact that one's boss is a real hard case or tough to get along with may not be pleasant, but it is okay as long as there is something to learn. In my case, I have worked for some terrible guys; they were poor communicators and slow of wit. But, as long as they meant well, had the interests of the project at heart, and had my personal welfare and advancement in mind, even if misplaced in some way, I would endure the pain and suffering.

I had a boss once who wanted me to produce an operational scenario for a ground system, for which I was the systems engineer. Indeed, in this case I was thoroughly qualified, both functionally as a user and as the analyst, operator, and systems designer. Yet, no matter how hard I tried, he didn't understand the architecture of the operations scenario. It was a terrible experience, truly. It took me at least 20 versions, 40 ways of presenting it to him, until he began to understand; he finally approved it. A much older and very experienced fellow engineer gave me some advice that I had never thought of. He said, "Mike, try to understand your difficulties with him in terms of a communications and computer software problem. He has a receiving rate of 16 bits per second, and one compiler. You transmit at 7.5 Kb/s, and you multiplex. It isn't that he's not smart; he's just *slow*. If you want to make him happy, go away and think about the data rate you are going to use, and select a language for which he has a compiler." My boss was a traditional, old-fashioned, no-nonsense American electrical engineer from the Midwest. I followed the advice my colleague gave me, and lo and behold, my boss was happy. In this process I had not only accomplished my objective, but over the terrible months of mental torture I had gained an insight and understanding into operations scenarios that I never had before. How absolutely important they are for certain methodologies and approaches to systems design.

12.11.1   Conquering the Organization

Another type of individual is the one who, upon employment, begins to study the organization like a military commander would study a tactical map. The objective of this individual is to identify the key positions in management, their occupants, and the strengths and weaknesses of each occupant. Then the individual marks out a route to the top, with intermediate steps to be achieved. This means, if possible, getting to the next higher position as fast as one can. There are many personal benefits in this approach. It means that there will be faster increases in salary and prestige and power, which to this type of individual mean more than expertise in any one technical skill or the assurance of a well-designed, well-developed product. Moving up the chain of command requires lots of work and risk. This type usually does good work, but unfortunately just good enough to get by, because profiling becomes a time-consuming activity. Going to meetings, however unconnected to one's work, and meeting important managers and "organizationally key communicators" who know someone who knows someone is important in establishing good communications interfaces, "uttering the right noises," and making friends with the powerful. The trouble with this type of individual is that few in this category are intelligent enough to pick up the technical, managerial, and leadership skills on their way up to the lofty management positions they wish to achieve to be useful to the company. The years they spend in organizational politics make them politicians and not engineers or scientists, managers or leaders.

Interestingly enough, as careful as the U.S. Army and the sister services are in their evaluations of officers to prevent this type of individual from rising into high positions, they often fail to prevent them from getting into the top ranks, where apprenticeship and experience are very important.

There are exceptional brains, of course, who simply absorb knowledge at such a rate that they do not need experience, but these are very rare. So if an organization acquires managers who skip rungs up the ladder, it is no wonder that sound planning, organization, and execution of tasks and project are not present. This is most evident when employee morale is low, and when trust in management and from management down to the employee doesn't exist. This lack of trust comes from a lack of communication, which is the result of a lack of good leadership. Good employees leave and the poor performers remain. The upper management, having bungled or failed to exercise proper authority in the interest of the project or company, now resort to "consultants" to tell them what needs to be done. Consultants are very expensive, and are no guarantors of success. Some of the books that are written on management are really very good. However, many of the authors have little to no practical experience in hands-on management. It is, in many ways, the "teacher of responsibility" when a young soldier dies with his head on your lap because he failed to follow your orders, or because you as the commander made a mistake in judgment.

Positions of leadership? *No!* There are positions of management, and effective management requires leadership, but leadership is an attribute of the human character. You can acquire positive leadership qualities, which can make you into a good leader by study, apprenticeship, and the practical exercise of its functions over a period of time, but it requires a quality of caring, and in Kant's words, an understanding of duty. This word, *duty*, is almost sacred in its meaning and definition. It is the driving motive of pure ethics. It has no likes and dislikes; it has only the obligation to produce the best effort for an agreed-to price. Those who dismiss this word from their minds are, according to Kant, unethical. That's a heavy concept indeed.

13 Management of Software Systems Development

Management is the hardest of all jobs to do well. This chapter encompasses some review, but also covers those key elements of management that are not discussed in the other chapters of this book. I try not to cover management subjects about which much has been written by some very outstanding authors and experts in the field.

A well-managed project reflects the abilities, character, and personality of the manager. And, a well-managed project is reflected in the quality of its product and by being on schedule, and on budget. Poor and downright bad management is easily identified because it fails to meet the criteria of good management: a quality product, on schedule, on budget, at low cost, with a highly motivated workforce possessing high morale.

The obligation of those in positions of management is to provide the best possible product at an agreed-to cost and within an agreed-to schedule to the sponsor or customer paying for the service or product. On the surface, it is an easy definition.

Management is a position of high responsibility, accountability, and authority. Managers, from the smallest five-person team leader to the President of the United States, have the obligation to deliver to the customer the best possible product they can provide for the compensation they receive. The key philosophical idea here is *obligation*.

Without getting into the leadership aspects of management, the English words "obligation" and "self-respect" are rarely used in the context of management. In his work, *The Critique of Practical Reason*,[1] Immanuel Kant presents the thesis of pure ethic as a categorical imperative of duty/obligation, which he asserts is an attribute of self-respect. This really means "the will to do what is good," which is coupled tightly to the idea of responsibility. Briefly, therefore, self-respect is represented in the American phrase, "I have to look myself in the mirror in the morning," implying that if I have no self-respect, I don't like what I see. There are, of course, lots of managers who have no self-respect, and have no problem looking into the mirror in the morning; the workforce knows who they are.

---

[1] Immanuel Kant, *Die Drei Kritiken*, Alfred Kroner Varlag, 1975, Stuttgart Germany, Kritik der Praktischer Vernunft, page 243.

The Cognitive Dynamics of Computer Science: Cost-Effective Large Scale Software Development, by Szabolcs Michael de Gyurky

13.1 SELF-RESPECT IN THE MANAGER

SELF-RESPECT in the manager means that he will strive to do the ultimate good for the company and for the workforce. This means that if there is a way to increase the quality of a product, lower the cost, and shorten the delivery schedule, the manager will see to it that it is done. A person with self-respect will speak up, and will equally expect his subordinates to do the same, and even if it is understood that such a view is subjective, it will nevertheless contribute positively to the solution of any problem. A lack of self-respect means that if a person has a solution to a problem, but is silent and passive and does not contribute to the solution, he is not true to himself and is not behaving ethically.

This is a critical issue, especially today, when great losses have been incurred by the American investor and taxpayer because of a lack of "philosophical" ethics, the pure ethic of which Kant speaks. An ethic is lacking, because it is not acceptable or tolerated by the people as a whole. An ethic is not pleasant; it is in fact very burdensome and dangerous to stand up and give one's opinion. It is far easier to go to an "Ethics Hotline" and report behind an individual's back, as is encouraged today. But to an American, one who has been brought up and raised in the American tradition, this kind of "hotline" is really a cowardly act, performed by what we used to refer to as stool pigeons, informants, and squealers. Americans hate this more than bank robbery. A squealer loses his soul, or has none to begin with. The informants and stool pigeons controlled the German people and kept the Nazis firmly in control, just as the squealers and informants of the Communists kept the Russian people and the other nations they controlled under subjugation. There is no substitute for honesty and courage; it is the hallmark of American democracy. If you are a competent and good manager, the workforce will never let you down, and you will be protected even when you make mistakes, by taking up the slack. This is a wonderful attribute and character of the American engineer, worker, and scientist, and I have seen it happen many times.

To be a good manager, therefore, definitely means letting every subordinate speak his professional opinion, even if it is unpleasant, unwelcome, or even if it happens to be wrong. This is very stressful to the manager. However, discouraging or not permitting free dialog means the possibility of missing just one key element of information that could make or break a project. The dictators in industry cost a lot of money to the shareholder; in politics they cost a lot of lives and misery in addition to money.

13.2 THE ETHICAL WORKPLACE

The ETHICAL workplace is as important to product quality as the funds themselves. The American workplace is being bombarded with seminars and workshops about ethics. What fundamental conclusion can be drawn from the fact that workers are being forced to attend classes on ethics and take tests to make sure that they have been indoctrinated? The inference is that the workforce is perceived by upper-level management as being "unethical." The buck always stops (or should stop) at the top.

It is the upper levels of management that must understand the meaning of ethics. Ethics in its real meaning is a philosophical concept. I have yet to attend a seminar on ethics that mentions or in any way refers to Aristotle or Immanuel Kant. Without these, a class in ethics is nothing more than a half-backed laundry list of what you must do and not do or else go to jail. It is an insult to the intelligence of the American working professional to be given a laundry list without being taught the tremendously deep, meaningful, and intricate concept of ethics as both a philosophical concept and a cognitive process. I have yet to find an individual presenting such classes who knows what the meaning of ethics is.

An ethical environment means many good things in management. It makes working pleasant and encourages good teamwork. Good teamwork is a work effort multiplier, in that it produces a better product because team members, even when they compete with each other, also look out for the welfare of their colleagues and co-workers. In my way of working, the workplace that the manager provides for the employees is as attractive a place to be in as being at home with one's family. The manager with self-respect looks out for the welfare of the individual employee.

The individual employee should be completely confident that all he has to do is a good job, and the manager will plan for the next job ahead. The increase in morale in such an instance is truly inspiring. When a manager sees the productivity in an individual falling, he should inquire. Maybe there is something that the manager can do to help; maybe he is sick but has no sick leave and needs the job to pay the bills. Perhaps the individual begins to start the day very early, and work late. Asking why, you may discover that the home life of the individual is falling apart, and he is happier at work than at home. Just asking, genuinely, if there is anything the manager can do will make the individual appreciative. This builds loyalty[2] and increases product quality. This aspect of the personal attributes of a manager is, again, leadership. We often misuse the word leadership, by saying "individuals in leadership positions" or "corporate leadership"; most of the managers I know have few to no leadership attributes, and therefore are not leaders.

13.3   NARCOTICS USE IN THE WORKFORCE

The use of narcotics by members of the workforce has a staggering impact on cost and product quality. It takes a trained eye on part of the manager to see if someone is using narcotics; to prove it is a little more difficult. There are legal issues, of course, since our legal industry seemingly doesn't concern itself with the loss of public funds due to the impact of poor performance, absenteeism, and declining individual health resulting from the use of illegal narcotics.

But regardless of how our legal industry condones the use of drugs in the workplace as an impact on cost and product quality, this is nevertheless a very great

---

[2] See Chapter 12, on leadership.

problem to quality, schedule, and cost in the American workplace. The legal industry must somehow care about the danger the drug-free worker and engineer finds himself in when there are no controls in a workplace. The sad fact is that a person talking with a colleague has no idea who he is talking to, a conscious state of Dr. Jekyll or a Mr. Hyde.

While still in the U.S. Army, I was awakened in the middle of the night by a scream for help from the house next door. I jumped out of bed and ran up the fire escape to where the screams for help were coming from. It was a young woman in the corner of her kitchen with a young man, his back to me in the door, about to attack her with a meat cleaver.

When he heard me, he turned around with a fantastic grin on his face, and came at me. Lucky for me, I was 32 and at the height of my physical and mental strength; he weighed about 150 to my 175 lbs. I was able to disarm him quickly, but to hold him down on the floor until the sheriff's deputy arrived was terribly difficult and required all of my strength and skills as a Green Beret captain. It is worth mentioning that it took the deputy about 20 minutes to get there, and when he came in, at about 2:00 A.M., he stood in the door, laughing happily, hands on his hips, saying, "Howdy Cap'n! Don't you recognize me?"

I replied that I didn't, and that I needed help fast; I couldn't keep this guy under control. He insisted I recognize him. "No I don't, who are you? Give me a hand, please!"

"Well, I'm so and so, remember? I was the Orkin Man, just got this here job last week!"

Great! I needed police help, and I get the Orkin Man who is going through on-the-job training in hopes of becoming a policeman. "You got any handcuffs on you?" I yelled.

"Yes sir, I think so!"

"Well give them to me, *now!*" He finally gave me the handcuffs, and I put them on the guy. Thank God my friends, a couple of Georgia State policemen, were in the area and arrived shortly thereafter; I was finally off the hook. One of the interesting things about this incident was that there was not a muscle in my body, including my facial muscles, that didn't hurt after this. I can remember clearly that I was in pain for something like two weeks. The Georgia State policemen later told me how lucky I had been. The guy had been high on PCP.

This is a serious problem, and workplace safety is a serious matter. And, it is an ethical matter. The employer is required to provide a safe working environment for the employees and can be held liable if he does not. I am surprised that state and municipal governments, as well as companies, forbid cigarette smoking but do not bother with going to the trouble of mandating checks for narcotics and other habit-forming drugs in the workplace. Even for the security of the employees they do not bother.

It is a matter of ethics within our legal industry, which is probably the reason for this neglect. Narcotics are so widespread that they pose a threat to the health of our industry, our country, and our national security.

I am not sure if the problem of narcotics in the workplace ranks with poorly qualified management; I suspect it exceeds it. In any case, it threatens our productivity in all of our industries, not just software. It takes a very experienced manager to identify the user of illicit drugs in the workplace. We modern Americans like to make light of the issue of narcotics by calling them drugs, which makes them sound less harmful than if we call them by their real names. If one considers the kinds of legal drugs some of us are prescribed by our physicians, and remain under for the rest of our lives, it is bad enough. The side effects of these legal drugs are often terrible. For my conditions of dengue fever, malaria, and Marie-Strumpell disease[3], the Army was ever-ready to provide me with all the painkillers I needed: Darvon, codeine, quinine, etc. Eventually, I threw them out because they made me even sicker, and I needed to work with a clear head. So, I decided to live with the pain; I exercised and used nothing stronger than Bayer aspirin.

We have become a nation of junkies and are loving it. The leading heroes of the sports and entertainment industries are narcotics addicts. Okay, they entertain us, but in the workplace it makes the environment unsafe, the quality of the product poor, and the cost go through the roof. Let's not kid ourselves. If it is true that "America's business is business," then we are losing our livelihood to those nations and workers overseas who are not as addicted to drugs (narcotics) as Americans are. If we must support a large segment of the population because it is drugged up, it is still cheaper than keeping such people in the workplace, ruining our products and productivity. Out of the simple reason of national and corporate self-preservation, we need to eliminate narcotics from the workplace.

There is a lot to be said here about languages and the play on words, as a teacher. What do the words "drug" and "narcotics" mean in other languages, and how is it connected to the way we treat "drugs" as opposed to "narcotics" and places where people sell and buy drugs? This has teaching and relational implications as to how we label things that are "good" and things that are "not good." It is important philosophically because that is how we learn as children. Does it mean that if something is "bad" then we won't touch it? By no means. However, some of us will not touch it if it is bad. I have personally never touched mind-altering drugs. People will immediately say, "But you like booze, and that is a drug." That too is a philosophical issue open to debate. A drunk clearly does not belong in the workplace. One can smell the alcohol on a person's breath, and tell him to go home. But cocaine, morphine, and the others like cannabis are not so easy to detect. Only by knowing a person's performance and programming pace and style can I detect that something is wrong.

The German word for narcotics, for example, is *Rauschgift*, which translates roughly into "a poison that causes a 'rush' or a 'high'," which is accurate. So, should the young German take drugs, he is at least alerted to the fact that it is a poison.

We start going to "drug stores" when we are kids for a soda or a milkshake, and get used to the word "drug" in a very benign way. So calling a spade a spade might help.

---

[3] Marie-Strumpell disease, a.k.a. ankylosing spondylitis, is a degenerative rheumatoid arthritis, primarily of the spinal column.

The use of narcotics among the managers and workforce will destroy a company. One has to ask how many of the great American companies and corporations that went belly up during the past 40 years did so as the result of narcotics use. The use of narcotics is a mortal danger to a company, far more so than alcohol. There is nothing to it if it is just a glass of wine or a beer at lunch. But the use of heroin, cocaine, angel dust, marijuana, etc., is much more dangerous. The reason why they pose such danger is that the inexperienced manager, team leader, or even a fellow worker is not really aware of to whom, or with whom, he is talking. This is the Dr. Jekyll and Mr. Hyde syndrome. You make a serious correction, counsel an employee for performance, coming in late to work, absenteeism, or you make a remark in jest, thinking that you are talking to Dr. Jekyll, but you are actually talking to Mr. Hyde. You have placed yourself and maybe the entire workplace in mortal jeopardy. The manager is responsible for the physical safety and welfare of all employees. You must assume the responsibility and accountability for everything around you that falls under your authority and ensure that you are aware around the periphery of the organization as well.

The fraggings in Vietnam were not done by clear-headed people; they were done under the influence of narcotics. I can assure the reader, that having spent 34 months there, half of which was as a rifle company commander, I know what I am talking about. On combat operations there were fewer problems with the troops because they seriously policed themselves and beat up very badly those they caught using drugs. Everyone knew that drug use by even a single person jeopardized the safety of the entire unit and the lives of their fellow soldiers, due to inaccurate shooting, slow reflexes, carelessness, falling asleep in night ambush positions, or getting lost on patrol. But once in the rear area, which was usually a Landing Zone (LZ) or Fire Support Base, a company commander's hands were full. You could, of course, "outfox" the potheads, and that was a challenging task that kept me busy night and day.

13.4 SPOTTING NARCOTICS ADDICTS

How do you spot narcotics addicts? Besides the dilated pupils, inconsistent attention span, and the level and quality of participation in the design team meetings, look for compromised alertness, erratic behavior, and unwarranted mean-tempered responses to questions. These indicate the use of narcotics.

Then there is the issue of absenteeism as an indicator of narcotics use, manifested by a chronic lateness for work, and a low quality of work. The easiest way I have found to spot a real user is by watching someone who is a good programmer program. I can monitor a programmer working in Honolulu on my networked workstation, and tell that he is "not normal," because of the simple mistakes and errors the individual makes and the rhythm and flow of the work.

I once had to get on a plane, fly out to Hickam AFB, Hawaii, and let a contractor go, all because of his drug use[4]. I also told him that once he dried out in a few months, I'd hire him back, because he was very good, and he had done a very good job for me during the first year on the job. I have schedules to meet, and I don't have the luxury to pay for sloppy work, which then takes complete rewriting by three people so that the deliveries are on schedule and meet the quality control criteria.

13.5   COURAGE AND DYNAMIC ENERGY IN MANAGEMENT

The issues of courage and dynamic energy in management and command hearken back to the leadership issue, but need brief coverage here as well. Managers who are lacking in courage and are afraid to confront people lose time and money. If the product and the funding matter to the company, upper management can always move these people up (and out of the way) to positions of "special assistants" to the staff. In this way, they are far less costly than when they are in positions requiring leadership over four or five people, and obstruct getting the task done.

A good manager's day is rarely done. If the problems inherent in design, production, and testing don't preoccupy his thinking, then it is the settling of disputes between subsystems, between good people, or planning ahead. A manager is always at least six months ahead of the project and people, and thinking and planning even one year into the future. The good manager has the positive leadership trait called *initiative*; he rarely finds himself reacting to conditions he has not anticipated and is always the initiator of action based on the information he receives from his staff and employees.

Management is in some respects the equivalent to what we refer to as leadership in the military. The military call their managers leaders because in addition to their administrative and accounting responsibilities, they lead from the front in combat. This means that they must be prepared to give their lives in the achievement of the tactical objective. This act of leading from the front and paying the ultimate price is a matter of fact, because the concept of self-respect is not lost on the civilian counterpart of the American soldier. Be the individual an engineer or scientist, a programmer or administrator, he will say, "Show me." This really means, "I want to know how much you know, how hard you work, and how much you care for

---

[4] This incident was a painful experience for me, because I not only liked the individual, but I had personally hired him. The dilemma is always the issue between the obligation to the customer who pays for the product, and the obligation to the employee whose welfare is always on a good manager's mind. In this case my deputy and my systems engineer would only have been able to have a good talk with the individual. This was therefore an obligatory trip for me. My systems engineers came with me, to insure that technically I was correct in my assessment of the individual's work. His code was full of errors, and would have caused us serious delays in delivering the system version. This was not an isolated incident. In delivering a system of the size of GDSS, without the traditional documentation in place, to accidentally overlook faulty software could have meant serious cost overruns. The system was delivered, just in time for the massive airlift required by Operation Desert Storm.

the project, for me, for what I do and what I think. If I find that you are interested in what I do and think, and in my product, and take the time, then you'll earn my respect and loyalty. But if you exercise your authority through intimidation,[5] or show a lack of interest or consideration, then I'll do the work I must just to get by, and do it as long as I can, or until you run out of money."

In the military, the commander has recourse to the application of severe discipline under the law, which is called "The Uniform Code of Military Justice," or as it was called in the past, "The Articles of War." A manager doesn't have this kind of authority. So the civilian manager in many ways needs even greater leadership attributes and managerial acumen than his military counterpart.

In order to ensure the achievement of tactical and strategic objectives, the commander is given through the military courts full authority over the individual to obey orders and carry out instructions. Failing that, for reasons of negligence, sloppiness, or outright dereliction of duty, the individual winds up before a court martial, goes to prison if convicted, and could even lose his life. The country, our way of life, and the protection of our democratic institutions demand this type of discipline. In war, the country's future is at stake.

Now take the manager of a project in industry. This individual is appointed to manage an enterprise, and that means that it must be accomplished in such a way as to enhance the reputation of the company or corporation he works for. The responsibility of achieving a high-quality product at a reasonable cost to the customer rests squarely on the manager's shoulders. Not only that, but the corporate profits are equally important, and not just to the organization. People have invested their hard-earned savings in company stock, and often the investors are planning their retirement years on those investments. So the manager is the equivalent of the general in the field, fighting to achieve the objectives of the corporation and the investors. If he cannot manage their projects, the corporation suffers damage or defeat, and goes down the tubes.

Yet, all of the manager's responsibilities are achieved without the help of a set of laws we refer to as military justice. In fact, the manager is severely constrained by civil code, and by the difficulty of firing lazy, uncooperative, and often incompetent employees. The threat of the lawsuit hangs over many a manager's decisions, much like the possibility of a soldier's getting hit by a bullet or by an enemy artillery barrage or air strike, and getting wounded or killed.

For the manager without the recourse of military justice, all project and corporate objectives are achieved by ability alone. Either he has or doesn't have what it takes to attain the achievement of the objective: a quality product, on time, and on budget. This ability is the summation of leadership, experience, academic endeavors, and expertise in the field in which the individual has spent his apprenticeship; it may be as diverse as computer science and software design, accounting and planning. However, it must include communicating, directing, and understanding human beings, and understanding them well. It must include having infinite patience to listen to every subjective well-intentioned argument, based on sound

---

[5] See Chapter 12, on leadership. Subheading: "Personal Struggles."

knowledge, years of experience, or a flash of intuition[6] on the part of a junior engineer who has found a solution to a problem that can save the project a load of time and money. At worst, it can be an argument by a senior engineer intended to mislead for whatever reason; I have seen this and experienced it.[7] I must admit that it took me a long time to accept the fact that people I have trusted and have known over many years will do this.

However, it is a crucial ability to discern right from wrong and to take lessons from all sides through the process of dialectic argument.[8] (I actually prefer to call this process *poly-dialectic* because the process is ideally among the manager and 10 or 12 individuals representing that many knowledge domains.) At any rate, only through such a process can one reach an acceptable reality understood by all to about the same degree. This acceptable reality is a *design object*.

This process requires enormous amounts of physical and mental energy called dynamic energy and is both a leadership and management attribute[9] that forces the logical object to materialize with all the attributes postulated by diverse subjective views. In the manager, dynamic energy as a bottom line means that the individual is physically, mentally, and spiritually strong enough, not only to keep up with every member of the project, but to be ahead of the entire pack and drag them along. Just to motivate a 10-person team is difficult; to motivate 200 or more requires enormous reserves of energy. If you have ever gone home after a day's work and decided that you are too tired to work out, and plopped down on the bed "just until supper," yet didn't wake up until the following morning, then you are aware of dynamic energy, and how your people seem to thrive on your mental and physical resources. By the way, this should rarely happen, because working out in the gym and running a number of miles every day is a good means of dealing effectively with management stress. I increase the mileage and the gym time when the workload stress increases. This was the way I dealt with stress in the Army, too.

13.6   THE TRAVELING MANAGER

The manager who knows his business, and who is concerned with the product and the welfare of the company he works for, spends almost all of the working day managing and leading, for there is little time for travel. Based on my experience of the past 25 years, the following holds true:

The number of frequent-flyer bonus miles on a manager's account is directly proportional to the cost overrun and schedule slip of his project.

You can quote me on this one, because I haven't met a manager yet who can manage effectively from the seat of an aircraft, from a hotel room or gourmet

---

[6] Immanuel Kant: *Kritik der Reiner Vernunft*. "The only irrefutable hypothesis is the human intuition."
[7] See Chapter 5, on Project Control.
[8] Hegel, Georg Wilhelm Friedrich, *Wissenschaft der Logik*, Volume I (The Science of Logic), Felix Meiner Verlag GmbH, 1990 Hamburg Germany.
[9] Eugene E. Jennings. *An Anatomy of Leadership*.

restaurant any more than I have met a commanding officer who did well by managing and commanding from an aircraft. Maybe a theater commander or the commander of a field army can do so, but as a commander or manager close to the work to be accomplished, you must physically be present to get an understanding of the situation. "It is in the nature of things."[10]

The reason you have a deputy or systems engineer is so that he can do your traveling and your interfacing with others. The deputy and systems engineer know as much as, if not more than, the manager on the technical and administrative status of the project. They generally lack only one attribute that the manager has, and that is the power of coercive authority. This authority comes with paying salaries, hiring, and firing. Disputes among headstrong engineers and scientists are not settled easily. The manager, and only he, has the authority to get all the parties together by edict to listen to the arguments. He listens attentively, weighs the technical conflict with the cost and schedule impact in mind, and makes a decision.[11] Failing to resolve lower-level design conflicts or conflicts between subsystems will cause serious impact on a schedule due to delivery dependencies. The manager therefore can travel only if it is an absolute necessity, provided funding and schedule are an issue. So, as the project manager, you send your deputy or systems engineer in your stead. If you don't trust him to say as he sees fit to the corporate stem-winders and to your superiors, you shouldn't have hired him in the first place.

The successful completion of a project requires tireless attention to every detail, and the position of manager cannot be delegated. The manager is the only authority obeyed, even if with resistance at times, because only he has the authority to fire or withhold a salary increase. A systems engineer has only the power to coordinate, and draws his real authority by demonstrated knowledge, commitment, and his ability to persuade.

13.7   THE MANAGER AS ARCHITECT

The manager of a successful project also must be its architect at three critical levels:

- He must be able to visualize the system and the architecture in its completeness, however subjective it is initially.
- He must be able to visualize the organization, all of its components and its members, with the requisite skills that will be required to build such a system. This includes the infrastructure of the parent organization and the contractor organizations.
- He must be able to visualize the process, methodology, and techniques to complete the project successfully.

---

[10] Napoleon Bonaparte
[11] See Chapter 12, on leadership.

In fact, this methodology is very similar to the way Napoleon I handled his adversaries in his campaigns. He knew his project objectives and every nuance of his army, his logistics and his schedule, and he organized to accomplish his objective. He selected and assembled an experienced staff over many years, assembled the resources, selected the methodology appropriate to the situation, and completed the project in a fast and cost-effective manner.[12] This was the Battle of Austerlitz. Later at Waterloo, his old, experienced staff were no longer with him, and his dynamic energy was no longer what it was at Austerlitz, nor were his resources.

There is something to be said for approaching a project in the way one approaches a military campaign. They are very similar even to the point of taking casualties due to carelessness. If the planning is poor, the execution of the plan is worse. There is nothing more stressful to even the finest and most knowledgeable workforce than trying to "make a silk purse out of a sow's ear." A small percentage of people, maybe 15%, will stay late trying to make it work; they will work weekends and late into the night—all while the poor type of manager is traveling to meetings around the country. These dedicated workers have what is called self-respect to do the ultimate good; they will at all costs make their part work, because they are professionals. However, soon their health is affected; they eat too much in the way of fatty foods, like I did, to compensate for the level of stomach acid. Their cholesterol count goes through the roof, and they later die of heart attacks and cancer brought about by the unnecessary stress. Managing high-technology software-intensive computer science projects is tough enough when you are organized; they become nearly impossible when you are not organized and you don't have a solid plan to make use of a proven methodology. The "casualties" become great. Your experienced staff give up after a while, and look for other less stressful jobs that are more rewarding professionally; the less-talented people, however, remain. Replacing people takes time. New people take time to familiarize themselves with the technical design, to get to know how the organization works and how the "rules apply." Productivity slows to a crawl, and the cost overruns soar. Yet, companies, corporations, and even the government agencies, military included, promote and appoint individuals who do not have a track record of accomplishment or experience to go with the position.

13.8   THE PHENOMENON OF DECISION MAKING

Finally, there is the phenomenon often referred to by different names but which manifests itself in a manager's inability to make a decision. If any single fact permeates an organization at the workforce level, it is that the manager can't make a decision. Decision making is one of the key aspects of good leadership and management. See Figure 8.

---

[12] Henry Lachouque, *Napoleon's Campaigns.*

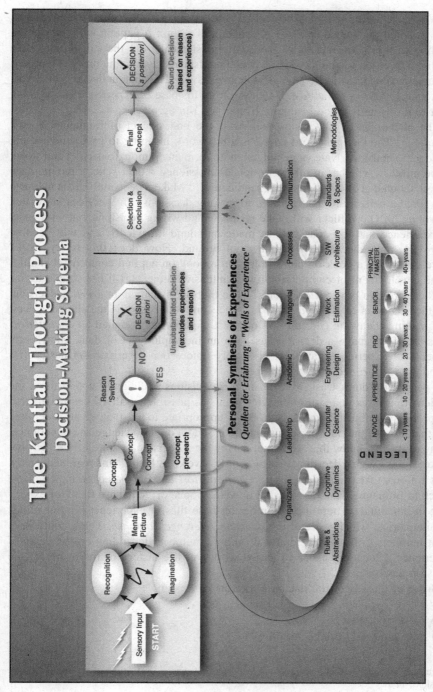

Figure 8. The "phenomenon of decision-making" schema.

183

Why is decision making so critical? It is because it sets the course of the project, such as when the course is set by the captain of a ship. A captain will call out the heading to the helmsman, after the quartermaster calls out the calculations of a heading. To ensure that everyone on deck understands clearly, the order is repeated and acknowledged, with an "Aye, 154 degrees, aye." The captain doesn't run below deck and ask others for advice. He knows from his base of experience and training what to do, if he is a good captain. If not, you run aground.

The phenomenon of decision making is the first subject of Immanuel Kant's critiques.[13] The German word *Urteil* is a big word, meaning to pass sentence on, to judge, to make a private value judgment, to form an opinion, to decide, and so on. In the military, whether in officer or noncommissioned officer school, the message always shouted at and drilled into a candidate is, "Make a decision!" This message is to force a person into getting used to making decisions. The services know that the young NCO or officer will make mistaken and wrong decisions, but with years of experience the decisions will be made on sound knowledge and will become improved, more accurate, and better all around. How does this really work? Since this is not a book on philosophy, but a book on applied cognitive dynamics in the development of computer software-intensive projects, I'll use simple terms.

There are two types of decisions:[14] The first one is called an *a priori* decision, and the second is called an *a posteriori* decision, both based on the subject's decision making. Drawing carefully on our past experiences is called an *a posteriori* decision. If we make a decision based on an incomplete set of data, knowledge, or personal experience database, or simply ignore our experience in haste, it is called an *a priori* decision.

I personally don't trust my *a posteriori* decisions sufficiently not to force the participation of as many different viewpoints as possible, so that I can understand the problem or object better. It is probably appropriate to say that we all accept the fact that most of the time our decisions are based on our knowledge and experience. Many of us also know that we sometimes make a decision in spite of the fact that we know it is a wrong decision; in other words, "we knew better" and regretted it later.

It follows that sound decisions are *a posteriori* and are based on experiences, which to Immanuel Kant are located in wells, pools, or "database files" of experience in our minds. There are a number of these files of experiences in our minds and memories, which we call the *decision reference database*. There could be a great number of these files, almost an infinite number, depending on the years of experience, education, age, and varied work and life history of the owner of the decision database.

Some of these decision database files are, for example:

- Life experience
- Academic discipline/education

---

[13] Immanuel Kant, *Kritik der Urteilskraft* (*ein Kritik des Erkennens*). The Critique of the Ability to Make Decisions. 1790.
[14] Ibid.

- Apprenticeship-acquired technology
- Management
- Administration
- Organization
- Communication
- Leadership
- Architectural design
- Ethics
- Methodologies
- Understanding people
- Work estimation
- Software standards
- Languages
- Cognitive mechanics and philosophy

Now, all of these files are important to the management of a successful project, because they give the project manager the initial reference data set when confronting a problem in need of a solution. The manager-architect can analyze the situation and know with relative certainty where to go to get more information on a subject, and how to assemble all the relevant people to get an even clearer understanding to support his *a posteriori* impression. All solutions are not perfect, nor complete. However, when a problem has been thoroughly examined from as many sides as possible, the object has been enhanced sufficiently enough to provide what I call an *acceptable reality* for a relatively sound decision. Once this has been done, the likelihood of having to backtrack on a faulty design later is minimal. The fewer mistakes we make in our decisions, the lower the cost of the project.

We accumulate our particular experience databases at individual rates, based on the time and effort spent seriously pursuing the acquisition and storage of clean data (sound experiences) in each one of these files. Some of these files are full, such as for example, the academic discipline/education file, when one is a world-class physicist with the degree of Ph.D. and perhaps a Nobel Prize. However, some of the other files, or wells of experience, are only half-full, and some are empty, such as the file on software architectural design, leadership, apprenticeship, management, and administration.

When a decision is made rationally, *a posteriori*, that decision is based on a value judgment formed as a result of the synthesis of all experiences drawn from the individual's experience files. With a little luck, if his files are sufficiently full in all the categories needed for that particular decision, then that decision is an effective one.

The *a priori* decision, however, means that the process of forming a value judgment based on a synthesis of the sum of data in the experience data files has been bypassed. Such a decision is faulty, because it either bypassed the experience files completely, if they exist, or there were insufficient experience files in a number of the categories needed for a sound decision. It could also be true that only a few files were available, and out of these only a small number were sufficiently complete.

I may have suspected in my early life some of the cognitive mechanics that form the underpinnings of decisions, but it took Immanuel Kant to validate my suspicions. The truth is, of course, that we would all like to be perfect in every field. Unfortunately, we are not, nor can we be. The higher one goes in management, the broader the requirement for many experience files in the experience database of the individual. Engineering firms require engineers at the helm, and scientific research organizations require scientists at the helm. Rare are the individuals who can bridge the distance between broad-based knowledge and detailed expertise. There are a very few on the Bell curve; they are in the outer 1.9%, and they are the genius exceptions who have been provided by nature with the added reserves of physical and mental energy to perform at both ends of the scale.

Yet companies appoint the wrong managers and destroy themselves in the process, as managers have immense impact on the success or failure of a company. During recent decades we have seen TWA, Pan Am, and Eastern Air Lines all go down the drain, not to mention other companies of the recent high technology scandals. You can be sure of one thing, it was due to the manager and the management, not the workforce.

The dynamics remain the same, however. In management, as in technology, there is always a solution to every problem, and it takes a good manager to see that a crisis does not occur. The good manager is always on the job and anticipates, much like a good general in the field, watching every move the enemy can make, and looking for indicators of these moves and feigns.

13.9   THE CONCEPT OF "ABILITY"

Next, we come to a concept called *ability*. It is not just a word for one's academic qualifications or the way one presents oneself and one's experiences, or even one's track record, but a combination of all of the above, and more.

Ability is also integrity; it is the sum of all the parts, plus loyalty, intelligence, knowledge, and love of truth. The manager as architect must love the truth. Loving the truth means that in any design there has to be a balanced acceptable reality. The system must encompass the range of postulates of every member of the design team for the object to have sufficient substance to be built cost-effectively. This requires a balancing of the accomplishment of the mission (a quality product, on time and on budget) with the welfare of the workforce (the employees, engineers, scientists, administrators and secretarial staff who make it all happen). Taking care of the employees' welfare (not coddling them, but assuring their meaningful employment) is a full-time job. It is also the hallmark of a successful corporation or enterprise. It is through attentive, dedicated, and success-oriented management that young, talented employees are trained, apprenticed, and guided to higher positions in the organization; these are the ones who make the company strong and competitive. If you train your workforce, again not by coddling, such as with jingoist slogans like the communists and Nazis did, but by good example, with honesty, integrity, and intelligent and professional methodology to perform successfully, you'll have not only a smart workforce, but also a loyal one. In this manner you don't lose your brain trust, those skills that made your company great. Even looking at it from a selfish as opposed to a romantic point of view, you safeguard your retirement, the stocks you have invested in, and you can be proud of the company you work for.

13.10   MANAGER: ADMINISTRATOR OR LEADER?

One of the issues I have pondered for a very long time is just what percentage of management is leadership, what percent is administration, and what percent is accounting.

The most condescending slur in the American engineering world is to refer to a manager as a "bean counter." This is not always fair, or always well-placed because it all depends on the individual person's ability to do the job. Simply because a person happens to be a bean counter doesn't mean that he doesn't have positive leadership attributes or great analytical skills. What in fact happens in management is that it is here that all of the intellectual and mechanical domains that are discussed in this dissertation converge and synthesize.

So, just exactly how do these percentages affect cost and schedule, success and failure?

After the Vietnam War, we had a tendency in the military to use the term "management" more than the terms "command" or "leadership." Leaving the infantry and Special Forces, I went into Psychological Warfare. There I had the intention of learning new skills, such as writing propaganda messages, newspaper editorials, area studies, doing radio and television program preparation, and of course, computer science. It was at Fort Bragg where all of these opportunities presented themselves, at the John F. Kennedy Center for Special Warfare. This was also the place where most of my friends were. All paratroopers and Green Berets have called Ft. Bragg home for a few three-year assignments, whether in the 82nd Airborne Division, one of the units of the XVIII Airborne Corps, or a Special Forces group. Being there as a writer meant undergoing the severe and justified criticism of my editors who were far junior in rank, but infinitely better writers and more qualified than I. This required the learning of humility, not just grammar and composition, and living with abuse from the customer's editors in the offices of the Joint Chiefs of Staff, where many of our products went. If I was to succeed as a writer, I had to shut up and listen and submit to criticism, which was usually justified. However, at times this criticism turned intentionally mean-spirited, typically by those who thought that infantry officers were not a civilized or well-educated group of people, Green Berets especially. This was also the opinion of some of the intelligence officers of the era, who joined the Army and received commissions so as not to get drafted.

Then I was given a computer science project of severely abstracted architectural requirements. In typical fashion, if you want to be a computer science project manager, you had to learn all the necessary skills that your soldiers who are doing the work have. This meant going to school and learning systems engineering, architectures (hardware and software), learning to program in three language modes (assembler, simulation, applications), and writing technical documents day and night, seven days a week, for six months. At that time in the military, you did not manage or command organizations you were not qualified in tactically or technically. It was an extremely difficult thing to do, making the transition from infantry to computer science; it was physically and mentally exhausting, since you were at it from 6:30 A.M. until 10:30 P.M. every day. The only reason you got off at 10:30 is because that is when the computer center closed the window, and you couldn't get the results of your program until 6:30 the next morning. Not only did you have to learn to design and code, but to type also, because you flowcharted, programmed, and punched up the cards. Typing errors were fatal to a program, as they are today, but at least if someone looked over your flowchart and code, written with a No. 2 pencil, they could tell you if you had made a mistake before you punched the cards. Today these controls are gone, and the mistakes are still made.

In the service, being able to compare the newly emerging idea of management, as opposed to command or leadership, was an interesting experience. I thought that perhaps it was the technical work that made management more important than command, and wondered if the services were becoming more and more technology oriented, and what part leadership played in all of it. These were important questions for which my curious mind needed answers, not so much from an academic perspective, but from a professional perspective. As a professional in uniform, I wanted to build a quality system, on a reasonable schedule, and at a reasonable cost.

I was to learn rather quickly that leadership was the major part of management. In fact, I figured management to be around 80% leadership, because you had to motivate people in uniform to do the technical work, to improve themselves technically, and to produce. You cannot order an American soldier to do an outstanding technical job if you can't do it yourself, or "find him out" when he is trying to "get one over on you." American soldiers and fellow citizens are all individualistic; the good ones always challenge their leaders. If you find them out and tell them about it, and have a sense of humor, they respect you for it and do their work, and do it well. But simply ordering them doesn't work very well. Then the remaining 20% of management turns out to be about 10% administrative work: signing papers, going to meetings, taking care of personnel problems, planning work, and coordinating actions. The remaining 10% is accounting, which is looking after the budget and the burn rate of the project, and figuring out how much money you have, and where the problems are in the technical work being done that affect your budget.

The administrator type of manager, unfortunately, is today the norm in software development; this type is the "bean counter." There are many reasons for this. For one, it is a corporate decision to put a "manager" in charge of a project, because the individual has had a string of successes in other management assignments. This is probably the best reason for doing so, but there are also poor reasons for assigning a manager, such as when the individual needs a job, or simply because he is well liked: "He is a nice guy," and "He gets along well with upper management."

These last reasons, currently active on the American software scene, are disastrous to budgets. Americans, whether in or out of uniform, are anarchists at heart. If you don't know more about most things than the employee or soldier under your command, you quickly earn their contempt. They want the involvement of their manager, the genuine interest in their work done for you, not through some intermediate manager or supervisor alone. They will still do their assignments (most of them will, not all), but don't ask them for more work, or quality work. Leaders get that kind of respect, not the guy who goes to meetings and falls asleep at the conference table.

13.11 AUTHORITY, RESPONSIBILITY, AND ACCOUNTABILITY

Authority, responsibility, and accountability are the manager's obligations! Anything short of this is just "playing manager" in the manner that children play office. Why is American business in trouble? Why are companies going bankrupt? Why are workers, white- and blue-collar alike, losing their jobs? It is because we have people at the heads of projects and companies who have no qualifications in the key requirements of management: leadership, organization, communication, and academics.

In American management, there are two sources of authority. One is receiving it as an appointment. The second source of authority is receiving it out of respect and trust from one's peers and colleagues; this is bestowed authority. This is the American way. This is also little understood by most who recently came to this country, and less and less understood by Americans born in this country. I have often been told by some senior people, "Give me the authority and I'll show you how I can do the job." I have tried very hard to explain to these people that in the American workplace it is your peers who raise you up. Unless you have their respect and confidence, the authority you have will not be a contributing factor to a quality product at a reasonable cost. Not on any of my projects will a person rise to the top just because I happen to like him, nor will he be confined to the lower ranks because he happens to disagree with me on almost all points or is a general pain to be around, even if he holds my opinion in contempt for the duration of the project. If the individual is efficient, effective, productive, and intelligent, even if a general pain to have around, I'll promote him, based on contributions he makes to the project. That is the ethical thing to do.

Promotion in an organization where quality and money are important should only be possible based on merit. *Merit!* Think about this terrible word! The entire world of engineering and management is thrown onto its ear by this one nasty little word, merit. Think about American corporate leadership: Where would our economy stand if our leaders were promoted solely on merit?

13.12 THE ISSUE OF CONTEMPT

The issue of contempt is worthy of discussion here, because it is an important phenomenon. I have had a great number of successes in combat operations, peacetime military, and in engineering. There is nothing that impressed me more than an individual who exuded "contempt," provided he was not drunk and not conceited by imaginary personal virtues. The guy who showed contempt always aroused my attention, and thereby made me focus to see if the contempt was justified or not. The phenomenon of contempt in an individual is usually based on an innate belief that he is smarter, more expert, and more capable to do the job others have been made responsible for. They don't cuddle up or "kiss up," as we Americans like to refer to the phenomenon of mirroring. In fact, they are so tired of the incompetence they see that it isn't worth their effort to even make a suggestion. In the military, there is an option a commander has in his toolbox called the Uniform Code of Military Justice. Individuals who exhibit silent contempt are subject to punishment because it infringes on the discipline required in a military unit.

There were occasions when I had to remind an insubordinate young man that he had to be careful, and when I had the time, I'd explain to him the possible consequences for exhibiting contempt of rank and the ramifications under the UCMJ. But, I'd always explain and tell him why he needed to watch himself, and this was always sufficient in my experience. Then, over time, I would watch the individual; usually he would receive greater responsibility, which he would embrace, and volunteer for more. People like this, if one actually takes the time to get to know them, are highly intelligent, aggressive, unselfish, and take on responsibility. They complain little if at all, regardless how tough the assignments are, and take pride in their work. Such people became great individuals, these terrible troublemakers of mine, and in combat they kept our casualties down. On engineering projects, they kept the cost down. The only problem for a manager is to tolerate them initially, to get to know them, and then put them into positions where they are the most effective.

It is a sorry manager who cannot tolerate people who are talented but whom he doesn't happen to like. In such cases, the manager, no matter how high in an organization, has a low self-esteem, is unsure of himself, and is insecure in his position, which he probably achieved in a "Princely"[15] fashion, as opposed to achieving the position through merit. A manager who has achieved through merit is self-confident, comfortable in his position, and generous to a fault with the great and contemptuous individuals in his organization. Such a manager welcomes criticism, because he knows his limitations and relies on brutal honesty, at times, from his subordinates to keep a handle on his projects or corporation.

Authority then, once you have it and are able to exercise it, is always available when push comes to shove. But, what one must never forget is that the responsibility for performance, success, and failure go to the manager, and the manager alone. The manager who points a finger and says, "It's not my fault—the contractor failed to deliver the subsystem!" doesn't belong in management, but in something less responsible. A company's greatest assets are its managers and leaders, nurtured carefully from its pool of employees. They are the ones who ensure the continued

[15] Machiavelli, Niccolo. *The Prince*. See also Chapter 8.

viability of the company, by managing systems that are of quality, and keeping the customers happy and coming back for more.

13.13 MANAGEMENT: THE FULCRUM OF PROJECT EXECUTION

Management, regardless of how you slice it up among leadership, administration, and bean counting, is the fulcrum of project execution. It is the mix of the ability and energy of the manager that makes something happen or fail to happen, that makes it profitable for the client or expensive, with the cost being difficult to recover. There are many great books on management, and I'm not going to quote from these; each stands on its own merits.

I look at management with fascination as opposed to ambition. My interest was not to climb to the top, but to do some very difficult work in software development, some very large in scope, and try to implement cutting edge (or beyond) technology on very short schedules, and with very limited and *a priori* agreed-to budgets. These projects are more like puzzles to me than jobs. They were real-life management equivalents of puzzles, like jigsaw puzzles, where an expertise and intuitive understanding of leadership, accounting, and administration are in harmony with one's ability in understanding the nature of computer science, the underlying philosophy. This includes understanding the development of architectures, the selection of standards, methodologies, and of the organization required to do the work.

I wanted to experiment and try out new approaches, while still being required to deliver a system and be accountable and responsible for a serious and important technical product.

Everything in management interested me, such as the workings of the organization and the mistakes made in hiring or placing a person into the wrong job. If misplaced in an organization, even a highly qualified and great performing individual can cause extensive damage to a budget and schedule.

Everything in the context of this book is motivated by the issues of budget and schedule. If these are unimportant, this book does not apply. Take the time to watch how people under immense pressure and stress behave, think, decide, and act. You will see that the ones who are motivated are driven by a desire to excel technically. This is true of engineers, administrators, and even bean counters proud of their professional selves and the work they accomplish to earn their salaries.

13.14 THE ASCENDANCE OF MEDIOCRITY

On the other hand, there are those who do an outstanding job in faking their work; they produce nothing, and have no qualms about "pulling one over on the boss" and bragging about it. This is the undermining of projects without reason;

it demoralizes the workforce and presents many problems in the path of the manager who cares to finish the job. The manager must understand the motivation of people to do what they do, and must know how to motivate them to do a better job through constant teaching and supervision. The successful and profitable design team meeting in reality is a classroom where the manager-architect teaches the system and holds spot quizzes to see if he is getting through. These on-going sessions do not take place in a hostile environment, but in a truly academic atmosphere of frank, open discussions, with leadership and discipline provided by the manager as architect and teacher. To be a project or corporate manager and not to know what is going on in the corporation is a tragedy to the stockholders and the customers of the project.

One is appointed to positions of high responsibility because one is expected to be on top of everything! Period.

If there is one glaring reason for the failure of great companies, it is the mistake made in this regard: appearance versus ability. It has long been noted that in modern industrial society, "leadership (management) would not be founded on sincerity and superior ability, and that form and not substance will prevail."[16] John Stuart Mill also was convinced that in the future (i.e., our time today), mediocrity would ascend to high leadership and management positions. Indeed, mediocrity, as he had predicted, has become fashionable in industry. We have reduced the selection of managers to a set of "scientific" rules; on the top of the qualifications is "being a nice guy."

Indeed, one of the first things that is asked is, "Is he a nice person?" I know so many "nice guys" in management who never tell a person to "buzz off" (in so many words) when told an opinion or that their design is flawed or that they are wasting funds and time. What they do is go behind the scenes and tell your decision makers not to promote so and so because "he is not a nice person," or "he won't be a good fit on the board of governors," or "he uses off-color language." Shame on this attitude, but this is the attitude that currently prevails, and jobs are going overseas.

To many managers I have known, management means only having a big office with executive furniture, a secretary, and plenty of frequent flyer bonuses. I am dead serious. I have met this manager type in the Army, the Navy, the Air Force, and at GE, TRW, CSC, Hughes Aircraft, in NASA and DOE, and almost every other place I have consulted or worked. The many truly dedicated lower-level managers and staff bring their systems to a successful conclusion by working day and night, carrying 80% of the workload, while the remaining 80% of the staff do 20% of the workload, and slum it. Some of our managers are so utterly lacking in ability that one wonders how in the world they got to head up large projects and companies. Why ask the young engineers? Why and how they succeed in getting into these positions of influence is partially covered in Chapter 12, on leadership.

Good, efficient, cost-effective management is clearly the most difficult of all jobs and professions. It requires intelligence, motivation, education, apprenticeship,

---

[16] Eugene E. Jennings. *An Anatomy of Leadership*. McGraw-Hill Book Company, 1960, New York.

experience, integrity, energy, and a good track record acquired over a long period of time. Yet, people are often appointed without any of these qualifications. There are people who fail constantly at doing a good job and yet rocket to the top. One of the examples I like to use for my design team lectures is the great career of Robert S. McNamara. He built the doomed Edsel for Ford, then for the Air Force and Navy he built the very problematic F-111. Then he got us into Vietnam, knowing, as he said recently, that "we couldn't win" (we could have, of course). And then he became head of the World Bank after which the U.S. dollar went down the tubes. No small wonder, considering his lifelong string of failures. I'm sure that he would have made a great professor, and has an equally great mind. He lacked only managerial acumen and leadership skills.

Management in computer science and related projects, such as software systems, is more difficult than managing the development of a new model of an automobile or the aeronautical design of an aircraft because software is an abstraction of a portion of the human thought system. It is part of the thought system that you are trying to replicate. This is like the mental process of calculating the mathematics of pointing an antenna at a spacecraft 800 million miles away for the transmission of commands, and then moving and pointing the antenna to the correct azimuth for the spacecraft to be able to receive the commands. All of this is a purely mental activity translated into code. For the manager-architect, it is imperative to be able to visualize in software terms what the overall design is to look like, what the mathematical equations are to represent, and then to write the job descriptions with the required qualifications for each position to be filled. The selection of the mathematician with the correct skills (such as applied and theoretical mathematics, great communication, energy, commitment, and the ability to work as a team) is crucial if you are to maintain a budget and schedule.

13.15   THE PITFALLS OF STAFFING UP

Many years ago, back around 1982, a dear friend and I had developed a concept for a very large-scale war gaming system for the Department of the Army. Dr. Joseph P. Fearey had built our Deep Space Tracking station in Madrid, Spain, and developed the first orbit determination algorithm at JPL; now he wanted something new to do, something different. I had finished my job as the General Science Data team chief on the Voyager Project with the wonderful and exciting Jupiter encounters, and wanted to try something different also. Joe was and is the genius of the mechanics of game theory because he has a doctorate of philosophy in economics. I was the systems architect, largely because I had a very broad military background, with three years of combat experience. We went on a pilgrimage to visit Dr. Martin Schubic at Yale, who is an economist and was the guru of game theory of that age. We wanted his opinion on our idea and hoped for his blessing on our concept for an interactive, event-driven military simulation. Much to our delight, Schubic thought that we were on the right track, and in fact said that conceptually we were about four years ahead of the pack in military simulation and gaming theory. This effort turned out to become the Joint Theater Level Simulation (JTLS),[17] and I understand that it is still in use, by the sponsor.

Now came the hard part. We needed mathematicians at the doctorate level with experience in game theory. I ran a bunch of ads in the papers, and had some responses, but still had three positions I couldn't fill. There were two guys at 29 Palms whom we wanted, but they had nice homes and big yards, and the area around JPL, La Cañada Flintridge, was too expensive. As is my habit when I'm staffing up, I take home about 100 or 200 résumés and read through them casually in the quiet of my den. Then I select 10 to call. Out of the 10, I'll fly out two or three for an interview. Using this approach, I found what appeared to be a great résumé. The individual had his Ph.D. in mathematics, and in number theory at that; that is what Joe said he needed. The degree was from the Technical University in Basel, Switzerland. "Hot dog!" I thought. "That's where Freddie Nietzsche taught classical Latin and Greek." I had a real find; I was a genius at finding great talent. I was very excited. He was an American, so security clearance wouldn't be a problem. I set up an interview and looked forward to meeting a very special person. I was also in great need. The project was somewhat behind schedule because we were short of mathematicians.

Then came the momentous day. He had set the time for 3:30 in the afternoon. At the time, I had not thought it significant that he wanted to meet during the hot, lazy hours of the afternoon. I picked him up at the reception center, and we were walking over to my office. He certainly was everything I had hoped for: articulate, well groomed, in a three-piece suit, and had super intelligence. As we walked to my office, I told him about the great opportunities we had at JPL. I showed him the Galileo spacecraft from the viewing area of the spacecraft assembly facility (SAF), and told him that this place, JPL, was the most exciting place to be on the planet, and that after a while he could have his pick of exciting and challenging work on the Laboratory. In the process, just out of curiosity, I asked him which language he had done his doctoral work in at Basel: German or French. He answered that he had done it in German, so I enthusiastically switched to speaking in German. I rattled off that I really liked German as a language, and that I really preferred it over French or English as a technical tool for learning, and that most of my reference books were German books. He responded with a *Ja!* and *Ja!* to everything I said. To my consternation, I realized that he didn't speak a word of German! By the time we got to my office, I was embarrassed, while he was totally cool and casual. Joe was not around to help me with the interview, so I gave him a partial differential equation and asked him to solve it for me on my blackboard. Well it turned out that I knew more algebra than he did, and I'm no mathematician. Meanwhile he was totally unflappable, so I had to tell him that I regretted to say that I had made a mistake, and escorted him back to the reception center. I do hate to say it, but had I not gotten into the issue of languages, and since it was a hot 4:00 P.M. by the time the interview started, I might have just let his résumé and diploma speak and instead talked about trivia and how great our retirement benefits and our dental plans were. Wow! I would have hired him.

---

[17] See Chapter 10.

I also have to say that the previous experience is only a small portion of the répertoire of lessons I have learned in staffing up a project. Some of the experiences in the Army were worse, and very relevant. The most important work of a manager is to select and staff up with personnel who are fully qualified for the positions they are to fill. The academic qualifications are rarely avoidable; if it calls for a Ph.D., MS, or BS/BA in mathematics, molecular biology, chemical engineering, or computer science, then that is what you need. Generally, the doctorate, when under three years of experience, belongs to the hands-on implementation of mathematical algorithms and their proofs. However, in a project the ability to communicate well, to interact well with a team, and timeliness to work (which means commitment) are almost equally important. Never select people because you like them, their attitude, their outward appearance, or above all someone who is pleasing. Write down each academic and technical qualification, along with the experience required, over how many completed tasks and projects, in terms of lines of code, modules, languages, and the documentation. Look at the examples of each. Be sure that there are no more than two incomplete tasks or projects in a career, especially not when their participation in the workforce is under 10 years. The inability or unwillingness to start a piece of work and stick with it until completion indicates a lack of stability.

Never staff up faster than what you need to work a phase of a specific task, especially during the requirements and design phases. From the beginning of selection onto a project, a person must know what his job is, what the performance expectations are, whom to see for input material data or instruction, when the product will be required, and by whom. In software, unlike in electrical or mechanical engineering, a personal schedule is rarely necessary, because it is too time consuming to maintain.

13.16 SALARY ISSUES

The salaries of experienced personnel vs. those of novices is an interesting issue and a phenomenon of the subjective impressions others have about production and personnel. I am often criticized by colleagues who tell me that my staff cost much more than theirs, which is true. However, my software production is far higher than anywhere I have checked, based on the telephone calls I get from defense project managers, and from companies that in the past have invited me to consult on the particular issue of low-cost software, high production, and quality production on the cutting edge. How do I do it? I have arrived at the conclusion that a highly proficient team has three times the productivity of one that is not as expert. This has many additional bonus factors, besides being small and efficient. It enables me to hire a few select junior engineers or administrators and apprentice them to the senior experienced ones. It also gives me the time to supervise and teach them. I don't have to teach them how to program; it is assumed (and hoped) that they received that skill at their universities. It is their senior programmer/senior design engineers who teach them how to design sound modules, teach them their domain (e.g., telemetry processing), teach them how to write well in technical English, and what standards we use and why they are important. So, I don't just hire an expensive programmer, I also have in him a teacher, a designer, and a number of potential software wizards all at a reasonable cost. We also have time to cross-train the various SDEs and SPs on other data sets. Certainly the cost of completing a system at $20 per line of code, with salaries ranging from $45 to $85 an hour, is worth more than paying $35 to $40 for programmers and paying $750 or more per line of code, which is the going rate for both DOD and NASA for spacecraft ground systems.

There is also an observation I have made over the years, and it is that many engineers and managers, for a variety of reasons, prefer to hire younger and less experienced people. One reason for this is that they feel more secure that they know more than the hiree, and therefore have a knowledge clout over the new young employee and can intimidate him with knowledge and experience. The other reason is that people are usually insecure in their positions, and need to have less experienced employees under them. This is not much of a problem in electrical and mechanical engineering, or in structural dynamics, and so on, but it is in software. Our technology has a cyclic turnover rate of about four years, and the only technical inheritance from one project to the next is the system architecture portion that we call Common Software Services, and the methodology used. The platforms, languages, and operating systems tend to change every four years or so.

Then there is the issue of apprenticeship in salaries. In most engineering disciplines, in particular computer software, it is not the level of the academic degree that is paramount, but the years of experience of the individual. In fact, my experience shows that the higher the academic degree, the more narrow and highly specialized the worker. Ph.D.s as a rule in my organizations are the "knowledge workers"—the highly specialized designers of complex, intricate software routines and device drivers. They require years of apprenticeship to qualify into leading positions, which they are not used to. I have also found that some of my best computer software designers have had no academic degree at all, and it hurt them in their ability to get a good salary at JPL where, because of our engineering orientation and association to Caltech, we are very much focused on academic pedigree.

13.17   CONTRACTING OUT WORK

Contracting out work in software-intensive systems is a reasonable thing to do; I have done it almost my entire career, both in and out of the service. There is much that is important about contracting out work that has bothered me over the years, as the contracts affect cost.

One can use individual contractors to augment the workforce or design team, in which case they are full-time working personnel participating in the work as though they were employees. This is my general approach to software implementation.

However, one can also contract out the entire work to software companies, and leave the implementation to the company that gets the award. This is the approach that makes it so expensive in this country to build software that the jobs are going overseas. The entire process is flawed. This process is almost so bad as to give the impression of an urge on part of DOD to squander funds, because funds are not to be taken seriously. This is a nightmare to anyone who has any level of conscience about the responsibility of handling public funds. The sign over the door of the project manager should read: *WELCOME TO SOFTWARE HELL!*

13.18 EVALUATING PROPOSALS

I first encountered the process of evaluating proposals from industry while at SHAPE in Belgium. When DOD or any government organization goes out for a Request For Bid (RFB), it is almost always poorly written. The structure of the document does not lend itself to proper expansion to the DOD standard compliant format for requirements and design documentation. The document mixes science, engineering, and organizational and management functions to an incredibly confusing degree. This makes it nearly impossible to understand, and makes the preparation of a proposal difficult. On top of that, the language it is written in is wanting. Even if written by individuals with a native fluency in English, it is in usage poor, inconsistent, and vague. Now, if the equivalent approach to a legal brief were to be used in a case to be tried in a court of law, it would never be accepted; it would have a disastrous consequence. Yet, we are talking about documents that represent hundreds of million dollars in value. Why then the negligence in the preparation of a proposal that could cost the American or NATO taxpayer so much money, and even lead to litigation that has no chance of winning and no chance of recovering the spent funds? I have seen so many poorly written requests for proposals and bids that I am not surprised that almost all budgets are overrun.

There are several solutions to this problem, and I use them whenever I can. The most important thing for a Request For Proposal (RFP) is that it be prepared with precision, in compliance with a standard. After this, my team and I prepare the Functional Requirements Document (FRD) and Software Requirements Document (SRD). These go into the RFP, and while the RFP is being responded to, we independently prepare the Software Design Document (SDD-1) and a Work Implementation Plan (WIP). When the bids come in, we can evaluate them as to our best professional estimate in rational schedule and cost. Low-balling and high-balling are excluded. It is also we who prepare the Software Test Plan (STP), which is based on the SRD, and is the only way the sponsor can certify that he has received what has been asked for and paid for. Moreover, if the contractor fails to be on schedule and budget, I can recover the system and complete it myself.

It is essential to remember that the only reason for a company to have an information systems division (computer science/information technology), whatever its mission (building aircraft, satellites, engines), is to make it easier for the company to do its business effectively. The information systems division has a limited number of expert and experienced computer scientists. They are there to ensure that all of the divisions and organizations within the parent company are fully supported with qualified people, and that the software they are provided is first rate and meets all of their requirements. In a corporation that makes its living by producing aircraft engines, the design, manufacturing, and testing organizations rely on the computer science engineers to ensure that their needs are fully met, so they can concentrate on the mechanical engineering, metallurgy, propulsion, and structural aspects of the jobs.

An Information Systems Division (ISD) is important to any organization where computer science and software development play a significant role. It is the ISD that prepares the user requirements, the detailed software requirements, design documentation, and interface specifications among the systems, if any. This package is then offered up for a competitive bid in the marketplace. Why not do the implementation internally? It can be implemented internally, of course, and in an emergency it should be, but there are a number of arguments against it. My biggest argument is that software implementing contractors are much more numerous, available, and better programmers and much more current than those who are employees of large corporations. Independent contractors who make their living designing and writing programs depend on producing a quality software product for their income. (There are exceptions to this rule, and I cover these dangerous exceptions in other parts of this book in detail.) Therefore, contractors are like "fast guns for hire." They may cost a lot, but the job gets done and they move on. They must keep current with the latest technology and latest tools and COTS packages in order to ensure that their reputation remains above reproach. They are hired based on their performance and reputation. There is among serious software managers and software engineers a "communications network" based on reputation, expertise, and reliability. This network runs on trust and professional pride. When you need good people, you call your friends nationwide; among the top guns, almost everyone knows everyone, or knows somebody who does.

So, a company building aircraft engines does not need computer scientists who do the things they normally do, but who do the things that the company needs them to do. This means that while they keep current professionally, they also do more of the requirements, design, and testing, ergo quality control for their company, rather than just sling code. Once a bid package is out for the RFP, they keep busy by preparing a test plan based on the software requirements document, and an internal work implementation plan. This has many benefits, because it is done in isolation, and when the proposals come in with the bids, the implementation plan of the bidders can be compared to the one prepared internally. This methodology will immediately identify which bid is rational and which is not.

13.19   COST BIDDING TOO EARLY

Years ago, I used an internal Work Implementation Plan for a DOD sponsor who unfortunately did not understand, and would not understand, DOD-STD-2167A. After the contract was awarded and published, by sheer coincidence I attended a meeting together with the proposal managers of two of the three bidding companies. The two managers had known me from my assignment at SHAPE in Belgium. They knew that I had prepared the requirements, the architectural design, and the interfaces; they also knew my habit from the military that I prepared a Work Implementation Plan and figured the cost of the system to within ±10%. After the meetings of the day were over, when they were about to depart, they couldn't help but ask me what I had estimated the system at, and said that if I told them, they'd tell me how much their companies had bid. I was intrigued for many reasons. For one, I wanted to know how close our estimates had been, and they, being professionals, also wanted the information. Secondly, as a JPL designer and manager, this was an opportunity for me to see how close industry was to estimating true software costs.

We agreed to write down two items of information on pieces of paper and put them into a cup. The two items of information were (1) total cost in dollars, and (2) total development time in calendar months. Mind you, these guys were serious professionals; one represented one of the largest American aircraft companies, and the other, one of the largest software and hardware contractors in industry. The result of our little exercise was not only impressive, but encouraging. My estimate after completing the requirements and design was $62.5 million, with a development time of 6 years. The other two estimates were $64 million, and $67 million. I can't recall the schedule of either, but they were close, perhaps 8 to 12 months more than mine. Yet, the contract that the DOD agency awarded had been announced in the papers at just $16.7 million; those two guys were miffed, to say the least.

We talked about the difference for some time over coffee and donuts. The conclusion was, of course, that the winning company couldn't complete the system on that schedule and on that budget, especially with the management that was in place at the sponsoring agency. In fact, the system was never completed, and the contractor ended up suing the sponsor for mismanagement. For me it was a big lesson learned. It showed that most bidders are honest, hard working folk, who are proud of their products and are willing to put forth a true best effort. It also showed that when going out on a bid, you must have completed the FRD, SRD, SDD, and SISD before you can determine what your budget is. If you need the system, prepare these documents professionally. Then, if the budget doesn't stretch, descope your requirements and design by 10%. It is up to the successful bidder whether his people want to work as cost-effectively as we do, and have a greater profit margin, or to try to complete the project at the pace they select as being suitable for their workforce.

14 Four Case Studies of Low-Cost Systems

For those who have managed or designed and participated in the development of software systems, it is nothing new to say that each system is unique, as each one carries with it its own special problems. For those who are young software professionals and computer scientists starting out on their careers, it is important to understand the pitfalls and inhibitors to low-cost development and how to deal with them. In fact, it is important to have at least an idea why things don't get done. No one told me when I started out in computer science what to expect from the workplace environment, from the sponsor, or from colleagues and subordinates. It would have been easier for me to have known beforehand.

I have added this chapter with the intention of sharing with the reader information elements that are generally only found in military "after-action" reports. As mentioned in Chapter 4, an after-action report is a detailed description of what went right and what went wrong in an exercise (FTX/CPX) or combat action. It highlights interesting items, incidents, and activities that went according to plan and those that did not. These after-action reports are the tools that provide the participants of an exercise or combat operations the insight into events that are overlooked in the heat of actually participating in an event. The presentation of an after-action report is to be as objective as possible. What is important, however, is that it is through the after-action report that the analysis starts in the mind and forms the formalized template or hypothesis in the database of the mind. It increases the information in the files Immanuel Kant refers to as "wells of experience," and provides the foundations for decisions, both *a priori* and *a posteriori*, for future events. This exercise of information sharing is also the partial template that is the foundation of methodology in the toolbox of great engineers and scientists. Unforeseen events are dealt with by referring to a number of similar experiences in the past, whereas the process of inferring solutions to new problems and applying them effectively is called creativity.

I didn't start collecting data on systems development until the JTLS project, and these have survived only in summaries. As I started to build GDSS, I was more aware of the need to keep a good record of events and technical problems so I

The Cognitive Dynamics of Computer Science: Cost-Effective Large Scale Software Development,
by Szabolcs Michael de Gyurky
Copyright © 2006 by John Wiley & Sons, Inc.

wouldn't make the same mistakes twice. This of course proved to be very valuable, because I found that even if I didn't make the same mistakes twice, I made other mistakes to replace the ones I had avoided. Thus, it is my conclusion that the manager-architect who makes the fewest mistakes will be the one whose software quality is highest and whose product is cheapest. There are no perfect managers, engineers, or developers.

There are many reasons for overrunning a budget, slipping a schedule, and having many bugs in one's software releases. The main reason of course is the relative expertise of the manager-architect, which includes lack of experience, dynamic energy, a work ethic, and the lack of positive leadership attributes. The other inhibitors are the lack of understanding and experience on the part of the sponsor or customer, and interference in the work process on the part of peer groups and "stakeholders," as well as subordinates and employees. The poor approach to systems engineering and the interference with and outmaneuvering of the manager are not always badly motivated or done with malice; they are often the result of a mental limitation. All brains are not programmed the same way, nor have the same databases or well-developed reason as others. There are very intelligent, well-intentioned people who lack expertise in certain fields who try to force their will on a methodology. A design and implementation organization that is not appropriate can cause great harm in terms of budget, schedule, and product quality. These people can pose enormous problems to getting the job done.

For example, back in 1968 in Vietnam I was engaged in the only really terrible ambush I have ever been caught in. I and my platoon were so busy fighting that I had not even been aware that my reserve platoon, which I had hidden in a dry gully, had been pulled out and airlifted by my commanding officer, my own brigade commander. He was flying in his command helicopter over my position at about 3,000 feet, looking at the battle below. I was surrounded, and with all the gunfire, artillery, and close air support noise, I was unaware of the airlift HU1-Es coming in behind my back and airlifting out my reserve platoon. He was playing company commander, and put them down in another surprisingly devastating ambush of a large North Vietnamese unit, well entrenched just for that purpose. Unaware of this, I called my reserve platoon, because I needed their help to reinforce the platoon I was with, and they were not where I thought they were. Now the platoon leader of my reserve platoon was asking for help, and he and his men were in trouble about a mile away from where I was, separated by jungle and a wide river, totally out of my reach to help them in any way. It was a terrible two days.

Clearly, my commanding officer did not have the intention of endangering me or my men. He was just a man of limited ability, an engineer type, managing and trying out some ill-conceived hypothesis from his perch at 3,000 feet. His hypothesis turned out to be wrong, an *a priori* decision that was as wrong as Arthur Schopenhauer predicted *a priori* decisions to be, for he and his staff nearly got me and my men wiped out. This doesn't mean that his intentions were not good; he just was not an expert in his field. He had been in the Corps of Engineers and had made a branch transfer to the Infantry to be able to make general.

So keep in mind that just because a project manager is inept, and just because corporate management interferes with negative impact on your work, they are not always trying to keep you from getting your job done. They may simply be well-intentioned morons, who kissed their way to the top.

So here are four case studies of systems that I managed, from start to completion. Each could have a 300-page book written on it, but I present only the highlights for the purpose of reinforcing the other chapters in this book.

A note is in order here. The following four case studies necessarily involve many technical issues particular to the software trade. Some of these issues are discussed at length. The reader who is not interested in such details may safely skip over them without loss of understanding.

14.1 CASE STUDY ONE: THE JOINT THEATER LEVEL SIMULATION (JTLS)

The Joint Theater Level Simulation (JTLS) is a NASA equivalent Class C system, developed on a short schedule as a proof of concept system for the support of Theater Level Command Post Exercises (CPX) and Field Training Exercises (FTX). JTLS supplemented the FTX with realistic data supplements to aid in the training of Theater and Army staffs in the performance of their staff duty assignments in time of war. Additionally, it was designed to permit the Theater and Army staffs to gain insight into strategic realities and operational trends in a fluid combat environment, both as a learning tool and as a planning tool.

Software Development Standard: None used. The system was the first of its kind, and the sponsoring organizations had no one who understood DOD-STD-2167A at that time.

Documentation: Nonstandard. Little time was available to field the system, with the immediate involvement of numerous "stakeholders." All architectural design documents were discarded because of the lack of customer familiarity with computers (a typical problem with armed forces personnel at the time). We designed a Functional Design Document (FDD) and a User Analyst Guide (AG), done by Dr. Joseph P. Fearey. The system was a proof of concept where the tactical and technical expertise was at JPL. The documentation totaled approximately 5,000 pages.

System Size: Approximately 120,000 source lines of code, 180,000 total lines of commented code.

Languages: SIMSCRIPT II.5, the C programming language, and INGRES.

Total Cost: $7,800,000.

Cost/Line of Code: $43.35 per commented line of code.

System Description: JTLS was a "first of its kind" attempt to use computers to transliterate realistic combat events at the war theater level into useful and understandable information, for the use of staff officers and commanders. This was done as a proof of concept. It started on a DEC VAX 11-780 and 8600 running VMS 4.1, and used VT-100 and VT-220 text terminals and Graphover 9500 graphics display terminals.

Note: As in all first of the kind prototypes, neither Dr. Joe Fearey nor I had the foggiest idea of how many "stakeholders" and nonperforming government agencies (well-funded agencies, without producing a product) there were in the "theater of operations" we had entered. These descended on us like a squadron of dive-bombers from the carrier *Kaga* on the Yorktown at Midway. We had to work at a rate fast enough to deliver before they sank us for the same simple philosophical reason and phenomenon that Napoleon used so often: "A glutton will defend his dinner like a hero!"

In the end, with the help of great contractors, JPLers, and consultants like Col. Trevor Dupuy of treasured memory, we delivered. The system is, as far as I'm aware, still in use by the Pentagon, but not for its intended purpose. It was designed for theater warfare, as a staff exercise tool in support of the FTX, and not to detail combat events at corps or division.

However, it served its purpose in proving that combat operations, planning, and execution can be modeled effectively, and if well used can save lives and money. This of course takes the human at his best. When people don't use tools as intended, then it produces the wrong results.

The Joint Theater Level Simulation[1] was something that I had wanted to design and implement from the time I was serving in Vietnam. The concept (or *Begriff*, as the Kantian definition is more precise) started to take on substance while serving on the war planning staff at CINCLANT. It then took on the final object architecture in my mind during my three years at SHAPE. However, it was my experience on the Voyager Project at JPL that rounded out the concept of a war game. In particular, it was the way we used simulations like the command simulator (COMSIM) and sequence generation (SEQGEN) that synthesized with my experience at SHAPE and enriched the vision into a doable concept. I envisioned it as a driver for our large and very important Command Post Exercises of WINTEX and Able Archer.[2]

---

[1] *The Joint Theater Level Simulation*. JPL Highlights 1985. Jet Propulsion Laboratory, California Institute of Technology. Page 56 by S. Mike de Gyurky.

[2] WINTEX and Able Archer were the two major Tactical and Strategic Field Training Exercises (FTX), and Command Post Exercises (CPX) of NATO's operations plan for the defense of Western (Allied) Europe against the Soviet Union and the Warsaw Pact. They were held annually and cost huge resources in the displacement of personnel and the preparation of manually generated exercise scenarios. These two FTX/CPX included countless military units from all NATO countries except France. They included all of the military headquarters from Supreme Headquarters Allied Command Europe (SHAPE) down to divisional levels, spanning from CINCLANT (Commander in Chief Atlantic) in Norfolk, VA, to CINCMED (Commander in Chief, Mediterranean Sea) in Naples, Italy, to Eastern Anatolia, and the North Cape. The preparation for and the execution of such a large military exercise cost huge resources in time and money. At the time I was assigned as Staff Officer for Command and Control Systems, to Colonel Joseph Bullers USAF (1976–1979), I had the additional duty of conducting the situation briefings to the SACEUR (Supreme Allied Commander Europe) and the NATO Secretary General.

In doing the requirements for and the design of the Allied Command Europe (ACE) Command, Control and Information System Architecture, I became very familiar with the physical system (manually used), the information handling, the data contents, and their use. I started to think about it, and developed in my head a concept for building a computer simulation to drive the FTX and CPX automatically and provide the participating staffs with realistic information and environment.

My initial vision, or as Kant and Schopenhauer term it, *Anschauung*, was substantially different from what it finally turned out to be. There were several reasons for this.

I was too new to JPL to have a sufficiently large "wheelbase" (political pull, coercive power, authority) to exercise the kind of control I needed; later on I would have the approach to the detailed design, the development process, and the methodology for building the system. But this lack of authority also had a positive side, because there was a most important object lesson for me to learn that otherwise would have eluded me. It was one of the most important lessons for me in my three decades of designing and building software-intensive systems.

This lesson became the most important driving force toward developing the common software services (CSS) layer. The lesson was learned on JTLS and implemented for the first time with GDSS, which immediately followed the completion of JTLS. The lesson learned was brought to its full sophistication much later on the Jason 1 Satellite Telemetry, Command, and Communications Subsystem in 2001.

This most important design lesson that I learned is the importance of modularity and layering of the software architecture. The technical term for this software is Common Software Services.

14.1.1 The Beginnings of JTLS

After completing my assignment as Team Chief of the Voyager General Science Data Team on the Voyager project in 1982, Dr. Joe Fearey and I wrote up a concept of operations (CONOPS) for a military exercise support system. We found a supporter of this concept here at JPL at the Assistant Laboratory Directorate level. At the time, we at JPL liked to do work on military programs. One reason was that JPL had started its existence as an Army ordnance laboratory before NASA came into being. Second, we experiment, develop, learn, and integrate many new technologies on defense programs, which we later use on flight projects. After a technology proved effective on a class B subsystem,[3] it was then adopted into our flight projects as proven technology. We also have an opportunity to push the technical envelope to the limit, which we cannot do freely on a flight project, because of the risk factor involved.

Once we complete a DOD project, and deliver the product, we do not maintain it. Upon delivery of the system to the customer, the customer turns it over to a contractor of their preference and we at JPL move on to other, one of a kind projects.

I traveled around with Dr. Fearey, looking for someone interested in developing a war gaming system. We found a sponsor at U.S. Readiness Command (now CENTCOM) at MacDill AFB in Florida. After completion, it was very well received and adopted by the Joint Analysis Directorate (JAD) of the Office of the Joint Chiefs of

---

[3] Class A systems are segments, the loss of which will have catastrophic consequences or result in the loss of a spacecraft.

Class B systems are segments, the loss of which will not have tragic consequences to a project or result in the loss of a spacecraft.

Class C systems are those systems that can be recovered and corrected, and then reset or placed back into duty.

Staff (OJCS) as the standard gaming system for joint and specified commands for the analysis of theater-level plans. JTLS was the first major piece of gaming software to become a part of the OJCS's Modern Aids to Planning Program (MAPP).

Insight and *understanding* are not only philosophical terms, they are key concepts to event-driven interactive systems. Through the use of such systems as JTLS, a military staff can get a better understanding of the soundness of a military plan. Using a spacecraft and operations simulator, we can gain a better understanding of the status of new software before we uplink it to the spacecraft during cruise, prior to a planetary encounter.

Architecturally, JTLS was designed to provide its users with an environmental realism (user interface) similar to those encountered at the theater-level battle staffs of that period, where few, if any, staff officers of the combat arms were computer-literate.[4] JTLS requires a minimum of three players: a Game Controller, a Red Team Commander, and a Blue Team Commander. The only computer users were located at workstation terminals, VT100s, at the Controller's Team; these we called Systems Terminals. The messages to the Red and Blue teams to and from the combat forces simulated by the computer were provided through the Controller. Since the workload was very heavy, due to the message traffic from ground and air units, and could overwhelm players at high game speed, a limit of 26 players could be added as part of the Red and Blue Commander staffs. See Figure 9.

JTLS's initial configuration was developed, coded, tested, and delivered to the U.S. Readiness Command, MacDill AFB, Florida, in approximately 16 months. The final version, JTLS 1.5, a significant enhancement over the baseline version, was delivered to JAD with the acceptance testing accomplished at the Naval Post Graduate School in Monterey, California, on October 1, 1985.

14.1.2   Estimating the Cost of War

Preparation for the execution of a game was a time-consuming task. Digitized terrain, still in its infancy at JPL, was prepared by the JPL Image Processing Laboratory from maps provided with 1:1,200,000 resolution. The user prepared the air-ground-naval database that included all organizations, units, weapons systems, attrition coefficients, movement rates, weapons performance factors, and the consumption rates for critical items like rations, fuel, and ammunition through the Scenario Preparation Program (SPP). For a theater such as Central Europe, game preparations required the effort of two engineers covering an average period of six work months. Prior to running JTLS, the scenario database was passed through the Scenario Verification Program (SVP) to validate its correctness and integrity.

---

[4] The JTLS User Interface environment provided the using Theater or Field Army Command Post with manually posted displays and verbal input to the "Game Controller" who received the game truth from the Model Interface Program (MIP), and input the orders from the Red Commander and Blue Commander through the MIP into the Combat Events Program. In this way, the Battle Staff of participating units could be located in tents, in trucks (as was the practice), or in bunkers. This provided field realism and permitted noncomputer-literate officers to perform their duties in the same manner as they were trained to do.

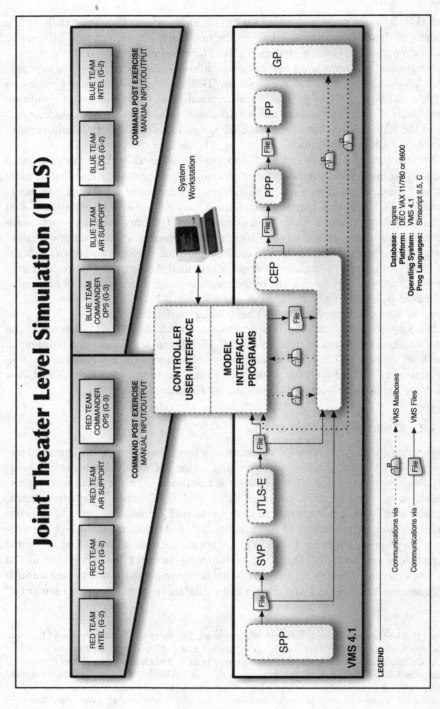

Figure 9. JTLS—examples of an operating system-dependent architecture.

The JTLS graphics capability freed users from manually updating the situation maps, and provided a clearer view of the overall tactical situation. Users were provided with terrain detail, unit identification, combat strength and location, and indicated their direction of movement via arrows.

The JTLS Post Processor (PP) recorded the data generated during the Command Post Exercise and the execution of the game, providing the users the capability to analyze the exercise results. By the way, to my mind the original idea was that even if nobody cared about the issues of fighting a war, if I could provide a CPX supportive game that would enable the JCS to calculate the cost in dollars and cents, maybe they would present the Congress with an estimated cost, *a priori*. Perhaps after looking at the bill before starting, they would say, "Nah, we can't afford this war. Forget it." Anyway, the user may identify the most effective weapons system through air-to-air combat, the type of weapon producing the greatest number of tank losses (figuring into the equation, it is hoped, the loss of tank crews, five soldiers per tank), and the amount of fuel and rations used during a period of time at $1.50 per gallon of JP-4 and diesel.

What had started all this thinking about the cost of a war was the decision process of President Eisenhower in not going to the aid of the French at Dien Bien Phu, when the entire Joint Chiefs of Staff wanted to, and the Cabinet as well. He flatly asked the Secretary of the Treasury what it would do to the National Budget; to be specific, would we go into the red?

At the following cabinet meeting, the Secretary of Treasury informed President Eisenhower that sending in troops and materiel to get the French out of their colonial jam (which most Americans didn't sympathize with anyway) would put our finances in the red. President Eisenhower then replied that we couldn't afford to go to war. Well, to me that was the best answer I have ever heard about a war. I loved this attitude of President Eisenhower's, that we won't go to war, because it will put our national budget into the red! I figured that if I could build a war game that permitted even a ballpark figure of the cost of a war to be contemplated by our president, he could ask for a simulation run, and get the dollar cost. Based on this, the president then could tell the Cabinet, "Okay, let's do it. We can afford it, so let's proceed." Or conversely, he could say, "No, we can't go to war. We don't have the money in our budget!"

All of this is for cases, of course, where we have not been attacked or have declared war. Needless to say, I was naïve. Since I was only a Green Beret major, I had no idea that people simply liked to go to war, for too many reasons to go into here.

What it did provide was the relief to the budget required for the funding of the CPX and FTX to the Army and Air Force during the Cold War. What had been a time-consuming and manpower-intensive process had been greatly simplified through the advances in technology, particularly in modeling techniques, computer simulation languages (such as the advances from GPSS to Simscript), and computer platforms and operating systems, particularly the leap from the PDP-11 to the VAX 11-780 and VMS.

JTLS, in its final configuration at the time of delivery, comprised 120,000 source lines of code, with about 60,000 lines of comments. It ran on the DEC VAX 11-780 and VAX 8600 platforms using DEC's great VMS 4.1 operating system. The major technologies that enabled us to build it, in addition to the truly outstanding talents, were Simscript II.5, the C programming language, INGRES (a relational database management system), and the system workstations (including VT100 terminals). Each graphics workstation was composed of a Sony video monitor, a digitizer pad, a Graphover 9500, and a Sony videodisc player, which contained the terrain map representation.

14.1.3   Starting up the Effort

Nothing is ever easy! After many failed attempts at finding a sponsor, we ran into some imaginative Air Force officers who wanted to get going at once. No sooner had the word leaked out that we were going to build a war game, the "stake-holders" got into the act. We, Dr. Joe Fearey and I, certainly hadn't the foggiest idea that there were so many stakeholders in the business of war gaming. With all of the heavy funding that the DOD had invested in war gaming, no one had anything worth mentioning to show for the money. But they had powerful lobbies. There was one functionally good product called the McClintic Theater Model, which had been built by some very talented individuals.[5] It was the automation of a military board game like the "Eastern Front" or "Gettysburg" games. One of the stakeholders immediately forced us to build on this system and enhance its capabilities with improved movement and attrition algorithms. This game was written in 12,000 lines of Fortran and ran on a PDP-11 (then my favorite machine).

But this was a great inhibitor to us, because it shunted aside my modular and global architecture, and forced us to use an old system, which was dated. There were several reasons for this, the first being control over development. Government agencies rarely if ever yield to the troops in the field. US STRIKECOM at McDill was a "field" organization, and not a Defense stem-winder establishment. The old Napoleonic dictum, "A glutton will defend his dinner like a hero," was making itself felt. I, being thoroughly naïve, and not understanding politics, just defied them and went about my business trying to build on the McClintic model, while ignoring the stakeholders as much as I could.

The thing that was paramount to the few brave visionary officers at McDill AFB was that we simply had to swallow our pride and prove by any means possible that an interactive, event-driven, computer simulation was not only doable, but that it was far superior to anything the stem-winders at DOD had. We were proved correct. With all the problems we had to solve, we also had things going for us. The DEC VAX 11-780 and VMS 4.1 had just come out and had great compilers for C and for Simscript II. I knew only GPSS, but this was far better. I had to yield on the issue of my large, elaborate modular hardware and software architecture called MEDUSA to something simple, just to get the system built and prove my hypothesis on war gaming. It was politically a very unsavory experience. When Army guys finally got involved at the War College and in the Pentagon, it was like going from Air Force

---

[5] Ray Macedonia, Fred McClintic, and James F. Dunnigan.

heaven to software purgatory. Let's face it; Army officers are bound to simple and uncomplicated rules. The requirements of infantry and artillery require courage and initiative, but not a very creative mind.

14.1.4 Costly Lessons Learned

There are a few things that influenced our development effort that must be mentioned here. I personally was committed to completing a couple of projects I was managing, including the design of a large architecture for long-range threat forecasting. Fortunately, we had Tom Hayes, a very experienced senior spacecraft engineer, available to manage JTLS. We also were fortunate enough to have recently hired Hubert Henry, who was an outstanding modeler and systems engineer in my group. So the Joint Theater Level Simulation had the required "troika" of experts: the Technical Manager, the Systems Engineer, and the Military Modeling Architect, (in Dr. Joe Fearey).[6] Without these three individuals, the system would not have taken on development momentum, and it would have increased the cost by a factor of three.

We (including me as the Group Supervisor of the Software Systems Engineering Group) had to re-evaluate our schedule and design objectives after we collectively, and with the support of the sponsor, finally decided to drop the McClintic Theater Model and build a new system now designated as JTLS. In order to make up for lost time, the programmers began to program their applications directly on top of the VMS 4.1 operating system. This was to prove very costly.

Although I was aware of this activity, I was on the sidelines because of my other commitments. Furthermore, we had no idea what impact this was going to have on debugging the software, on testing, and on putting in modifications to the programs.

There are innumerable valuable services and functions provided by modern virtual, multiprocessing, multitasking operating systems, such as interprocess communications, shared memory, timing, threading and synchronization, process control, start, termination, suspension, prioritization, file services, global variables, and debugging functions. But, when programmed to directly, these services so embed the application programs as to make removal for modification almost impossible without bringing the entire development system to a standstill. This is a big problem!

After Tom Hayes, Hubert Henry, and Joe Fearey delivered JTLS 1.0 to the sponsor, and I had just completed my projects, Tom and Joe went off to begin work on a

---

[6] One of the most difficult hurdles we had to overcome was the finding of competent modelers and hiring them. A "modeler" generally is an individual with an M.S. or a Ph.D. in economics or mathematics, specializing in game theory, number theory, or something similar. The individuals who are hired for the lead modeler positions must have four to eight years of military experience to understand tactics, organizations, logistics, and the application of firepower, command and control, and movement. If you then add the required working knowledge of systems design and programming, such an individual is not easy to find. We did work hard to find such individuals, though, and the JTLS team did a great job of finding them and training them on the job.

new military simulation project. I returned to JTLS and delivered the final product, JTLS 1.5. The idea that we had come up with had taken root, and the U.S. Army wanted more and better models. Modeling is a great learning and teaching tool, not only in the military, but also in most other professions.

The customer wanted the product fast, and the modifications to the applications had to be implemented. This process was laborious, time-consuming, and expensive. Some of the programmers had so deeply embedded their programs into the OS that they almost had lifetime jobs. This approach to programming, the use of the operating system directly, is dangerous to the schedule and budget. It seats the applications programs so tightly into the OS that debugging is very time-consuming, and the reprogramming of an applications program is costwise prohibitively expensive.

I have a hard time with the concept of lifetime jobs, especially where it concerns me personally. I can never do a project longer than 4 years. After that, I have to complete it so I can move on to something new and interesting, with new and bigger problems to solve. However, as we struggled to deliver the JTLS product, I had an idea. I had to design a layer of software that separated the applications programmers from the operating system, and thereby give me control over my development process. It had to be so effective that if a subsystem didn't fill my expectations, I could unplug it without affecting the rest of the system and replace it with a better subsystem within a matter of hours. (I was able to first apply this approach to great advantage on the GDSS project. See Case Study Two.) I owe this idea to the JTLS development effort.

The other factor affecting cost was the fact that gaming concepts had to be learned by the implementers, prior to the start of the design and programming. For this purpose we bought military board games and played them to gain a better insight into the gaming discipline. Some of these board games were outstanding, accurate, and fun to play and use as teaching tools. This taught me the key to winning the Battle of Gettysburg, playing as the Confederates.[7] Not that winning at

---

[7] Interested? Here's the basic scenario: There is a Union Cavalry Brigade from Massachusetts under the command of a lawyer named Beauford. At the time, they were armed with the latest Spencer repeating rifles. (These were originally called Henry Repeating Rifles, after their inventor. The patent was bought by Winchester from Spencer.) The men in Beauford's Brigade are mounted on horseback, are of high mobility, and coupled with this kind of firepower, are quite formidable.

When the tired, barefooted, ill-equipped Confederate infantry comes onto the battlefield at Pepperton Pike, they get beaten back. Gen. Longstreet, recovering from wounds himself, doesn't attack but waits for the rest of the divisions to catch up. Meanwhile Beauford's Brigade keeps the Confederates from moving ahead and continues to inflict heavy casualties on them, keeping them out of Gettysburg and Seminary Ridge.

Playing as the Confederates, I attacked and continued to attack as the Confederate divisions arrived. This continued and piecemeal attack on Beuford's Brigade causes some increased casualties, until they are reduced to about 60% of their mobility and firepower. Then when Gen. Lee arrives with the rest of the troops, they can occupy Gettysburg, Seminary Ridge, and Little Round Top, and dig in, before Gen. Meade arrives with the main body of the Union Army. Now, this strategy causes heavy Confederate casualties, but not as severe as later in the battle with Picket's abortive and bloody charge. In the board game, if you do this as the Confederates, you do win at Gettysburg.

Gettysburg would have won the war for the South, but it might have given the Union reason to negotiate.

Development of the system could never have been done without my friend, Dr. Joe Fearey. He was the gaming expert, with the mathematical knowledge to match. JTLS was a first of its kind in war-gaming simulations and was accomplished by JPL engineers such as Joe Provenzano, Dr. Chris Roach, Mike DiLoreto, Paul Firnett, Larry Hawley, Jay Braun, Felicia Gordon, and John Flynn, to mention just a few. There was also management, with consultants and contractors of great talent provided by Merrie Computing, Rolands & Associates, Inc., and CACI. Especially important for the understanding of the art of war was Colonel U.S. Army (Ret) Trevor Dupuy, who became a trusted friend.

14.2   CASE STUDY TWO: THE GLOBAL DECISION SUPPORT SYSTEM (GDSS)

The Global Decision Support System (GDSS) is a Military Command and Control System (MCCS) built for the United States Air Force, Military Airlift Command (MAC). It was built on a very short schedule and limited budget. It was a matter of very serious urgency that the MAC have a state-of-the-art MCCS for the tracking and control of all of its assets around the world. The basic estimate for such a system was a cost of $200 million and a schedule of 7 years, which was not acceptable to HQ/MAC. So, the development schedule was set at 21 months, and the budget capped at $16.5 million. The question before the Air Force and JPL was whether it was possible to build a system of this complexity under such a short schedule. We decided to give it a try and to build it as a prototype for the all the uniformed services.

Software Development Standard: DOD-STD-2167A, waived by USAF due to schedule restrictions, and replaced by the Rapid Development Methodology developed by S. Mike de Gyurky.

Documentation: GDSS FRD, TIP, Concept of Operations, GDSS Design Book, and GDSS User Guide, one of each per application subsystem. The GDSS Technical Bulletin, Design Book User Guide, GDSS Interface Control Document, GDSS System Message Manual, GDSS Test Plans, all documented in 5,000 pages.

14.2.1   GDSS System Size

At Final Operational Capability: 7 October 1987. 492,000 source lines of new code.

Total cost: $16.4 million.

Note: The customer was so pleased with the GDSS product that they requested one more year of additional requirements to be added to the baseline.[8]

At End of Project: 30 September 1988. 971,600 source lines of new code.

---

[8] See Figure 12, the official GDSS memo of recognition.

Final Cost: $27.0 million.

Languages: GDSS was programmed in Ada, C, and Fortran.

Cost/Line of Code: $27.80 per commented line of code.

14.2.2   The History and Background of GDSS

This is a brief encapsulation of the Global Decision Support System (GDSS) built for the U.S. Air Force's Military Airlift Command, between December 1986 and October 1988. GDSS was an extremely interesting puzzle to solve, the solution to which was at least partially rooted in the Allied Command Europe (ACE) CCIS.

I had just returned from delivering the Joint Theater Level Simulation to one of our customers when I was informed that we were stuck with this project, and what the circumstances surrounding it were.

Our section and division had inherited the responsibility of building a command and control system for the U.S. Air Force (USAF), specifically for Military Airlift Command (MAC). There were several important functional and technical factors that made it nearly impossible.

The schedule from start to completion was to be 21 months. There were to be three software deliveries, the first was to be in nine months, and the other two in six-month increments.

GDSS was to be a large, geographically distributed, near real-time system that would enable the Numbered Air Force bases of MAC to control its resources efficiently and reduce the cost of operations. (MAC is the largest airline in the world, transporting cargo and personnel around the world under all political and climatic conditions.) The network was to link the following Air Force bases:

- HQ/MAC at Scott AFB, Illinois
- 23rd NAF at Hurlburt AFB, Florida
- The ANG at Andrews AFB, Washington, DC
- The 22nd NAF at Travis AFB, California
- The 21st NAF at Maguire AFB, New Jersey
- The 834th ALD at Hickam AFB, Hawaii
- The 322nd ALD at Ramstein AFB, Germany

For the duration of the development I would add JPL as an NAF-like node. Each node would need to contain the identical functional task groups:

- **Operations**, which is responsible for flight scheduling.
- **Transportation**, with personnel ticketing, is responsible for cargo handling, loading, and unloading.
- **Command and Control**, which is responsible for flight following.
- **Logistics**, which ensures that en route mechanical failures are serviced promptly.

- **Crisis Action**, which is responsible for the management of threats and emergencies.

GDSS was to be designed to accommodate 400 sorties on a daily basis. In the event of war, with the addition of civilian cargo and passenger aircraft, it must accommodate up to 1,600 airlift sorties per day.[9]

GDSS had to link to the World Wide Military Command and Control System (WWMCCS), which was based on Honeywell 6060 computers, and from there to AutoDIN. We were going to use TransLAN (DDN/PSN) for development, with a development bandwidth available at 7.6 KBS. At the operational stage, the network would be provided a two-way bandwidth of 28.8 KB between NAF nodes and 19.2 KB to the two ALDs (Air Lift Divisions).

A state-of-the-art user interface with both graphical and alphanumeric displays was to be provided. There was an additional large-scale situation display at the HQ/MAC Operations Center using two Visulux Laser Projectors, projecting a 32 × 15-foot-high resolution display onto a motion picture quality screen.

Funding was set at an upper limit of $16.5 million for software development, with the Air Force providing computer hardware (DEC VAX 8600s, disk drives, terminals, MicroVAX-II and IV minicomputers, and the operating systems).

The system was to provide all office automation services possible to reduce the workload of the staff required to run MAC manually (36 Officers and NCOs per shift, three 8-hour shifts per site). GDSS had to be "survivable" and operational in case of a worldwide conflict with the USSR.

14.2.3 Expediting the System

To expedite development, the system was to be implemented with "vanilla" Digital Equipment Corporation hardware and software if it would help to get the system completed on budget.

There was a reason for expediting the development. The tremendous pressure to get this MAC CCIS done was caused by a failure in our military command and control system. During the 1983 Grenada operation, an Air Force Colonel on the ground in Grenada had to use a public telephone to call Pope AFB in North Carolina, get patched through to Ft. Bragg in California, and then had a patch put through to the airlift commander of the U.S. Airborne Task Force with the paratroops of an 82nd Airborne Division to provide the latest tactical information on the drop zone. With all the funds spent by the Department of Defense on command and control systems, we did not have an integrated command and control network between the services and joint tactical commands. Thus, JPL

---

[9] During Operation Desert Storm, the Force Generation and Staging Phase, the addition of allied transport aircraft pushed the sortie generation to 6,400 per 24 hours. GDSS was able to handle the load without problem. Also during this period, an additional ad hoc node was added to GDSS, a mobile one stationed in Kuwait. Again the automatic systems software accommodated the addition without a hitch. We received compliments for this technical feat, unprecedented in its day.

had the privilege to do the job, within 21 months, and under the cost ceiling of $16.5 million.

The basic requirements presented a number of implied requirements that were not stated. A system such as the one the Air Force wanted could not be accomplished at the time, in 1986, without a few completely new technology thrusts.

14.2.4   The Euler Sphere

A uniquely new way of looking at a systems architecture was called variously the "Euler sphere" or the "GDSS donut." This was in reality nothing new, as it had been first used by the mathematician Euler. This is a representation in the form of spheres as opposed to boxes and was of enormous help to me to express what I wanted, and what was needed to get underway.[10] But, its successful application and use depended on the level of intelligence of the team members, in particular in the area of translating abstract concepts into practical and programmable software entities, which they would then be able to put into code. The visualization of the technical manager as architect is very important, but of equal importance is the intelligence of the team. I was very fortunate—by sheer luck I had a team of unequalled ability, vision, and skill. This was essential in creating the Globally Distributed Mini/Super-Minicomputer System (GDMSMCS), based on Digital Equipment Corporation (DEC) VAX 8550, 8600 and MicroVAX-II computers and peripherals, using at that time the best operating system available, VMS, and other DEC software as a design baseline.

14.2.5   Beyond State of the Art

GDSS was the beginning of the term *Methodology for Rapid Development*. At the time, it was absolutely state-of-the-art technology, using a new approach to architecture articulation, as well as a new approach to development methodology and process, which is still valid today. Keep in mind that DEC computer hardware and software at the time of the GDSS development period were the best in the industry.

What follows are some of the technological highlights and innovations that made GDSS such an unprecedented feat of engineering in its day.

14.2.6   A Replicated, Survivable, Synchronous Database Management System

No such thing as a replicated, survivable, synchronous database management system existed at this time. This was a most unique approach to database design. The GDSS DBMS, instead of having one master database that updated the others, had all master databases that continually maintained each other in a current state.

---

[10] Arthur Schopenhauer. *Die Welt als Wille und Vorstellung* (The World as Will and Imagination), Hoffmans Verlag AG, Zurich 1988. also Deutscher Taschenbuch Verlag, Munchen 1998 pages 76–83.

When one or two local databases had a problem of any sort, the user still would transparently have access to the remote replicated and synchronized surviving database of any of the other sites.

14.2.7   The Ultra Large Screen Display System

The Ultra Large Screen Display system (ULSD) provided the MAC decision makers with a worldwide view of all MAC assets, their location, and status. The ULSD utilized two Visulux 1050 laser projectors driven by a MicroVAX II through a 32-bit graphics frame buffer. The image was 32×15 feet of high-resolution graphics rear-projected onto a semitransparent motion picture screen. The ULSD was backed up by a new invention by Dr. Don Wedding: large monochrome plasma displays.

14.2.8   The Local Area Networks

GDSS is composed of eight LANs. The GDSS Wide Area Network Configuration figure (Figure 10) shows one LAN at each of the GDSS sites, including the JPL development LAN. The LANs used DEC Ethernet hardware and DECnet-based communications software.

14.2.9   The Wide Area Network

The wide area network used TransLAN hardware that functioned as a datagram repeater, passing all datagrams through the WAN unchanged. Ultimately, when the interface was developed during FY 1988, we switched to the Defense Data Network, DDN (Figure 10).

14.2.10   Distributed Client/Server Technology

The system team came up with a novel distributed hierarchical client/server model of communicating between GDSS elements, locally and remotely. This allows any GDSS application to act as sender or receiver to/from a GDSS server process. The servers then communicate to the destination, thus extending a local node's "reach" to any of the nodes connected at the time. In this way, each node is made aware of the other GDSS nodes that are online, enabling them to synchronize databases automatically among themselves.

14.2.11   Message Bus

GDSS also is noted for its origination of the message bus or middleware paradigm, which allows an application to communicate to any other through standardized high-level function calls, thereby hiding the communications-specific protocols from the applications programmers. Automatic message queuing and "store and forward" technologies allow messages sent to offline destinations to be retained (archived), and delivered when they come back online. And, due to the restricted

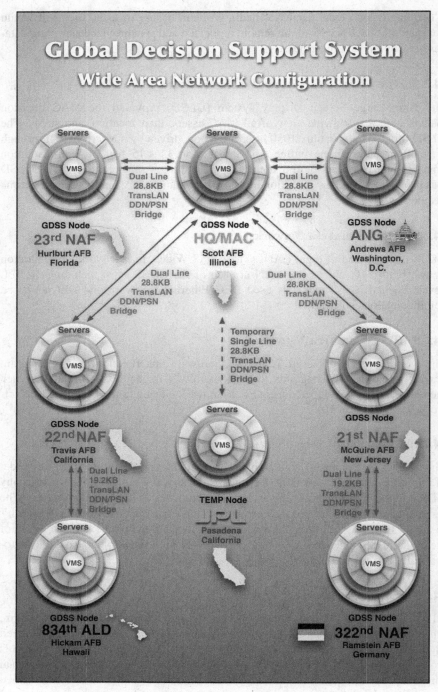

Figure 10. The GDSS wide area network topology.

network bandwidth, GDSS employs a run-length compression scheme for all message packets sent remotely.

14.2.12   The GDSS Software Architecture

The GDSS system software design allows users, after the appropriate authentication procedure has been completed, to use any terminal to gain access to the desired GDSS function. The GDSS Integrated Software Functional Diagram, Figure 11, known as the "GDSS donut," shows the system-level software architecture of GDSS. I'd like to note here that I found it easier to describe to my team how the system-level architecture should look like using Euler's approach rather than agonize over block diagrams. Fortunately my team understood, while upper management didn't. But then, upper management did not have to build the system, I did.

At the center of the GDSS donut (Euler sphere) is the VAX/VMS operating system, which provides process connections between all GDSS system and application support software.

Surrounding the VMS core is a circled layer of COTS packages, commercially available off-the-shelf layered software products. Contained within this level of software is a variety of compilers,[11] the Configuration Management System (CMS), the relational database (DEC/RDB), the All-In-One office automation software, the DECnet message protocol software, and a variety of other software productivity tools and packages.

The next circle outward is called the GDSS System Software. This common software services layer provides the software connectivity between the inner circles and the next outward circle, which contain the system servers (the first-ever large-scale distributed client/server technology) and the replicable, survivable, and synchronous DBMS (built as a team effort between JPL and DEC).

Outside the GDSS System Software layer is the GDSS System Server layer. In this layer are the server processes that control the underlying operation of GDSS, acting as bridges between the GDSS software applications and the inner layers, the DBMS, and the network.

The GDSS software applications surround the GDSS system server layer. In this way, all applications can access the DBMS and the servers needed to perform their assigned tasks. The users are connected to their local systems via a LAN, and to remote systems via the GDSS Node Network Connectivity (GDSS WAN) and the External Systems Network Connectivity. GDSS also ensures that all system hardware and network addresses are accessed by logical or virtual addresses rather than by hard-coded physical addresses.

---

[11] Note re: compilers for Ada, C, and Fortran. Approximately 50% of the GDSS software was written in Ada, a wonderfully stable language, especially ideal for spacecraft onboard computers using the RAD 6000 series 1750A architecture. The balance of the GDSS software was written in C and Fortran, augmented by a variety of software preprocessors. This was not my usual approach to development, but on a very tight schedule, all usable, mature COTS packages had to be exploited.

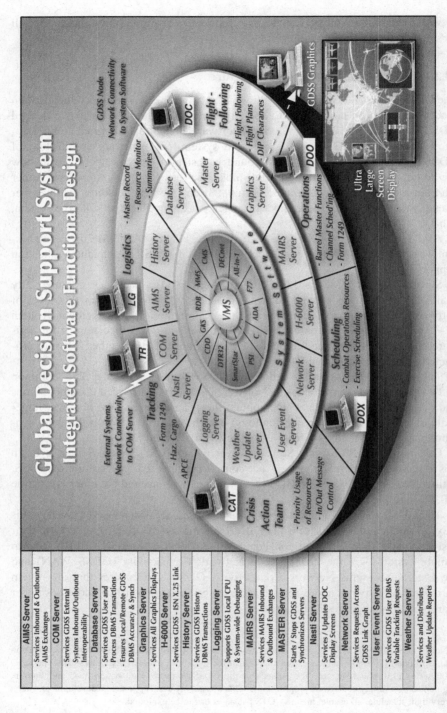

Figure 11. The GDSS software functional design.

DEPARTMENT OF THE AIR FORCE
HEADQUARTERS MILITARY AIRLIFT COMMAND
SCOTT AIR FORCE BASE. ILLINOIS 62225

General Bernard P. Randolph, USAF   18 NOV 1987
Commander
Air Force Systems Command
Andrews AFB, DC 20334-5000

Dear Randy

As you know, I am not a technical expert in the computer or
communications world, but I sure know when things are going
right. The impressive results and enthusiasm generated by
the Global Decision Support System (GDSS) program have been
a success story of the first order. I am convinced the reason
for this success can be directly attributed to the strong
partnership between MAC and your Electronic Systems Division.
In fact, our combined efforts have been so productive that the
JCS and DOD command and control counterparts want us to extend
the Prototype Model Command Center effort another year to usher
in additional technology.

During "ESD Day" at HQ MAC, Dr Allen from Jet Propulsion
Laboratory, Lt Gen Chubb, and I agreed the GDSS program should
continue. As part of the agreement, MAC and ESD would share
the expenses. We're on course and on schedule. ESD contributed
$1.7M in FY87, and I know they're currently working the balance
of their funding for this year.

Randy, I cannot thank you enough for the superb support ESD has
given MAC. The GDSS program has literally propelled our top
three echelons of command out of the dark ages and is now serving
as an example for the other CINCs and JCS. Soon, the Information
Processing System will join GDSS to complete the task at our
lower echelons.

Please extend my appreciation to Nick and his professional crew
who have so steadfastly advocated our C4S needs.

Sincerely

DUANE H. CASSIDY   cc: ESD/CC
General, USAF
Commander in Chief

Figure 12. Official GDSS recognition from General Duane Cassidy.

14.2.13 Accepting the Challenge

When I was asked whether a serious command and control system with military imperatives could be built within 21 months for under $20 million, I was taken off-guard. I had never thought about such a short schedule, limited level of funding, and global scale. However, I did think about solving the problem of developing the ACE CCIS at SHAPE in Belgium, which was huge and very costly. I told my section and my division that it could be done, but that I was not going to apply for the job. I had just delivered the Joint Theater Level Simulation to the Army, and it had not been a picnic. I really love the Army, it was my teacher, it paid for my education and taught me everything imaginable, but my fellow combat arms officers are not known for their creativity (with a few notable exceptions, of course). It took extreme patience to explain theoretical concepts to them. I was worn out after three years of hard, grinding work.

I told them that if I were to do it, they would have to *order* me to do it. And if they did that, there would have to be waived rules, and lots of trust on their part. Then I would do it out of duty and out of friendship. I knew some of the big problems already. At SHAPE, my boss, teacher, and mentor Col. Joseph Bullers (who had been Gen. Curtis LeMay's command and control officer at SAC) and I were fought at every turn. We were in Operations Division, Command and Control Branch. The Information Systems Division did not want the users to be involved in determining what we needed to do our jobs. Then there was the big power of WWMCCS with their Honeywell 6060 machines, while we came to the conclusion after the completion of the requirements, that the DEC PDP-11, in 1977, was the best for the task. Naturally, I was shot out of the water; we got H-6060s.

As it turned out, I was told that like it or not, I would *have* to do GDSS. JPL's reputation was on the line, and without a responsive, fast, trouble-free CCIS, Military Airlift Command would not be able to respond effectively to a worldwide crisis. So, I agreed.

14.2.14 Initial Conditions

The first thing I did was to fly up to Scott AFB, HQ/MAC, and talk with the Chief of Staff. He was curious. "Can it be done?" he asked.

I told him that it could be done, but the Air Force would need to waive my favorite standard, DOD-STD-2167A, and I'd follow the "Joint Logistics Commanders Guidance, For the Use of an Evolutionary Acquisition Strategy in Acquiring Command and Control Systems," which was just about to be published, and about which I had talked to a Brigadier General at Ft. Belvoir, Virginia.

This meant that there would be no "throwing over the wall" a system unfamiliar to the user. If we were going to build this in 21 months, then all users of the system would need to work with my JPL development team on a daily basis, as needed. This condition also applied to DEC. GDSS would be a vanilla DEC system, with DEC benefiting from the development of the products. DEC was to be the sustaining engineering contractor, so they would have to work with us as the third member of the team. The COS agreed, we shook hands, and the GDSS Design Team JPL-MAC-DEC came into being. This shows right off the starting line that when a customer is serious about wanting a product, it will support the developer wholeheartedly. It also shows that it takes a team of serious people to get the job done. Without the Chief of Staff behind the system, it would have taken the original Air Force estimate of $200 million and 7 years. I fully believe that this is a true and honest estimate.

A group of very talented DEC engineers was assigned to work under my control. At first, they felt that they would be the "go between" for the project manager (me) and DEC. For the sake of unity of command, it was made clear that for the duration, they would work for me. It was okay; this idea worked fine.

The next issue to be solved was the architecture. The design team had to have a systems structure to focus on and get to understand. This was not a trivial task. My old friends who were experienced in DEC VAX/VMS first of all felt that it was their prerogative to take charge of the system, and to let me count beans, travel, and go to meetings. This too is understandable, because these are the things managers typically do. (By the way, travel and meetings are the by far the largest consumers of time on a project. In Chapter 8, on cost estimates, I go into detail about this.) So for a manager on a very tight schedule, there has to be a creative approach to the issue of meetings and reviews as well as travel, with the objective of getting the maximum benefit out of them.

14.2.15 Rapid Development: A Totally Different Approach

A totally different methodology is required in a rapid development environment than in a traditional one. The methodology is unique; it is *not* "prototyping" as some people who do not understand the difference like to call it. A prototype system may be the end result of the effort, such as GDSS became for the DOD, but it is not a "methodology."

I spent an inordinate amount of time trying to explain to a few highly placed managers the difference between the rapid development methodology and a traditional one; it was useless, because the Kantian "wells of experience"[12] were not there. Without the experience on part of the listener, there is no understanding: "You have eyes, but you cannot see. You have ears, but you cannot hear." If there is no experience factor in the listener, and no analytical ability of abstract concepts, he will subjectively interpret what you are trying to explain. Your transmission is simply dumped into the mental trash bin by the reasoning of "I don't know, and I don't understand."

As an analogy, the difference between traditional development and rapid development is like the difference between the military command and control measures and operational rules of an Armored Division versus the role of a Cavalry Regimental Combat Group in its Corps Covering Force Mission. The armored division is large and cumbersome. Even when led by a very talented commander like Rommel

---

[12] Immanuel Kant, *Critique der Praktischer Vernunft* (Quellen der Erfahrung).

or Patton, it must have detailed planning for maneuvers, fire support, logistics, close air support and traffic control in the form of detailed operations, plans, and orders; otherwise, there is chaos and confusion. The preparation of these plans and orders requires a set methodology with coordinated procedures, and it takes a lot of work and a large staff. The Cavalry Regiment, on the other hand, is commanded by one regimental commander from his Jeep or helicopter. More often than not, he may be miles away from his Battle Command Post (CP) with nothing more than a map in his lap, a driver, and his radio, with one or two recon sections for security. He maintains the situation in his head and makes drawings on his map to keep track of his cavalry squadrons (battalions) that may be 10 to 20 kilometers away. He talks to his squadron commanders who are also most of the time driving and operating in a similar manner away from the Combat CPs.

The CP is then like the rapid development systems engineering team, with software engineers, technical writers, and a systems engineer who is like the operations officer of the regiment. They keep track of all design issues approved on the spot, and articulate them much like a situation report (SITREP) or intelligence report (INTREP). There is no time to have large all-encompassing reviews of the operational plan and the situation, because the situation is fluid. In the Covering Force of an Army Corps, the mission is to search for and locate the enemy, and if destroyable, to destroy or at least to delay him. The U.S. Armored Cavalry Regiment has all of the combat assets a Corps has, but in small numbers. It has cavalry troops, tank companies, self-propelled howitzers, combat engineers, ordnance, and an aviation company. A rapid development computer software project has all of the assets a large traditional project has—the manager-architect, the systems engineer, the principal design engineers, technical writers, testers, configuration managers, administrators and secretarial support—but on a far smaller scale than a project.

In this respect the rapid development project organization is also made up of people with much more experience, initiative, and independent mindsets, much like the cavalry. In the cavalry, you must make decisions fast; even down to the recon section leader (a midlevel noncommissioned officer, usually an SFC), initiative is everything. The manager-architect/regimental commander must have the mental elasticity to understand the tactical and technical situation to such a degree as to make sound decisions. Only the best in the Army command Armored Cavalry Regiments, and only the best technical managers in industry can be entrusted with Rapid Development Projects.

When done well, a review takes a lot of time to prepare and to present, usually at a minimum one week to prepare, and two days to present. On traditional systems it sometimes takes two months, involving nearly the entire staff, and several days of presentations. This costs a tremendous amount of time and money away from doing work.

In a rapid development environment, the "design team" (i.e., the Command Post equivalent) is in session from 0800 hours until 1300 hours, when there is a break for lunch. Any time a manager or a number of reviewers have a need to understand the status of the design or the progress of the implementation, all they need to do is come into the "war room," sit down, and listen. They have every right to ask questions for their own understanding of the project status, and may by their questions contribute to the project by bringing to the attention of the design team issues that might have been overlooked. But holding separate reviews, dumbed-down to a staff that is technically no longer qualified to evaluate the technical design, and which lacks the years of hands-on experience required to understand and evaluate the organization, operating procedures, and methodologies to get things done on time is a gross and irresponsible waste of time, because time is money. It is also unethical, because "dumbing down" of a funded project to any audience is unethical. I don't recommend costly reviews except one before the delivery of the software product version.

14.2.16 There Can Be Only One!

In any case, when your most trusted colleagues, who are all very good in their fields, tell you that they will do your work for you, you are in a bind. In this case, this was difficult in the extreme because we happened to have some of the finest graphics, database, and operating systems software engineers in the world. The problem was that they didn't understand that I had a schedule, and they couldn't visualize the architecture in the way I did. Each one of them saw the system as all database, or all systems functions, or all communications, but not as one integrated, balanced, systems architecture. Nor would any one of them yield to any other; all wanted to be in charge and to dominate the evolution of the system. So, regrettably, I had to push them out of the way.

This resulted in much "weeping and gnashing of teeth" and open serious threats, along with accusations that I would never get one delivery out the door. This kind of thing feels somewhat like when one is playing on the home team against formidable opposition (technical, schedule, and funding problems) and your own fans boo, hiss, and threaten you. It takes a Babe Ruth to step out and do his thing, confident that his intuition is telling him what he needs to do, and how he must do it, even when his best friends are dismayed.

There can only be one in charge! The proverbial "buck" stops at the manager's desk. Accountability and responsibility cannot be delegated!

So, I listen to the opinions of expert colleagues, appreciatively and graciously, and look for the technical solutions they have in mind, and evaluate them as to their validity and technical soundness. Consider the questions: Does it fit into my schedule? Does it fit into my funding? Does it make sense? Are they being sincere and unselfish and trying to be genuinely helpful, or are they following their own agendas? If they want to validate a concept of their own, or are not well intentioned, the answer is *no!* End of message! If I had a dollar for every time I have been misled or lied to by people I trusted, I would be a wealthy man. Indeed, in the end, when a manager fails, those who misguided him simply find another job, while the manager is now a "loser" in reputation. I thank God I have never been unable to deliver a quality system on time and on budget, except once. In that case, the upper management was too strong, and cancelled the project just two months before delivery.

However, in that program office, funding is no issue, and the prevailing attitude is, "If you deliver, the jobs and org chart go away, so don't deliver."

14.2.17   GDSS End-to-End Architecture

Meanwhile, the GDSS program office wanted an end-to-end systems diagram so they could understand what I was doing. I understood their need. To get it done, I gave my contracting company and my systems engineer a week to prepare for me a Level I systems architecture. Now, my contracting company was a major software outfit. And, I had persuaded my systems engineer to join me on the project. He was one of my best friends at the time, and was absolutely a superb programmer with a Ph.D. in mathematics. Now a week on a nine-month schedule is a long time. When I arrived, I had an existing development team of about 45 persons charging to the account. This is a very impressive burn rate when nothing is getting done but going to meetings and lunch, with some travel thrown in. At that time TWA was having a drive for passengers and was giving triple mileage for every trip taken. There were almost weekly meetings at Scott AFB in Illinois, and many more at Maguire AFB in New Jersey. Then there was Ramstein AFB in Germany, with all the Bratwurst and Bittburger beer, not to mention Hickam AFB just outside Honolulu, with the Bar of the Royal Hawaiian (where we used to drink while going back and forth to Vietnam, a true nostalgia trip).

But I couldn't sleep. I saw my funds oozing away like the sands of an hourglass, and nothing getting done except the accumulation of frequent-flier bonus miles into the accounts of well-meaning engineers with nothing to do.

When the week was up, we had a meeting and there was still no end-to-end diagram. I gave them until the following meeting, and waited anxiously. At the next meeting there was *still* no end-to-end diagram, so I told them that they had one final week or they could pack their bags. By the end of the third week, there were excuses that they couldn't "put their arms around the system," so I fired my systems engineer and the contracting company.

Then, using the Euler sphere, I drew the architecture on my whiteboard, and drew the Level I systems architecture. Then, I went next door where four young people, whom I had been watching for over three weeks, were gathered closely around their terminals, doing their thing. I asked them to come into my office for a minute. I pointed to the diagram I had drawn, and asked them if they understood what I had depicted, and whether it made any sense to them. Their eyes lit up. There were questions, and we had a discussion about the addition of the functions, many of which I was still unfamiliar with. Then I asked them if they could fill in the blanks. They said yes, and left with a copy of the sketch.

14.2.18   Architecting the Development Effort

Having set the systems architecture design in motion, the next problem to solve was the one of architecting the development effort. The problem that presented itself was that there was no time to prepare a set of functional or software requirements, much less the software design document. The writing, reviewing, and approving of the software interface specifications and the preparation of test plans and user guides were out of the question. Even if I had not asked for the waiver of DOD-STD-2167A, there was no hope of getting GDSS done in a traditional or close to traditional fashion.

I went to the section manager and told him I needed one of our conference rooms as an office. He was reluctant to give it me, but finally agreed to. I picked one without windows, and asked the section administrator to have Facilities cover all of the walls with cork. I got myself a large round table that would seat all my key engineering and administrative staff plus a few more, around 10 to 12 people. This was going to be the "war room."

The individuals to whom I had given the Euler systems diagram returned after about two days, by which time the "war room" was ready. They had taken the systems architecture diagram and done a great job filling in the blanks.

At 0800 sharp I called a meeting of all the individuals who had impressed me with their knowledge and desire to get the system done. I tacked the system central architecture onto the middle of the wall. Then the dialectic approach to the systems design started, very much like I had read so long ago in the *Republic* of Plato. I wanted to establish firmly an architecture that reflected the subjective vision of every member of the GDSS design team.

The "fleshing out," or as Immanuel Kant called the process, the *adding of substance to an object* (i.e., the *architecture*), had started. No one can build a system as complicated as GDSS without a design, however, there was no time for a requirements document or a design document. The walls of my office had to be the repository of the requirements and the design combined. The process was difficult because the key people were anxious about sitting down and laboriously going through the dialectical design process; they wanted to get to work and program with their people what they had on their minds. This would not do. You can't program something for which there is no design. The design team session went on until 1300 hours. Much was accomplished, but there was one really glaring problem in the methodology approach: Many on the team, the programmers and hardware engineers, were not being utilized and the burn rate doesn't allow for people to sit around without being productive.

14.2.19 Inferential Systems Architecture

Since there was no way to take time out for the formal design process, I asked that each subsystem use a couple of DEC terminals and have either the subsystem team chief or a member of his team start laying out the user's data display on the computer. The Air Force had agreed that an Air Force user or operator, usually an officer or senior NCO, would work as a partner with the subsystem team chief and his team. As a starter, I had appointed the principal design engineer of the Command and Control Subsystem (AF designator "DOC"), along with a very fine young software designer who was one of the senior programmers on her team. I told her to have her team develop the user interface and the screenfaces for her subsystem, and start a prototype programming effort of the design in Fortran as soon as there was a screenface and module identified and designed. The inferring of an entire systems architecture from the user screenfaces and the user interface is a practical approach to systems design when there is little breathing room on a schedule. This is specifically how I managed to get the ACE CCIS sized.

The methodology now demanded that each morning the design team be in session from 0800 hours until 1300 hours. This meeting would be ongoing for the duration of the project, until we felt that it was no longer necessary to have it every day. There was no other possible way to control the development and keep track of the design. Every morning, each senior design engineer would present the design of his subsystem, discuss it, report on the problems encountered, finalize the design and put it on a Macintosh, print it out, and tack it on my wall. The current design was always on the wall, and people came and went freely, upgrading the "situation map" if you will, while the design team was in session.

14.2.20   The GDSS System Software Layer

There were many things to solve in the methodology if I didn't want to lose control and have the system development run away from me. The most important of these was the GDSS System Software layer.

The GDSS System Software layer (which evolved into the Common Software Services of the TOPEX and Jason 1 TCCS) was the result of a very unpleasant experience I had in the building of the JTLS system. As is usual with the implementation of software systems, as soon as the funding starts people above push the manager as well as the implementing engineers. Everyone wants to start work. The manager who is inexperienced and lacks sufficient self-confidence is unable to stand up to the upper management bureaucracy and to the "experts" he has hired or inherited. Everyone starts to go in his own direction; there is no control, certainly not sufficient control. As milestones loom on the horizon, even if the manager is unhappy with many of the staff, he is unable to let them go or sideline them because of delivery issues. If the software is poor and undocumented, and is hooked deeply into the operating system, the manager is totally helpless, and the programmers are completely safe, knowing that in order to replace their system, it will have to be completely redone, and for that there is no time. Additionally, if it is a subcontractor's personnel who did that segment, you have to pay almost whatever they demand, because if they leave, your system is almost useless.

Since this had happened to me before, I resolved that the only way I would ever let anyone program is through an intermediate layer I was going to place atop the operating system. I described the concept to my system team (who had the Euler diagram), explaining that what I wanted was for them to build a layer of software on top of VMS that would provide an abstraction of the needed services provided by VMS (e.g., shared memory, timers and timing, process control, etc.), as well as clearly defined interfaces, coding conventions, and practices for the applications programmers. No one would program on any application or element who did not follow the rules, and who did not pass the scrutiny of the system software senior design engineer and his senior programmers. They immediately understood what I wanted, and went off to do the design and implementation of this layer at once.

Before applications programming can start, there first had to be a common software layer, and well-defined interfaces, conventions, and rules. If at any time in the development phase a subsystem was flawed or not up to the high quality I expected, it could be unplugged and replaced without affecting or inhibiting performance and usage of any other part of the system. If I wanted to, I could have a new module or subsystem programmed, unplug the current one, and replace it without losing much in the way of time or performance. It also enabled me to let go of poorly performing personnel and replace them without fear of missing a delivery milestone. Fortunately for me, there were relatively few people I had to let go, because I inherited outstanding ones and added some excellent new members to the team.

All of these things were, of course, going on simultaneously and not sequentially; there was a torrent of activity at all times, from early morning to late at night. The "troops" were beginning to enjoy the dynamics of the environment, with the exception of the continuous session design team; that really bothered most of them, but they knew that this was mandatory and for many reasons a *sine qua non* to success.

14.2.21   Applications Language Selection

As the system software layer started to take shape, and the Ethernet communications layer was activated, the team began to bother me about what programming language we were going to use for the programming of our applications. So I asked what they, the team, wanted to use. I gave them a week to come up with a recommendation. They did; they wanted to use Ada.

"How many of you can program in Ada?" I asked them. "Raise your hands."

No one raised a hand. So I asked them why they wanted to use Ada. They said they wanted to learn it, and that the DOD preferred Ada and had good results with it. There was one major factor, and that was that they would acquire another skill. Well, I told them that I'd think about that for a while, and then called the first "all-hands meeting" of GDSS. All of the team would attend, including secretaries and administrators. This was in the fourth week of the project, a month after New Year's Day, and we had just lost a Space Shuttle. I wanted to discuss with the team the overall methodology and rules, as well as organize the team for the duration of the project.

The first issue was the rules by which we would work. My office would always be open, and even if the door was closed, if the issue was important, you could interrupt me even if the division manager was there. This would be no "dog in the manger" type of environment; everyone would share information freely, and I would help out by talking and monitoring down to the programming level whenever I felt like it.

14.2.22   Project Documentation

Due to a lack of time, the only documents we would deliver with each software release would be a user guide for each subsystem. This meant that I would need a great technical writing team, one that was made up of software engineers who also knew how to write in fluent, clear and concise, unambiguous technical English, in addition to being expert technical editors. There were several reasons for this. One was that I needed to provide the customer with documentation that exceeded commercial standards in ease of understanding and quality. I had a good software engineer who knew how to write well in English, so I took him off programming and made him the team chief of the technical writers. Technical writers in any but the most leisurely project environments are essential and big cost reducers.[13]

The all-hands meeting brought out a point: we could not do the design documents until we completed the delivery of the system. The user guides would be ready with each software delivery, but we would only have a rough idea of the details required to maintain the source code. We talked; all 45 members of the development team participated fully. We all finally agreed to the following rule: No one, but no one, seriously, would be permitted to leave the project until I gave my permission to leave for another job. After the final software delivery was tested, installed, and operational we would describe the detailed design in a hybrid design document called the GDSS Design Book. Each subsystem would have one, and there would be an overall design book that pulled all of GDSS together. This item was to be designed during the period we were developing. All agreed to remain, and did. We were now bound and determined to prove that a system like GDSS could be accomplished in 21 months and be easy to use and maintain. This was a great and creative team effort. Everyone would share equally in the work and the pride of having built it.

14.2.23   Finding an Ada Expert

I looked into the issue of using Ada, but real expert practitioners were hard to find. So I sent the programming members of the team to a one-week, fast-track class in Ada, and procured a number of Ada instructional video tapes. Good, experienced programmers learn a new language like Ada fast. Best of all, I found a guy who was one of the top Ada gurus in the country at the time, and hired him away from a large company. This project was going to be the largest Ada project up to that time, in lines of code, and I told him that if he was as good as he and others said he was, then he couldn't afford to miss this chance to participate. He said, "I'll be there." He was instrumental in teaching the rest of the team, and in answering questions on Ada. He knew the structure, the syntax, and the application. There was no question he was unable to answer. He was our Ada guru, and a great one at that, and we all owed him a debt of gratitude.

---

[13] See Chapter 7, subheading "Engineers as Technical Writers."

One serious aspect of Ada as a programming language is that it is a demanding language to program in. By "demanding" I mean that it will not compile sloppy work. Once it has compiled and linked a program, a module, or a software element, it is steady as a rock. Granted, on the occasions during test and integration when a software bug does appear, it is hard to correct the problem; better said, it is "work-intensive."

Why was it important to GDSS that I had the common sense to select Ada? It proved that Ada afforded far fewer programming bugs than did Fortran or C. It had one additional important impact. At the time we started to program our applications seriously, in March 1987, programming was done online. This meant that the discipline in programming I was used to was gone. In the approach I learned, you first described what a module was to do in good technical English on paper. Then, you flowcharted the module with the help of an IBM template. This was followed by writing out the code to the right of the flow chart with the use of a No. 2 pencil. Finally, you commented the code with the same pencil, before keypunching the cards and submitting them to an operator. Well, that era was gone.

What did this mean? This meant that even with a team chief or senior lead programmer, it was nearly impossible to check and oversee the work performed by individual programmers, quite a few of whom were sloppy. In this way, many bugs enter a subsystem and the results are a costly waste of time spent on debugging.

Not only are the time and money spent on debugging bad, but they mean that the program, module, or subsystem is essentially "subjective" in its organization; that is, it represents entirely the viewpoint of the programmer, without input from someone else with more experience. So the program can be sloppy, very sloppy, awful, and, finally, useless. It can be greatly excessive in the lines of code it contains to express the function it needs to perform. It can be convoluted and almost impossible for anyone but the programmer who wrote it to maintain, and more often than not, even that individual will forget what he has written, and why. I have had the experience where one programmer had repeated the code for an undocumented algebraic equation eight times in the same program. It was obvious from the reconstructed equations that he had simply forgotten what he had done and why. This may work out on a large, fast computer with plenty of memory, but it is out of the question on something with a smaller architecture. It will slow the thing to a crawl.

So Ada, at least, put the guys into a disciplined environment; they had to be careful, and this forced attention to detail on them. Those who couldn't handle the environment left for other jobs.

14.2.24 Testing and Database Design

Testing was another matter that was critical. I had my deputy, who was a computer hardware wizard, set up a replica of the entire USAF MAC network using Ethernet and TransLAN connecting DEC MicroVAX-IIs (Q-3s and Q-5s) and one DEC VAX 8600. The Air Force actually provided 17 MicroVAXes. This was great, because I could model the MAC network in our laboratory, a nice, well-designed place, and each team had its own MicroVAX to develop its subsystem, without polluting the development network at large. Once the testers accepted a unit-tested module from a team, it was installed via magtape onto the clean simulated network. The number of terminals on the SimulatorLAN was identical to the functional positions/stations used by the MAC Operators in the performance of their jobs at Scott, Travis, Maguire, and the other AFBs. Thus, when the MAC duty officers and noncommissioned officers came to JPL to sit down with their engineering counterparts (on a bimonthly basis, or as needed), they were doing their functional jobs in building their computer displays.

The large documentation team (composed of nine technical writers and one editor) would have a current user manual for each station ready. This had many uses. First, of course, it made the use of the system easy to learn, so it was a training tool. However, it was also the main testing tool. In the absence of a formal test plan, a functional capability had been developed; it either worked as described by the user guide procedurally or did not.

Then there is the all-important factor of the evolving systems design. We derived the database requirements from the screenfaces. The screenfaces and keyboard action routines reflected the desires and needs of the users rather than the senior design engineer designing it. The users felt happy to get exactly what they wanted in the format and presentation of the data. They were brought in from the beginning; if they liked it, it was just as much a product of their efforts as it was ours, and so our success was theirs. Having user involvement in an implementation from the start saves lots of time, and time is money. There is nothing worse than a system that is user-unfriendly, convoluted, and complicated, and there are many of them around with poorly written user guides, in bad technical English.

Having defined the database requirements, the database team set about designing a distributed, replicated, point-synchronized relational database system, based on DEC RDB. At the time, we had benchmarked all three major DBMSes (Ingress, Oracle, and DEC RDB); all were about on equal footing in performance and schedule. DEC, however, agreed to team with my database team, exchange design data on a weekly basis, and build DEC RDB together; it was at the convenience of the customer, MAC, who needed this capability. Two people on the database team were DEC employees detailed to JPL, and three were Category A contractors, working in much the same way as any JPL employee.

I should mention here that JPL had at the time a restriction on the number of JPL billets allocated to a project. I was allocated only 9 billets; this is why out of 73 members total on the GDSS Project, only 7 were JPL employees.

As RDB developed, it revealed an interesting fact: there were more database developers on the JPL GDSS team than there were at DEC in Nashua, N.H. This was one of the most exciting development subsystems on GDSS, because no one in industry had what we were building, and frankly, it never occurred to the database team that they couldn't build an RDB, together with the close cooperation of the system team. It was an amazing thing for me to watch. Sometimes we would be working and having fun until 11:00 P.M., myself included. I had to come in on weekends and chase them out of the building. One of the accusations on performance statistics that I received was that the team doing the study could not give an accurate estimate of cost, because the entire team worked overtime and on weekends and holidays behind my back for free, just to show the world in industry what American engineers are capable of doing.

So then this, too, brings up the issue of architecting the organization to do the job, and using a methodology appropriate to the schedule, funding level, and the people available. I am certain that my habit of providing a work environment to the engineering and administrative workforce that is stimulating, challenging, exciting, and as pleasant as or nicer than being at home makes for a great product. Selecting the correct development methodology is very important.

14.2.25   Additional Difficulties

Unfortunately, although the Air Force had waived DOD-STD-2167A, a reorganization at JPL brought about a program manager who wanted to impose our JPL-STD-D-4000. I checked it out; all the D-4000 was at that time was an outline, though the engineers who eventually built D-4000 did an outstanding job. I was to use it later on the implementation of the TOPEX Telemetry, Command and Communications Subsystem, as well as the Jason 1 TCCS. It was not that D-4000 was not good; it was just that it didn't even exist. The program manager had probably not even checked if it existed, and if it did, he didn't understand that in a rapid development environment the architectural vision and the design is in the head of the manager-architect and those of his key principal design engineers and systems engineer.

An interesting phenomenon ensued. We were going to build the system, on time and on budget, as I had promised my boss and the Chief of Staff at MAC. Yet, this new program manager was out to stop me at all cost. He reorganized the structure above me several times, and even tried to relieve me. The problem was that the customer loved the product, as it was coming off the assembly line on time and on budget. It was a high-quality system, it had a great user guide, and my boss was happy with my performance, so I remained. (The idea that someone without any substance can work his way up a management structure is discussed in Chapter 12, on leadership.)

When the project was completed, installed, and delivered to the sponsor, a study was done on the software development factors.[14] I include here the performance factors taken at the time of release 3.0.

As it turned out, the sponsor liked the system so much that I was given an additional year of funding to add some interesting extended functional capabilities to the system. This last delivery had some novel technical features and also some very important lessons for me personally.

A most interesting event occurred. As soon as software release 3.0 was in testing, still undocumented but working fine, I was offered $50 million by an individual

---

[14] National Aeronautics and Space Administration, Jet Propulsion Laboratory, California Institute of Technology. Pasadena, Ca 91109. JPL SSORCE/Engineering Economic Analysis, Technical Report No. 1. A Productivity Analysis of JPL Software, July 1989, by Jairus Hinh et al.

representing a consortium. The offer was to give me $50 million and then to move my team and me into another facility in Pasadena and make a commercial version of GDSS. I responded at once that it was not mine to give away, that it belonged to the USAF and to Caltech. The individual with the offer argued that I had completed my obligation; it was public domain, built at taxpayer expense. I refused, and he became very angry and left in disgust. I suppose he had no idea of the meaning of the word "integrity."

However, about six months into the building of the final version of GDSS, release 4.0, I was talking with a highly-placed friend of mine who was an executive with TWA. He was telling me of a product they had that did similar functions at about 1/5 of the functional capability and scale of GDSS. The reason he told me was because he was angry—after they had sold it to another major airline, for $750 million, the company had not used the funds for reinvesting in upgrades that he felt they needed on TWA. So there you go—the people who offered me the $50 million to commercialize GDSS would have sold it to airline companies for probably $1 billion per license, and were trying to cheat my team and me. That is life.

At last, with all the documentation done, and the system installed and running, we had our final review. The review board was made up of good engineers and the applicable program office managers; they were happy. Still, the guy who chaired the board and never understood the system, the technology, or the development methodology was angry. We had an argument with the sponsor present (we were a big team, JPL, USAF-MAC, and DEC), and he told me he didn't believe I had a methodology or a process, and told me (as a last gesture of defiance) to write it down. My team wanted to have a record of the development process and methodology anyway, because they were justly proud of what they had done. So it was documented in JPL publication D-3216.[15] This is a very interesting and helpful document, because it compares the traditional approach specified in DOD-STD-2167A that we all like to follow to a methodology that is unique and different, and which in a pinch can save the taxpayer 7 out of 8 dollars.

We in software development do not always have the leisure of going at an easy pace. Furthermore, our jobs are going overseas because our companies and firms believe that jamming 16 foreign programmers into one room at the Fast Software Motel is cheaper than having it implemented by American software engineers. There is no one who can produce better, more reliable, easier-to-use, and lower-cost software than we do here in this country.

Look at Figure 8, the diagram on decision. The fault lies in our technical management, who in large part are not experienced in all the fields required to manage at low cost, and who have no positive personal qualities of leadership. If, on the other hand, this is the kind of manager America wants, then fine companies will

---

[15] *The Global Decision Support System Software Methodology: Comparison of Non-Standard Software Development Approach to DOD-STD-2167A.* 17 February 1989. Prepared for U.S. Department of the Air Force Military Airlift Command and U.S. Department of the Air Force Electronic Systems Division, through an Agreement with the National Aeronautics and Space Administration by Jet Propulsion Laboratory, California Institute of Technology by Tom Collins, Louis Hirsch, Joseph Galinsky et al.

go the route of DEC, TWA, and Pan Am. It is all management and leadership, not technical expertise, that makes for winners and losers.

The GDSS design team was a truly well-integrated team, in every sense of the word! The Team was made up of three organizations: Jet Propulsion Laboratory, Digital Equipment Corporation, and the USAF Military Airlift Command. I have rarely worked with better and more professional engineers, operators, technical writers, and administrative support personnel than the ones who worked on this project.

Among the many individuals who deserve special mention are Dan Wenrick, Rodney Iwashina, Mark Tarbell, James Brownfield, Larry Johnsen, Henry Judd, Dan Zink, Sebastian Van Alphen, Bill Cline, Tom Collins, Louis Hirsch, Joe Galinsky, Matt Ward, Diane Melin, Elaine Blomeyer, Ken Clark, Sushil DaSilva, and Larry Garcia. There were many more, of course, whose contributions were indispensable; my special "thank you" to all of you.

14.3   CASE STUDY THREE: THE TOPEX TCCS SYSTEM

The Ocean Topographic Explorer (TOPEX) Satellite, Telemetry, Command and Communications Subsystem (TCCS), is a Class A System, developed on a very short schedule and low budget.

14.3.1   The TOPEX TCCS System

Software Development Standard: JPL-STD-D-4000 employed throughout.
Documentation: FRD, SRD, SDD-1, User Guide/Software Operators Manual,
Test Plan, totaling 13,000 pages.
System Size: 196,169 commented lines of code.
Languages: C, Macro, and Fortran.
Total Cost: $5,400,000.
Cost/Line of Code: $27.50

TOPEX, the Ocean Topographic Explorer Satellite (or Poseidon, as the French call it), was decommissioned on 18 January 2006. It performed its science mission nearly flawlessly during its 14 years of operation.

14.3.2   System Description

The TOPEX TCCS is a flight-quality telemetry, command, and communications subsystem of the TOPEX ground system, with a NASA communications center monitoring function added for the support of the TOPEX project. The TCCS is based on Digital Equipment Corporation VAX 6410 computers running under the VMS operating system. It has the capability of processing data rates of 512 KB/s and has two NASCOM Front End Processors (NFEPs) for data storage and formatting. See Figure 13.

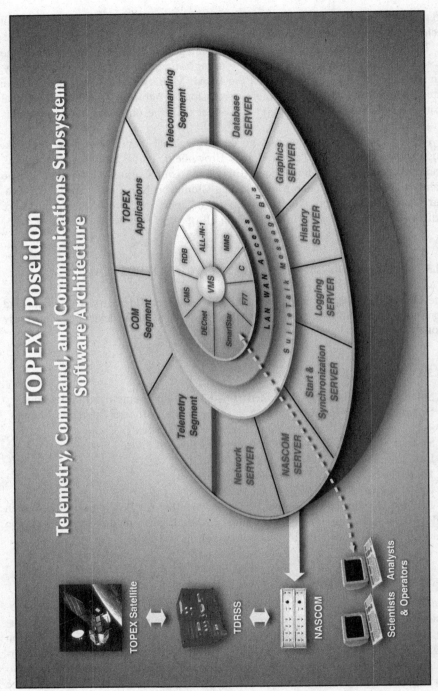

Figure 13. The TOPEX software architecture.

234

The objective of the effort was to complete the TCCS within 27 months, at a cost of under $6.0 million. There was a task contractor in place, Computer Sciences Corporation (CSC). This contract had two separate segments, one being a task contract, the other a TSEP, from two separate organizations of CSC.

Although JPL-STD-D-4000 was not mandated by the project, I chose to apply it strictly.

14.3.3   The Initial Conditions

My part of the development was to start in December 1989 and be completed by March 1992. The computer hardware and software had been ordered and was scheduled for delivery in June of 1990, but wasn't actually received until September 1990, very close to what I had anticipated. Nor were there any facilities for the development available except those of the contractor.

There were three documents available that had been prepared during the preceding 24 months: an FRD, an SRD, and an FDD. However, since no standard had been used in their preparation, they were not properly structured, organized, or content-wise sufficiently developed to be used in their existing form.

At the beginning of the project, there had been a number estimated as to how much work would be involved, in the form of source lines of code (SLOC), since I find this approach a good one to use as a means of quantifying work (there are others, but I view the SLOC metric as the best). After the completion of a project, we add the comments to the SLOCs and come up with lines of code (LOC), since most of my senior design engineers and senior programmers feel that commenting takes as much time as programming does. I agree with this, and I cost a project after completion overall on dollars per LOC.

The estimates varied from CSC, at 47,000 SLOC, based upon their experience with the UARS spacecraft. The systems engineer's estimate was 92,000 SLOC, and my estimate was 130,000 SLOC. (The final total turned out to be 196,169 SLOC.)

14.3.4   Project Constraints

There were a number of constraints. CSC was to be used as the subcontractor because we needed a task contractor. The CSC contractor team was also going to reuse[16] the UARS software on TOPEX. The experience the CSC design team gained on UARS was also of great value to the TOPEX project. Also, adequate in-house facilities at JPL were not available, and I was limited to no more then seven JPL billets altogether.

The already available IBM PCs and Macintoshes were to be used for the definition of the requirements and the design.[17] Also, JPL-STD-D-4000 was to be used

---

[16] "Reuse" is a very misleading and costly word! Out of 47,000 SLOC of Perkin-Elmer Fortran, we were able to force-fit in 7,000 SLOC. These 7,000 SLOC caused more work to fit in than had we simply reprogrammed them in C. I have had the same experience on every project I have done.

[17] Requirements and design must be traceable both horizontally and vertically in the system, down to the software module. Also, it is a waste of time and money to use a system for documentation other than the one you are going to use for development.

"as far as practical."[18] There are some tough lessons to be learned in these three areas, software reuse, using PCs for requirements and design, and using JPL-STD-D-4000 "as far as practical" if cost and budget are limited.

14.3.5   Implementation Considerations

Although it is almost never fully appreciated on projects, there is a glaring lack of computer scientists on all project staffs. Almost all cost overruns and schedule slips are directly traceable to the computer software area. Nothing runs without computer software, not aircraft, not spacecraft, not even automobiles. Yet for some reason, mechanical and electrical engineers, and above all, scientists, have little appreciation for computer science and software. The TOPEX project was no exception.

At first, the TOPEX project manager and staff had an idea of the significance of the tight schedule, but not a full appreciation. Why? The most likely cause is a lack of understanding of the complexity of software; that is, not being able to understand it and therefore ignoring the issues impacting it. This of course is understandable. We all have a hesitation in trying to understand something with which we are unfamiliar. Wasting 24 months "thrashing around," then waking up to a 27 months' distant launch date and getting into gear (not appreciating that I, too, along with every other manager, no matter how good, also have a "thrashing period"), is an indicator of the absence of solid planning.

Then there was the idea that the hardware would arrive someday, and the software would happen as if by magic. Computer hardware and software, and all COTS packages, like compilers and tools, must be available at startup. Staffing up, with its associated "burn rate," yet without solid work getting done is poor practice and a waste of time and money. It forced me to bypass the bureaucracy and borrow all of the needed equipment, software, and COTS packages on the promise that I would buy it all. There is plenty of danger here from those in the bureaucracy who run the procurement process without much regard for the objective of our existence, which is to be there at the launch date, ready for liftoff and mission operations.

Finally, there is the availability of work areas. Even with plenty of time, work space is important. The work space is often as important as the architecture of the organization. It either enhances or hinders the work getting done. Each project has its own unique requirements, with respect to software technology, hardware, schedule, and budget. Cost estimates that do not consider these requirements are flawed.

TOPEX TCCS had office and cubicle space available for individual employees, but no office for me, or for a work "war room," which the nature of a TCCS requires. The work on the development of a TCCS generally takes about 48 months on the average. On TOPEX, all I had left was 27 months to launch.

---

[18] "As far as practical" is an incomplete directive that will cause a lot of confusion and waste of money and schedule. What it means in reality is "everybody does his own thing." You either commit to a standard, or you don't. When everybody does his own thing, the interface specifications are a nightmare to write, and very costly to connect to!

At times, as the manager at the subsystem level, I was overwhelmed by the sheer weight of the bureaucracy against getting anything done. I had to keep in mind the reason I was given the job in the first place, namely, to get it done, and be there for launch. If one keeps that in mind, everything else falls into place.

I simply took over a medium-sized conference room for my office space, and another large conference room for my war room. This got many people angry, above me, below me, and along side of me. How dare I do such a thing, take over territory! It is easy, as I often have to explain; "I have a launch date to meet!"

As I have said, each project has its own unique requirements, thus a "cookie cutter" approach seldom works. One must have many templates and wells of experience to pick the right approach, and then modify it or synthesize it with several other schemata and come up with a new one that works efficiently.

This I did. It worked out fine. There was objection from all hands, but since many of them had worked for me before, they trusted that it would work out and that it would enhance our work and the need for coordination.

14.3.6 Development of TOPEX TCCS

My part of the work in developing the TOPEX TCCS started late one evening at the end of November 1989. I was called in by my division manager for a talk.

(The reason I am going into detail is to show how cumbersome and disjointed projects can become by simple oversights and perspectives of an incomplete object. This is important for anyone desiring to build at low cost. The lessons learned contain many nuances that are rarely told, and therefore the lessons are incomplete.)

Out of the blue, my boss told me that I had to transfer to a different section in our division and complete a satellite telemetry, command, and communications system that was behind schedule and over in funding. He also added that I had no say in the matter, since he saw that I was not enthusiastic about TOPEX.

He told me that the mission of the satellite was to acquire, process, and verify altimeter sea surface height data. Data sets would then be distributed to principal investigators who would map the mean and variable geostrophic surface current of the world's oceans. The studies would then give indications of the effect of ocean temperatures on global climates.

The work was being done in our division, and my boss said that all there was remaining of the budget was $5.6 million, and the schedule was now down to 27 months to launch. Normally the TOPEX Ground System would have been a part of the services provided by the JPL Deep Space Network and our Space Flight Operations Facility (SFOF); however, because of time constraints and budget considerations, and because TOPEX-Poseidon was a partnership between NASA and the French Centre National d'Etudes Spatiales (CNES), it had to be completed on time for the launch and within the budget remaining for the job. As division manager, he was responsible for the work in his division, and he intended to get it done. He had seen my work in building systems fast and at cost over many years, and he decided that he wanted me to do it.

The spacecraft was being built here in the U.S. by Fairchild Aerospace, a distinguished American firm whose WWII planes I used to model out of balsa wood as a kid. It seems I was always immursed in modeling.

The TOPEX spacecraft (or better said, *satellite*, to distinguish it from great interplanetary spacecraft like the Voyagers and Viking) was to be launched from the Colony of French Guiana, from the Launch Facility at Courou, on an Arianne IV-42b Launch Vehicle, so there was an international side to the operation. The cost of this included that of the launch vehicle and the launch pad reservation. Each extension of the launch pad cost around a million dollars per day, for up to a week's delay; then you were forced to go to the end of the line. Such costs incurred are very burdensome to a project. At JPL, we have never had a delay in launching due to the ground system not being ready. The TCCS therefore had to be ready.

14.3.7 Agreeing to Do the Job

The TOPEX TCCS is a subsystem of the TOPEX Ground System (TGS) that supports satellite management during flight operations, and geophysical data production and distribution. The TCCS provides the functionality required to capture, process, and display telemetry data, transmit commands to the satellite, communicate with it, receive data from it, and make the data available to the other subsystems within TGS and to agencies external to TGS.

The TGS consists of five subsystems, including TCCS:

- Mission Planning (MP)
- Scheduling and Sequencing Subsystem (MPSSS)
- The Navigation Subsystem (NAVS)
- The Science Data Subsystem (SDS)
- The Satellite/Sensor Performance Analysis Subsystem (SPAS)

If I were to accept the job without asking for more money or schedule, my boss promised me I'd get a promotion to Engineer Level 8, a great incentive to get it done. Senior Research Engineer and Senior Scientist was the only way to make E-8 without becoming a "stem-winder" or line and project manager. Stem-winding was something I was not good at, either in the Army or at JPL.

I agreed to do the job, not that I had a choice, but I was curious. I had never built a Class A system. The telemetry, command, and communications subsystem of a ground system is the only Class A system on the ground, in that a wrong or faulty command error can cause the loss of the spacecraft.

There were many interesting problems associated with this project. The first was that I had never built a spacecraft ground system before. When I was given the job, some of the senior engineers told me that there had been a lot of talk about me having no experience in spacecraft flight projects, except for being Team Chief of the Voyager General Science Data Team, which was career-wise a dead end at JPL. We, like any organization, have our power groups and elite areas. With us it has been traditionally the spacecraft engineering folk who were at the top of the list, and admittedly they were the geniuses, because they designed and built interplanetary spacecraft. Once JPL "outsourced" that skill function, things changed. My reply was that as far as I was concerned, computer software is computer software. For someone else with limited experience, however, it may be true that building a spacecraft ground system would be daunting.

If all you have done in your working life is build spacecraft, then that is probably all you know how to do. Computer science and software were not considered critical or important skills at the Laboratory. This bothered some of the guys, but not me. I knew better.

14.3.8   Ground Truth

The ground conditions at start of work are very important, so I must discuss them for the sake of lessons learned.

The "ground truth," as we call it in the Army, is the real enemy situation, the friendly situation, and the terrain. I use these terms because these three factors are the reasons Americans build software that is so terribly expensive.

The enemies in this case are the well-meaning and well-intentioned people who, because of their subjective mindset, will do everything to stop you from getting the job done. What is getting the job done? It is the accomplishment of the mission: being at the launch pad, with the spacecraft sitting aboard the launch vehicle, fueled, and all systems functioning flawlessly, ready for liftoff. That is the accomplishment of the mission at NASA and at JPL. Anything short of that is a poor job.

Now, people will say, as they often do, "How come you're so outspoken?" To tell it the way I see it is to add emphasis to the theme of success and failure as we did in the Army. Keep in mind that we are engineers, being paid high salaries at taxpayer expense; Kantian and Aristotelian ethics demand that we earn our daily bread by doing the very best we can for the individual who pays our salary, i.e., the American taxpayer. This is a strange concept to many of my colleagues around the country, where managing means a big office, executive furniture, and lots of frequent-flier bonus miles.

14.3.9   Start of Project Development

To start things off, I met with my systems engineer. He was a very nice and smart person, to my good fortune. He introduced himself and told me that he was delighted to have me assume the job of technical manager, and that I would be making all the programmatic decisions, and he would be making all the technical decisions. I replied that *I* would be making *all* decisions. I know that this was a real downer for him and for me as well, as it has been for most of the people who have worked for me as systems engineers.

I then took a four-day period to read the FRD, SRD, and SDD that I had been given by my immediate supervisor, who was the division representative for the project. My new section manager and another group supervisor met me in the section manager's office to give me my instructions, and to get some feedback on my estimate of the work. When asked what I thought of these three all-important documents, I replied that they contained lots of good and important information, but were FRD, SRD, and SDD in name only. They had little structure, followed no standard, and the contents were in poor and ambiguous English.

They got upset and angry with me. I told them that it was okay, I'd fix the system, after all that is why I was told to do this job. It is a fact of life that if you want to get your work done efficiently, people will resist you and try to stop you. The harder they resist, the more assured you should be that you are on the right track. If they don't resist, then your approach is their approach, and it will not lead anywhere. You might as well have remained doing the job you had been doing before you arrived.

A 27-month schedule for implementation of a Class A ground system is not long, and $5.6 million is not much for such a job. A two-year period had already passed, and about $2.0 million had been spent with nothing to show for the effort. This was going to be a very difficult job.

The team was physically separated. The contractor had a facility in town, made up of two separate competing divisions of the same corporation. The only inherited hardware on the JPL side consisted of two Macintoshes, three IBM PCs, and a couple of printers. The selected ground systems hardware, which to my good fortune was Digital Equipment Corporation equipment, had been ordered. They were supposed to be delivered in June of 1990; launch was to be in May of 1992. This, of course, meant that I would be in trouble, because the delivery would be at least four months late. Development couldn't start until the hardware was delivered, and that was not good enough.

There was no development facility for the TCCS, and the although the design team was made up of very intelligent, hardworking, and capable people, unless they were organized properly and had a set of procedures to work with, they would simply thrash and go to meetings. This is a dangerous phenomenon. Compounding this problem, the section was busy doing "the routine"—leaving my action item requests at the bottom of the in-box.

As luck would have it again, the section manager left, and an interim section manager was put in place to continue supporting the Deep Space Network. Fortunately, I also had the support of a friend who was the Chief Administrator of the Division; in this way, as in the Army, I could get things done, and untangle the logjams. It is always the initiative, the taking of risks, versus the choice of staying within the bureaucratic rules and not getting the job completed. Yet if I risked getting it done, I would make enemies of those who do not dare, whose name is Legion. There was this terribly clear choice: Was I going to have the TOPEX TCCS ready for my project manager, my division manager, and the customer or not? My project manager had also taken a big risk. He had decided because of the cost and schedule factor to bypass the Deep Space Network Multi-Mission

System, in defiance of his boss. He would go with a custom-made spacecraft ground system, using NASCOM to the White Sands tracking station, and then going through TDRSS Satellite Communications to link with the TOPEX spacecraft. Bypassing the DSN was not very convenient politically. So much depended on my getting the job done, and getting it done well, and having it on time for launch. The idea was of launch-readiness: "We're ready!" not just, "Well, we're about as ready as we'll ever be." This had by 1990 slipped somewhat in the minds of many of our engineers. The ground system manager was also supportive, and to my luck, while we had just lost our ground system engineer, we were appointed one of the very best systems engineers ever, Don Royer, dependable, technically super, and current. He was a delight to work with and helpful whenever I needed his skills.

14.3.10 Architecting the Environment

The first thing I needed was my large office/conference room where I could tack the design on the walls. I like to look at designs "at a glance." This has a lot to do with perception and the art of aesthetic design[19] or logical symmetrical forms. I believe, contrary to some views, that the beauty of art is not restricted to paintings, music, and architectures, but applies to software design as well. I see computer software architecture as a form of art, like a beautifully designed bridge. A bridge has many beautiful philosophical implications. It is a means of getting from one side of something to another. What we do in software is always build bridges, from the ground to a spacecraft for example. To be a successful architect, one must be able to view this electronic bridge phenomenon with the eye of the human reason.

It is not strange then that the *Critique of Pure Reason* is so important to building clean, harmonious systems architectures, as opposed to throwing together a bunch of this and that, which looks like a pile of rubble to the mind's eye. Most of our computer software systems are thrown together as if they were beaver dams. In a way, it is fortunate that most people are not equipped with the ability to visualize the software in the space allocated to them by the human reason. They would die of fright if they saw it. Software is an abstraction of the human thought system and the human thought process. Some of us are well organized in our mental process, and some are not.

The next task was to architect the working environment, to lay out an office in such a way as to reduce turnaround time in the process of developing the software requirements and the design. Since I had no previous experience in building a ground system, the design had to be flawless and the process careful. We could not make mistakes that would cause us to backtrack and do guesswork corrections of our mistakes. This made me think of a new approach to the development problem: the architecting of the environment, the creation of a true software engineering war room. This was easier said than done.

I took over a medium-sized conference room for my office, because as a work habit, my office serves also as a conference room, which is always in session,

[19] Immanuel Kant, *Die Drei Kritiken*, Kroner Verlag Stuttgart , 1975. pp. 290–293.

regardless of how busy I am. My team members, when technical or administrative issues arise, simply come in and sit down and talk things over. I always listen, even when I'm taking care of my own business. This method allows me to be aware of issues and conflicts in detail, and doesn't disturb me in the least. I took over a very large conference room that was serving as a technical library and converted it to a "war room" (or "design hub," as it is sometimes referred to). This is where all of my team do their work and hold detailed discussions.

Actually, I got the idea of setting up my projects from the SHOC (SHAPE Headquarters Operations Center) while serving at SHAPE, Belgium, in the Operations Division. The Supreme Allied Headquarters Allied Powers Europe (SHAPE) had a huge official War Room, and all of the Cells (Operations, Intelligence, Logistics, Personnel, Communications, Ground Forces, Air Forces, Maritime Forces, etc.) had their offices around this large "arena." They had large glass windows, as well as a door with direct access to the War Room. On the walls were the situation maps in very large relief.

In my briefing studio were closed-circuit television cameras and PDP-11 computers; from here I could brief remotely, to monitors at all major commands in Europe, including the Secretary General of NATO, SACEUR, and the NATO Military Council. It was, my boss told me, very close to the way the Strategic Air Command War Room had been set up for Gen. Curtis LeMay. So the idea of a design hub came from here; I modified the concept for engineering work and on a much smaller scale.

In my version of the war room, the personal working cubicles of the engineers were located along the walls of the conference room; they faced the wall, away from the center. This is where their personal workstations or terminals were to be located. A space was allocated for a high-speed printer as well. At one end of the design center was a large motion picture screen for projecting the design images onto the wall, with a large copyboard for drawing. In the center of the war room was a very large conference table, with sufficient chairs to accommodate about 20 individuals, the CSC subcontractors included. See Figure 14.

14.3.11 Hardware Procurement, Software Procurement

At this time it was clear that if we were going to meet the launch date we had to have working software, which meant we had to have working hardware, the delivery of which was at least 9 months away. Working with the burn rate I had inherited, and with most of the employees either idle or going to meetings, this was not productive, and I would run out of funds long before launch. I had to procure my own hardware, and thereby bypass the Project and the Laboratory bureaucracy.

Since I had to scrounge up my own hardware, I first assigned a technical writer to write the Automatic Data Processing Plan. The ADP plan was still a mandatory process required by the government, NASA, and JPL. I needed right from the start four DEC workstations, the kind that had proven themselves so handy and effective on GDSS. I called the JPL DEC representative, and told him what I needed and that I had no approved ADP plan, but I needed the workstations, printers, and terminals quickly because there was no time to waste. He had quite a few "floaters" around

Figure 14. The TOPEX "war room" environment.

243

the Laboratory, and he reassigned these to me. I then called a friend of mine who was at the time the section manager of the Institutional Computing Section, and asked him to connect me via DECnet to the GDSS VAX 8600. This he did, and I had now the compilers for C and Fortran that I needed, as well as VAX Document. We had used VAX Doc among other tools, like VAX Office, VAX Mail, and VAX Phone, all of which were great work enhancers, but by now had become obsolete. In particular, the troops disliked VAX Doc for the documentation task, but my budget was tight and we had to get going. All this had taken about six weeks to do, while I was out recruiting those members of my GDSS team who were available and whom I trusted.

Again I was in luck. A senior engineer and programmer who had been on the GDSS System Software team was available, so I hired him to do the Common Software Service layer and gave him one of the VAX workstations. Next was an Ada programmer; he was ready to go for another exciting adventure in software development, and I gave him the job of developing the Communications subsystem. He, too, received a VAX workstation, and the two set about to do the most important task of getting communications going with the simulator at GSFC, and getting the VAX ready for the applications of telemetry and commanding, plus, of course, the user interface development. Yet another programmer was available for the user interface, and I hired him on as the senior design engineer for that subsystem. Meanwhile, our systems engineer was busy getting the NASCOM front-end processor developed and delivered by the Goddard Space Flight Center.

Since the TOPEX TCCS was a vanilla DEC System, with the VAX 6410s running VMS, the architecture was easy to visualize for those of us who had built GDSS.

The technical writing team was in place, with three excellent technical writers. Although a software standard was not mandated by the TOPEX project, I decided that the JPL-STD-D-4000 would be used throughout, and that we would tailor D-4000 so that it would keep us under development discipline, but not to the extent that it would increase the workload on the developers. The use of D-4000 would also prevent the need for frequent code walkthroughs, and prevent mistakes that would force us to stop what we were doing and backtrack into our code.

14.3.12   The Relationship with the Contractor

The president of the Computer Sciences Corporation's Science Division, with which we had a contract, was very helpful and enthusiastic. He provided me with a CSC manager to take over from our current systems engineer. He was probably one of the best systems engineers I have ever met anywhere. I asked him to take over the development of the requirements and the design, with my special timesaving caveats. His leading the requirements and design of the TOPEX TCCS was a great achievement.

The systems engineer is extremely important to a project; at a minimum, he needs to be the alter ego of the manager and be able to interpret technically what the manager-architect explains his vision to be. The systems engineer is at least one factor closer to the technical detail of the work. Any disconnect between these two people is costly to the project. CSC also provided some truly great senior design engineers for commanding and telemetry, with CSC programmers filling out the team.

The relationship between the CSC contract and JPL made for an integrated team. This was demanded by the budget and schedule. The accountability and responsibility as the JPL manager was mine. The work could now begin. After organizing the task, I went to see a respected friend and colleague who was the manager of the section that provided spacecraft operators and analysts. I asked him to give me an operator and analyst who would help design the user interface. I explained that it was the operators who had to be happy with the display and the interface, not the designers, since the operators would know better what made them happy and what they were comfortable seeing. SmartStar was already selected as the screen design software we would build on, so we were not going from scratch. My friend, however, was overcommitted, as sometimes happens, so the arrival of our operator and analyst was delayed about six months. Just as I had predicted, they didn't like what we had done, and so we redesigned the user interface to suit them. One of them, a senior operator from the Voyager project, demanded that we provide him with text-based VT-220 terminals, not a graphical VAX workstation, because that was what he was used to. This of course didn't happen. (Anecdotally, on one of my earliest projects, which I had designed at the Laboratory in 1982, some development is still being done using the ancient VT-220s. Interesting.)

I was also lucky that I did not need to design the TOPEX TCCS from the user interfaces, like I did on GDSS. Spacecraft ground systems were fairly well known by that time. I had two very good systems engineers, one for the NFEP, who also knew the TOPEX satellite, and an equally outstanding systems engineer who had the expertise with the CSC senior design engineers from the UARS satellite. We had a great technical writing team to develop the requirements and design, following the tailored interpretation of JPL-STD-D-4000. From the FRD through the SRD and FDD, the documentation was extensive and detailed, but we didn't have to backtrack on fixing big mistakes, which would have cost us time and money.

The software testing area made for an interesting insight on TOPEX TCCS. Before the actual delivery of the software releases in the past, we always prepared a test plan. The test plan covered the requirements stated in the software requirements document, and as is usually the case, required by a software standard.

14.3.13   Test Plan Scheduling

We programmed following the SRD, until to my surprise the first major test date loomed on the horizon. This was the testing with the onboard computer of the satellite at Fairchild. It turned out that many of the required capabilities were not ready, while those that weren't to be tested until later (e.g., during vacuum chamber testing) were available now. This caused us to stop what we were doing and complete the mandatory test for that scheduled event. This was repeated with the vacuum chamber test also. Again we had to stop after we were informed what capabilities were going to be tested. The proper procedure for avoiding this kind of wasted time, effort, and associated stress is to prepare an overall test schedule, detailing all capabilities to be tested, and then use the Software Requirements Document as the guideline to prepare the test plan for that particular system test. Along with the test plan should be the user guide appropriate to the test plan. In this case, it is the user guide or user manual that should contain the procedures for the proper exercising of the individual test cases required to see if it works or not. The preparation of the software capabilities and the test plans did cost us some time that we could have saved by having all the test parameters available to the team before we started development. In fact, the development of the architecture can be scheduled in a way so as to accommodate each major test with the software delivery. This is a big saving measure to keep on schedule and keep down cost.

14.3.14   Adherence to a Standard

I cannot overemphasize the fact that rigorous adherence to a software standard, when properly applied, will save time and money, as well as reduce the frustration level on a highly complex task that is to be accomplished over a relatively short period of time. A well-designed and implemented set of requirements and design provides a baseline for problem analysis and solutions that can eliminate the need for code walkthroughs, and facilitate the coordination of action items by eliminating ill-defined and ambiguous requirements.

The TOPEX TCCS design team used the D-4000 standard as a guideline to define the documentation set appropriate to the task. Once we had the "documentation tree" in place, the entire team as a group in session developed the table of contents (TOC) for each book in the documentation set. In this way, the TOC served as a checklist for monitoring the progress of the design. A well-designed and robust system resembles an edifice, like the architecture of a bridge or building. The successful implementation of a system (if we mean by success that it is a quality product, on time, and on budget) depends very much on the selection of an appropriate underlying architectural philosophy upon which the system will be built.

As in all of my projects, this too was a special team effort, composed of Jet Propulsion Laboratory and Computer Science Corporation personnel. The team members were great talents, the most memorable of whom were Rodney Iwashina, Willie Huo, Art Rinaldi, Phil Coffman, Ken Clark, Mike DiLoreto, Jerry Hill, Mike Kotska, Tom Collins, Louis Hirsch, Joe Galinsky, Don Royer and his ground system engineers, Al Hofmann and the TOPEX operators and analysts, and Anil Agrawal.

14.4   CASE STUDY FOUR: THE JASON 1 TCCS SYSTEM (JTCCS)

Software Development Standard: JPL-STD-D-4000 employed throughout.

Documentation: FRD, combined SRD/SDD, Software Test Plan, combined User Guide/Maintenance Manual, totaling 7,000 pages.

System Size: 803,000 lines of new code, written by the team in C++, Java, TCL. 400,000 lines of legacy code also integrated into the system.

Cost/Line of Code:

$9.65 per line of code (new and legacy code, at different rates).

Total Cost: $8,773,643 at software delivery.

14.4.1   The Jason 1 TCCS System

The JTCCS subsystem was nominated to represent Jet Propulsion Laboratory at the NASA Software of the Year Competition, in Fairmont, West Virginia, for the year 2002. Alas, we did not win. One of the criteria for winning the competition is that the software be used by several users, and not only by the developing project. Try as we did to sell it to other projects, we failed. I attended symposium after symposium, and held demonstrations and briefings lauding the benefits of elegant, robust spacecraft ground systems at under $10 per line of code; there was simply no interest. This is another lesson you the reader should be prepared to accept: No matter how good your systems are or will be in the future, you are doing it for your project and for your colleagues and co-workers only. Don't be disappointed if others in your peer group across the country have no interest in your product, regardless of how low the development cost, how elegant, open, or extensible the design, how easy the maintenance, or how low the software failure rate; they will never take your product and use it. The conservation of private or public funds is not one of the major concerns to most people. "The longer the job lasts, the better." That is just a fact.

Every system I have ever built or managed the development of has been unique, even if it served a similar function, such as spacecraft command and control. Jason 1 TCCS is no exception. It is similar in its functional application and architecture to the TOPEX TCCS, but is quite different. Why? The first reason is that the requirements were very different. The second important difference is that the state of the art in computer hardware and software had advanced dramatically in the time since the TOPEX TCCS implementation was started. There was one additional major factor, and that was the lessons learned over eight years and the experience of the team. One factor was constant, however, and that was my mandating the use of the JPL-STD-D-4000 software development standard.

As I write this book, the Jason 1 satellite, which is a follow-on to the TOPEX-Poseidon satellite, is in orbit and performing its mission nearly flawlessly. This is a tribute to the entire Jason project team, from the project manager on down to every member of the project in CNES, NASA, and JPL.

14.4.2   System Description

The JTCCS is a flight-quality, beyond state-of-the-art (for 2003) Class A telemetry, command, and communications subsystem with an equally elegant user interface to match. Truly a great system, it is the culmination of 17 years of experience in building command and control systems. It is by virtue of the systems requirements a high technology, very low-cost TCCS, designed to support multiple spacecraft. The multiple spacecraft requirement was intended to provide continuous support for four generations of Jason-class satellites over a period of 20 years. It is currently hosted on a DELL Power Edge 400 series computer running Windows/XP, but it was designed and implemented to be platform- and operating system-independent, permitting the seamless changeover to the new platforms and operating systems that will come available over the next 20 years.

The JTCCS flies the Jason 1 satellite through three Low Earth Orbiter Terminals ("Leo-Ts") located at Poker Flats, Alaska, Wallops Island, North Carolina, and Aussaguel, France. It comprises 803,000 lines of code, written in C++, Java, and some Macro and SQL. The total time and cost of development was 36 months and $8.8 million.

I received a total of just three JPL billets for the job, so in the main it was accomplished with Category A contractors, most of whom have worked with me for 17 years. Early in the development, my team was outsourced to the Information Systems Development Support (ISDS) contractor that our division manager had put into place to help the division with the overflow of work. The ISDS contract was originally with AverStar, which then became InfoTech, and finally Titan, Inc. Throughout all of these transitions, the ISDS Manager worked successfully to make JTCCS a resounding success. I am mentioning this because the relationship between contractor and sponsor can have a dramatic and often crippling impact on the budget, the quality of the project, and the schedule. In our case, the ISDS team was superb in its teamwork, organization, and coordination. The methodology used in this management approach is worth writing a book about and is only discussed in generic terms here.

14.4.3 The Initial Conditions

The Jason 1 TCCS project had a reasonable schedule, which started on 14 December 1998, with launch scheduled initially for May 2000. There were several reasons we built another separate ground system once again, and did not use the Deep Space Network. The first was that the Earth Sciences program office wanted to operate both TOPEX and Jason 1 on the same system and out of the same facility, thereby making the work of the operators easier. Flying two spacecraft off the same system also reduced the learning curve for operators and reduced the number of operators required to fly the spacecraft. This, of course, reduced overall mission operations cost. The second reason was implementation time. In the field of interplanetary spacecraft ground systems that are very complicated and costly, development time is very long and costly as well. Satellite command and control systems as a rule don't have large budgets. The third reason was that when you build a unique system, the project manager and ground systems manager have more control over the development effort, and have options available to change the requirements in the "middle of the stream" without impacting delivery, and without having a huge impact on the budget.

The only real constraint was that we were going to fly Jason 1 on the same system with TOPEX. Since we had ported TOPEX for reasons of maintainability and efficiency from the VAX 6410 to DEC Alpha machines running OpenVMS, this was not a problem. We also had no mandated software development standard to follow, so it was up to me. Being familiar with JPL-STD-D-4000, and always preferring to use a standard, I decided to mandate it for the development of the TCCS. The one minor constraint was that since I was allocated so few JPL billets for the work, I would have to do it with contractor personnel, which was fine, since almost all of my computer scientists are contractors, or work-producing consultants.

14.4.4 Implementation Considerations

As a starter, the Jason 1 satellite was completely different from TOPEX-Poseidon. TOPEX had been U.S.-built by Fairchild Aerospace, and Jason was brand new, with a spacecraft bus called Proteus; it was built by Alcatel, a French company under contract to CNES. This new spacecraft bus was to be a new series of spacecraft for French commercial satellites, and had many new functional requirements and new and different instruments from TOPEX. During a design one wishes to satisfy a number of different design objectives for multiple missions; however, there are vague or unclear requirements for the spacecraft ground system. Anticipating problems, I decided after much discussion with the design team that the common software services package would have a strong first priority. This was lucky for us. As we began to build our design, we decided that object-oriented design should be incorporated throughout, even though we were already using a tool, EasyCASE, that did not support object-oriented design very easily. We had already done a lot of work in design and programming, and we couldn't switch to Rational Rose, which I was using on another project of similar size. Keeping the individual design team members happy by accommodating their individual needs to gain experience on new design tools and languages is always a part of my approach when I develop a system. So in the case of the design tool, I didn't yield, but as far as using C++ and Java, I did. This revealed another problem. Although we all liked DEC Alpha and OpenVMS, the software was too slow in execution. The Ground System Manager, who was like a full partner, asked me if we could port the system onto DELL Power Edge 450 computers running Windows-NT, and see if this would make a difference. Once the common software service layer was in operation, the porting went smoothly, and was accomplished in one day. The speed of execution went up by a factor of ten! Amazing! And again, this was thanks to the fact that we had many things going in our favor.

We were following a strict design approach using JPL-STD-D-4000. We had a great technical writer, who was using a design tool for structured design. He was able to shoehorn in the objective design we were pursuing, and this allowed us to know where we were at any time with reasonable certainty. This permitted me to make reasonable decisions to save time and money. Having several projects running in a group, all of which follow strict software developments standards, permits shifting people from one project to the other without losing track or control of the design and implementation schedule. When the French company announced the delays in the delivery of our spacecraft, I shifted some of my team to another large software project that I was developing for another customer. This saved the budget on Jason 1 TCCS by reducing the burn rate to an acceptable level. You can do these kinds of things if you follow standards, are disciplined, document the work in an orderly fashion, and have an experienced group, with experienced engineers who work well as a team. This enabled some of our engineers to build the software for the satellite instruments and other ground support equipment that were required for advanced testing while the spacecraft was being built.

The intention of using Alpha machines and OpenVMS had been a good one. In this way, we had the computer hardware and the software development tools already available. We were also familiar with the application languages. During the years between 1992 and 1998, object-oriented design had come into its own, along with C++, Java, and such design tools as Rational Rose and EasyCASE. Furthermore, as we started the design process, my team of technical writers seriously objected to using VAX Doc, which we had used on TOPEX and GDSS. They said that EasyCASE had built-in design advantages, such as the tracing of requirements to design, the numbering of modules, etc. It was a real time-saver. So I agreed to use EasyCASE.

Now, however, the considerations of software execution speed, new instruments on the spacecraft, the fact that we were not using TDRSS satellites for TCCS, and the delay in spacecraft availability made the project decide that we would not fly the TOPEX and Jason satellites off the same system, but we would build a totally separate and new system! Had we not used JPL-STD-D-4000, and had we not documented what we were doing with discipline, it would have caused a severe overrunning of our budget. However, all things considered, we were building the most advanced and flexible system ever built for a satellite/spacecraft, within an agreed-to budget. This fact negates any complaints about "creeping requirements" impacting budgets and schedule.

Indeed, the results of the system were amazing. The only inheritances that were truly constant from GDSS through TOPEX to Jason 1 were:

- The methodology we use in building systems.
- The design process of improving and using a common software service layer.
- Selecting a software standard and tailoring it to suit our budget and schedule. In this case it was JPL-STD-D-4000, which from the very beginning helped us lay out the JTCCS documentation tree and the contents outline.
- Documenting what we do carefully, as a team, through the use of superb technical writers, who had the authority of the systems engineers. Here I reiterate the idea that all projects of any size above 100,000 lines of code, if done efficiently, need at a minimum two systems engineers.
- Keeping the team small, for clearer oversight, good control, and facilitated optimal communication and coordination between developers.

- Using the design hub methodology to facilitate the design, implementation, and testing process.

14.4.5 The JTCCS Architecture

The technical feature that makes the JTCCS so successful and different from all other systems is its architecture. See Figure 15. What we have achieved is a truly modular and layered architecture that makes the JTCCS totally operating system- and platform-independent. For the first time, when we started the design process, the state of the art in computer platforms, operating systems, and design and development tools had reached a level of sophistication that permitted us to actually create our vision and make it happen. The layering provides an abstraction between the application "plug-ins," the operating environment, and the various COTS packages we use. This enhances the "plug and play" nature of the architecture allowing for the replacement of the sub-layers with little effect on the applications. For example, it is easy to unplug the Talarian product and replace it with our own IPC mechanism or with any other product without affecting the application code.

The most important component of the JTCCS architecture is the Common Software Service (CSS) layer. Architecturally viewed, the CSS layer sits on top of the operating system. See Figure 16. The services the operating system provides are platform-specific. The CSS layer provides the identical services in an abstract format separating the operating system from the application programs. The services that are used in a multithreaded, multiprocessing application include

- Interprocess communications (IPC)
- Shared memory functionality
- Timers and timing functions
- Thread and synchronization functions
- Database access functions
- The message database that defines the structure (field names, data types, and length) of messages passed between processes
- Process control functions (starts, terminations, suspensions, priorities, etc.)
- File services functions
- Global variable functions
- Debugging functions

The CSS enables the JTCCS to be ported seamlessly to almost any operating system and platform. It also permits unplugging the support applications and replacing them with a newer version without interfering with other applications or the overall operation of the system. Some of these services are abstracted a step further from the operating environment via a COTS package or other implementation layer.

In case of JTCCS, the Talarian SmartSockets package was selected as the COTS solution for providing interprocess communications. Likewise, because we were

Figure 15. The Jason TCCS software architecture.

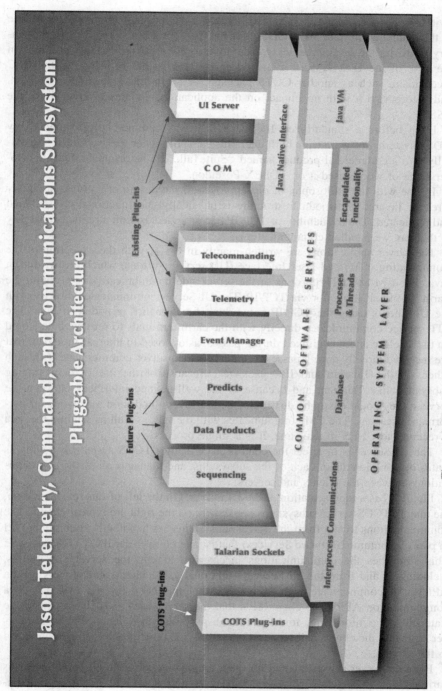

Figure 16. The Jason TCCS pluggable architecture.

253

switching between MS Access and MS SQL Server for database chores, we chose as the database interface APIs ODBC for the C++ processes, and the complimentary JDBC for the Java processes in order to make the software changes minimal. In the case of the IPC services, it would easily be possible to select another IPC mechanism, such as another COTS package, or an in-house developed solution, and incorporate it with no impact on the application modules layered above the CSS.

Long before a standardized IPC capability was commercially available, my GDSS systems software team built one. This capability later was expanded successfully into a commercial product named "SuiteTalk" by its original GDSS developers, one of whom used it on TOPEX-Poseidon.

In line with the philosophy of our approach to the design of software architecture, the layered and modular structure is physically and functionally distributed and replicated. The availability of TCP/IP has provided us with a refined capability in the way we handled communications.

The server applications are written mainly in C++, with the exception of the Commanding (CM) and User Interface (UI) server portions, which are written in Java. The CM and FTP portions of the server side communicate directly with the Earth Terminal Simulator via TCP/IP. The UI Server communicates directly with the UI Clients using the TCP/IP networking functionality provided in Java. The FTP service communicates directly with the earth terminals to retrieve data stored on the satellite and downlinked during passes, as opposed to the real-time data that are received directly during passes. The servers themselves communicate with each other via the Talarian and IPC packages. Because of the use of a messaging subsystem like Talarian, and because of the well-defined interfaces between the servers, they could easily be distributed across several nodes on a network for performance reasons. The CM communicates with the ETs as well as sending the data it receives to CNES in real-time. It is a single process.

The UI Server is in effect the central piece of the JTCCS system. It maintains status information about each of the subsystems and manages all of the communications between the clients and servers.

Figure 17 is a representation of the UI Server. On the left of this representation, the major JTCCS server subsystems are shown; on the right are typical clients. The communications to and from the server subsystems are handled by a common API (a part of Common Software Services) that is layered over the IPC COTS package. This simplifies the communications mechanism among the server subsystems, including to and from the UI Server. Additionally, the clients and servers use an API set to communicate with each other that has been layered over the Java communication APIs. The client APIs that the server uses are defined to provide state and value information to the various displays that the clients contain. The server APIs that the clients call request data or provide directives to be communicated to the servers.

For each server subsystem and for other major functions, the UI Server contains various "data managers." These data managers are responsible for the application-specific functionality that is visible to the clients. For example, from the server side,

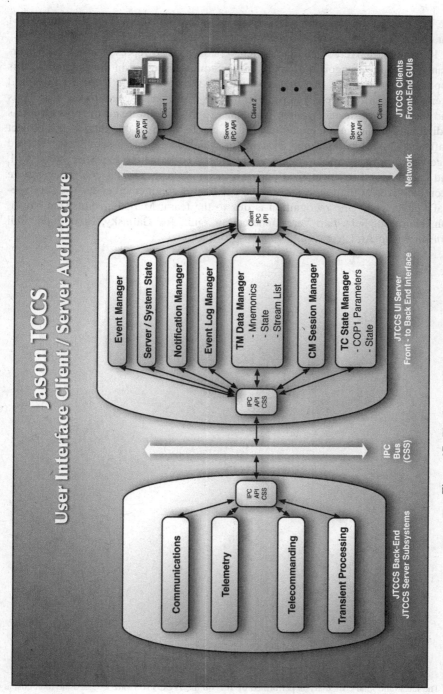

Figure 17. The Jason TCCS UI client/server architecture.

255

the Telemetry Data Manager contains the list of TM mnemonics for the various TM parameters, and the current values of each.

In its final, delivered and operational version, JTCCS represents the best performance in all the categories of cognitive dynamics addressed in the chapters of this book. It is to be noted, that the experience of the design team members increased over the years from project to project, moving from one success to the next. This had the effect of developing the personal expertise of the team members both as individuals and as an integrated team. It is also to be noted that the Jason 1 project staff and the Jason 1 Ground System (of which JTCCS is a subsystem) worked together with unequalled efficiency. Had it not been for the expertise, good will, and commitment to excellence on every person's part, JTCCS could never have been delivered at the low cost of $9.65 per line of commented code.[20] A very special "thank you" and recognition is due to the team: Mark Fujishin, Don Royer, John Guineau, Sebastian Van Alphen, Dan Zink, Joe Galinsky, Hank Judd, Phil Coffman, and Anil Agrawal.

---

[20] The latest and final cost analysis performed by JPL on the JTCCS software assessed the total cost at $9.65 per commented line of code (LOC).

15 Operations, Operators, and Users: Their Impact on Cost

There are two salient reasons for considering the users and operators of a system early on. The first reason is that it is the users who determine whether they like a system or not. When delivering a system to an Air Force or NASA sponsor, if the users are happy and appreciative, the system will be accepted without much inconvenience or delay, allowing the builder to go on to the next job instead of thrashing, making corrections, and fixing problems that cause other problems. It is the first dictum of American business that "the customer is always right." If this is what made the United States great in the business world, why is it then that to many minds the dictum should read "the customer should be happy that he is getting anything at all"?

The second reason for involving the user early in the definition stages is that the user interface to the system (computer screenfaces, and keyboard/mouse action routines) is actually one of the determining factors of the systems architecture, such as during a rapid development project (as mentioned in the GDSS case study of Chapter XII). It is from the user interface, as functionally described by the end user, that the remaining parts of the architecture are developed through inference (e.g., the communications requirements, the database requirements, etc.) and integrated into a well-balanced design.

Visualizing a system "from the outside in" is one of the two major approaches to architectural design. In my education and early work in automatic data processing, learning how to design the user interface played a major role. I have designed and built an entire system, GDSS, completely from the contents, format, and scope of the user screen formats, so well explained in a small book I reference here.[1] Many of the older books have become technically obsolete, but the process and methodologies they contain are as applicable today as they were when they were written.

In fact, on the GDSS project, there was no other way open to me, due to the schedule and funding constraints. This option was also the only methodology and approach by which I was able to establish the scope and architecture of the

---

[1] Wilbert O. Galitz, *Handbook of Screen Format Design*, Information Sciences, Inc, Wellesley Hills, Massachusetts, 1981. This is a valuable book in the library of any software architect.

The Cognitive Dynamics of Computer Science: Cost-Effective Large Scale Software Development, by Szabolcs Michael de Gyurky
Copyright © 2006 by John Wiley & Sons, Inc.

Allied Command Europe (ACE) Command, Control, and Communications System (CCIS) in 1977. I designed, from the outside in, all commands from the user screen-faces at SHAPE Operation Center, through CINCLANT, CINCMED, and CINC-NORTH. At the time, in 1976, computer science was still in the "automatic data processing" phase. Designing from the outside in was not taught back then. It was "top down" or "bottom up" how one designed and implemented. We have come a long way with our technology, but the techniques, methodologies, and processes remain the only transferable commodity.

Thus, the users of a system must sit down with the senior design engineer of a particular segment of a system. This allows the users to describe in detail how they work, what information they need and how fast, how they would like the screen-faces to be designed, and how the data are to be configured. If they get what they asked for, they will be happy because the layout reflects the organization of their minds, and how they view (*Anschauung*) the data they need to work with.

This is much like the way an automobile is designed on the inside. It may be the prettiest, sleekest, fastest car ever, but if the inside is ugly or doesn't correspond to the taste of the driver, it will be a constant irritant and will be gotten rid of soon.

15.1   THE OPERATIONAL REQUIREMENT

The Operational Requirement (OR) also plays an important role in the systems design and the estimation of cost. It is from the OR that the systems requirements are derived, and from the Systems Requirements (SR) that the functional requirements follow. It is a relatively simple issue from a computer science engineering point of view: Only the customer know what he wants, and only the customer can declare that he is happy with the product. By "customer," in the case of the OR in the military, it is the sponsoring staff officer or program manager, usually a lieutenant colonel or colonel. It is the program manager who receives from a service branch the operational requirement and then compiles from the end users (e.g., finance, ordnance, missile command, or satellite ground systems users) what they need to operate the system effectively. The process is usually extracted from the military standard that is mandated to be applied.

Then, upon completion, the evaluation criteria follow: Does it do the job? Are the requirements specified as to what it must do, and to what degree? Is it easy to use for the operators and the analysts performing their duties? These are very important questions, because it is the operators (through the user interface) who perform the routine and tedious work over long periods of time. Only they can say that the system is okay or not okay. The same holds true of the analyst who uses the engineering data ("housekeeping" data) or science data (instrumentation-acquired data) to correct technical malfunctions, and read and use the data provided by an instrument for scientific research. Yet for some reason, this idea of the users being involved from the very beginning in the development of a system (at least at the time of this writing) is almost always ignored.

15.2 THE LACK OF AN OPERATIONAL REQUIREMENT

What if there is no Operational Requirement to be used as a starting point? This happens sometimes, and the results are very costly.

In the absence of an OR, the manager-architect is forced to develop a Concept of Operations (CONOPS) in controlling costs. Whenever you begin to build a system, and have in fact subjectively visualized the system before anything has been set down on paper, you must perform a task that is truly complicated and difficult to do. Often, you will receive vaguely and poorly written operational requirements from your customer. You must sketch out and elaborate on what the system is to do, and how it will be used. The manager-architect takes whatever OR he may have and develops the CONOPS. This is a very important exercise, because although it may wind up being radically different after the proposition is presented to the design team, it is the starting point. Who will use the system? How will it be used? Where will it be used? How frequently will it be used? Will it be used out of fixed or mobile installations? Will it require a degree of survivability, and if so, from what type of threat? What type of communications will it use, common user networks or user-specified unique communications networks, and why? What about the extra expense? Can the extra expense be justified?

15.3 THE OPERATIONS SCENARIO

Now we come to a really difficult but often big money saving exercise called the "operations scenario."

The operations scenario gives scope to the system. Why redesign the technical system without considering how the operators and analysts will make use of it? If the requirements are not complete (and often they are not), then the consideration of who will use it, maintain it, and improve on it becomes an important factor in the architecture.

There are many ways to build an Operations Scenario. My way is to take a time-line snapshot of a two-week period of activity using the system, and insert into it the timeline of every user position involved with the system. Then I describe in the clearest, most unambiguous manner possible what every one of the users does at any given moment. There are usually three shifts in an operational system like military flight controllers, for example. With modern computer technology, high-speed laptops, and wireless, handheld mini-computers, a scenario may not be important, but there are instances where the ability to build a scenario is very important, and not knowing how to do it can affect the budget in a big way.

It is well worth the time and effort (if time and effort are important) to sit down and work out the time and activity flow for each position using the system. It should start at an arbitrary time zero. All positions are identified, such as Operations Chief, Shift Chief, Spacecraft Engineer, Science Data Engineer, Data Communications Engineer, Systems Engineer and Scheduler, and operators for flight following, logistics, and intelligence.

This is only an arbitrary list and may not apply to every case; however, each operator and analyst position has a task that requires certain actions be performed. An acceptable operations scenario, worked out meticulously by the operations team under the chairmanship of the manager and systems engineer, should cover one month. The timeline should be on an hourly basis, and describe who performs which task, and when, and which tasks may be shared or combined into one. It should describe dependencies for actions performed and decisions made by individuals, and data requirements upon which decisions are made. Emergency and out-of-the-ordinary events must be included to identify and anticipate "what-ifs" and the countermeasures needed to correct them. Finally, upon completion, and based on the operations scenario, the user requirements are compiled, which of course can seriously impact the overall cost of the system.

15.4 THE COST OF OPERATORS AND ANALYSTS

Recently there has been a great concern about the cost of operators and analysts required for running military operations centers, satellite operations centers, and the like. There are many reasons for this concern in the military; one is that it costs lots of money in personnel salaries. Another is that these personnel could be utilized in other assignments where they are more urgently needed due to the shortages in filling billets.

This bears discussion since it is an important funding issue and impacts directly on efficient and effective systems design. Operators are very important people in every endeavor, not only in software. To begin with, they are specialized in using the system, and they know how to use it optimally. There will be no machines for the foreseeable future that will replace them. (It will take 10 years to build a cognitive autonomous system, and it will not be cheap. The cost of a true robot system, one that can learn, make decisions, and do most of the things we humans do will be approximately $1.2 billion. That buys a lot of operators who earn between $60,000 and $90,000 per year.)

With the automation of the command centers on GDSS, we reduced the staffing requirements in 1987 from 36 persons per shift to 12 per shift at all the numbered Air Force bases; that's a big savings in personnel. On satellite ground systems here at JPL, we went from a TOPEX operations crew at launch of 20 individuals, to a present Jason/TOPEX team of 3 operators per shift. Again, that's a big savings.

However, the highly qualified and experienced operator analyst cannot be replaced by either a robot or automaton, because the human thought and analysis function is intuitive to a very high degree, and regardless of how highly skilled our robots will be, it might be hundreds of years before they acquire intuition.

The *simulator*, as a driver of a system, is potentially one of the greatest tools and certainly a wonderful investment for those managers who are concerned with schedule, budget, and quality. I'm talking about large expensive systems, like satellites, air traffic control systems, and antiballistic missile defense systems, all of which have immense data throughput.

Let's think a minute about what a Project Operations Center (POC) is, such as we have at NASA or JPL. In military terms, it is a Command Post (CP) or a battle headquarters. For those who can visualize a combat command post, know its components, and understand the workings and functional organization of a project operations center and how it works, it becomes clear that they are functionally the same. Both deal with receiving intelligence (telemetry), posting the data, analyzing the data, making decisions, and uplinking commands (issuing orders), which are most often well conceived, but sometimes not. The results can be the accomplishment of the mission objectives of the spacecraft or satellite, or the loss of the spacecraft. In combat, this relates to those units executing a tactical maneuver and winning (or losing) the battle. At Waterloo, Napoleon issued almost all of the right commands that would have won the battle, but the communications "uplink" was impeded. For a variety of reasons, misinterpretations and failures occurred on the part of his staff and commanders to take initiative and make correct decisions of their own. This analogy of the military command post and the project operations center has a definite validity.

During my tour of duty at SHAPE[2] in Belgium, the idea came to me of building a simulator to drive a command post exercise or field training exercise at the theater headquarters level, and linking it electronically with the major subordinate battle headquarters. SHAPE is located within walking distance of the city of Mons, and a mere 15 minute drive from the environments of the battlefields of Quatre Brass and of Waterloo. In themselves, these two battlefields are as fine a study subject of military command and control, clear unambiguous communications, planning, and execution as one could want.

15.5   THE VOYAGER PROJECT OPERATIONS CENTER

My acceptance of an offer from Jet Propulsion Laboratory, to be the Team Chief of the Voyager project's General Science Data Team, brought me to Pasadena, and into close proximity to the Voyager Project Operations Center. The Voyager ground system fascinated me because its organization, technology, innovation, planning, and operating procedures all reflected the very best in American engineering and engineering practices. The formality of the standing operating procedures evidenced that many of the managers were World War II veterans who knew organization and process control, and were also technically on the cutting edge. Learning how the two Voyager spacecraft were commanded, how the sequencing for the cruise and encounter phases for our scientific experiments were planned down to the second, and how we received the telemetry data were all exciting to me. I was busy learning about the data produced by the instruments on board, and the integration of the data packages into the data transmission streams. Other important aspects of flying a spacecraft are the processes for the preparation of

---

[2] My assignment was staff officer for command, control, and information systems, in the Operations Division of SHAPE.

Science Data Records and Engineering Data Records and their distribution to the principal investigators around the country, at first on magnetic tape, then by line transmission. Then there was another item that stood out, the simulator COMSIM.

In my mind, my intuition took over. The antithesis was my experience with military command, control, and communications, which largely was manual with the Honeywell 6060 computer mainframe-based WWMCCS.[3] That system ruled the entire domain of command and control with an iron hand, and consistently defeated my military colleagues and myself in our attempts to modernize and upgrade it to state of the art, current with the times.

The thesis was the Voyager state of the art system (in its day, in 1979). A synthesis emerged in the background of my mind. The new thesis was a military command and control system that integrated JPL command, control, and communications with a simulator that would drive our normally very expensive CPX/FTXs (Command Post Exercises / Field Training Exercises). The benefits were obvious. The system would add realism to the CPX and FTX, and make it not only a teaching tool for battle and logistics staffs, but give insight into tactical problems. The additional bonus was that if the participating headquarters were linked by secure communications, they would not have to travel, but could participate from their permanent locations, saving lots of money, per diem, separation allowances, and fuel.

15.6 WAR GAMING

It so happened that sometime in 1981 I had to see a person I didn't know who wanted to ask me a couple of questions on military command and control for a project he was working on. I was reluctant to get involved because I was, at least in my conscious mind, committed to spaceflight, and had put the military out of my mind.

I decided to walk up and talk with the guy, who was a senior engineer. We started to talk, and for some reason I commented that it would be a practical thing if he would add a war gaming simulation to this thing he was working on, which was called "Command and Control Utilities." This was a simple name for what was at the time a big problem, namely, survivable networks.

It turned out that the minute the words "war game" came out of my mouth, he became enthusiastic. He was a military history enthusiast and had built the Deep Space Tracking Station outside Madrid. He was an abstract thinker, had a super intellect, and was a problem solver. We became friends for life. After this, I started

---

[3] That famous quote from Napoleon Bonaparte is again appropriate, here regarding my attempts while in the service to change WWMCCS: "Even a coward defends his meal like a hero." This quote is for those young, intelligent, and highly motivated engineers who try to upgrade an existing system for sound reasons, but who are rejected and defeated at every turn.

thinking about the problems of survivable networks and simulations, and we talked about these ideas more as a hobby on our own time. But the new thesis started to emerge, and that was the Joint Theater Level Simulation, JTLS. We conceived it, designed it, and built it here at JPL. The details are discussed in a previous chapter since JTLS proved a watershed for my thoughts on software architectural design. The Joint Theater Level Simulation is still being used, and is still in production, run by the contractors who built the Combat Events Module of the system. Here at JPL, having undergone several changes in its morphology from JTLS to JESS and then to Corps Battle Simulation, it continues along with Voyager as the longest-running projects on the books.

The simulators for theater combat, combat support, and combat service support are not critical Class A systems, the failure of which have catastrophic consequences. Rather, they are large complex electronic sandboxes, or board games, which enable the participants to visualize the battlefield in all its tangible aspects, such as terrain, rivers, towns, and roads. They then superimpose onto these the less-tangible elements, such as the combat units and logistics units, which enable the participants viewing the simulator to gain insights into the possibilities open to both sides of a conflict. War as business is a competition, and a consumer of resources, with endless possibilities, options, and variations to moves in the attempt to gain superiority over the competition.

That means that the command center staff officers from the commander (or manager) on down to the operators and analysts receive all the data and information they need in the proper format and with the correct contents, and at the rate they need it, in exactly the manner they would were the system online and the satellite in orbit and in operation. The only difference is that a computer generates the data; it is not the product of the system proposed to be built. Almost all simulators have their value; I have used some that were almost worthless. A systems simulator should be as accurate for an antiballistic missile defense system as for a Boeing 747. It should provide real, live, and true data; the system does not cause a disaster except if the operator fails.

A great spacecraft mission simulator, like a combat simulator, should be architecturally so generic as to accommodate many different spacecraft systems with their ground control all replicated in software. To accommodate new requirements and new spacecraft, the only change that should be needed is to modify the space-craft database, the antenna database, and communications. A GUI interface should permit the addition of new desired screen formats. I was told that JTLS was of great help to the staff when the Iraqi invasion of Kuwait occurred. They had run a simulation CPX/FTX twice with a similar scenario and force structure. When the invasion happened, and we decided to get the Iraqis out of Kuwait one way or another, the SOCOM staff knew what resources they needed to do the job, and how to do it with the lowest possible loss of life and materiel. In the same way, a project manager should be able to run the simulator for a planetary mission and get a very good idea about how much it is going to cost. It would save a lot of hassle, simulating everything from launch to fly-by or landing, including the science experiments conducted in space or on the surface of a planet.

15.7   THE VALUE OF SIMULATION

What about the benefits of the system simulator? That depends, of course, on what kind of system you are interested in. The Project Operations Center commands and receives telemetry from a spacecraft, as well as monitors and maintains remotely the proper operational status of the spacecraft, the ground systems software, and perhaps even the antennas in the network.

First, to the operators, the simulator provides a training tool that permits operators and analysts to use the system early on, to become familiar with the user interface, and become experts through practice.

Second, the operators participate in the development of the system, by providing feedback in the form of design change requests. These are issued to the design team, the manager-architect, and the systems engineers, and provide insights into the operation of the system that were overlooked in the requirements.

Third, as the system's first release comes online, the operators and analysts already know what to expect and are able to test it more effectively. This means that there is a simulator that drives the command center for the purpose of operator and analyst training, user requirements, and insight to the designers.

Additionally, the system simulator is configurable to permit software testing and mission operations training. A spacecraft simulator, with a launch vehicle simulator interface configured separately, can be used as the test bed for the real products coming off the assembly line. The test bed is used by the operators and analysts in accordance with the procedures set forth in the operations manuals, user guide, and systems software manuals. Unlike the operations simulator, no fancy stuff is done on this system. Test plans and the procedures are executed in accordance with the "dos and don'ts" established in the UG/SOM SSMM. As anomalies and problems are corrected by the developers, and as they are duly tested and accepted, the requirements and design documents are upgraded to reflect the system as it is in the build. This will avoid a lot of thrashing and wasting of funds.

15.8   FUNDS: A PERSPECTIVE

Let me digress for a minute and be boring for once, and relate to you a humbling experience. The other day I was walking with my wife through the neighborhood supermarket, doing our customary Sunday shopping, because that is when we have time. I observed a couple of old ladies, in fairly worn clothes, with coupons in hand, critically examining the costs of some laundry detergents, and looking at the coupons several times. Then finally they picked the cheaper one, which was, by their facial expressions, not their desired choice, but clearly what they could afford. I was fascinated, as I always am with things like that. It was the difference of 25 cents. I suddenly felt upset and ashamed. Here were a couple of elderly taxpayers who had paid their dues, pinching their pennies; only God knows how little is left at the end of the month for food and medication. At the same time, our young managers overrun their budgets by many millions of dollars; some of these overruns go into the hundreds of millions. They like the big cars, Porsches, perhaps Mercedes, and live extravagantly, all at the cost of the taxpayer. Let me say this also: Unless your funds are from the corporate sponsor direct, or from shareholders or private funds, it doesn't really matter whether the funding agency is DOE, DOD, or NASA; you are spending that old gentleman's or lady's money. If you can't manage your budget, if you can't deliver a quality product, find another job. I'm a true believer in saving the taxpayer money, and I consider the taxpayer to be my customer.

There was another incident many years ago at Ft. Bragg that relates to this. As was my usual custom, I went running late one afternoon through the tank trails on the military reservation. My runs were usually 6 miles (a far cry from my pre-Vietnam days of 12 miles a day), in addition to the daily physical training, and two-mile runs with the battalion. Sometimes, keeping me company on these runs was a personable West Point lieutenant. I was a major by now, and I really liked the kid. He was intelligent, well-educated, and on his way to getting his M.S. from one of our best universities. He had been a track star at the Academy and was also very young, as lieutenants usually are. He was the weapons platoon leader of one of the rifle companies in the 82nd Airborne Division.

Suddenly, as we were about halfway through our run, he stopped and exclaimed with exasperation, "Sir, I wish to register a complaint!"

I stopped, and said, "Speak!"

"Sir, with all due respect, I have a problem with you addressing the janitor in the barracks as 'sir.' Many of the other officers think it is out of line!"

I was surprised at this outburst, and replied that the janitor happened to be much older than I was. This in itself deserved my respect and courtesy. I then added, "He is an American taxpayer, and he pays our salaries."

Then the Lieutenant replied, again with exasperation, that he himself was also a taxpayer, and he would never call an old, decrepit, individual "sir" who was without any stature as far as he was concerned.

I explained to the young officer that this was a grave flaw in his outlook, and that as he matured he would either suffer for it, or recognize how wrong he was. After all, my cousins had gone to the Academy also, and received their education at public expense. All should have been grateful to the people, regardless of their social standing, for the great education they received. We remained friends, and continued to run together in the evenings until he departed to complete his Master's degree.

I wanted to relate these experiences as an indicator of where I stand as a soldier and engineering manager entrusted with public funds. We need to get back to some of our traditional American ethics and roots. We need to fight our way back to being honest and responsible individuals entrusted with public funds, whilst enjoying great salaries and benefits.

16 The Autonomous Cognitive System

16.1 INTRODUCTION

To build a truly intelligent, autonomous system is the "Holy Grail" of computer science. Chapters 3 through 15 have addressed the elements of cognitive dynamics required for the design and implementation of elegant and robust computer software systems at low cost and on schedule. Chapter 14 uses four real-world examples of large, complex, software-intensive projects to illustrate how quality software is built on schedule and on budget.

Now we arrive at the final chapter of this book, and I can't resist stepping out of the main theme of low-cost software development. The successful use of Euler spheres and Leibnitz circles as opposed to block diagrams as tools in software design and implementation permits the visualization and illustration of complex architectures. The application of cognitive dynamics based on the philosophy of Kant, Schopenhauer, and Hegel permits us the creation and presentation of a valid architecture for an autonomous and intelligent system. The design and implementation of computer software is no longer cast in the concrete of hierarchical logic. The tool needed to articulate the dynamic nonhierarchical nature of the architecture of the human thought system and human thought process is available and is proven to work flawlessly. The representation of functional relationships in the form of the sphere as opposed to block diagrams has given to me the visualization of a system that is an entirely elastic and creative approach to systems design.

In the mid-1990s I realized that a totally autonomous system was within our reach. We could build one; the state of the art in technology has just reached the level for autonomy to be built. Then, too, the state of the art back in 1986 had just reached the level of making GDSS doable. However, there are several philosophical issues one must consider before beginning the construction of an autonomous system.

The first issue concerns what the term "autonomous system" really means. To me, an autonomous system means that the system is technically totally competent, but is no longer under my imperative control. I can direct or command it to do

The Cognitive Dynamics of Computer Science: Cost-Effective Large Scale Software Development, by Szabolcs Michael de Gyurky
Copyright © 2006 by John Wiley & Sons, Inc.

certain things for me, but if it doesn't want to do it, it won't, and there is little I can do to impose my will on it. It is in every respect humanlike, except in appearance and physical instantiation.

The second issue, as discussed in the preceding chapters, is the realization that being humanlike is not necessarily a plus! I have seen such stupidity in human beings as displayed in their actions that I wouldn't want these attributes to be present in an autonomous system I built.

But if I build an autonomous system that is not prone to *a priori* decisions (i.e., decisions that can be catastrophically wrong), then I'll have built what Friedrich Nietzsche refers to as the "superman."[1] It is not foolishness to talk about this issue, because the ethical questions are clear. It can be built, so I must talk about it and all the pluses and minuses associated with it. As Hegel put it, "The world is driven by dialectics, and everything unto itself has its own contradiction in its nature." Thus, one of the major tasks for the design team of an autonomous system is to design in the functions allowing for external control. Since I can build an autonomous system, I must define, at least cursorily, what I mean by the term "autonomous system."

16.2 THE SCALE OF AUTONOMY

16.2.1 Category IV Autonomous Cognitive System: Superman

The CATEGORY IV AUTONOMOUS COGNITIVE SYSTEM represents the highest possible replication of the human cognitive system. Such a system operates totally on its own. This is the "superman" of Nietzsche, a model of our human cognitive system, a true android.

Primary Attribute:
- Fully Operational Synthetic Reasoning

Derived Functions:

- Its system segments are dynamic functions. The architecture is dynamic in all of its segments, subsystems, and components.[2]
- It is self-directed.

---

[1] Friedrich Nietzsche. *Also sprach Zarathustra*, Alfred Kroner Verlag, Stuttgart, Germany, 1988.
[2] Segments are either dynamic or hardwired functions, depending on the time available for implementation and the funding for development. Certainly, if one were to do a proof of concept, a number of functions (e.g., self/nonself-discrimination, motion detection, etc.) would have to be designed and programmed using hierarchical logic. When the real system is built, however, the functions must be designed to be dynamic in the internal architecture of a segment. The monadic "process cognitive" segment referred to as dual operating systems (the Will and the Genius) must always be dynamic.

- It can on its own recognize problems needing to be solved, form courses of action, select a course of action, and make a decision, which it carries out without human advice or intervention, if that is what it wants to do.
- It has the ability to synthesize all external and internal sensory perceptions and formulate preferences.
- It is able to acquire data and convert data to knowledge.
- It can dynamically reallocate memory and resources in order to concentrate on problem solving and learning and acquiring new information.
- It is able to perform self-state analysis, and perform self-repair. It can request a spare part, or perform its own self-repair.
- It is capable of making the tools for the manufacture of its own parts, to test them, and install them.
- It is capable of working in a weightless environment, as well as in one without an atmosphere. As such, it can go where Homo sapiens cannot.
- It can work for indefinite periods of time on its own.

16.2.2   Category III Autonomous Cognitive System: Perseus

The CATEGORY III AUTONOMOUS COGNITIVE SYSTEM represents a limited replication of the human cognitive system, with limited synthetic reasoning. This is the "Perseus" system.

Primary Attribute:
- Limited Synthetic Reasoning

Derived Functions:

- Its systems segments are hardwired functions, except for the internal monadic communications subsystem, which is dynamic.[3]
- It is task-directed and designed to intelligently perform operations, science, and engineering functions.
- When it has problems or tasks it is not capable of doing, it must ask for instructions and direction as to what to do.
- It has a limited synthetic reason and the limited ability to synthesize external and internal sensory perceptions.
- It also can acquire data, convert the acquired data to knowledge, recognize problems and conflicts, select courses of action, and make decisions, which it carries out on its own.

---

[3] For overcoming the issue of whether or not to build a totally autonomous thinking, learning, and deciding system with a true will of its own (such as one that can develop preferences, likes, and dislikes), the functions should be designed as hardwired, with hierarchical logic. However, the internal monadic operating systems (the Will and the Genius) must still be dynamic.

- It can dynamically reallocate memory and resources for solving problems and for learning and acquiring new information.
- It can perform self-state analysis, but can only perform limited reprogramming and limited self-repair mechanically.
- It can work in a weightless environment without an atmosphere, and can go where we humans cannot go.
- It is a system that can work for extended periods of time on its own.

16.2.3   Category II Autonomous Cognitive System: Robot

The CATEGORY II AUTONOMOUS COGNITIVE SYSTEM is a system that performs limited autonomous tasks, which are sequenced into memory and uplinked periodically. This system is the "Robot."

Primary Attribute:
- Hardwired Reasoning

Derived Functions:

- Its systems segments are hardwired functions, with no internal monadic subsystems.
- It can perform only the tasks that its functions provide.
- It can acquire data within the span of functions for which it is designed, and convert these data into knowledge.[4]
- It can recognize problems, but it solves problems by sequentially following instructions provided by humans.
- Its internal communications are hardwired.
- It can only synthesize external and internal sensory perceptions as programmed, and only such functions as motion and obstacle avoidance.
- It is under human control through external communications.
- It can work in a weightless environment without an atmosphere, and can go where we humans cannot go.
- It is a system that can work for limited periods of time on its own.

16.2.4   Category I Autonomous Cognitive System: Automaton

The CATEGORY I AUTONOMOUS COGNITIVE SYSTEM is a system that performs only as instructed by humans through communicated instructions. This is the "Automaton."

Primary Attribute:
- No Reasoning Capabilities

---

[4] Knowledge: used here to mean a summation of experiences and abstract information.

Derived Functions:

- Its systems segments are all hardwired functions.
- It can perform only the tasks that it is commanded to perform, and which are provided by its functions.
- Its external sensing is interpreted by humans. It can acquire raw data, but must relay the data back for interpretation by humans.
- It has limited onboard memory.
- It is an extension of human sensing and human manual functions. As such, it is an extension of the human facility to observe and perform manual tasks remotely.
- It can work in a weightless environment without an atmosphere, and can go where we humans cannot go.
- It is a system that can work for limited periods of time on its own.

16.3   "I WILL, BECAUSE I CAN"

There are problems that remain, even with the Superman autonomous system. Suppose that one is built, and it no longer likes the builder. I have a real problem with that. The other problem I have is that we humans are imperfect. We in our species span a scale from genius down to moron and idiot. What if the system we build makes moronic mistakes like we do?

Then, is it fair to the Superman or even Perseus system that it should be as unhappy as most of us are? I have never met a human being who wanted to be born. Most of our trouble in this world comes from us being unwilling guests or visitors to this often sad experience called life. These are ethical questions I must solve before I build. Nietzsche probably never guessed that his superman need not be a biological product, born of human biology, but rather born of the human mind, and built (at least version 1.0) by human hands.

This chapter, introducing autonomous cognitive systems, is essentially based on Immanuel Kant's *Three Critiques*. As such, this is an enormously complex chapter. The fact that autonomous cognitive systems can be built does not mean that it is cheap or easy. There is the categorical imperative of "I will, because I can." If I build it, what kind of Pandora's Box am I opening? Who will build it first? To what use will it be applied? What will the positive and negative impacts be? Who will control it? Will it control us?

I have to admit that I could not forgo to touch on this subject here, at the conclusion of this book. The temptation is too great to share with the few whose intelligence is matched by vision, creativity, and energy, and who will, just by reading this final chapter, gain an access to true cognitive autonomy. The enormous scope of the subject is restricted to a mere introduction in this book, to be perhaps followed by a volume of its own. Nonetheless, the architecture described in this chapter is quite achievable.

16.4 TOWARD COGNITIVE DYNAMICS

A totally autonomous system is where computer science is headed, and that is one of the reasons for this final chapter. There is also one rare human philosophical attribute or function without which this concept cannot be understood, and that is imagination, or to use the German word, *Vorstellung*. This is probably disturbing to say, but it is a fact. There are many facets to autonomy, but by my definition autonomy is a system that is completely independent of anyone, or at least independent to the degree that it can learn, decide, and act on its own without human intervention, and do so for extended periods of time (e.g., years).

That today's electronic digital computation, as a model, has too many limitations for our future needs is another disturbing fact. An autonomous, self-contained system requires magnitudes higher throughput and processing capacity than we have today, and this implies a process cognitive computation,[5] based on the human model. Such a computer will in its Initial Operating Capability (IOC) be a process cognitive system, though likely implemented using digital technology. But in its Final Operating Capability (FOC), it will be an integration of biological-chemical-electrical computation into a new system. This integration of cognitive philosophy, digital computation, biology, chemistry, and electrical processing is called Cognitive Dynamics. It will perform many of the functions and tasks we humans do, without needing direction.

16.5 BUILDING AN AUTONOMOUS SYSTEM

Do we really need such a system? I am not certain. However, since it will be built eventually, somewhere, by someone, it might as well be built here in the U.S., by American computer scientists. The subject is immense and excruciatingly difficult to contemplate, let alone to try to describe in one chapter; then again, the philosophically important ability of *Anschauung* on the reader's part to "visualize" it is a necessity.

This chapter will probably be expanded to a Level III architecture in separate volumes of its own. Much of this approach is simply following the software management plan for developing systems, such as those addressed in Chapter V. It is a logical approach, and I will use the language and terminology used in software development standard DOD-STD-2167A for the sake of convenience, and because I am familiar with it and feel comfortable using it. This chapter is dedicated entirely to the description of the architecture of the autonomous system I refer to as cognitive dynamics, for the sake of convenience.

[5] See Footnote 11 in Chapter 2.

What type of applications could a Cognitive Dynamics System be used for? I certainly would find its use in areas where we humans cannot survive or work. One of these is probably the exploration of the solar system and deep space. Another is the elimination of toxic and radioactive waste. The cleaning up of this home of ours, our Earth, is essential to our longevity, provided we bring our populations under control.

We are now quite capable of building such a system. Technically, I believe, it is no more difficult a leap than when we started building GDSS, and had to invent the technologies we needed to complete it. But there are many difficulties ahead, of course. The problems will pop up here and there, only to be solved, each in its own turn. This is all the more exciting, since problem solving is what makes humans happiest, especially the solving of very difficult problems. Our own limitations are our abilities to "visualize the system" and all of its segments so we can build it.

16.6   AN APPROPRIATE MODEL

An autonomous system needs an architecturally complete model first (or one as complete as possible), with clearly defined subsystems/segments and components that we can understand. This makes it necessary to invent a few new terms. What better model could we come up with than an architectural representation of the human thought system[6] and the human thought process? So, any autonomous system I build has the human thought system as its model, and is therefore biological in nature. We are trying to build a system that is capable of sensing, analyzing, learning, making decisions, and taking actions on its own that are reasonable and intelligent. Human beings are not perfect, so we will never have a "perfect system," but we need to model a human thought system for this and not, say, that of a dog. Some friends and colleagues of mine actually suggested that instead of using the human model I should use a dog model, which they thought would make the system much simpler. As Schopenhauer points out so definitively, animals are the slaves of the present, and cannot reason in time, past or future.[7] We cannot send the equivalent of a dog to the planets and expect it to do research! The problem that building such a biology-based system will bring with it is the challenge of testing and proving the mathematical algorithms. The proofs will need to be based on biology. This requires a test environment, a system in itself.

The architecture of the autonomous system has evolved in my reasoning from three distinct directions. In the first direction is the evolution of how I began to visualize complex systems architectures, starting with GDSS. The second is the

[6] Arthur Schopenhauer. *Die Welt als Wille und Vorstellung*. Page 7. Deutsche Taschenbuch Verlag GmBH & Co. KG, 1998, Muenchen, Germany.
[7] Schopenhauer, Arthur: *Die Welt Als Wille und Vorstellung* (The World as Will and Imagination) Book Two. *Die Objektivation des Willens* (The Objectivization of the Will) Page 655. Deutsche Taschenbuch Verlag GmbH & co. KG, Munich, Germany. April 1998.

hypothesis of Immanuel Kant, as he declares in one of his writings, "There will come a day when all visible and invisible phenomena in the Universe will de described in mathematics." I felt immediately happy that I understood what he meant, and this hypothesis of Kant's simply added substance to my subjective visualization of the design. I believe that this hypothesis of his was then and is now correct. The third is the sudden realization that an autonomous system is within our reach technically; I had a model for one, which I inferred from Kant, Schopenhauer, and Hegel.

This visualization of the architecture of an autonomous system and the conclusion of its validity is the process whereby we build and form according to necessity,[8] drawing on our knowledge and understanding of architectures and on our creative skills to formulate an abstraction of the thought function and process into an understandable object (i.e., a "design object" sufficiently defined as a 'thesis' from which to begin work).

There are a number of problems that have made this architecture necessary. None of the technical fields we use today in computer science is sufficient to accomplish autonomy. (Artificial intelligence is an important but small part of autonomy. It is as important as the rivet is to a supersonic aircraft.) Autonomous functions, in their simplest form, are mathematically so intensive that there is no hope of having a computer light enough to be mobile on Earth, much less for launching into space.

The architecture of the autonomous system (i.e., the Cognitive Dynamic System, or CDS) is based on *Die drei Kritiken*, the three critiques of Immanuel Kant. Properly stated, the architecture is an abstraction, reconfiguration, and expression in modern computer science of these masterpieces of the great teacher.[9] Let's approach autonomous systems as we would approach any software job or project, by asking what the system level requirements are.

16.7 SYSTEM-LEVEL REQUIREMENTS FOR AUTONOMY

The two basic requirements for an autonomous cognitive computational system are:

- A very large system throughput capacity, and
- A very large CPU availability

Additionally, the internal communications (interprocess communications) and the common software services must have a neural-network-like coupling with an object-oriented topography. The system must also have low energy consumption, and have distributed and replicated scalability. The autonomous systems architecture is visualized as a man-made model of the human cognitive system at

---

[8] Kant. *Kritik der Teleologische Urteilskraft*, Die drei Kritiken, pp. 316–320.
[9] Kant. *Die drei Kritiken*. Eine kommentierte Auswahl von Raymund Schmidt. Alfred Kroner Verlag (Publisher) Stuttgart, 1993, Germany.

the *phenomenological* level, capable of performing a given number of cognitive functions, such as thinking, learning, deciding, and acting to an acceptable level of reality. The building of this autonomous system will advance the state of the art in computation technology from silicon toward bio-based computing within the next decade.

Some of the benefits of this system will be the assured availability of safe and interference-free computational systems support to a user owning such as system. It is inherent in the nature of such a system that it is invulnerable to inadvertent or intentional intrusion or penetration, because it will have, as the human system does, the capability of self-defense against intrusion, and active and decisive countermeasures against intruders.

The acquisition of external sensory data and the conversion of such data to mathematical representations in the internal sensing function will enable the system to convert the data into knowledge. It will then apply the knowledge to the solving of problems intelligently and rationally. It will be able to take action, execute tasks, and solve problems completely on its own, such as to assemble several courses of action and select the one most likely to succeed. One of the most important attributes of the autonomous system is its ability to perform self-repair, and to reprogram itself.

16.8 ARCHITECTURAL DOMAINS FOR AUTONOMY

The autonomous systems architecture is composed of the following two major architectural domains. See Figure 1, which is a composite visualization of these domains.

16.8.1 Domain I: The Human Thought Architecture Model (Functional Architecture)

This is the architectural interpretation of the Human Thought Architecture Model (HTAM), and is a representation of all of its subsystems allocated to a space in virtual memory. The space is elastic and accommodates each subsystem according to the computational needs it performs for any given task. The major Domain I subsystems are:

THE SENSORY SUBSYSTEM, composed of two major segments:

- External Sensing Segment
- Internal Sensing Segment

THE FUNCTIONAL SUBSYSTEM, composed of the following major segments:

- The Reason Segment
- The Rules Segment
- The Abstraction Segment
- The Action Segment

- The Concepts Segment
- The Decision Segment
- The Knowledge Segment
- The Contemplation Segment[10]
- Other major segments

16.8.2   Domain II: The Human Thought Process Model (Common Software Services)

This is the architectural interpretation of the Human Thought Process Model (HTPM) and is a representation of all of the process cognitive computations and communications within the HTAM. It is an adaptive, self-regulating, computational paradigm, required for such a complex and large system, and is the underlying technology for performing mathematically-intensive tasks at extremely high speeds.

The major Domain II subsystems are

- The Control Semaphore
- The Will
- The Genius
- The Common Software Services

The CONTROL SEMAPHORE is much like the conductor of an orchestra; it directs the activities of the monad classes or monad networks. It also orchestrates the operations of the Will and the Genius.

The WILL is a world unto itself, a system within a system. In fact, it is the primary "operating system" that controls functions and segments, very much like a traditional operating system controls process execution and access to resources.

The GENIUS is the secondary operating system, also a system within a system, but which does not control. It is a hyperspace super-processor that synthesizes data and information, and hands it over to the Will for disposition.

The COMMON SOFTWARE SERVICES subsystem, or monad network, is akin to the traditional input and output subsystem, yet is a process cognitive computational system in its own right. It has evolved over almost two decades from the initial version in GDSS, through all of its uses and refinements and improvements to its present concept. Its implementation is not constrained by technology, but by computer speed and memory.

The major modification to the CSS comes from the Leibnizian hypothesis referred to as a *monad*. A monad, as Leibniz defined it, is a subatomic particle containing all the elements and information in existence. Here in this architecture, it encapsulates those key cognitive functions, which along with other monads, form an autonomous orchestra approach to high-speed work distribution and efficiency, under the control of the operating system, which acts as a concertmaster.

---

[10] Michail Zak. *Physical Model of Immune Inspired Computing.* Jet Propulsion Laboratory M/S 126-347, Pasadena, CA 91105.

The monad is the primary active element of the process cognitive computational system. The space allocated to the monad in virtual memory is elastic and depends entirely on the communications load it is required to accommodate. Individual monadic nodes group logically to form a monadic network called an *idea basis*. Monad sets that encapsulate such an idea basis are themselves related to each other via participation in a yet larger network called a *thought basis*. When the monad hierarchy elaborates (replicates) itself, the result is a layer upon layer (basis upon basis) network of abstract intelligent processing within the Common Software Services layer, and within the segments as well, performing their work towards solving problems.

Monads are classified into four basic types (refer again to Figure 1):

- SENSOR MONADS, which are dedicated to sensory functions, internal and external sensing of light, motion, mass, thermal energy, etc.
- COMMUNICATIONS MONADS, which are dedicated to input/output functions between the segments.
- MAINTENANCE MONADS, which are dedicated to status checking, programming, reprogramming, and discarding unneeded, obsolete, or expired monads.
- EXECUTOR MONADS, which are dedicated to performing functional work, such as geo-bio discrimination, motion detection, and self-repair at the systems level.

According to the Leibnitzian concept, there are countless monads in the universe; they act independently of each other, but do their work in concert and harmony. They communicate without a hierarchy, but are not simple "repeaters," since they perform tasks and work under a divine ordered logic. As the Functional Subsystem is not hierarchical, in that all of its segments are priority-bounded by task ordering, the monad is the ideal CSS entity for the Cognitive Dynamic System. The types of "work" performed by the monads of the CSS are function-specific to communications, sensing, maintenance, and command execution.

All monads, as extensions and elements of the control logic of the operating system, have the following architecture in common:

- FUNCTIONAL OPERATIONS SET, which classifies monads into the function-specific work they do (e.g., communications, sensing). The functional operations set includes a mathematical instruction.
- NLT CLOCK that regulates the "*No Later Than*" completion of an operation, which if not updated, auto-terminates the monad (a form of monadic "apoptosis").
- FUNCTIONAL STATE FILE SET, geared to the state of the activity being performed at any given time.
- COMMUNICATIONS FILE SET, which contains the monad's internal and external references.

- *MONAD SYSTEMIC DATABASE SET*, which contains the systemic memory of events, targets, temperatures, and attitudes related to its work.

- *REPLICATION AND MUTATION DATA SET*, which enables a monad to replicate itself when required by an event. For any event where the quantity of work required within the NLT period exceeds the capacity of the monad to perform on its own, the monad replicates itself to the number required for the performance of the event.

The human immune system is also a cognitive and autonomous system unto itself. It creates and commands into action specific types of phagocytes and lymphocytes (among many others), the goal of which is to perform an immune function (e.g., to neutralize an invading pathogen). Likewise, the autonomous cognitive system initiates and commands into action specific classes of monads to collectively perform a complex task (e.g., identify a foreign entity, assess risk, select a course of action, take action).

As stated earlier, an individual monad is related to other monads as a node in a more specialized network. Each monad may encapsulate a collection of other monads, called a *basis,* from different levels that are function-specific. Such a collection of monads operates on its own distinct levels or frequencies. It is the monad linkage of functional association and its structural arrangement that enable the process cognitive paradigm.

16.9   IN SUMMARY

This brief chapter on autonomous cognitive systems is essentially based on Kant's works. This is an enormously complex subject, and it is difficult not to have it "run away" into a level or two lower, or with a higher resolution than this. All computer scientists who are practitioners and who build will understand the necessity of evolving an architecture with the discipline of a standard, and so will understand what I'm talking about.

To those who understand what I have outlined in this chapter, it is already a given, as it is to some of my colleagues. Some will say, "Why didn't I think of it?" or "This is it! I've got a lot of learning to do to get the details, but I think I know what needs to be done." I'm fortunate to have friends and colleagues who understand all of this because of their experience of working with me and with each other as a technical team.

To those who don't understand it, I'm sorry; you probably never will, simply due to the time required to read the classical philosophers and the time required in the experience of design and development. I wish I could be more encouraging, more defensive, even humble for the sake of those readers who are so eminently qualified, who have great reputations in the fields of AI and IT, but I can't. It has taken me most of my life to get to this point. So, as sad as I feel, if you don't get it, in the immortal words of Arthur Schopenhauer: "Don't feel bad; put it down and forget it."

There is certainly more than one possible architecture to autonomy, and more than one methodology and process to achieving such a system. But to build on the architecture presented here will be far easier than to start slogging through Kant, Schopenhauer, and Hegel. The foundations will certainly not be based on Kant. I have to admit that it all started with Aristotle, and his "Categoriae."[11] I picked it up at the Parkersburg, W.V. Carnegie Library one summer afternoon in 1955, and had to buy myself my own copy, which was not cheap for a kid of 17. It was the beginning of a great adventure, leading through to Kant. It has taken me forty-four years of work, millions of lines of code and many large systems produced to get to this point of producing computer software at or under $10 per line of commented and documented code. It has also taken this long to evolve an architecture to the point where an autonomous system can be built. It will not be cheap, quick, or easy, it is true, but it can be built at greatly lower cost than that which is being expended on DOD and privately-funded research programs that do not have an architecture that can be implemented.

The technology in building the autonomous system is a synthesis of cognitive dynamics, theoretical and applied mathematics, molecular biology, object-oriented design and programming (initially), neural network technology (initially), and instrumentation design.

I don't believe there is a great technical problem in building such a system. The great obstacles will be in the organization of the workforce, in inter-team and external communication, and in the management methodology; thus the theme of this book. It will eventually be built, probably at great cost, with much trial and error and friction. Almost anything can be built by throwing enough money at it; the real issues, as always, are schedule and funding.

---

[11] *The Works of Aristotle. Volume I, Categoriae and De Interpretatione, Analytica Priora, Analytica Posteriora, Topica and De Sophisticis Elenchis.* Oxford University Press, London: Geoffrey Cumberledge. 1928, reprinted in Great Britain by Lowe & Brydone, Printers, Ltd, London, 1950.

Epilogue

THE SCIENCE OF COMPUTER SCIENCE

As computer software professionals, we are consistently inundated with new terms and concepts. This is an indicator of several things. One is that we really don't fully understand the scope and philosophical foundations of our discipline, and that we are trying to find these. Another is that we feel like we are really neither a science nor an engineering discipline, a fact that our colleagues in industry and academia are only too willing to reinforce and affirm.

What is also interesting is that as much as our discipline grows in scope and importance to technology, industry, and to the benefit of human living, we are still regarded as an apparition. It seems that either we don't fit into what people in academia consider "real science" or "real engineering," or that we ourselves have not taken the time to think about just were we do fit in.

Everybody I know in mathematics, engineering, chemistry, biology, astronomy, and the other "legitimate" sciences designs software and programs, even if only at the program, routine, or module level. This obscures the role of computer software professionals in our industry and in our national laboratories. In most cases, management does not know exactly where software professionals fit in on a project, what the scope of their work is, and where their responsibilities lie. The demarcation between the software profession on the one side, and physicists, mathematicians, and biologists who can program and design modules on the other is so obscure that it is invisible.

The result is that a physicist, biologist, or engineer winds up managing a software-intensive system or the computer software component of a project. The impact, of course, is that projects often cost twice as much as the original estimate. Management is the toughest of all jobs, provided the job of management is taken seriously. If the cost of a project is of little or no importance, then this issue is moot.

THE PROFESSIONAL SOFTWARE MANAGER

If cost and schedule are important, then the question arises, "What does it take to be a serious professional software manger?" Is it sufficient to have an academic degree

The Cognitive Dynamics of Computer Science: Cost-Effective Large Scale Software Development, by Szabolcs Michael de Gyurky
Copyright © 2006 by John Wiley & Sons, Inc.

of, say, Doctor of Philosophy, or a *doctor de rerum naturalis* (natural sciences) to become a manager of a software-intensive project? Would it not be better to have a doctor of computer science as an academic degree, in addition to the required years of management experience? Certainly, it is a rare doctor of management who, without the qualifications and experience in an engineering or other discipline, can be an effective project manager in software development. Again, any manager can get the job done if schedule and funding are of little or no importance, but if schedule and funding are important you need a professional.

Would it be possible for a software professional to pass himself off successfully as an astrophysicist? Highly unlikely! Then why is it that mechanical and electrical engineers or physicists pass themselves off as software managers, team leaders, and software cognizant engineers, fields they know very little about? Then the schedule slips start, and the cost overruns follow, until the corporation heads overseas to get their software development done.

There are many great software professionals I know who happen to be engineers and scientists, but the good ones have 20 years or so of experience in building software and delivering products. The reason for all this confusion in software development is that we, as computer software professionals, don't fully understand where we fit in. Nor do we understand that our discipline is a legitimate science on a level with biology and physics. If anything, we tie together the sciences, because all of the disciplines require software.

COGNITIVE PHILOSOPHY IN A MODERN TECHNICAL CONTEXT

The human thought system and human thought process have been explored to an incredible detail by the great thinkers of humanity. All of science was initially philosophy, the love of wisdom. We have forgotten our roots, because it emerged into the modern world as "automatic data processing" or a calculating tool. We progressed into becoming an analytical tool, and rapidly spread into different specialty domains such as data communications, operating systems, database technology, and applications programming.

In the rapid evolution we underwent in the past 30 years, we even failed to see the similarity of the early process of memory allocation for specific tasks in the CPU to the way our brains evolve when we teach children arithmetic rules, history, and other knowledge functions. This manner of working and thinking reflects back on the way we think, both consciously and subconsciously. This is also the domain of cognitive philosophy.

The cognitive philosophy of Immanuel Kant, Arthur Schopenhauer, and Georg Wilhelm Friedrich Hegel is much like the raw data in a core dump: One must read it, partition it, and then apply and use it. It is not easy to read these three great philosophers; if you have been raised on television, they will remain forever inaccessible to you.

What must be done to use cognitive philosophy effectively in our work is to create a level of abstraction and transliterate the philosophical terms, functions, and processes into modern technical terms. I did this by reading through the great works of cognitive philosophy three times or so, taking notes, and flowcharting and creating context diagrams of their contents. This process allowed me to understand the information better and apply it to my work. This new understanding of cognitive philosophy in a modern technical context became a tool that I have used and applied very successfully. I call this new tool and theory in advanced computer science *Cognitive Dynamics*.

Visually it is the layer sitting on top of cognitive philosophy, much like the "Common Software Services" layer sits on top of the operating system (as described in the chapters of this book, particularly Chapter 14). One should not program applications directly to the operating system unless one is prepared to incur great costs.

COGNITIVE DYNAMICS IS THE UNIFYING THEORY

It is my hypothesis that cognitive dynamics, sitting on top of the works of the great cognitive philosophers, forms the unifying theory for the next phase of evolution of computer science.

Computer science today and henceforward is a legitimate science because it is an *abstraction of the human thought system*. It is extremely complex because it is a synthesis of electro-biological and chemical operations, performed at incredible speeds, in the narrow confines of the human brain and body. The branch disciplines evolving from computer science, such as artificial intelligence, information technology, and neural networks, are like Doric Columns without a unifying foundation or a mutually converging roof point. They are evolving without converging. The convergence, or roof, is the concept of "total autonomy" which architecturally is more like Gothic architecture, than Greek, with most of the cognitive attributes of an intelligent, rational human being.[1] Although it may be unfair to build a totally autonomous system,[2] humanlike in its cognitive functions, it will be done because of the categorical imperative, "I will, because I can," and because of our need to explore places where we as biological species cannot go.

THE ISSUE OF SOFTWARE COST

Many of the very best professionals in our field cannot find jobs. This is because of the bottom line: we are too expensive at $700+ per line of code. Yet we at the Jet Propulsion Laboratory have proven repeatedly that quality software can be built as

---

[1] The "intelligent, rational human being" factor is a very important point. It would not be difficult to build an autonomous system at the level of a moron, or say, an idiot. These are real scales of human intelligence, and not put in frivolously. All human beings are not able to fly a space shuttle or to teach at a university. Rational intelligence with a high learning and *a posteriori* decision capability are therefore legitimate design objectives.

[2] Unfair to the autonomous system, that is.

low as $10 per line of code, on schedule. So where is the problem? Could it be that the managers of software development projects are not software professionals, or that they lack the experience, understanding, and desire necessary to keep costs low and on schedule?

Let's look once more at what I mean by *cost per line of code*.

The cost per line of code includes:

- **All commented lines of code** (because we understand that the useful commenting of code can be just as time-consuming as programming).
- **All salaries** from the software manager on down, including contractors.
- **The cost of all facilities**, such as office space.
- **The cost of computer hardware and software**, COTS packages, software tools, & utilities.
- **The cost of documenting** the requirements, the design, test plans, software interface specifications, user guides, maintenance manuals, and, of course, the project implementation plan.
- **The cost of all travel and per diem** paid to employees and contractors alike.

And to think that all this can be done in the U.S for around $10 per line of code!

Any software manager of a corporation, government agency, or national laboratory that pays over $50 per line of code today for the above-listed items should not be managing! To do so shows either a total disregard for the funds they have been entrusted with by the customer, or a total lack of ethics (or at best, a total lack of understanding of what ethical conduct means). It is the sacred duty for an honorable professional manager to deliver to the customer a quality product, at the agreed-to cost, and on the agreed-to schedule. There are no acceptable sniveling excuses or finger-pointing at "subcontractors" and "creeping requirements." These things simply don't exist. All "creeping requirements" means is that the manager does not know how to prepare the stated and implied requirements or how to infer the derived requirements from the stated and implied requirements. It is that simple.

THE PARADIGM SHIFT OF COGNITIVE DYNAMICS

As we enter the new age of computer science and pass through the paradigm shift into fully autonomous systems, a great number of the unimaginative and inexperienced managers, architects, and systems engineers will be left behind. This is a serious business, computer science. It is a legitimate science that stands shoulder to shoulder with physics, mathematics, and biology. Unless people accept this, our computer-related jobs will go overseas, along with Levi's jeans and Zenith television sets. We cannot let this happen, because computer science is the future.

The paradigm shift of Cognitive Dynamics in computer science has arrived, if not for building an autonomous cognitive system outright, then certainly for building elegant systems that are inexpensive and easy to maintain.

Glossary of Acronyms

ABMDS | Antiballistic Missile Defense System
ACE | Allied Command Europe
ADP | Automatic Data Processing
AFB | Air Force Base
AI | Artificial Intelligence
ALD | Airlift Division
API | Application Programmable Interface
ATP | Acceptance Test Plan
AUTODIN | Automatic Digital Network
BG | Brigadier General
CBS | Corps Battle Simulation
CCIS | Command and Control Information System
CCPRC | Coding Conventions/Programming Rules and Conventions
CDD | Conceptual Design Document
CDS | Cognitive Dynamic System
CENTCOM | U.S. Central Command
CINCLANT | Command in Chief, Atlantic Command
CINCMED | Command in Chief, Mediterranean Command
CINCNORTH | Command in Chief, Allied Forces, Northern Europe
CM | Command Processing Subsystem (JTCCS)
CNES | Centre National d'Etudes Spatiales (French)
COMSIM | Communications/Simulator Subsystem
CONOPS | Concept of Operations
COS | Chief of Staff
COTS | Commercial off-The-Shelf (ready products)
CP | Command Post
CPX | Command Post Exercise
CSC | Computer Software Component
CSC | Computer Sciences Corporation
CSS | Common System Services
CSSS | Common System Services Subsystem
CSU | Computer Software Unit
DBMS | Database Management System
DDD | Detailed Design Document
DDN | Digital Data Network
DEC | Digital Equipment Corporation
DECnet | Digital Equipment Corporation Network
DOC | GDSS Command and Control Subsystem (AF)
DOD | Department of Defense

DOE	Department of Energy
DSN	Deep Space Network
E-8	Engineering, Level 8 (JPL rank)
ET	Earth Terminal (Jason)
FOC	Final Operational Capability
FRD	Functional Requirements Document
FTIP	Final Test & Integration Plan
FTP	File Transfer Protocol
FTX	Field Training Exercise
GDMSMCS	Globally Distributed Mini/Super-Minicomputer System
GDSS	Global Decision Support System
GDT	GDSS Design Team
GSFC	Goddard Space Flight Center
GUI	Graphical User Interface
HQ/MAC	Headquarters, Military Airlift Command
INTREP	Intelligence Report
IOC	Initial Operating Capability
IPC	Interprocess Communications
ISD	Information Systems Division
ISDS	Information Systems Development Support
IT	Information Technology
JAD	Joint Analysis Directorate
JCS	Joint Chiefs of Staff
JDBC	Java Database Connectivity
JESS	Joint Exercise Simulation System
JTCCS	Jason Telemetry, Command, and Communications System
JPL	Jet Propulsion Laboratory
JTLS	Joint Theater Level Simulation
LAN	Local Area Network
LOC	Lines of Code (plus comments)
MAC	Military Airlift Command
MAPP	Modern Aids to Planning Program
MCCS	Military Command and Control System
MPSSS	Mission Planning, Scheduling, and Sequencing Subsystem
MS	Microsoft Corporation
NAF	Numbered Air Force
NASA	National Aeronautics and Space Administration
NASCOM	NASA Communications System
NAVS	Navigation Subsystem
NCC	NASA Communications Center
NCO	Noncommissioned Officer
NFEP	NASCOM Front End Processor
ODBC	Open Database Connectivity
OJCS	Office of the Joint Chiefs of Staff
OR	Operational Requirement

PDP	Programmable Data Processor
PIP	Project Implementation Plan
POC	Project Operations Center
PP	Post Processor (JTLS)
PSN	Packet-Switched Network
RDB	Relational Database
RFB	Request For Bid
RFP	Request For Proposal
SAC	Strategic Air Command
SDD	Software Design Document
SDE	Senior Design Engineer ("Cognizant" Design Engineer, JPL)
SDS	Science Data Subsystem
SFC	Sergeant First Class
SFOF	Space Flight Operations Facility
SHAPE	Supreme Headquarters Allied Powers, Europe (NATO)
SISD	Software Interface Specifications Document
SITREP	Situation Report
SLOC	Source Lines of Code (minus comments)
SMS	Software Management Standard
SOCOM	Special Operations Command
SOM	Software Operations Manual
SP	Senior Programmer ("Cognizant" Programmer, JPL)
SPAS	Satellite/Sensor Performance Analysis Subsystem
SPO	Special Program Officer
SPP	Scenario Preparation Program
SQL	Structured Query Language
SR	Systems Requirements
SRD	Software Requirements Document
SSD	Software Specifications Document
SSMM	System Simulator Maintenance Manual
STP	Software Test Plan
SVP	Scenario Verification Program
TCCS	Telemetry, Command, and Communications System
TCP/IP	Transfer Control Protocol/Internet Protocol
TDRESS	Tracking and Data Relay Satellite System
TGS	TOPEX Ground System
TIP	Test and Integration Plan
TM	Telemetry processing subsystem (JTCCS)
TOPEX	The Ocean Topographic Explorer (satellite)
TRANSLAN	LAN Translator, DDN to/from PSN
TSEP	Technical Support Effort Personnel
UARS	Unmanned Air Reconnaissance System (spacecraft)
UG	User Guide
UI	User Interface
ULSD	Ultra Large Screen Display

USAJFKCSW	John F. Kennedy Center for Special Warfare
VAX	Virtual Address Extension (DEC)
VMS	Virtual Memory System (DEC)
VT100	Virtual Terminal 100 (DEC)
VT220	Virtual Terminal 220 (DEC)
WAN	Wide Area Network
WINTEX	Winter Exercise
WIP	Work Implementation Plan
WWMCCS	World Wide Military Command and Control System

INDEX